LONDON FOR EVERYMAN

I pray you, let us satisfy our eyes
With the memorials and the things of fame
That do renown this city.—WILLIAM SHAKESPEARE.

London, thou art the flower of cities all.—WILLIAM DUNBAR.

It was a pleasant sight to see the City from one end to the other with a glory about it.—SAMUEL PEPYS.

Dear, damned, distracting town.—ALEXANDER POPE.

If you wish to have a just notion of the magnitude of this city, you must not be satisfied with seeing its great streets and squares, but must survey the innumerable little lanes and courts. It is not in the showy evolutions of buildings, but in the multiplicity of human habitations which are crowded together, that the wonderful immensity of London consists.—DR. JOHNSON.

When a man is tired of London, he is tired of life; for there is in London all that life can afford.—DR. JOHNSON.

Streets, streets, streets, markets, theatres, churches, Covent Gardens . . . lamps lit at night, pastry-cooks, and silversmiths' shops . . . inns of court with their learned air, and hall, and butteries, just like Cambridge colleges, old bookstalls, Jeremy Taylors, Burtons on Melancholy, and Religio Medicis on every stall. These are thy pleasures, O London with-the-many-sins.—CHARLES LAMB.

"We doan't come to Lunnon to do nought but 'joy oursel, do we?"—JOHN BROWDIE (CHARLES DICKENS).

LONDON
FOR EVERYMAN

BY

WILLIAM KENT

WITH 48 PAGES OF COLOURED MAPS

"What London hath been of ancient time men may here see, as what it is now every man doth behold."—JOHN STOW.

LONDON & TORONTO
J. M. DENT & SONS LTD.

FOREWORD

I COULD weep like Diana at the fountain, to adapt Shakespeare's only reference to Cheapside, at what I have been compelled to omit from this book. I would fain have written in the shorthand staccato of Mr. Jingle to include more. But whilst his account of Rochester in the evergreen pages of *Pickwick* may raise a smile: "Old cathedral—earthy smell—pilgrim's feet worn away the old steps—little Saxon doors — confessional like money-takers' boxes at theatres—queer customers those monks"—the method would offend the literary ear for which I have an ingrained respect. Therefore this book must be regarded as an attempt only to whet the appetite of the Londoner and his country cousin.

The story of "Eyes and No Eyes" need not have only a rural setting. I met the latter in London a short time ago. When, at a committee meeting, a London ramble was proposed, he arched his eyebrows, and said with scorn, "I work in the City." Doubtless he did, but evidently he did not there observe and muse. Those who come to my book with an appetite for it will enter into the spirit of Leigh Hunt's remarks: "I have seen various places . . . which have been rendered interesting by great men and their works . . . I seem to have made friends with them in their own houses, to have walked and talked, and suffered and enjoyed with them. . . . Even in London I find the principle hold good in me. . . . I once had duties to perform which kept me out late at night, and severely taxed my health and spirits. My path lay through a neighbourhood in which Dryden lived, and although nothing could be more commonplace, and I used to be tired to the heart and soul of me, I never hesitated to go a little out of my way purely that I might pass through Gerrard Street and so give myself the shadow of a pleasant thought." I quote these remarks because, whilst I can hardly hope to add much to the knowledge of London's great buildings—covered so thickly with palimpsests of printed sheets—I may haply help to make the stones of its streets cry out to those who tread them, more history than they have previously known.

I have endeavoured to avoid treating the wanderers in London as physically of the family of No-Eyes. I have not transcribed inscriptions which are as readable to them as to me. I say this lest it should be supposed that those not quoted have no interest. In short, I have tried to help those who will help themselves.

In conclusion, I can but hope that the "Everyman" ramblers, who have been kind enough to express enjoyment of rambles which I have personally conducted, will also derive enjoyment from those conducted by literary proxy through the medium of my book.

W. K.

October 1930.

CONTENTS

viii   *CONTENTS*

LIST OF MAPS

DISPOSAL OF TIME

THIS guide has been prepared for those visitors to London who, like Omar Khayyám in the world at large, are impressed with the little time they have to stay, though I hope that their position will be different from him in one respect, that once departing they will return at least once more. This accounts for my distinction between Day and Evening Walks. Very few buildings are open after 6 P.M., and so I suggest that the day-time should be exclusively devoted to them, and the evenings reserved for streets. There is an additional reason for this course. Some thoroughfares are congested with traffic in the day-time and an evening walk is more congenial.

The primary axiom for time-economy is travel by tube, wherever possible. The traffic blocks thus avoided may easily compensate for time consumed in walking to a station. The visitor should beware, however, of the intricacies of the underground system, and provide himself with a map which can be obtained at the stations. Provided your station is on the inner-circle obviously you must arrive there in time; but if you travel the wrong way it may be at loss of time and temper. There is no need either to pay undue importance to the label "Non Stop" on tube trains. The uninitiated are apt to imagine that these travel from terminus to terminus. In fact, they pass only intermittent and unimportant stations, and, if there is no official to consult, little harm is likely to result from boarding on chance. It may be useful to give a list of the more central inner circle stations, and an indication of their whereabouts. West to East: South Kensington (two minutes walk from museums), Sloane Square, Victoria, St. James's Park, Westminster (opposite Houses of Parliament), Charing Cross (on Victoria Embankment), Temple (on Victoria Embankment), Blackfriars (near bridge), Mansion House (corner of Cannon Street and Queen Victoria Street), Cannon Street (at Cannon Street Southern Railway Station), Monument, Mark Lane (two minutes walk from Tower of London).

With regard to trams, they are cheap, but of little use, so far as the programme of this guide is concerned. The exceptions are in the cases of journeys to Greenwich, Hampstead, Kew, and Hampton Court; and, to the first two places, if the journey is made in the middle of the day, at least fifty per çent can be saved in fares, but the routes are not attractive and the time consumed considerable. The London County Council issue one shilling all-day tickets every day. With these one may travel on any tram until any time over their system. Some L.C.C. trams, however, run over other companies' lines, e.g. to Croydon, Hampton Court, and Kew, and these, and the other cheap tickets to be mentioned, do not operate beyond the county boundary. The L.C.C. also issue from Sunday to Friday (public holidays excepted) on all trams leaving the central London termini between 9.30 a.m. and 4 p.m., and all cars arriving thereat between 10.30 a.m. and 5 p.m., a twopenny ticket for any distance, and a penny ticket which covers a longer distance than at other times of the day. The latter facilities are operative also on the omnibuses when they traverse the same route as trams. They do not, however, issue the shilling all-day tickets. With regard to omnibuses, a map of the system should be obtained from a conductor or inspector. Bus tops, as Mr. Gladstone said, are excellent for sights, if they cannot be commended in crowded streets for speed.

The following are the fares for taxi-cabs:

A distance not exceeding ⅔ of a mile, and time not exceeding 7½ minutes.   .   .   .   . 6d.

Exceeding ⅔ of mile or 7½ minutes, for each third of a mile or time not exceeding 3¾ minutes . 3d.

For any less distance or time   .   .   . 3d.

Extra payments, bicycle, mail-cart or perambulator 9d.

Other package carried outside   .   .   . 3d.

EXTRA PERSONS

Each additional person beyond two (one or two children under ten to count as one person)   . 6d.

(You can generally make peace with the driver by a tip of about twopence in the shilling.)

With reference to the river, James Howell wrote delightfully of this: "It is most proper for the City of London, who lies perpetually by her bed's side, and therefore in a fit posture to be watchful of her." Some visitors might well say that Londoners watch too much, and use the river too little. There are, however, frequent trips from Westminster Bridge to Kew, Hampton Court, Richmond, and Greenwich, whilst daily for a shilling, the visitor can go to Tower Bridge and back in a motor boat. Except in the case of Greenwich, however, the river route entails a considerable sacrifice of time.

A point always to be borne in mind is the almost right-angled turn of the river at Westminster. This is impressed upon one's mind by the delights of unexpected views of St. Paul's Cathedral. For this reason it does not follow that two places upon one side of the river are most easily linked up from one bank. Dickens helped us to realize this in *Our Mutual Friend*. Mr. Riah, when on a journey from St. Mary Axe to Smith Square, Westminster, to see Jenny Wren (see p. 156), crosses first London Bridge and then Westminster Bridge—very wisely. Lastly, it will help the visitor, I think, if he bears in mind the two parallel highways, and how continuous they are. On the north: Oxford Street, New Oxford Street, High Holborn, Holborn, Newgate Street, Cheapside, Bank. South of these: Parliament Street, Strand, Fleet Street, Ludgate Hill, Cannon Street, Queen Victoria Street, Bank.

WHERE TO STAY

THE following list contains merely a selection from a large number of hotels. They are taken from the handbook of the Hotels and Restaurants Association of Great Britain. In the case of those marked with an asterisk, accommodation can be obtained for a single day, without meals, for a sum between 6s. and 10s. 6d.; in the others the terms run from 12s. 6d. to 21s. for single rooms.

Bloomsbury District :
    *Cosmo Hotel, Southampton Row, W.C.1.
    *Midland Grand Hotel, adjoins St. Pancras Station.
    *Hotel Russell, Russell Square, W.C.1.

West End :
    Burlington Hotel, Cork Street, W.1.
    Grosvenor Hotel, adjoining Victoria Station.
    Hyde Park Hotel, Knightsbridge, S.W.1.
    *Regent Palace Hotel, Piccadilly, Circus, W.
    Hotel Washington, Curzon Street, Mayfair, W.1.

Strand District :
    *Adelphi, Adam Street, Strand, W.C.2.
    Arundel Hotel, Victoria Embankment, W.C.2.
    *Charing Cross Hotel, Charing Cross Station, W.C.2.
    *Strand Palace Hotel, W.C.2.
    Savoy Hotel, Strand, W.C.2.
    Hotel Victoria, Northumberland Avenue, W.C.2.
    Waldorf Hotel, Aldwych, W.C.2.

City :
    Anderton's Hotel, Fleet Street, E.C.4.
    Cannon Street Hotel, E.C.4.
    *Great Eastern Hotel, Liverpool Street, E.C.2.

Board residence is advertised in most papers, and for those of small means the Young Men's Christian Association, 13 Russell Square, W.C.1., and the Young Women's Christian Association, 252 Regent Street, W.1., may be useful.

WHERE TO DINE

THE following restaurants are of historical interest:

"Cheshire Cheese," Wine Office Court, Fleet Street.

For its history, see p. 162. A great feature is its pudding, referred to in the *Forsyte Saga*, where Soames and Winifred partake of it. The pudding season commences on the first Monday in October, when some distinguished person is asked to preside and make the first cut. Those who have performed the ceremony include Lord Oxford, Lord Haldane, Viscount Grey, Lord Rosebery, Sir Herbert Beerbohm Tree, Dean Inge, Mr. Stanley Baldwin, Jack Dempsey, Augustine Birrell, Conan Doyle, and the Bishop of London. A collection of the churchwarden pipes smoked by some of these celebrities are in a room on the top floor. The pudding is served daily at midday and at 6.30 p.m. This (1930–1) is the 155th season. It takes sixteen hours to cook, includes steak, mushrooms, larks, oysters, etc., and is large enough to supply ninety people.

"Cock," Fleet Street.

The old tavern and restaurant was on the other side of Fleet Street and disappeared on the construction of the Law Courts branch of the Bank of England in 1887. Of this Tennyson wrote in *Will Waterproof's Lyrical Monologue*:

> O plump head-waiter at the Cock,
> To which I most resort,
> How goes the time? 'Tis five o'clock.
> Go fetch a pint of port:

When Tennyson (who at the time had chambers in Lincoln's Inn), was mentioned to the waiter he said he did not remember the gent! The sign displayed is not the original one. This is preserved in the dining-room on the ground-floor. One of their specialities is an Old Cocke Pudding.

"George" Inn, Borough High Street (see p. 181).

"George and Vulture," George Yard, Lombard Street.

It was originally simply the "George." Probably the name of the bird was added after it was rebuilt as a consequence of the great Cornhill fire of 1748. The tavern may have acquired a vulture as an object of curiosity and probably it was desired, to distinguish it from another "George" in the neighbourhood. Dickens introduced it into *Pickwick Papers*:

Mr. Bob Sawyer, thrusting his forefinger between two of Mr. Pickwick's ribs and thereby displaying his native drollery and his knowledge of the anatomy of the human frame at one and the same time, inquired: "I say old boy, where do you hang out?" Mr. Pickwick replied that he was at present suspended at the 'George and Vulture.'"

This was, of course, after Mrs. Bardell's intrigues had caused him to leave the "domestic oasis in the desert of Goswell Street," as Sergeant Buzfuz called it. There is still a Pickwick room, but there are no longer residential visitors.

Simpson's Restaurant, Bird-in-Hand Court, 76 Cheapside.

"Simpson's" originated in 1723. The founder was George Simpson who, in Bell Alley, Billingsgate Market, initiated a fish "ordinary" for the purpose of catering for the luncheon needs of the Custom House officials hard by. Later on, the business was transferred to the present site, where it has been for probably about one hundred and seventy years. The original Simpson, it is said, instituted a Cheese Guessing Competition for the amusement of his guests. At any rate, this has been a daily practice from time immemorial. The cheese, which, being in use for customers, daily dwindles, is mounted upon a stand made out of a beam taken from Nelson's old ship *Victory*. All the diners are invited to guess weight, size, and girth, and if anybody succeeds in doing so his name adorns the wall, and champagne and cigars are supplied to each guest. Difficult as the feat might seem, in the course of twenty-eight years, the period of office of a recent chairman, it was performed nine times. The chairman opens the proceedings punctually at one o'clock with grace, and usually tells a funny story. Ladies are now admitted. The meal consists of soup, four courses of fish, sweet, etc., and the price is two shillings. The fish ordinary is not served on Saturdays.

Two other restaurants where one may feed in an antiquarian atmosphere are 12 Clifford's Inn and Essex Stairs Tea Rooms, 24 Essex Street. Scotch visitors will feel at home in the Thistle Restaurant, Tothill Street, Westminster.

With regard to more prosaic restaurants, in London where there is variety enough to satisfy that classical diner, the Emperor Heliogabalus, it would be invidious to single out any. It may, however, be mentioned that there are vegetarian restaurants at Chandos Street (near Charing Cross)—Eustace Miles Ltd.; at Furnival Street, Holborn— Food Reform; at Tottenham Court Road (No.231)—Shearn's; in Gray's Inn Road (No. 269); at 137 High Holborn; and in Fyfoot Lane, Queen Victoria Street. There are Italian, Chinese, and French restaurants in Soho.

Most of the higher-class restaurants are open also on Saturdays and Sundays. A number of the multiple shops, which cater for people of more moderate means, close at week-ends. The following are open Saturdays and Sundays: Lyons's, 213 Piccadilly, Maison Lyons, and Oxford Corner House, Oxford Street; Strand Corner House; 5 Ludgate Circus; 152 Bishopsgate; Slater's, 212 Piccadilly; A.B.C., 454 Strand.

In the multiple shops tips ("to ensure promptness" the word originally meant) are not permitted, but there is usually a staff box on the counter. In other cases about twopence in the shilling will suffice.

B

AMUSEMENTS

PLAYS of every description may be produced at almost every London theatre, so that it is not possible to be certain of the type of play that may be found at any of them. The following list indicates the sort of play usually to be found.

Evening performances usually begin at 8, 8.15, or 8.30. Matinées begin at 2, 2.15, or 2.30. For details see daily papers. All seats are bookable at the theatres marked with an asterisk.

ADELPHI, 410 Strand. Musical Comedy.
ALDWYCH, Aldwych. Farce.
AMBASSADORS', West Street, Shaftesbury Av. Comedy.
APOLLO, Shaftesbury Avenue. Comedy.
CAMBRIDGE, Great Earl Street. (New theatre.)
*CHILDREN's, Endell Street. Children's Plays.
COMEDY, Panton Street, Haymarket. Comedy.
COURT, Sloane Square. Comedy.
COVENT GARDEN, Royal Opera House.
CRITERION, Piccadilly Circus. Comedy.
DALY's, Leicester Square. Musical Comedy.
DRURY LANE, Catherine Street, Strand. Spectacular Plays.
DUKE OF YORK's, St. Martin's Lane. Comedy.
EMBASSY, Swiss Cottage. Repertory Company.
FORTUNE, Covent Garden. Comedy.
GAIETY, Strand. Musical Comedy.
GARRICK, Charing Cross Road. Comedy.
GLOBE, Shaftesbury Avenue. Comedy.
*HAYMARKET, Haymarket. Comedy.
*HIPPODROME, Cranbourn Street. Musical Comedy.
HIS MAJESTY's, Haymarket. Spectacular plays, Comedy.
KINGSWAY, Great Queen Street. Comedy.
LITTLE, John Street, Adelphi. Comedy.
LYCEUM, Wellington Street, Strand. Popular Drama.
LYRIC, Shaftesbury Avenue. Musical Comedy.
LYRIC, Hammersmith. Comedy, Operetta.
NEW, St. Martin's Lane. Comedy, Musical Comedy.
"OLD VIC," Waterloo Road. Shakespeare, Opera.
PALACE, Shaftesbury Avenue. Musical Comedy.
*PHŒNIX, Charing Cross Road. Comedy.

*PLAYHOUSE, Northumberland Avenue. Comedy.
PRINCES, Shaftesbury Avenue. Musical Comedy.
*PRINCE EDWARD, Greek Street. Musical Comedy.
*PRINCE OF WALES, Coventry Street, Piccadilly. Musical
    Comedy.
QUEEN'S, Shaftesbury Avenue. Comedy.
REGENT, King's Cross. Comedy.
*ROYALTY, Dean Street, Shaftesbury Avenue. Comedy.
SADLERS WELLS, Rosebery Avenue. Shakespeare, Opera.
ST. JAMES'S, King Street, St. James's. Comedy.
ST. MARTIN'S, West Street, Cambridge Circus. Comedy.
*SAVOY, Strand. Comedy, Musical Comedy.
SHAFTESBURY, Shaftesbury Avenue. Musical Comedy.
STRAND, Aldwych. Comedy.
VAUDEVILLE, 404 Strand. Comedy, Musical Comedy.
WHITEHALL, Whitehall. (New theatre.)
WINTER GARDEN, Drury Lane. Musical Comedy.
WYNDHAM'S, Cranbourn Street. Comedy.

There are also the following private theatres:

ARTS, 6 Great Newport Street.
GATE, 16A Villiers Street.
GRAFTON, 133 Tottenham Court Road.

Principal West End and Central London Cinemas :

An asterisk denotes cinemas where important new films
are put on for a run prior to general release.

ALHAMBRA, Leicester Square.
*ASTORIA, Charing Cross Road.
AVENUE PAVILION, Shaftesbury Avenue.
    (Specializing in News Films.)
*CAPITOL, Haymarket.
*CARLTON, Haymarket.
DOMINION THEATRE, Tottenham Court Road.
*EMPIRE, Leicester Square.
LEICESTER SQUARE THEATRE.
*MARBLE ARCH PAVILION.
*NEW GALLERY, Regent Street.
*PLAZA, Haymarket.
POLYTECHNIC THEATRE, Regent Street.
    (Usually specializing in educational or
    unusual films.)
*REGAL, Marble Arch.
*RIALTO, Coventry Street.
STOLL, Kingsway.
*TIVOLI, Strand.

There are also Variety Theatres, Music Halls, etc., as follow:

COLISEUM, St. Martin's Lane, near Charing Cross. Varieties.

HIPPODROME, Cranbourn Street, Leicester Square. Revue, etc. ·

HOLBORN EMPIRE, 242 High Holborn.   Varieties.

MASKELYNE'S; Langham Place, W.   Mystery, Conjuring.

PALLADIUM, Argyll Street, Regent Street.   Varieties.

PAVILION, Piccadilly Circus.   Varieties.

VICTORIA PALACE, Victoria Station.   Varieties.   Revue.

Matinées are usually at 2 or 2.30.   In some houses there are two performances a night, beginning about 6.15 and 8.45. Smoking is allowed, and usually seats are cheaper than at theatres.

There are good concerts from time to time at Albert Hall and Queen's Hall, Langham Place.   At the latter there is usually during August and September a continuous series of promenade concerts, the price for admission being 2s. There is particularly good church music at Westminster Cathedral.   There are regularly organ recitals at the city churches, particularly St. Stephen's, Walbrook, and St. Michael's, Cornhill.

A LONDONER'S CALENDAR

January 1.	The New Year is greeted by jollification outside St. Paul's, chiefly by Scotchmen in the spirit of Burns.
,, 30.	Service for the "Royal Martyr" at Charles I's Statue, Charing Cross.
February.	Shrove Tuesday, noon. Tossing pancake at Westminster School.
,, 3.	Blessing of throats at altar of St. Blaize, St. Etheldreda's Chapel, Ely Place.
Maundy Thursday (day before Good Friday).	Distribution of Maundy Money in Westminster Abbey.
Good Friday.	Twenty-one widows pick up sixpences from tombstone of St. Bartholomew-the-Great Church (11 a.m.).
March 31.	Oranges and Lemons service at St. Clement Danes' Church.
End of March or beginning of April.	Oxford and Cambridge Boat Race.
Saturday nearest April 23.	Shakespearean celebration. Service at Southwark Cathedral. Ramble round Bankside with scenes from plays.
April 25.	Anzac Day. Service at St. Clement Danes' Church.
April (or thereabout)	Stow Commemoration service at St. Andrew's Undershaft Church— arranged by London and Middlesex Archæological Society.
Last Saturday in April.	Football Cup Final.
Last Sunday in April.	Procession from Newgate to Tyburn to celebrate Catholic martyrs there.
Wednesday following Easter week.	Spital Sermon at Christ Church, Newgate Street.
May.	Royal Academy opens at Burlington House.

Ascension Day.	Beating Bounds, St. Clement Danes' parish, etc.
May 29.	Inspection of Chelsea Pensioners at the Royal Hospital.
June 24.	Procession of Knights of St. John from St. John's Gate, Clerkenwell.
About last week.	Cricket. Test match at Lords when touring team is in England. Tennis tournament at Wimbledon.
July 10.	Procession of Vintners from Vintners' Hall, to Church of St. James, Garlickhithe, or St. Michael's, Paternoster Royal.
„ 10–20.	Cricket. Oxford *v.* Cambridge. Gentlemen *v.* Players. Eton *v.* Harrow at Lords's.
August 1.	Race for Doggett's Coat and Badge, London Bridge to Chelsea.
About 3rd week.	Cricket. Test match at Kennington Oval if touring team is here.
September 21.	Visit of Blue-coat boys to Christ Church, Newgate Street and Mansion House.
„ 29.	Election of Lord Mayor.
October 12 (or thereabouts).	Re-opening of Law Courts following visit of judges to Westminster Abbey.
October 16.	Lion Sermon at St. Catherine Cree Church.
October (end of).	Sunday nearest All Saints' Day (November 1). Fish Harvest Festival at St. Dunstan's-in-the-East Church, Lower Thames Street. Thirty-nine different kinds of fish are displayed, and it is afterwards presented to Guy's Hospital.
November 5.	Gunpowder Plot sermon at St. Mary-le-Bow Church.
„ 9.	Lord Mayor's Show.

SHORT HISTORY OF LONDON

THERE is a story of James I, which we owe to a contemporary, James Howell, which may provide a starting-point for a short plunge into the great stream of London history. The king was refused a loan by the corporation, whereupon, in high dudgeon, he threatened to remove his court to another place. "The Lord Mayor calmly heard all, and at last answered, 'Your Majesty hath power to do what you please, and your City of London will obey accordingly: but she humbly desires that when your Majesty shall remove your Court, you would please to leave the Thames behind you.'" London's river, like Tennyson's brook, has flown on whilst men have come and gone—Celts, Romans, Saxons, Danes, Normans, Englishmen. If the river could become oracular, like Nathaniel Hawthorne's arm-chair, it could a tale unfold. What the tale might be Mr. John Burns once suggested by his happy phrase of "liquid history."

The Thames is truly the alpha of London's histroy. Doubtless its proximity to the Continent, its useful tributaries —the Fleet which entered the river at Blackfriars, and the Wall Brook which joined it a little west of where is now Cannon Street Station—dictated a site to the first British settlers. When we recall, too, the existence of Ludgate Hill on the west and Cornhill on the east, it is difficult to believe, with some, that the Romans found a barren site where is now a teeming population. It is unlikely that the Romans would have occupied an entirely new site, and any advantages it held for them would surely have been partly revealed to the Britons. Their settlements were probably a succession of villages, and it is significant that there have been numerous finds of neolithic pottery and Bronze Age weapons at Mortlake, Hammersmith, Wandsworth, and Battersea. Tangible relics of pre-Roman times may be seen in the London Museum. There is a gold coin of Cunobelinus (Shakespeare's Cymbeline), King of South Britain from about 5 B.C. to A.D. 40, and a currency-bar used as a medium of exchange before coins came into use.

13

It must not be assumed that before the advent of Julius
Cæsar in 55 B.C. Britain was such a tight little island that
nobody had ever landed. The "fortress built by nature,"
as Shakespeare called it, may not previously have been
invaded, but it was doubtless visited from time to time.
Cæsar's visit in 55 B.C. was but a coastal survey, and in the
following year it is doubtful whether he saw the site of
London. / Cæsar then retired from Britain after making
terms with its chieftans, and London history definitely
starts with Aulus Plautius, who—at first assisted by his
Emperor Claudius (who brought part of the famous Præ-
torian Guard and a squadron of elephants)—completely
subjugated the country between A.D. 43 and 50. Roman
London stands to-day, in the minds of most people, for three
things: roads, a bridge, and a wall. Watling Street, with a
name still preserved on a city thoroughfare, is the best known
of the Roman roads. It ran from London to Chester, and
its importance was subsequently indicated when it was made
a dividing line by the Treaty of Wedmore in 879, between
the territory of Alfred the Great and Guthrum, the Danish
king. In one year, 1013, it is twice referred to in the *Anglo-
Saxon Chronicle*. The present Watling Street must not be
regarded as following the same course. After the fire of
1136 it was deflected to avoid a market which had sprung up
where is now Budge Row. Other Roman roads were the
Viainal Way, which led from Bishopsgate to Camulodunum
(Colchester) and the east, and Ermyn Street, the great north
road from the same gate. The first London Bridge (most
likely a wooden structure) was probably erected in the early
period of the Roman occupation. Mr. Gordon Home points
out that Dion Cassius, the Roman historian, in his account
of Aulus Plautius's campaign, says that the Romans forced
the passage of a bridge which he thinks was situated east of
the present one. At any rate, the evidence of coins found in
the river gives a date not later than A.D. 70. London
Bridge was, extraordinary to relate, London's only permanent
link with the south bank of the Thames until Westminster
Bridge was completed in 1750. The wall is usually assigned
to the last decades of the first century. It was probably erected in consequence of the British rebellion under
Boadicea, A.D. 61. The character of its construction,

revealed by successive excavations, particularly the use of fragments of statues (some thus embedded can be seen in the Guildhall Museum), justifies the inference that it was a hurried defensive measure. The wall ran from the Tower north-ward to Aldgate, thence to Bishopsgate, and then along the course of the thoroughfare now known as London Wall. After this it passed southward to Aldersgate, thence west-ward to Newgate, and so southward again to Ludgate, and back along the river's bank to the Tower. It was from twenty to twenty-five feet in height, over three miles in circumference, and enclosed an area of about three hundred and twenty-five acres. There is a bastion in the graveyard of St. Giles's Church, Cripplegate, whilst the vestry of the Church of All Hallows, London Wall, is built upon another. At both places the wall is visible to all. There are many subterranean examples, notably in the bonded warehouse of Messrs. Barber, Trinity Square (near the Tower of London), and under the yard of the General Post Office premises at the corner of Newgate Street and Giltspur Street. The latter can be seen upon application to the Postmaster-General. The names of all the gates are still commemorated in London's nomenclature. Moorgate and Cripplegate did not apparently exist in the Roman era.

We can visualize the Roman city by placing the prætorium, or governor's residence, near the Wall Brook, the Forum and Basilica (remains of these have been discovered) in the neighbourhood of Leadenhall, surrounded by the handsome houses of the merchants such as those Tacitus mentions as having been along the banks of the Wall Brook. Their elegance may be imagined by inspecting the contents of our museums, where will be found specimens of beautiful mosaic pavements. The best is in the Guildhall Museum. It was found near the Mansion House, at the time of the construction of Queen Victoria Street in 1871. In the same museum will be found the remains of hypocausts for central heating, and elsewhere Roman baths. The best known of the latter is the one in Strand Lane, and the fact that it existed so far from the Wall is an indication that Roman law was as effective for safety in the suburb as in the city. The collection of domestic articles in the museums suggests that the amenities of civilized life were not much less to the Romans than to

ourselves.   There are writing materials, pens as well as styles,
Samian ware (a beautiful red-glazed pottery that took its
name from the Mediterranean island of Samos), saucepans,
spoons, tweezers (for extracting superfluous hairs), delicate
glass bottles, hand-bells.   One relic of particular interest—
in the Guildhall Museum—is a brick inscribed in Latin which
has been translated "Austalis goes off on his own every
day for a week."   The interest to us is not mainly that
Austalis was a micher (to use the word Shakespeare put into
the mouth of Falstaff) or an early apostle of ca' canny, but
that a Roman bricklayer could write, an impossibility to
the English hodman until the nineteenth century.   The
inscription may be compared with the curious one found
scratched upon the window of St. Catherine Cree Church,
Leadenhall Street, during restoration in 1920: "Thomas
Jordan cleaned this window and damn the job I say 1815."
Images of Demeter, Athene, and Mithra, found in London,
indicate the variety of religious cults followed by the Romans.
There were probably a few Christians in the Roman legions,
and as Cornhill was in the very heart of Roman London we
need not be too sceptical about the tradition that St. Peter's
Church was founded in the year 179.   London was repre-
sented by a bishop at the Council of Arles in 314, and
Tertullian (160–230) refers to British Christians.

There was a paucity of events in the Roman era, but two
may be mentioned.   First, the rebellion of Boudicca
(Boadicea), Queen of the Iceni (modern Norfolk and Suffolk),
whose army burned London.   In 1774 labourers excavating
in Walbrook brought up wood ashes mixed with soft earth and
mud, twenty-two feet below the present surface, and it is
conjectured that these were remains of that conflagration.
Boudicca was eventually defeated in a battle which is
believed to have been fought in the neighbourhood of King's
Cross, formerly known as Battle Bridge.   She committed
suicide and according to some is now "pyramidally extant,"
to use a phrase of Sir Thomas Browne's, in a tumulus on
Hampstead Heath.   To moderns she is best known as the
subject of a fine statue by Thornycroft, and by the lines of
Cowper inscribed thereupon: "Legions Cæsar never knew
thy posterity shall sway."   Readers of Defoe's *True-born
Englishman* will, however, have their doubts about descent.

The second event was the usurpation of Allectus, a Roman general who, in 296, was attacked by an imperial force which sailed from the harbours of Gaul.   One of its divisions, first lost in a fog, found its way to London, and the fine specimen of a Roman galley found on the site of County Hall, Westminster Bridge (now in the London Museum), has been connected with this event.

London disappears from history for a time after the departure of the Romans (about A.D. 440).   The *Anglo-Saxon Chronicle* records that in 467 Hengist and Eric, his son, chiefs of the Saxon invaders, fought against the Britons at Crayford, that four thousand Britons were slain, and that the residue of their army fled to London.   Then again history is silent until 604, when Ethelbert gave Mellitus the bishopric of London, a date associated with the founding of St. Paul's Cathedral.   The Teutonic invaders—Jutes, Angles, Saxons— were non-urban in habits, but it is hardly safe to assume from the silence of the records that London was entirely deserted. In mere "abstracts and brief chronicles of the times"—our only authorities—the absence of reference to London signifies little.   In the museums may be seen swords, spears, axes, and shields dating from Saxon times.   Perhaps the most interesting relics are in the London Museum—bones from fourteen graves found at Mitcham two feet below the surface. In one of these was also discovered a fine specimen of a brooch in the manufacture of which the Saxons were particularly skilful.

At the end of the eighth century came Vikings from Norway and Denmark, and from 839 they more than once plundered London.   In 886, however, Alfred the Great fortified the city, making substantial repair of its walls.   The existence of St. Clement Danes' Church in the Strand probably commemorates a suburban settlement of Danes permitted by Alfred.   In 1017 the whole of England admitted the sovereignty of the Danish king, Cnut, and London finally made a truce with the Danish forces.   Perhaps the most piquant relic of these times is the stake in the Guildhall Museum from the trench which Canute made through Southwark for the passage of his ships in order to circumvent the citizens who were defending the City from London Bridge. Also, in the same museum, is a carved stone, showing two grotesque animals intertwined, bearing an inscription which has been translated: "Konal and Tuki caused this stone to be laid." It was discovered on the site of Messrs. Cook's warehouse in St. Paul's Churchyard in 1852, and is believed to be of Danish origin. London's nomenclature, apart from St. Clement's Church, has a few other Scandinavian associations. There was, until very recently, St. Olave's Church, Tooley Street, and there is still one in the city, while on the north of London Bridge is the Church of St. Magnus the Martyr. Olaf, King of Norway at the beginning of the eleventh century, became its patron saint and Magnus was his son. In Nicholas Lane (King William Street) will be found the graveyard of St. Nicholas Acon. Readers of Ibsen will remember King Haakon in *The Pretenders*. Off Cheapside runs Gutter Lane, believed to be a corruption of that Danish King Guthrum with whom Alfred the Great made the Peace of Wedmore.

In this period Westminster became increasingly important. On Thorney Island there is said to have been a monastery since 604, and close by Edward the Confessor (1042–66) built a palace. From this we can infer that after Holborn, the oldest highways outside the City are the Strand and Fleet Street. The former is first mentioned in the *Anglo-Saxon Chronicle* under the year 1052. There is no extant reference to Fleet Bridge Street, as it was first called, before 1228, and it is probable that the one name was first given, quite appropriately, to the continuous thoroughfare parallel to the river which now has two.

William the Conqueror was the first king to be crowned in the abbey, which Edward the Confessor had been rebuilding. William gave London a charter—now preserved at the Guildhall. It indicated that London was to be under the ecclesiastical and civil jurisdiction of the bishop and portreeve, corresponding to a county sheriff, and included a promise to maintain the laws operative in the reign of Edward. A far more patent contribution of William the Conqueror's was the erection of what is now known as the White Tower of the Tower of London, a clear indication that his faith did not repose in a scrap of parchment. In the year of William's death a fire destroyed St. Paul's Cathedral and a great part of the City. William Rufus's contribution was the erection of a wall round the Tower, the repair of London Bridge, and the erection of Westminster Hall. The relations of the City with the Norman monarchs were fairly amicable and Henry I granted a further charter.

In 1136 occurred another great fire, the cathedral being again damaged, as also was London Bridge. Its successor, erected between 1176 and 1209, was the work of two architects, Peter, priest and chaplain of St. Mary Colechurch (which stood on the north side of the Poultry), and Isembert, a member of a famous brotherhood of bridge builders. The bridge came to be regarded as one of the wonders of medieval Europe. It had one drawback, however, and that was implied in the proverb that London Bridge was made for wise men to go over and fools to go under. The nineteen arches created such a strong current that shooting the bridge with a boat was an exhibition of foolhardiness. All Londoners who believed in "Safety First," dragged the boat round the bridge and re-embarked on the other side. This necessity remained up to the time the bridge was finally demolished in 1830, and we read of the practice in Pepys's *Diary*, Boswell's *Johnson*, and Dickens's *Great Expectations*. There were houses built upon the bridge; also a chapel dedicated to St. Thomas à Becket, who was murdered six years before it was commenced.

From about the same date and by reason of the same man, glorified by Londoners not only by reason of his death but also for his birth (in Cheapside), we get the first account of the City. Fitzstephen, à Becket's secretary, wrote a life of his master, and, in accordance with medieval ideas, a saint must have come out of a New Jerusalem on earth. So Fitzstephen, praising a famous man, praises also the city that begat him in the manner of a prospectus of a garden-suburb. Its climate was salubrious, its gardens well-furnished with trees spacious and beautiful. There were fields for pasture, and flowing streams "on which stand mills whose clack is very pleasing to the ear"; there were "excellent springs, the waters of which is sweet, clear and salubrious." There were in London and suburbs one hundred and forty-nine churches. There was also on the Thames side a restaurant so excellent that "those who wished to indulge themselves would not desire a sturgeon, or the bird of Africa, or the godwit of Ionia, when the delicacies that are to be found there are set before them." This old Fitz. was a bit of a romancer, but those who read his delightful account (so happily appended by John Stow to his famous *Survey*) cannot but be grateful.

One man who lived at the same time as Fitzstephen would certainly not have shared Fitzstephen's views of the charms of London life. This was William Fitzosbert, popularly known as Longbeard. In 1196 he protested against the heavy taxation imposed by Richard I, largely to pay his ransom from captivity, and declared that poor people were compelled to pay everything. When a riot broke out the justiciar was sent to arrest him. Longbeard and a few followers took refuge in the Church of St. Mary-le-Bow, Cheapside, where they laid in provisions and prepared for a siege. Neither threats nor persuasions brought them out, but at length, faggots being placed against the church door, he and his comrades were smoked out—like vermin. Though this occurred in Passion Week they were straightway dragged ignominiously through the City streets and hanged in Smithfield. Crowds flocked to his execution (one chronicler gives the number as fifty-two thousand, but it is doubtful if the whole population of London reached that figure) and shed tears at his end. After the execution it is said that the people carried away pieces of the scaffold and handfuls of the last patch of earth upon which he trod—as talismans to heal the sick.

But the soul of Longbeard, like John Brown's, went marching on. Powerful City families like the Bokerels, Farringdons, and Basings (names commemorated in Bucklersbury, Farringdon Street, and Basinghall Street) came to be opposed by the tradesmen, and from the year of the Great Charter (1215), the agitation for which commenced with a meeting in the cathedral of the barons and clergy— "a true Parliament of the realm, though no king presided over it," said E. A. Freeman—we find mayors bearing such names as Serlo le Mercer, Bartholomew the Spicer, Walter le Potter, Alan le Hurer (capmaker). By this time—it was a concession wrung from King John in hope of conciliating the City—London was allowed to elect its own mayor instead of his being a nominee of the Crown. This, however, was not then an annual election, as Henry FitzEylwin, the first mayor, held office from 1189 until his death in 1212.

The institution of the mayor—there is no evidence that he was called Lord Mayor before the time of Henry VIII—was a manifestation of the growing power of the craft-guilds whose nominee he was. These guilds were for trade protection and mutual assistance. Only members and their approved apprentices were allowed to practise their craft in the City and its suburbs; they punished bad work and regulated wages. They came into existence as a result of charters, but some organized without. These—known as adulterine guilds—were usually allowed to continue upon payment of fines. The City companies, thus originated, exist to this day, although only in a few cases do they exercise their ancient functions. One example is the Goldsmiths' Company which, in its fine hall—with a classical façade—in Foster Lane, puts a mark of approval upon certain gold articles. Another can be found in the licences granted by the Apothecaries' Company, from its seventeenth-century hall in Water Lane, to competent persons to dispense drugs. The first in order of precedence was the Mercers', whose hall is in Cheapside. The next in order is the Grocers', whose fine eighteenth-century hall and charming garden can be seen off Princes Street (No. 5).

An incident that left its mark upon London was the Wat Tyler rebellion of 1381. The Kentish insurgent and his followers caused serious damage to the Savoy Palace, in the Strand, and to the Priory of St. John of Jerusalem, in addition to which valuable documents were destroyed at the Temple and Lambeth Palace. Tyler was struck down by Sir William Walworth, the mayor, and the dagger with which the deed was done is still exhibited in the hall of the Fishmongers' Company of which he was a member. We must not misjudge Tyler because of the violence of his followers. Charles Dickens happily wrote in his *Child's History of England*: "Wat was a hard-working man, who had suffered much . . . and it is probable that he was a man of a much higher nature and a much braver spirit than any of the parasites who exulted then, or have exulted since, over his defeat." A far greater historical authority, Mr. G. M. Trevelyan, has written with similar sympathy.

A more famous Englishman was a contemporary of Tyler's—Geoffrey Chaucer. One could wish he could have given as vivacious a picture of a wanderer in the London he knew as of the Canterbury pilgrimage. Still, we can always associate him with three places—Aldgate, where he lived in rooms over the gate from 1374-6, the Tabard Inn, from whence the pilgrims departed, and Westminster, of which he was Clerk of the Works, and in whose abbey, by reason of his office rather than his poetry, his body was laid in 1400.

At the same time as Chaucer, lived the man who is perhaps, having regard to his fame with the unlettered, the best known of all Londoners, Richard Whittington. His poverty is more legendary than his cat. He came from a middle-class Gloucestershire family, and was apprenticed to Sir John Fitzwarren, a merchant adventurer. The steps of the ladder that led to his extraordinary wealth are lost in oblivion: Howbeit, Whittington rose to the top and was four times London's mayor. It is related of him that, having lent Henry V considerable sums of money with which to carry on his wars with France, he patriotically burned the bonds after entertaining his sovereign. With regard to the cat, a recent Lord Mayor was sadly in error in saying that the animal was unknown in the fourteenth century in England. It appears in the miracle plays of earlier date and in *The Nuns' Rule* (a counsel of ascetic perfection attributed to Poore, Bishop of Durham, and written about 1220) a cat is recommended to the nuns as a safer companion than a man. It may well have been, as Sir Walter Besant (who wrote a delightful book upon Whittington) suggested, that his good fortune started with the sale of a cat when the animal was more rare. It is remarkable that on Newgate, which was rebuilt by Whittington's executors, was a figure with a cat lying at its feet, and that during excavations in 1862 in a mansion in Gloucestershire, known to have been occupied by the Whittington family, was found a bas-relief of a boy carrying a cat in his arms.

Great as was the power of the City companies and the merchant princes, even they could not override the Church. In 1447, for example, the Goldsmiths' Company complained that their craft was being carried on illegally by criminals who had taken sanctuary in the Church of St. Martin-le-

Grand, Aldersgate Street, but nothing apparently was done. In 1450, Henry VI could not secure the person of Jack Cade because he had taken refuge in the same place. All the great religious orders were represented in medieval London. The Dominican or Black Friars had 'their priory, with its magnificent church, in the district which still bears their name. The Grey or Franciscan Friars settled at Newgate. The Minories—a thoroughfare near the Tower of London—commemorates the nunnery of the Minoresses, the female members of the same order. The Austin or Augustinian Friars had a house in Broad Street; the Friars of the Blessed Virgin of Mount Carmel, better known as the White Friars, had a house in the neighbourhood of Fleet Street, where the name remains; and the Carthusians one near Clerkenwell—Charterhouse being a corruption of Chartreuse. There were also the Crutched Friars (from the cross which formed part of the staff they carried); their name is still to be found in the City. Finally, there were the two great military orders—the Knights Hospitallers of St. John of Jerusalem, and the Knights Templars. The priory of the former was the origin of the village of Clerkenwell; the latter order was suppressed in the early part of the fourteenth century, and their property, between Fleet Street and the river, was shortly afterwards leased to the lawyers who still occupy the district.

A quarrel in these Temple Gardens is said to have started the Wars of the Roses, and the Tudor dynasty, which commenced in 1485 when those wars ceased, caused the greatest upheaval of our national life, and also, of course, affected London. Henry VII is associated with construction—notably the beautiful chapel bearing his name at Westminster Abbey—his son with destruction. The dissolution of the monasteries led to the despoiling of the ornaments of the Church of the Grey Friars at Newgate, to the destruction of the nave of the Priory Church of St. Bartholomew in Smithfield, to the dismantling of the Priory of Charterhouse, to the destruction of the fine churches of the Black Friars and the White Friars. By way of a small solatium, Henry VIII afterwards returned to the citizens the hospital of St. Bartholomew which had been attached to the priory, whilst Edward VI gave Bridewell Palace and the Grey Friars' Priory to the corporation, the former as a house of correction and

C

the latter as a school for poor boys. Queen Mary is associated in London only, alas! with Smithfield martyrdoms. The spacious days of Queen Elizabeth recall that monarch's desire for more space for London, and her prohibition of new buildings near the walls. In 1582 London's first waterworks came into existence; they were at the north end of London Bridge, the work of Peter Morris, a Dutchman. A little later there was erected upon the bridge Nonsuch House; it was entirely of wood and constructed in Holland. From Elizabeth's reign date also Middle Temple Hall (where *Twelfth Night* was performed in 1602), and Gray's Inn Hall (where *The Comedy of Errors* was performed in 1594). In 1576 the first theatre was erected in the fields at Shoreditch. It was followed by the Curtain, in the same neighbourhood, and by the Globe, on Bankside, in 1598. Appropriately enough, in the same year appeared *The Survey of London*, by John Stow, and it is as impossible to write upon the lore of the old city without quoting him, as to write a history of the English drama and ignore Shakespeare.

In early Stuart times London was beautified by specimens of the architecture of Inigo Jones—Palladian, as it was called, after an Italian Renaissance architect. He designed the Banqueting House, all that remains of the old palace of Whitehall (formerly called York Place, as the London residence of the archbishops — see *Henry VIII*), a west portico for St. Paul's Cathedral, Lincoln's Inn Chapel, and the west side of Lincoln's Inn Fields. The Civil War is matter of general history. London first sided with the king, but not for long. The Corporation protected the five members of Parliament who fled from Westminster to avoid arrest (a tablet in the council chamber of the Guildhall commemorates the event), and eventually raised troops for Parliament. The Puritan regime brought destruction. Away went the Eleanor Crosses at Charing and Cheapside; away went St. Paul's Cross, whilst the cathedral was used for horses and hucksters.

Every schoolboy, without the omniscience of Macaulay's, knows the two events in London's history with which the reign of Charles II is associated. The Great Plague (there had been many preceding—this was the last and worst) carried off seventy thousand of its citizens. The evidence of this to-day is the raised earth of many City churchyards, filled with its victims to overflowing, and in the registers of the churches. The curious should induce the courteous verger of St. Giles's, Cripplegate, to show his registers. In one month—July, 1665—six hundred and ninety-one burials resulted from the Plague. The Fire which occurred in the following year was a process of purgation. The known deaths were but six; the loss of property extended to eighty-four churches, thirteen thousand houses, and—to mention only the most important buildings—St. Paul's Cathedral, the Royal Exchange, the Customs House, Newgate Gaol, the greater part of Guildhall, and fifty-two of the Companies' halls. In short, five-sixths of the City was destroyed, only a small north-eastern segment being untouched. Amongst the City churches which escaped were St. Ethelburga's and St. Helen's, Bishopsgate Street, St. Catherine Cree, and St. Olave, Hart Street. In the latter church was buried, in 1703, Samuel Pepys, the diarist. To him we owe the best contemporary account of the Fire and the Plague (Defoe—who was born and died in the parish of St. Giles, Cripplegate—wrote a most vivid *Journal of the Plague*, but was a child of six when it occurred), and he also provided, with the particularity with which one might view the activities of a colony of ants through a museum showcase, the lives of Londoners, who like himself were neither saints nor scoundrels, between 1660 and 1669. Another diarist, who was Pepys's friend, John Evelyn, prepared a plan for the rebuilding of the City, as did also Sir Christopher Wren. Both had more to commend them from the geometrical than the historical point of view. There was to be a plenitude of straight streets; Ludgate Circus was to be the hub from which streets were to run off, equidistant, like the spokes of a wheel. Of the great main historical thoroughfares, only Cannon Street was to follow the old course, and even then for only part of the way. But the citizens would not wait for city-planners. They built more haphazard, but to our consolation they preserved more the past. Wren's ideas for the City were theory; his churches were the facts which actually became part of the new City. Those Londoners who think that Gothic is in architecture the only beauty which is a joy for ever, may nevertheless find delight in St. Paul's Cathedral, in the interiors of St. Stephen's, Walbrook, and St. Mary-le-Bow, or the spires of St. Dunstan's-in-the-East, St. Bride's, and St. Vedast's, Foster Lane.

James II's short reign added to London one landmark—perhaps I ought to say—sky sign—which still remains. On the north end of the Banqueting Hall at Whitehall there is a weathercock which he placed there. It was opposite his private apartments so that he might learn the direction of the wind while he was dreading the approach of William, Prince of Orange. These apartments and the whole of the palace, except the Banqueting Hall and a few adjoining buildings, disappeared in a fire in 1698. The residences of the quality tended to spread west. William III purchased Kensington Palace in 1689, and this remained the principal residence of the sovereigns until the death of George II in 1760. Meanwhile Bloomsbury Square, Cavendish Square, and Soho Square had been laid out as residential quarters, although there was still a remarkably rural aspect about London when De Saussure, a foreign traveller, described it in 1725. He mentioned the villages of Wandsworth, Islington, and Paddington, and it will be remembered that so late as 1768 Oliver Goldsmith, seeking rural tranquillity, far from the madding crowd of London, found it in a cottage off Edgware Road. You could see from Leicester Square (then called Leicester Fields) Temple Bar, and with a telescope the heads of the Scotch rebels of 1715 which adorned it.

In 1737 the Corporation commenced the burial of the River Fleet—a fitting demonstration of urban advance—by covering it in as far as Ludgate Circus, and in 1765 the rest of its course similarly disappeared from view. It must have been a foul stream. It was known as Fleet Ditch, and Pope wrote of it as "rolling its tribute of dead dogs to Thames." It had not worsened with age. In 1290 the White Friars complained that its stench overpowered their incense—and their priory was about a hundred yards from its course; in 1763 a Bromley barber, presumably in drink, strayed into it in the darkness, and was found the following morning not drowned but frozen. He was standing upright in the mud. The covering in of the Fleet synchronized with the erection of the Mansion House (the first building erected solely as a residence for the lord mayors), and as a consequence the Stocks Market, which had been on its site, was removed to the neighbourhood of the Fleet Prison and took its name.

One of the most piquant, though most sordid, spectacles of eighteenth - century London were the Fleet weddings, performed by disreputable clergy — usually prisoners for debt—who touted outside the prison for candidates for matrimony. They performed the ceremony without licence or question, sometimes even without knowing the names of the parties, in public-houses, brothels, or garrets. So many as two thousand nine hundred and fifty-four such marriages took place in four months; but eventually Lord Hardwicke's Marriage Act (1753) put an end to these misalliances. Those who wish to read more of this can do so in Besant's novel *The Chaplain of the Fleet*.

These happenings were symptoms of a general lawlessness. The watch, like the German clocks referred to by Shakespeare, needed watching that they might go right. The men who took the offenders to the watch-houses, one or two of which still remain (as at St. Sepulchre's Church), were hardly better than Dogberry and Verges. As Fielding—magistrate as well as novelist—wrote in *Amelia*, they were "chosen out of those poor old decrepit people who are from their want of bodily strength, rendered incapable of getting a livelihood by work. These men, armed only with a pole, which some of them are scarce able to lift, are to secure the persons and houses of His Majesty's subjects from the attacks of gangs of young, bold, stout, desperate, and well-armed villains. If the poor old fellows should run away from such enemies, no one I think can wonder, unless it be that they were able to make their escape." It is, in fact, on record that applicants for the post were rejected and reprimanded for being too sturdy for the job!

Two events connected with the Thames mark the history of the eighteenth century. In 1750 Westminster Bridge was completed, and it was followed, ten years later, by the first Blackfriars Bridge, which existed just a century. In 1760 the last of the houses on London Bridge disappeared. Nonsuch Palace, in a dilapidated condition, was then let out as business premises. The foundations of St. Thomas's Chapel remained until the destruction of the bridge between

1830 and 1832, and there was found beneath the masonry what were believed to be the bones of Peter of Colechurch, its first architect, who was buried there. In 1760 too, the London gates disappeared. Like the wall, for centuries they had been more historical than useful. Several were sold to a carpenter of Coleman Street, who gave one hundred and seventy-seven pounds ten shillings for Aldgate, one hundred and forty-eight pounds for Ludgate, and ninety-one pounds for Cripplegate.

The decade 1830–40 marks a dividing line between the London of history and the London of experience, and it is the limit of the recollection of all but a few to-day. At the commencement of the period the Metropolitan Police were introduced. In 1832 the Reform Bill became law. In 1834 the old Palace of Westminster was burned down, and it is piquant to recall that when it was proposed to erect the new Houses of Parliament on another site such as the Green Park, the Duke of Wellington vetoed it upon the ground that the river was a protection, and that it should never be placed where it could be completely surrounded by a mob. In 1836 the first train left a London terminus— it ran from London Bridge to Greenwich. In the same year appeared the first published volume of Charles Dickens. I may perhaps close this brief survey of London's history by remarking that despite all that has been done by men like Leigh Hunt, Augustus Hare, Rev. W. J. Loftie, Sir Walter Besant, and—in the present era—Wilfred Whitten, C. G. Harper, Walter G. Bell, and E. V. Lucas, writers like Dickens have done more than they could do to foster an increasing affection for what Lamb called the Old Jerusalem. This has been happily manifest in the interest taken in the new Regent Street, the fate of Waterloo Bridge, the proposed new bridge at Charing Cross, and the restoration of St. Paul's Cathedral. No doubt, Macaulay's New Zealander (whom Macaulay did not originate) was to see the ruins of St. Paul's, because there was felt to have been the cradle of the Londoner. Whilst, therefore, Australia— partly in the person of Grimmett, a New Zealander—may have captured the cricket ashes, no colonial will view the pyre of London, for "Everyman"—be he cockney or countryman—tends to love his city more and more.

DAY WALKS[1]

WALK I: *St. Paul's Cathedral—St. Botolph's Churchyard—Aldersgate—Shakespeare House—St. Mary Aldermanbury Church—Guildhall—Mansion House—Royal Exchange—Bank of England.*

CHRISTIANS regard wistfully the legend that upon the site of St. Paul's Cathedral was once a temple of Diana—"goddess of the Ephesians," and of the Romans as well. Its sole justification is the discovery, in 1830, upon the site of the Goldsmiths' Hall, north-east of the cathedral, of an altar bearing her image. It is, however, a small one, and most likely adorned a private house. The first authentic record of a church here is in connection with Mellitus, who became Bishop of London in 604. According to the Venerable Bede, under his bishopric, the church was erected by King Ethelbert, and one of the endowments given by him—the manor of Tillingham in Essex—still belongs to the Chapter.

The first building was destroyed by fire in 1087. The second originally consisted of a nave of twelve bays, transepts, and a short apsidal choir in the Norman style, but by 1240 the choir had been enlarged and rebuilt upon Gothic lines. The spire was four hundred and eighty-nine feet high (the present one is three hundred and sixty-five), and was not completed until 1513. After being thrice struck by lightning, it was destroyed by fire in 1561, and never rebuilt. The cathedral was the landmark of London, and Falstaff said of Bardolph: "This oily rascal is known as well as St. Paul's." Old St. Paul's fell into a ruinous condition, and in the reign of Charles I, Inigo Jones refaced it inside and out. He also added a classical portico to the west front, somewhat similar to Wren's subsequent design. Dr. Wren, as he then was, was appointed Assistant Surveyor-General of His Majesty's Works, and with a few others, notably John Evelyn, the diarist, was examining the cathedral a few days before the Great Fire of 1666 in which it was reduced to a ruin. The

[1] For particulars of hours of admission, fees, etc. see page 211.

first stone of the new cathedral was laid by Wren in 1675.
It was first opened for services in 1697, but the last stone
was not placed upon the summit of the lantern until 1710.
The master builder was seventy-eight—too old to make the
perilous ascent—and the work was thus crowned by his son.
In 1718, when he had been forty-nine years architect to the
cathedral, owing to intrigue, he was suspended.   He retired
to his house at Hampton Court, from whence he made a
pilgrimage once a year to sit beneath its dome contemplating
his work—"cheerful in solitude," wrote his son, "and as
well pleased to die in the shade as in the light." In 1723
he died at the age of ninety-one.

Those who first survey the cathedral, and perhaps after
experience of Canterbury, Salisbury, and other Gothic piles,
with feelings of disappointment, must remember that here,
less than anywhere else, was the architect allowed to follow
his own bent. Indeed, it might be said that one looks
around, as more than once invited, not only to view Wren's
monument, but a monument to the folly of committees from
whom Wren suffered much.

An itinerary may start with the Chapel of the Order of
St. Michael and St. George in the south aisle, which has a
beautiful screen of richly carved oak and an elaborate vaulting.
The Order was instituted in 1818 to honour men distinguished
in colonial and foreign affairs. A little farther on, on the
left, is Holman Hunt's picture "The Light of the World."
It is a modified replica of the original at Keble College,
Oxford. The most interesting monuments in the south
transept are General Abercromby's, and Sir John Moore's.
The expression of agony upon the face of the former figure
is lifelike, and the monument unique in the attendant
sphinxes, a reminder of the fact that the general received
his death-wound at Alexandria.   Moore's monument recalls
Rev. Charles Wolfe's poem—one of the best known in the
English language—and another fine description of his burial
in Thomas Hardy's *Dynasts*. Over this monument is a
thanksgiving window for the recovery from typhoid of the
Prince of Wales.   On the left, at the entrance to the choir,
is the statue of John Howard, the first erected in the cathedral.
His merits are fully and truly recorded upon the pedestal.
Charles Lamb made an unfortunate remark about this statue.

He had an idea that Howard was responsible for truant
Blue-coat boys being put into dungeons, and he wrote:
"Saving the reverence due to holy Paul I would fain spit upon
his statue." Howard certainly advocated solitary confinement, as a progressive step as compared with herding
prisoners together in small and foul apartments, but not for
children. Farther down the choir is a fine monument to
Dean Milman. The modelling of the forehead has em-
phasized the high mentality of the man who wrote an
admirable history of the cathedral, and histories of the
Jews and Christendom, whose candour caused a buzz of
theological hornets. The next monument is the only one
that in its entirety survived the Fire. It represents Donne
(1573–1631), a well-known Dean of St. Paul's, selections
from whose prose and poetry have been recently published.
Izaak Walton, a charming biographer, in his life of Donne,
related how one day he dressed himself in his funeral shroud,
stood upon an urn and had his picture painted. To remind
himself that mortality was the common lot of man, he kept
the painting continually by his bed, and after his death the
monument was similarly designed. We now pass through
the gate to view the altar and reredos. Over the doorways
leading to the apse are angels supporting the crossed swords
and keys, the arms of the diocese, and emblems of St. Paul
and St. Peter. The frieze over the crucifix bears the
inscription: *Sic Deus dilexit mundum* ("so God loved the
world"). The inscription over the north door, *Vas Electionis*
("a chosen vessel"), refers to St. Paul; that over the south
door, *Pasce oves meas* ("feed my sheep"), to St. Peter. The
section above has the Entombment in the centre, and the
Nativity and Resurrection on either side, with the crucifix
in the central position, and twisted columns of Brescia
marble supporting the entablature. Adjoining this is a
colonnade with a figure on the north of the angel Gabriel,
and on the south of the Virgin. Above the pediment is a
canopy with the Virgin and Child, with St. Peter and Paul
to the north and south, and surmounting them, the Risen
Christ. The bronze candlesticks are copies of those at
Ghent, which are believed to have been in old St. Paul's,
and the work of Benedetto of Rovezzano, who was brought
to this country by Cardinal Wolsey. The choir stalls,

adorned with Grinling Gibbons's carving, demand notice.
There are also a number of prebendal stalls, bearing in
Latin the name of the estate, or prebend, with which the
stall is endowed.   The title over one is *Consumpta per mare*
("swallowed up by the sea"), a catastrophe which occurred
about the time of the Norman Conquest, so that for some time
the occupant of the stall enjoyed the honour of office without
reward.   At the east of the north aisle is the Carnarvon
window.   One of the figures is said to have been modelled
from Mr. John Burns, a friend of the artist, Sir W. Richmond.
At the rear of the apse is the Jesus Chapel, so called after
one with a similar dedication in old St. Paul's.   The monument, altar and altar-piece and the lower range of windows
are a memorial to Henry Parry Liddon, Canon and Chancellor of St. Paul's, whose name was linked with Spurgeon's
and Parker's, a generation ago, as that of a prince of the
pulpit.   The altar-piece includes a copy of "The Doubting
of Thomas," by Cima, which is in the National Gallery.
The subjects of the windows are the Nativity and the
Martyrdom of Stephen.   The clerestory windows, with the
mosaics and other decoration of the apse, are part of Sir
W. Richmond's work.   The delicate ironwork of the gates
should be observed.   They were designed by Tijou, a contemporary of Wren's, and were made of the last iron obtained
from Sussex iron-fields.   Above the gates are mosaics: on
the north, "Melchizedec receiving tithes from Abram"; on
the south, "Noah sacrificing after the Flood."

We return to the nave by the south choir aisle, and notice,
on each side of the Milman monument, fragments from the
Temple of Jerusalem.   We will now pass across the entrance
to the choir.   The pulpit, beautifully designed in coloured
marble, is modern.   From this point we may look at the
paintings with which Sir W. Richmond adorned the dome.
They represent the burial, resurrection, and ascension of
Christ.   The spandrels portray on the west (south to north),
Isaiah, Jeremiah, Ezekiel, Daniel, and on the north the four
evangelists, St. Matthew and St. John after designs by
G. F. Watts.   Mr. John Burns has claimed that he also is
here, and the figure of St. Mark resembles his features as a
young man.   In a position corresponding with that of
Howard's statue on the south side, is one of Dr. Johnson, by

Bacon, a famous eighteenth-century sculptor. The figure is most impressive, but the garb is quaint. The Roman toga, it has been suggested, might be taken for a bathing towel swathed round the doctor's sturdy limbs as he made for the sea at Brighthelmstone, as Brighton was then called!

In the north transept, on the right, is a monument to Hallam, the historian, and opposite an artistic bronze tablet to the memory of Sir Arthur Sullivan (1842–1900). The marble portico leading to the north door bears Wren's epitaph, *Si monumentum requiris circumspice*—"If you would see his monument look around you." West of the transept is a statue of Sir Joshua Reynolds, first president of the Royal Academy. Then comes the list of deans since the Norman Conquest, and after that the Doors of Death, an impressive memorial to Lord Melbourne. Next of importance is the Wellington monument by Alfred Stevens. The equestrian statue was completed by Mr. Tweed in 1912 from Stevens's sketch model, now at South Kensington. There are bronze groups at the base of the curved pediment: "Virtue keeping Vice beneath its feet," and "Truth plucking out the tongue of Calumny." Past St. Dunstan's Chapel, and at the extreme west end, is the All Souls' Chapel with the Kitchener Memorial. The sculptor was W. Reid Dick, R.A. The altar was given by the Royal Engineers, the figure of St. George by Queen Alexandra's Imperial Military Nursing Service and the Territorial Army Nursing Service, and the large silver candlesticks by the London Rifle Brigade.

The crypt contains a most interesting series of graves. On descending, we see at once the gravestone of Robert Mylne (1734–1811), cathedral surveyor in 1766 and the architect of the first Blackfriars Bridge. On the left is a memorial to Sir John Goss, for thirty-four years organist to the cathedral. The epitaph is the opening bars of the anthem he composed for Wellington's funeral. We then reach the Painters' Corner, including graves of Turner, Landseer, and Millais. Van Dyck, the Flemish artist who was buried in old St. Paul's in 1641, is commemorated by a, mural tablet. On the right is the simple slab over the grave of Wren, with the epitaph placed there at the time of his death and repeated in the cathedral. On the right of

the entrance to the Chapel of St. Faith's is a beautiful
medallion of William Blake, inscribed with his famous lines:

> To see a World in a grain of sand,
> And a Heaven in a wild flower,
> Hold Infinity in the palm of your hand,
> And Eternity in an hour.

In St. Faith's Chapel, given to the parishioners when their
external chapel was destroyed, are seven monuments which,
not in their entirety, escaped the Fire. One is to Nicholas
Bacon, father of the famous chancellor. On the farther
side of the crypt is the Musicians' Corner, and after that we
come to a group of soldiers' graves, the latest of which is
Sir Henry Wilson's, with the inscription: "Murdered outside
his home, 36 Eaton Place, June 22nd, 1922." Close by,
Nelson's sarcophagus was made for Cardinal Wolsey. Not
inappropriately for the man who sang songs of the
sword, is a spirited bust of W. E. Henley, by Rodin,
whilst near by—in the centre—is a copper bust of George
Washington, the gift of the Sulgrave Institution, 1921. In
front of this is a large tablet to the memory of George
Cruikshank, illustrator of Dickens's earlier works. Its
detail is noteworthy. He is recorded as being born at "No —
Duke Street, St. George's, Bloomsbury," and as having "died
at 263 Hampstead Road, St. Pancras, London," whilst an
epitaph composed by his wife is dated 9 February, 1880.
Opposite is a tablet to the memory of Charles Reade,
"Author, Dramatist, Journalist," and close by are memorials
to Sir Walter Besant, one of the most genial and gifted of
London-lovers; G. M. Smith, to whom the *Dictionary of
National Biography* owes its existence, and Rev. R. H. Barham, author of the *Ingoldsby Legends*. Opposite these is
the grave of Sir George Williams, who founded the Y.M.C.A.
by setting apart a sitting-room in the premises of Hitchcock,
Williams & Co., St. Paul's Churchyard, for shop assistants,
and of George S. Nottage, the only Lord Mayor buried in
the cathedral. This honour was his because he died (1885)
during his year of office. At the end of the crypt is the
funeral car of the Duke of Wellington. It weighs eighteen
tons, and was drawn by twelve black horses. It was made
at Woolwich Arsenal, it is said in eighteen days, of metal
from guns captured by his armies. The names of his various

engagements are inscribed in golden letters. It has never been used since his funeral.

The Library and Whispering Gallery are worth a visit. In the former is the subscription list, opened after the fire, for the rebuilding. It is headed by Charles II's promise to give one thousand pounds per annum, but there is no record that the money was paid. There are also documents bearing the signatures of Wren and Archbishops Laud and Cranmer. The Whispering Gallery, a stage higher, will reveal its secrets under the directions of the guide. Sir James Thornhill's paintings in the dome can best be seen from here. They portray incidents in the life of St. Paul: (1) His conversion. (2) His preaching before Sergius Paulus and the punishment of Elymas the sorcerer. (3) The sacrifice of Lystra. (4) The conversion of the gaoler at Philippi. (5) His preaching at Athens. (6) The burning of the books at Ephesus. (7) The defence before Agrippa. (8) His shipwreck at Melita. From the stone gallery a wonderful panoramic view of London can be obtained. Also from this vantage point the external features can best be studied. Wren's design of a screening wall, to conceal buttresses, is manifest, and it will be noticed that the figures of the apostles are not full-bodied. The number of steps to the ball is six hundred and twenty-seven, about two-thirds of which take the visitor to the stone gallery.

Leaving the cathedral by the north door, and turning right we reach Newgate Street, on the other side of which is Aldersgate Street. A tablet on the right indicates the site of the old gate. A short walk brings us to St. Botolph's Church. This saint was the patron saint of travellers and his churches are always associated with gates. There are such churches still at Aldgate and Bishopsgate, and there was, prior to the Fire, one also at Billingsgate. This church is most unsightly, and its graveyard, sometimes called Postmen's Park by reason of its proximity to the General Post Office, is more interesting than the church. Under a long canopy will be found tablets recording the sacrifice of a number of humble heroes. They were placed here through the instrumentality of G. F. Watts, a small statue of whom will be seen, to commemorate the Jubilee of Queen Victoria, 1887. There are now fifty in all, a number having been added since Mr. Watts's death in 1904. The two last were unveiled by Mr. Lees-Smith, Postmaster-General, in 1930.

On leaving the churchyard, we may turn into Little Britain, the turning alongside it. On the first pillar of the churchyard wall, will be seen a plate representing the old Aldersgate. The side represented is that which faced north. The equestrian figure is James I, and on each side of him the prophets Samuel and Jeremiah. The texts quoted to justify this flattery, for which James had an insatiable appetite, were 1 Sam. xii. 1, and Jeremiah xvii. 25.

Leaving the churchyard, we walk along Aldersgate Street and turn down Falcon Street, on the right. On the right is a churchyard, and opposite is Monkwell Street, which here joins Silver Street. On a tavern is a tablet commemorating Shakespeare's residence in a house on the site, the only London address of Shakespeare's which can be verified by a document still extant. This discovery we owe to Professor Wallace, an American, who found in the Record Office the papers relating to an action, Bellot *v.* Mountjoy, in 1612. It appeared that Bellot had been apprentice to Mountjoy, a wig-maker, and had done the correct thing according to the canons of romance and married his master's daughter; the wedding was solemnized at the Church of St. Olave, Silver Street, the burial ground of which is the one mentioned. In 1612 the son-in-law sued his father-in-law in respect of a dowry of fifty pounds, alleged to have been promised but not paid, and amongst the depositions is one of "William Shakespeare of Stratford-on-Avon, in the County of Warwick, gentleman, of forty-seven or thereabouts." It appeared that Shakespeare had resided in the house when the marriage was mooted, and that the house was at the corner of Monkwell Street and Silver Street. It is not indicated which corner, but—perhaps with a sense that a tavern, even though modern as this, is more historic than business premises— the tablet has been placed upon the former. It must not, however, be assumed that Shakespeare borrowed the name of his landlord for his herald in *Henry V*, as this is his name in Holinshed's *History*.

We walk down Silver Street until Wood Street is reached, then turn to the right and take Love Lane on the left. This brings us to the Church of St. Mary, Aldermanbury. The first part of the dedication is indicated by a small figure of the Virgin Mary over the porch; the second part refers to the houses of the aldermen, which were hereabouts in medieval London. The church dates from 1677. Its interest to us is almost entirely in the pre-Fire building, which is associated with Shakespeare, for the reason that Heminge and Condell, who with much labour published the First Folio in 1623, were parishioners. Both of them acted before Queen Elizabeth, and to both Shakespeare bequeathed mourning rings. They were both buried in the churchyard: Heminge in 1630, Condell in 1629. The monument erected in 1895, justly commemorates them as well as the great dramatist. The bust is designed after the Chandos portrait (in the National Portrait Gallery). The First Folio is shown open with the title page similar to the original, and on the left, an extract from Heminge and Condell's address "To the great Variety of Readers"—"We have but collected them, and done an office to the dead, to procure his Orphanes guardians: without ambition either of selfe-profit, or fame only to keep the memory of so worthy a Friend and fellow alive as was our Shakespeare." On one of the sides of the pedestal is an account of Heminge and Condell; on the other a quotation from *Henry VIII*: "Let all the ends thou aim'st at be thy country's God and truth's." It was in the old church that Milton married his second wife, Catherine Woodcock, the "late espoused saint" of the sonnet in 1656. The one association of the present building is that here, in 1693, Judge Jeffreys was buried. He was first interred in the Tower of London, where he died (1688), but on the ground that he had been a distinguished parishioner, his body was exhumed. The text over his grave is "The Lord seeth not as man seeth." It perhaps represents the only hope that the infamous judge had of anything approaching eternal bliss! If we leave the church behind us we shall arrive at Milk Street, which leads to Cheapside. Shakespeare's only allusion to Cheapside is in the first sentence of this book, and as the "Mermaid" is dealt with elsewhere here we will leave him.

If we proceed down Aldermanbury, and turn left along, Gresham Street, we reach King Street; turning left we arrive at the Guildhall. It takes its name from the guilds referred to in our historical sketch. It was built between 1411 and 1426. Whilst the front was the work of George Dance, the younger, in 1789, the porch through which we enter dates from the original building. On its vaulting are the arms of Edward the Confessor (five martlets surrounding a cross), and Henry VI (lions, etc.). The hall was completed in the reign of the last monarch, and probably the "little cottage" which, according to Stow, preceded it, was erected in the reign of the former.

The Hall was badly damaged in the Fire. The roof was of solid oak, and according to a contemporary, the whole body was "in a bright shining coal as if it had been a palace of gold, or a great building of burnished brass." The Hall was rebuilt, probably a substantial part of the walls was again utilized, and in place of the old hammer-beam open roof, was substituted a flat one. This is said to have been designed by Wren as a temporary expedient. It remained, however, until 1864, when it was replaced by the present one, designed by Sir Horace Jones, the City architect. It has some resemblance to the pre-Fire roof.

Turning to the left, on entering, one of the fifteenth-century windows will be seen. It was uncovered during restorations in 1909. The west screen and gallery date from 1864. The figures of Gog and Magog were made in 1708 and cost seventy pounds. They apparently succeeded figures of wicker work and paste board carried in the Lord Mayor's show, when every great city had its symbolical giants. Gog is the figure armed with a globe full of spikes, fastened to a long pole by a chain—a weapon known in the Middle Ages as "the morning star." Magog is armed with a shield and spear and is arrayed in conventional Roman costume. The figures, which are fourteen feet six inches high, have their heads wreathed with laurel. It is probable that they were intended to represent Gogmagog and Corineus, who in the myths of the monks, fought the battles of the Trojan invaders against the early inhabitants of this island. They are both mentioned in the Bible (Ezek. xxxviii-xxxix. Rev. xx. 8).

The stained-glass windows are of great interest. The one next to Magog shows William the Conqueror holding in his hand the first charter granted to the City; Henry I presenting

the charter granting the County of Middlesex, and the right
of hunting in the forests; Richard I granting the charter
conveying to the City of London the conservancy of the
Thames; Edward VI presenting the charter of the four
royal hospitals. The next window—British inhabitants of
London with representation of the Tower of London; erection
of the Roman Wall beneath which is a view of Baynard's
Castle; Edward the Confessor recognizing the privileges of
the citizens, and below old London Bridge; Edward IV making
four citizens Knights of the Bath, and below representation
of St. John's Gate, Clerkenwell. The window over Nelson's
monument—Fitzwalter doing service as Bannerer, 1303;
youth swearing fealty at Paul's Cross, 1259; Henry Picard,
Mayor, feasting five kings: Edward III, and Kings of France,
Scotland, Denmark, and Cyprus, 1363; holding a great joust
on London Bridge, 1395; Edward I ordering gold to be
coined in Tower, 1344; the building of Guildhall; William
Walworth slaying Wat Tyler, 1381; Henry V making his
triumphal entry into London after Agincourt, 1415. The
door leads to the council chamber lobby and in the window
over it is a full-length representation of FitzEylwin, London's
first mayor, and of Whittington. The window over the
Wellington monument contains figures of Saints Andrew,
Bride or Bridget, Helen, and Dunstan, with London churches
dedicated to those saints with the exception of St. Helen,
who is represented by the Church of St. Sepulchre, Snow
Hill, as she founded the Church of the Holy Sepulchre at
Jerusalem. Beneath the figures are medallions containing
views of Holborn Viaduct, Blackfriars Bridge, the New
Meat Market in Smithfield, and Temple Bar. The handsome
eastern window was presented to the Corporation by the
Operatives of Lancashire and the Cotton Districts in 1870,
in acknowledgment of assistance during the cotton famine
(1862-5). The middle division on both tiers is devoted to
representations of historical subjects connected with the
City's history, such as the rebuilding of the City by Alfred
the Great, and the granting of the charter by William the
Conqueror. In the side division (north side) are Whittington
and Gresham; on the south, John of Gaunt, Duke of Lancaster, and Sir Thomas Stanley. In the tracery of the
main portion of the window are the shields of the twelve

D

great Livery Companies. The next window, on the south
side, represents the restoration of the City charter in 1688.
The following one shows Edward VI passing to Westminster
to be crowned, 1547, and below the reception of the five
kings already referred to. The window over Alderman
Beckford's monument shows the dream of Rahere and his
vision of St. Bartholomew which led to the founding of the
Hospital and Church of St. Bartholomew the Great. The
next window has for its subject the death of Wat Tyler,
whilst the second window from the west end is of particular
interest to Jews. It shows their banishment by Edward I,
and their petitioning Cromwell in 1656 to be allowed again
to reside here. The lower compartments represent the
swearing in of the first Jewish Lord Mayor, Sir David
Salomans, in 1855. The west window, unveiled in 1870,
was filled with stained glass by the Corporation in memory
of Prince Consort. The leading ideas and occupations of
the country are represented. The large monuments which
unfortunately in some instances obscure the windows are
self-explanatory.

The Lord Mayor is elected in the Guildhall on 29 September, and here is held the famous banquet on 9 November.
The Lord Mayor takes precedence of all but the sovereign
in the City, and even the latter must formally ask for
admission to the City at Temple Bar. The Council Chamber
and Aldermen's Room are worth a visit. The former has
some fine panelling and a statue of George III, by Chantrey;
the latter is the finest room in the Guildhall. In addition
to the panelling it has some paintings by Sir James Thornhill,
whose work also adorns the dome of St. Paul's Cathedral.
The Museum can be reached from the Guildhall, and before
descending the staircase, the tablet on the left of it should
be noticed. It enumerates the famous trials that took place
here: Anne Askew, the Earl of Surrey, the famous sonneteer,
Lady Jane Grey, Dr. Lopez, and Dr. Garnett. The last
two are particularly interesting to Shakespeareans. Lopez
was a Spanish Jew and was accused of poisoning Queen
Elizabeth, to whom he was one of the physicians. He
was executed at Tyburn in 1594, and the anti-Semitic
feeling aroused led to a revival of Marlowe's *Jew of Malta*,
and possibly also to the writing of *The Merchant of Venice*.

Garnett was one of the gunpowder-plot conspirators. On the scaffold he delivered a defence of equivocation. In *Macbeth* the drunken porter, the janitor in imagination of hell gate, says: "Here's an equivocator, that could swear in both the scales against either scale, yet could not equivocate to heaven."

The staircase leads to the crypt, only about half of which is now shown to the public. It dates from the time of the erection of the Hall and is a fine specimen of the architecture of the period. It is the most extensive in London. In the vaulting, Edward the Confessor's arms are again visible. It was fitted up in 1851 as a baronial hall for the purpose of a banquet held to celebrate the opening of the Great Exhibition. The City Companies' plate was used, there were mirrors in recesses, tapestries made from Bayeux examples, and City policemen in suits of armour from the Tower. Here are a number of Roman coffins, and a stone one found beneath the Guildhall Chapel, which was demolished in 1822. It evidently once contained the body of the City's trumpeter. The Museum, which is approached by a short passage from the crypt (from which the thickness of the walls will be observed), is of great interest. In the far left-hand corner will be found some Roman relics, including Austalis's tile (see page 16) and the mosaic pavement referred to in our history. In cases in the centre are such valued treasures as the sword of the French commander at the Battle of the Nile, presented to the City by Nelson whose accompanying letter is exhibited. There are other valuable autographs: Wellington, Garibaldi, Queen Elizabeth, Wren, and Dickens. There is also a copy of the purchase deed of Shakespeare's house at Blackfriars; the Corporation bought the original for the very modest price of one hundred and forty-five pounds in 1843. In the corner opposite the Roman relics are some fragments of the Eleanor Cross in Cheapside, whilst in a case in the centre will be found some spurious relics deliberately made for sale by workmen. There is in this museum a fine collection of tavern signs. The most interesting are the Bull and Mouth's from Aldersgate Street. One represents a bull within a large open mouth; on either side grapes, and above the arms of Christ's Hospital on whose ground the inn stood, while a bust of Edward VI, donor of the hospital, surmounts the whole. A tablet contains the couplet:

Milo the Crotonian an ox slew with his fist,
And ate it up at one meal—ye gods! what a glorious twist.

The other sign is near the staircase and shows a bull's mouth with two long rows of molars. This gives point to a delightful passage in Dickens's *Haunted Man* concerning Tetterby's baby: "It was a peculiarity of this baby to be always cutting teeth. Whether they never came or whether they came and went away again is not in evidence: but it had certainly cut enough, on the showing of Mrs. Tetterby, to make a handsome dental provision for the sign of the Bull and Mouth." The staircase referred to leads to another short flight. Beside this are statues of Charles I and Edward VI, which once stood outside the Guildhall Chapel. At the top of the stairs, from which will be seen a large painting of the death of Wat Tyler, is a room containing a valuable collection of watches and clocks, the property of the Clockmakers' Company. Passing this, we reach the Reading-room and Library—both open to the ordinary public. The Library contains about two hundred thousand volumes and pamphlets and some twenty-five thousand prints. After traversing the Library we descend some stairs and find ourselves in a passage in which is a fine collection of old insurance companies' signs. This passage leads to the porch where we first entered. The Corporation Picture-gallery need not detain the visitor unless his time is spacious. The Church of St. Lawrence, Jewry, is interesting. Annually on Michaelmas Day the Lord Mayor and Corporation attend here prior to the election of the new Lord Mayor. The dome of the church is a gridiron, in recognition of the fact that St. Lawrence is said to have been martyred upon one.

Returning to Cheapside and turning left we soon reach the Mansion House. It was erected between 1739-52, as the first official residence of the Lord Mayors, upon the site of the Stocks Market established in 1282. The architect was George Dance, the elder. The principal room is the Egyptian Hall in which many State banquets are held. It is necessary to make previous application by letter to the Lord Mayor's secretary for permission to view. The Royal

Exchange is the third building on the site. The first was opened by Queen Elizabeth in 1571, and burned in the Great Fire. The second was destroyed in the same way in 1838. The present building was opened by Queen Victoria in 1844. A statue of Sir Thomas Gresham, which Pepys records escaped the first fire, is said also to have survived the second. The grasshopper on the vane of the Royal Exchange was also on the previous building, some say the first also. It is part of Gresham's family crest, and was supposed to have been adopted by him because, as a child, he was lost in a field and discovered through the chirping of that insect. The crest has, however, been traced in the family at a much earlier date. The Royal Exchange is little used now as a meeting place for merchants, but every Wednesday the Wax Chandlers and the Chemical Makers assemble at their respective pillars. The interior court is open to the public. There are statues of Sir Thomas Gresham, Queen Elizabeth, Charles II, and Queen Victoria, and a series of frescoes representing scenes in the history of London. The Bank of England, a windowless building, was designed by Sir John Soane and dates from 1734. The charming little garden court is on the site of the churchyard of St. Christopher-le-Stocks Church, which was demolished in 1771—the first of Wren's churches to disappear. Members of the staff who died during the war are commemorated by a statue of St. Christopher carrying the Christ Child, unveiled in 1921. Every night a detachment of Foot-guards marches along the Embankment to guard the Bank of England. This dates from the "No Popery" riots of *Barnaby Rudge*, when it was threatened.

WALK II: *Church of All Hallows, Barking—Tower of London — Tower Bridge — Monument and Southwark Cathedral.*

Opposite Mark Lane station is the Church of All Hallows, Barking. It is the descendant of a church which was burned down in 1087. Charred wood from that catastrophe was found under the paving in 1923. The arches in the nave date from about 1210. The tower dates from about 1660, and the pulpit from 1613. It contains the best

collection of monumental brasses of any church in the
City. The most elaborate is in the centre of the nave
(under a mat), to the memory of Andrew Evyngar and
Ellyn his wife, dating from about 1535. Here were tem-
porarily buried some of the victims of the Tower: Bishop
Fisher for a few weeks until his body was taken to St. Peter's
Chapel; Henry Howard, Earl of Surrey, from 1547 until
1614, when he was reinterred in Framlingham in Suffolk;
Archbishop Laud from 1645 to 1663, when his remains were
conveyed to St. John's College, Oxford, of which he had
once been president. The church is associated with Barking
by reason of the fact that it was in the early period of its
history in the possession of the abbess and convent of
Barking in Essex. It is the church of Toc H, and the
chapel with its ever-burning lamp will be seen in the north-
east corner.

Turning left, we come to Tower Hill where there is an
enclosed plot of ground and, not far from the rails, a bare
patch. In its centre is a tablet with these words: "Site of
the Ancient Scaffold. Here the Earl of Kilmarnock and
Lord Balmerino suffered, 18 August, 1746." Why Lord
Lovat, who was executed later and was the last to suffer
by the axe, is omitted it is difficult to explain. He was the
last of a long line including Sir Thomas More, Bishop Fisher,
the Earl of Surrey, the Earl of Strafford, and Archbishop
Laud. The palatial building behind the green is the Port
of London Authority's, and next to it is Trinity House,
erected between 1793 and 1795 for the "Guild, Fraternity
or Brotherhood of the most glorious and undivided Trinity,"
which received its charter from Henry VIII in 1514. The
object of the corporation is to safeguard navigation and
control lighthouses, etc.

According to Shakespeare's Duke of Buckingham (see
Richard III, Act III, Scene i) it was on record that Julius
Cæsar built the Tower of London. What the record was it
is difficult to say. Stow, whilst throwing doubt upon its
alleged Roman origin, passed on the piquant suggestion of
Fitzstephen that its mortar was tempered with the blood of
beasts, and probably it was to Fitzstephen or some chronicler
who derived from him that Shakespeare referred, as at the
time *Richard III* was written Stow had not published his

Survey. Whilst, however, we must regard this as a myth, in view of the fact that the Tower stands at the eastern extremity of the City and of possible Roman fears of a flotilla assailing it from the river, it is likely enough that some kind of Roman fortification stood here.

The White Tower or Keep was commenced in 1078, and William the Conqueror entrusted the work to Gundulf, a monk of Bec in Normandy (from whose abbey Tooting Bec derives its name) who was afterwards Bishop of Rochester, where he built its castle. The present buildings are partly of Norman architecture, but, from the reign of Rufus onwards, our Norman and Plantagenet kings successively made additions to the fortress until Henry III's time (1216-72) when it finally assumed something of its present form. The chief alterations since have been the destruction of the Great Hall (probably the scene of Anne Boleyn's trial), south of the White Tower, which was demolished in Cromwell's time, of the Wardrobe Tower which disappeared in the time of Charles II, and the Lion Tower which remained until the 1840's. Sir Christopher Wren made some alterations which have met with justifiable disapproval. Believing the Tower to be entirely Roman, he decorated it in the Italian Renaissance style. Only two or at most four windows (in the south face of the top floor) can be taken to be in anything like their original condition. To Wren also we owe the cupolas on its four turrets, though from the illumination in the manuscript of Froissart's *Chronicle*, representing Charles of Orleans, grandson of Charles V, as a prisoner in the White Tower, it would appear that these somewhat resemble those previously in existence. The Tower has been prison, palace, and menagerie. In respect of the first it was so used up to 1820 when the conspirators of Cato Street were confined within its walls; as a residence for kings until the time of Charles II (it was always the custom for the night preceding the coronation to be spent there); as a menagerie up to the formation of the Zoological Gardens at Regent's Park in 1834. This was the year of Charles Lamb's death, and one of his pleasures was going to the Tower to see the lions when there was a holiday at the Blue-coat School.

We are reminded of this at the outset, as the ticket office was on the site of the Lion Tower, and where in the eighteenth century as many as eleven lions were kept. Long after the lions had gone it was a joke played upon country cousins to write out for them a formal order to see the lions washed! We reach first the Middle Tower, originally built by Edward I, but entirely refaced. Through its archway we reach the stone bridge, which leads to the Byward Tower, in part the work of Edward I and in part of Richard II. In the arch is the portcullis grate with the wheel for raising and lowering it. We pass on the left the Bell Tower. In 1928 there was revealed a part of the plinth of this tower believed to date from 1190 when it was on the river front. Here Sir Thomas More and Fisher, Bishop of Rochester, were imprisoned by Henry VIII, and the Princess Elizabeth by her sister Mary. Here Lady Arabella Stuart died half crazed and heart-broken in 1615. On the western wall which connects this with the Beauchamp Tower will be seen the Prisoners' Walk, along which Elizabeth took exercise. The Traitors' Gate, with St. Thomas's Tower, is now on our right. Here were landed prisoners who had been tried at Westminster, such as Sir Thomas More, Cromwell, Earl of Essex, Queen Catherine Howard, Lady Jane Grey, and the Duke of Monmouth. One other was the Princess Elizabeth in 1554. She sat down on the wet steps leading from the gate into "Water Lane" (as the thoroughfare in which we stand was called) and refused to budge unless she was promised her liberty. She was only induced to move after a long parley in the rain. St. Thomas's Tower was built by Henry III, and contains a small chapel or oratory dedicated to St. Thomas of Canterbury. We leave the Bloody Tower on our left and turning to the left enter the Inner Ward and get our first view of the White Tower. We notice, as we approach, the remains of the Wardrobe Tower, which at one time stored a portion of Queen Elizabeth's thousands of wigs and gowns. Here, for a short time in 1618, the year of his execution, Sir Walter Raleigh was a prisoner.

The original entrance of the White Tower was on the south side on the first floor, being reached, as usual in Norman castles, by an external stair. The outer walls vary in thickness from fifteen feet to eleven feet in the upper story. Many royal prisoners have been confined here—

David King of Scots and the Duke of Orleans already mentioned. On entering we find ourselves in what is known as the Record Room. At its southern end is the Crypt. On the walls are inscriptions carved by prisoners who took part in Wyatt's rebellion in 1554. Here are shown also instruments of torture, a model of the rack, and the block and axe—last used in 1747. We pass to the Small Arms Room.. The large opening in the south wall is the original entrance to the White Tower. It is now filled with glass. Ascending by the staircase at the south-west angle we reach the Chapel of St. John, built in 1080, the most complete specimen of Norman architecture. It is very plain now, but was once rich in decoration. The walls, in Henry III's time, were covered with rich tapestries, the floor was beautifully tiled, and the windows filled with stained glass. The few scraps of ecclesiastical finery left after the Reformation were dispersed or defaced by Cromwell, and in the reign of Charles II the chapel became a storehouse for State records, which it remained until they were removed to the present Record Office in 1857. There are no old fittings in the chapel now, but although the glass in the windows is fairly modern, being part of Horace Walpole's collection at Strawberry Hill, it is not so blatantly so as the harmonium! It was in this chapel that Queen Mary was betrothed to Count Egmont, proxy for Philip of Spain, in 1554. The triforium served as a place where the queen and the ladies of the Court could hear mass.

Leaving the chapel by the north door we enter the Sword Room. Here is one of the original fire-places of the White Tower. This room opens on to the Weapon Room and adjoins the Tudor Room. According to some authorities it was here—before the formal deposition at Westminster— that Richard II resigned the throne to Bolingbroke. In this room, in a glass case, is a helmet decorated with rams' horns sent by the Emperor Maximilian, some say to Henry VIII, others to Will Somers the king's jester, the registry of whose burial can still be seen at Shoreditch. The nature of the gift suggests that the latter theory is correct. We leave the Tudor Room by a north-east staircase and reach the Mortar Room. At the south end is the sub-Crypt of St. John's Chapel, which may have been at

times used as a prison. There is a tradition that here Guy
Fawkes spent his last hours. The adjoining apartment is
now called the Cannon Room, from the exhibits.

We now leave the White Tower, and the next place of
interest is Tower Green where private executions took place.
It was specially paved by orders of Queen Victoria. Amongst
those who suffered here were Lord Hastings (see *Richard III*),
1483, Anne Boleyn, 1536, Catherine Howard, 1542, Lady
Jane Grey, 1554, Earl of Essex, 1601.

All of these except the first are known to have been
buried in the Chapel of St. Peter-ad-Vincula (St. Peter in
Chains) close by. This chapel was first built by Henry I,
eight hundred years ago. There is, however, little of the
original work left and it was largely rebuilt in 1305-6, and
restored by Henry VIII. The chestnut beams of the roof
and most of the windows and arches are of the latter period.
Inside the door, on the left, is a brass tablet on which are
the names of thirty-four prominent personages who were
executed or died in the Tower and were buried in the chapel.
The first is Gerald Fitzgerald, Earl of Kildare, 1535; the
last Simon, Lord Fraser of Lovat, 1747. Beside this tablet
are the coffin-plates of the latter and one of the other
Scotch lords who were executed after the Battle of Culloden.
These were discovered when, in 1876, a committee of experts
went into the task of verifying the burials. Until then no
mark existed to indicate the place of interment, but now
are clearly inscribed the spots where Anne Boleyn, Catherine
Howard, the Dukes of Northumberland and Somerset, and the
Duke of Monmouth are buried. Lady Jane Grey and her
husband, Lord Guildford Dudley, are known to rest near
the foot of the Blount monument, but the committee considered it unsafe to verify this lest the monument should be
damaged. The names of those not verified but known to
be buried before the altar are recorded on a stone on the
floor just outside the altar railings.

Over the pulpit is a tablet to the memory of Sir Allen
Apsley, Lieutenant of the Tower when Sir Walter Raleigh
was a prisoner. Let into the wall is an old gravestone which
was brought in from outside and is to the memory of
"Talbot Edwards, gentn." He was in charge of the Crown
Jewels when Colonel Blood attempted to steal them in

1671. On the north wall of the chancel is a fine alabaster monument to two Lieutenants of the Tower, Sir Richard and Sir Michael Blount, father and son, who held appointments during the reign of Elizabeth. Amongst the family groups kneeling in prayer, one widow can be identified by a cap streamer and the other by the skull held in the hand. At the head of the north nave is a sarcophagus, on which lie the figures of Sir Richard Cholmondeley (Lieutenant of the Tower under Henry VIII) and his wife. It was made during his lifetime, but when the sarcophagus was opened no remains were found, and evidently Sir Richard, having severed his connection with the Tower, was buried elsewhere. There were in the sarcophagus, however, the remains of an old font and these form part of the one which will be seen on the left as we leave the chapel. This is the chapel of which Lord Macaulay wrote a memorable passage, in the course of which he said: "In truth there is no sadder spot on earth."

We now enter the Beauchamp Tower, so named after Thomas Beauchamp, Earl of Warwick, here imprisoned in 1397. There are ninety-one inscriptions on these walls, the oldest being cut by Thomas Talbot in 1462. Some, however, have been brought from other places in order to preserve them. On the ground floor, against the private door, is carved "Robert Dudley." He was a son of the Duke of Northumberland, executed in 1553, and brother to Lord Guildford Dudley who was executed the following year. He himself was condemned to death, but afterwards liberated and survived until 1588. On the left at the entrance is a carved cross with the other religious emblems and the name of Peverel, and the date 1570. This is supposed to have been cut by a Roman Catholic prisoner, perhaps a "Peverel of the Peak"! Over the fire-place is this inscription in Latin: "The more suffering for Christ in this world the more Glory with Christ in the next," etc. It is signed "Arundel, June 22, 1587." The son of the Duke of Norfolk who lived at Charterhouse and was executed in 1572 (see page 189), he died in 1595 after ten years' imprisonment. Near to the western recess is a long inscription by William Rame, 1559. It commences: "Better it is to be in the howse of morning than in the howse of

banketing." G. Gyfford (16) philosophizes: "Grief is over-
come by patience"; as also Poole (57): "To serve God—to
endure penance—to obey fate—is to reign," 1564; and
again (52): "A passage perillus maketh a port pleasant,"
1568. Nos. 48 and 85 are simply: "Jane." It is not known
that Lady Jane Grey was ever imprisoned in the Beauchamp
Tower, and this was probably inscribed by her husband,
Lord Guildford Dudley. In the window (66) is a rebus of
Thomas Abel, chaplain to Catherine of Aragon. His
determined advocacy of her cause offended the king. He
was executed for denying the king's supremacy in 1540.

On leaving the Beauchamp Tower, we take the passage
on our right and reach the Bloody Tower, so called from a
series of tragedies associated with it. The most familiar is
the murder of Edward V and his brother, Duke of York,
in 1483. Here Henry Percy, Earl of Northumberland, was
stabbed to death in bed in 1584, and in 1613 Sir Thomas
Overbury was poisoned. Famous prisoners were Ridley,
Latimer, and Cranmer, the three martyrs, Sir Walter Raleigh,
Archbishop Laud, and Judge Jeffreys. Raleigh was here
fifteen years and during his confinement wrote his *History
of the World*, an early copy of which—presented by Sir
Charles Wakefield, a former Lord Mayor—may be seen in
his old prison. Judge Jeffreys drank himself to death. It
has a portcullis still in working order though it probably
dates back to Norman times. Adjoining this gateway is
the Wakefield Tower where now the Crown Jewels are kept.
It was in an oratory here that Henry VI was murdered
whilst at prayer. Annually, on the anniversary of his death
lilies are strewn upon the spot under the will of an unknown
benefactor. Henry VI founded Eton College, and the three
lilies on its escutcheon are derived from him. Before leaving
the Tower we may walk along its river front and get a good
view of the Tower Bridge, which has been savagely attacked
by H. G. Wells. It was completed in 1894. The bascules,
to allow of the passage of large vessels, are raised about
fourteen times daily. The higher stage is no longer open
for foot-passengers. In view of the time taken in ascending
and descending the stairs, probably no time would be gained
by so doing as the bascules can be raised in one and half
minutes. The designers of the bridge were Sir Horace

Jones and Sir J. Wolfe Barry, and it cost the Corporation a million and a half of money. We now turn down Lower Thames Street, opposite the entrance to the Tower, and in about ten minutes we pass the Customs House and Billingsgate Market and reach the Monument.

The Monument was erected between 1671 and 1676 and was designed by Wren. It is two hundred and two feet high and the same distance from the house in Pudding Lane (first turning on the left looking east) where the Fire started. It was originally intended to surmount it with a statue of Charles II, but this being too costly, the present vase of flames was substituted. The bas-relief is the work of Caius Gabriel Cibber, father of the dramatist whose autobiography is in Everyman's Library. It displays a female figure representing the City of London, sitting on ruins in a languishing condition. Behind is Father Time gradually raising her up. Another female figure gently touches her with one hand, and points upward to two goddesses sitting in the clouds, one with a cornucopia, denoting Plenty, the other having a palm branch on her left hand, signifying Peace. At her feet is a beehive, denoting Industry. Underneath the figure of London is a dragon supporting a shield bearing the arms of the City. Over her head are shown houses burning, and behind Time is a group of citizens raising their hands in encouragement. Opposite these figures is Charles II in Roman costume with a baton in his right hand and a laurel wreath upon his head, commanding three attendants to go to London's relief. The first is Science—in her hand a figure of Nature with numerous breasts ready to give assistance to all. The second is Architecture holding a plan in the right hand and in the left a square and compasses. The third figure is Liberty waving a cap in the air. Behind the king is James, Duke of York, holding a garland to crown the rising city, an uplifted sword for her defence. The two figures behind are Justice with a coronet, and Fortitude, with a reined lion. Above these figures are houses being built, and underneath the stone pavement, is a figure of Envy gnawing a heart and emitting pestiferous fumes from its mouth. On the east side is a list of the Lord Mayors during the period of erection; on the north side an account of the Fire and the destruction it caused (thirteen thousand two hundred houses, four hundred streets, etc.), and on the south side an account of the provisions made for rebuilding. In 1681, through the machinations of Titus Oates, lines were added attributing the Fire to the Catholics. On James II's accession these were deleted. They were reinstated when William III succeeded, causing the poet Pope to write:

> Where London's column, pointing at the skies,
> Like the tall bully, lifts its head and lies,

and finally taken down in 1830.

There are two delightful references to the Monument in Dickens. Old John Willet, allowing young Joe sixpence for "the diversions of London," recommends him to go to the top of the Monument and sit there. "There's no temptation there, Sir—no drink—no young women—no bad characters of any sort—nothing but imagination." And Tom Pinch, exploring London, sees a lady and gentleman commence the ascent after putting a shilling in the keeper's hand (the Monument is the only London sight to get cheaper with the years—perhaps due to a fall in wind!), whilst he sat down and laughed. "They don't know what a many steps there is," he said. "It's worth twice the money to stop here. Oh, my eye!" The number of steps is three hundred and eleven, but some may think it worth the view.

We now walk over London Bridge to Southwark Cathedral, on the right. In about the year 607 a church was built upon this site and dedicated to St. Mary Overy, a lady of whom is related one of the most melodramatic of London stories. Her father was the ferry-keeper before the bridge was built and also a great miser. To save money he feigned to be dead, supposing that grief would diminish appetite. Instead, his household fell to feasting at the old man's death, and, like Daniel Quilp, he was minded to interrupt the premature merriment. Attempting to do so, he was met by a boatman who, believing he had met a ghost, applied an oar to its head and really killed the unfortunate actor. The ferryman's daughter Mary then sent for her lover, who lived in the country and had hitherto been forbidden the house by her father. On his way there he fell from his horse and was killed, whereupon in grief Mary assigned the oversight and profits of the ferry to a nunnery which she caused to be erected and entered herself. The word Overy is usually explained as meaning "over the water," but some consider it a corruption of "over the ferry." In A.D. 852 the nunnery was dissolved, and St. Swithun, Bishop of Winchester, established a body of secular priests. In 1106, the College of Secular Priests was dissolved, and the Canons Regular of St. Augustine were established. These "Black Canons" built a church on the site in the Norman style. In 1207 the Norman church was almost entirely destroyed by fire, and the friars built a Gothic church. In 1469 the stone roof of the nave fell in, and a new roof was built of wood. In 1540 the Augustinian Priory was dissolved and the dedication was altered from that of St. Mary Overy to that of St. Saviour. In 1830 the wooden roof of the nave, being in a dangerous condition, was removed, and for nine years the building was without roof and exposed to the weather. In 1839 the walls of the nave were pulled down and an unworthy church built on the site. In 1877, Southwark was transferred from Winchester to the diocese of Rochester. In 1889, Bishop Thorold of Rochester appealed for funds to rebuild the nave. This was done, the architect being Sir Arthur Blomfield, and his work so beautifully harmonizes with the rest of the building that most people visiting the cathedral are surprised to learn that the nave is a modern one. The work was completed in 1897. In 1905, the diocese of Rochester was divided and Southwark constituted a diocese with Dr. Talbot as first bishop.

We may commence a tour of the interior at the north aisle. The window at the extreme west of this aisle contains a figure of St. Augustine of Hippo, as patron of the Augustinian Canons referred to. The next window is to Goldsmith—for a short time a physician on Bankside. The Nativity is represented as illustrating Goldsmith's skill in delineating the joys of family life, and St. Patrick as the patron saint of his native country. Next is the Johnson window, commemorating the doctor's friendship with Thrale, whose brewery was in the neighbourhood. The scene is the Judgment of Christ. Pilate is asking "What is truth?" and Johnson was concerned with that question. Then comes the Sacheverell window. This stormy petrel

of the pulpit of Queen Anne's time was once a chaplain at
St. Saviour's Church.   Cruden, who is next celebrated, com-
piled a concordance and was buried in Deadman's Place,
Southwark, a burial ground now covered by Barclay & Per-
kins's brewery.   The Bunyan window is due to the fact that
Bunyan preached, late in life, in a chapel in Zoar Street,
Southwark.   The windows include a famous scene from the
Pilgrim's Progress.   We then come to the tomb of John
Gower, who died in 1408.   He was a benefactor to the
church and founded a chantry in the Chapel of St. John the
Baptist where he was buried.   Both have disappeared, and
the tomb stands upon the site.   Gower's head rests upon
the three volumes of his poetical works.   Horace Smith (of
Rejected Addresses fame) referred to the monument in 1825
as "from the dampness of its situation hurrying to oblivion."
Fortunately this has not happened, but it became very
dilapidated and a recent appeal to the literary men of
England for subscriptions for its restoration produced eight
and sixpence!   The explanation is that Gower is never read.
He is simply a name in the history of English literature,
whereas Chaucer is still a personality pulsating with the
life of his Canterbury pilgrims.   The window above the
Gower monument is appropriately dedicated to the latter,
and shows the Borough High Street and the "Tabard."   In
the north transept is a curious tomb of a quack doctor who,
with the assistance of a Merry Andrew, sold pills, said to
be composed of rays extracted from the sun, which were
guaranteed to cure a whole regiment of diseases.   He is
shown semi-recumbent with a full-bottomed wig, and a long
inscription aptly tells us that his praises all men's mouths
rehearse.   No doubt he was buried here solely as a parishioner, and the tomb erected from the profits of his pills.
We then come to the beautiful little Harvard Chapel, the
name given to a chapel dedicated to St. John the Divine
when it was restored.   The cost was borne by members of
Harvard University, in recognition of the fact that John
Harvard, their founder, was baptized in the church.   Harvard
men also gave the altar and the ornaments.   The window
is the work of an American artist, John la Farge, and it was
unveiled by Mr. J. H. Choate, American ambassador, in
1905.   The arms of Harvard College are on the left, and

those of Emmanuel College, Cambridge, where Harvard took his degree, on the right. In the centre is the only piece of old glass in the cathedral — the conjectural date is the sixteenth century. Here there are signs of the old Norman chapel in the shafts at the north-east corner, which helped to form the apse. On entering the chapel we pass through one of two Norman arches, the capitals of which exhibit "hatched" moulding. This is a very early form of decoration, common before chisels were used.

Entering the north choir aisle we come to the tomb of John Trehearne, servant to Queen Elizabeth, who died in 1618. The whole family is shown, his wife, who died in 1645, and four children below. The principal figures are holding a tablet upon which an inscription states that had Death been susceptible to persuasion, as he assured Everyman in the old morality play he was not, James I would have prevailed upon him to extend the earthly service of his porter! A little farther on is the effigy of a supposed crusader. It is a remarkably fine piece of oak carving, and may represent a member of the De Warren family, several of whom were buried in the church. It will be noticed that the sword is drawn five or six inches from the scabbard. It has been suggested that this refers to the practice of reciting the creed every morning, the sword being drawn and put back at the words "Jesus Christ our Lord."

The retro-choir, now the Lady Chapel, was erected about 1228, at about the same time as the choir. It is, however, still more graceful, and the clustered columns (each quite separate from the other as can be seen by passing a slip of paper between them) and the beautiful curves of the groined vaulting make it a delight to the eye. The windows are of interest. That at the north end is devoted to the Rev. Laurence Saunders, the Rt. Rev. Robert Ferrar, and the Rev. Rowland Taylor. Entwined about the robes of the third there is a scroll bearing the supplication from the Litany in the early prayer books against "the tyranny of the Bishop of Rome and all his detestable enormities." The corresponding window in the southernmost of the four eastern bays displays figures of the Rev. John Rogers, Bishop Hooper, and the Rev. John Bradford. The seventh of the martyrs is commemorated

E

in the central window on the south, viz. the Ven. Archdeacon Philpot, the three lights being filled with pictorial scenes from his trial. All except the last were tried in this chapel, the Consistory Court being set up about where is the first-mentioned of the windows. As a window, the best is one on the north side, in the Decorated style. The modern glass is by Kempe, but it is an excellent imitation of medieval work. The three lights contain figures of King Charles I, Thomas à Becket, and Archbishop Laud, held to be martyrs also.

Passing into the south choir aisle, we arrive at the tomb of Lancelot Andrewes. He ruled several dioceses and after translation to Winchester was "translated to heaven," according to a contemporary. He died in Winchester Palace (see p. 179) in 1626. The book the bishop holds was probably intended to represent his famous *Manual of Devotions*. He was a very learned man, and one of the translators of the New Testament. We now pass into the choir and examine the wonderful screen originally designed by Fox, Bishop of Winchester, about 1520, but misguidedly restored from time to time. All the numerous figures were inserted between 1905 and 1912. Space forbids a complete list, but a few are particularly interesting. The fourth from the left in the top row is the great Beaufort of *Henry VI*. This famous Bishop of Winchester, who was buried here, participated in the trial of Joan of Arc. The third from the left on the second row is Thomas à Becket. The next on the left is St. Swithun, the weather saint. The third figure from the right on the same row is Gower (note the inkhorn and pen). The first figure on the last row is Henry I, and the second Lancelot Andrewes. Next to him, on the right, is Bishop Fox, and lastly, Edward VII who, as Prince of Wales, laid the foundation stone of the new nave in 1890, and as king attended again in 1905 for the inauguration of the church as a cathedral. From here we get a good view of the monument to Richard Humble. The inscription states that he was "Alderman of London." He is attended by his two wives. The second was apparently more fashionable than the first as she sports a conical hat. His sons and daughters are represented in bas-relief on the north and south sides of the basement. The inscription, not easily read, is worthy of quotation:

> Like to the damask rose you see,
> Or like the blossom on the tree,
> Or like the dainty flower of May,
> Or like the morning of the day,
> Or like the sun or like the shade,
> Or like the gourd which Jonas had,
> Even so is man whose thread is spun,
> Drawn out and cut and so is done.
> The rose withers, the blossom blasteth,
> The flower fades, the morning hasteth,
> The sun sets, the shadow flies,
> The gourd consumes and man he dies.

The lines have been attributed to Beaumont and to Quarles. In the floor of the choir are stones bearing the names Philip Massinger, John Fletcher, Edmund Shakespeare, the latter a brother of William who was buried here with a forenoon knell of the great bell, costing twenty shillings, according to the monthly accounts of the church, in 1607. It is not known where either of the three was buried and the lettering is modern. We will now go to the south choir aisle. Here are stacked some interesting wooden bosses from the fifteenth-century roof which were taken down in 1830. In one the devil is shown swallowing Judas Iscariot who wears a kilt. The pelican feeding her brood from her breast was the usual symbol of sacrifice. There is a man with a twisted tongue, perhaps to indicate a liar, and a figure with swollen face, possibly intended for gluttony.

On leaving the south choir aisle for the north transept, we walk over some Roman tesseræ found eighty years ago in the churchyard. Above it is a memorial brass to Susanna Barford who died at the age of ten. The inscription is almost illegible and therefore worth quoting:

> And death and envye both must say 'twas fitt
> Her memory should thus in brasse bee writt.
> Here lyes interr'd within this bed of dust,
> A virgin pure not stain'd by carnall lust.
> Such grace the King of Kings bestow'd upon her,
> That now she lives with Him a maid of honour.
> Her stage was short, her thread was quickly spun,
> Drawne out and cutt Gott heaven her work was done.
> This world to her was but a traged play,
> Shee came and saw 't, dislik't and pass'd away.

She is described on the same brass as "the non-such of the World for Piety and Virtue in so tender years." On a pier by the transept door is a sculptured and coloured representation of Cardinal Beaufort's arms. Beaufort rebuilt the south transept and this largely accounts for the architectural differences as compared with the north transept. The next object of interest is the beautiful alabaster figure of Shakespeare. A light behind the head brings out its beauty. The courteous verger relates how a schoolboy once said, upon a taper being so used, that he had for the first time seen through Shakespeare! It will be noticed that in the background are Winchester Palace and the Globe Theatre. The window above was presented by Sir Frederick Wigan, Bart., in memory of his brother-in-law, Arthur Cecil Blunt. An allegorical figure of Poetry is shown, supported by Shakespeare and Spenser. Above the Muse the sacred Dove, a symbol of inspiration, is hovering. The next window is in memory of Philip Massinger; it was unveiled by Sir Walter Besant in 1896. The subject taken is from his play *The Virgin Martyr*, and represents an angel bearing flowers and fruits of Paradise from the martyr (St. Dorothea) to a sceptical lawyer who had asked for proof of survival. In the figure of the saint ladies should notice the Dorothy bag. Next is the Fletcher window. The subject was suggested by the dramatist's *Knight of Malta*. St. John the Baptist stands in the lower compartment as patron of the Knights of St. John, holding a standard displaying the word "Concordia." Then comes the Beaumont window, and the intimate relations between him and Fletcher are suggested by the design portraying David and Jonathan. Lastly there is a window to Edward Alleyn, player and warden of the queen's bears, who largely from that inhuman sport became rich enough to found the College of "God's Gift" at Dulwich. Alleyn is represented reading the charter of his foundation in the College Chapel, attended by Bacon, Inigo Jones, and other contemporaries.

The font is a modern one, but a piece of adjacent thirteenth-century wall-arcade should be noticed. On the other side of the nave, at this west end, is a case containing various relics, including Roman tiles and German bombs.

WALK III: *Westminster Abbey—St. Margaret's Church—Westminster Cathedral — Buckingham Palace — London Museum—St. James's Palace—Tate Gallery.*

A tradition has it, as companion to that of St. Paul's, that on the site of Westminster Abbey was once a temple to Apollo. Its alleged destruction by an earthquake, legally act of God, suggests the slender foundation for the story. The discovery of Roman flooring and Roman wall beneath the nave justifies the belief, however, that here was some kind of Roman building. The foundation of a church upon the site of the temple to Apollo is ascribed to the King Lucius who is supposed to have built St. Peter's, Cornhill. A second foundation is ascribed to Sebert, King of the East Saxons, who died in 616. According to a legend, carefully fostered by the monks, it was consecrated by St. Peter in person. He appeared to a fisherman who was casting his net into the Thames and who ferried him over from the Lambeth side. After the mystic consecration, St. Peter said: "For yourself, go out into the river; you will catch a plentiful supply of fish, whereof the larger part shall be salmon." In the Chapter-house to-day, starting from the top of the steps, will be seen a line of tiles adorned with salmon as an illustration of the story. The official title of the abbey to-day is the Collegiate Church of St. Peter, Westminster. History commences with the consecration of the Norman church and monastery of Edward the Confessor in 1065, a week before that king's death. Beneath the floor of the present sacrarium are chambers containing the bases of three clustered pillars. These, with a section of the wall of the apse beneath the Confessor's Chapel, are all the parts which are known to remain of the old Norman church, as distinct from the monastic buildings which adjoined it, of which considerable portions are still standing. Early in the thirteenth century a Lady Chapel was built by the Abbots of Westminster to the east of the Confessor's church. A little later Henry III commenced rebuilding. He had placed himself under the special protection of Edward the Confessor who had been canonized in 1163, and he determined to pull down the old church and build a new one as a fitting shrine for the body of his patron.

The demolition began in 1243 and the new church had been completed as far westward as the fifth bay of the nave when Henry died in 1272. To this, new burying-place the body of St. Edward the Confessor had been transferred in 1269. Not until 1376 was the completion of Henry's church attempted and not until 1528, under Abbot Islip, did the work reach its end.

Space forbids any description of the architecture of the abbey, and those who love this art—and all who revere old buildings must yearn to understand it more—may well acquire one of the books recommended in our bibliography for this aspect. We may, however, notice on entry the beauty of the triforium and the clerestory and remember that to the Catholic mind all this was symbolical. The lowest row of arches on which the others depend and from which they spring symbolized God the Father; the second row represented God the Son. The two arches under one signified the two natures under one Person. The circle with five points, called cusps, was a reminder of the Five Wounds. The highest tier of arches which proceeded from the two lower ones, lets in the light, and thus symbolized God the Holy Ghost who enlightens and teaches through the Church.

The North Transept is largely devoted to statesmen, W. E. Gladstone (d. 1898) being the last of these. On the left is a huge tomb of the Duke and Duchess of Newcastle, an admirable illustration of William Morris's remark that the abbey was a registration office for notorieties. Now, with a paucity of space in the abbey and a plenitude of literary patricians, the duke and duchess would have been denied this honour. In their day the literary world was small, and rush-lights apt to be treated as stars. Pepys said of the lady: "Her whole story is a romance and all she does romantic." She was a voluminous writer, and her servants had to be ever ready to transfer to paper the inspirations of their mistress. Her effigy holds an open book, a pen case and inkhorn, symbolic of her passion. The epitaph says she was "a wise, wittie and learned Lady, which her many Bookes do well testifie." The cream of them is included in a volume in Everyman's Library.

Standing by the brass rail which encloses the Sanctuary,

we notice the beautiful mosaic floor dating from 1268. The materials were brought from Rome by Abbot Ware. On the left are three tombs, with stone canopies, considered to be the most beautiful in the abbey. The nearest and smallest is that of Aveline of Lancaster (d. 1273), wife of the Earl of Lancaster (d. 1296) whose tomb is the farthest of the three. The tomb in the centre is of Aymer de Valence (d. 1324), the son of a half-brother of Henry III. On the right is the long tomb of Anne of Cleves, fourth wife of Henry VIII.

From here we have a good view of the two rose-windows. The north was entirely remodelled in the latter part of the nineteenth century, but the glass dates from 1722. The south window is the earliest of this type and was entirely remodelled under Sir Gilbert Scott in 1849–50. The glass, however, only dates from 1902. Leaving the Sanctuary and resuming our original direction we pass into the South Transept. At the side of a seat just before we reach Poets' Corner is a slab to the memory of Old Parr, here simply by virtue of longevity. He was alleged at his death in 1635 to have lived one hundred and fifty-two years. The earliest poet represented in Poets' Corner is Chaucer—in the eastern aisle. His canopied altar-tomb was not erected until at least one hundred and fifty years after his death in 1400. The lines on John Gay's monument:

> Life is a jest; and all things show it,
> I thought so once; but now I know it,

were placed there at his own request. The last to be laid here was Thomas Hardy in 1929. A monument does not necessarily denote burial in the abbey. Milton was interred in the Church of St. Giles, Cripplegate, Goldsmith in the Temple, and Coleridge at Highgate. In the western aisle is a monument to Casaubon (1560–1614). This "learned critic," as Fuller, the Church historian, called him, may have suggested to George Eliot that admirable portrait in *Middlemarch* of a parson-pedant. On the tablet are scratched the initials "I.W.," and the date 1658. This was done by Izaak Walton.

We pass now to the gates of the South Ambulatory which gives access to the most interesting parts of the abbey.

Immediately to the right is the Chapel of St. Benedict, the founder of the order to which the Westminster monks belonged. Close to the railings is the alabaster effigy of the great abbot, Simon Langham (d. 1376), who became a cardinal and inspired the erection of the existing nave. On the other side of the ambulatory is the reputed tomb of Sebert, King of the East Saxons (d. 616), traditional founder of the abbey. The canopy, however, is fifteenth-century work. The paintings on the back of the sedilia represent Edward the Confessor, the Angel of the Annunciation, and the Virgin. They date from the early years of the fourteenth century. Between the Chapels of St. Benedict and St. Edmund is a tomb said to contain the bones of Catherine, an infant daughter of Henry III (d. 1257), and other royal children. The next chapel is that of St. Edmund. The most conspicuous tomb is the Earl of Pembroke's (d. 1296). He was a half-brother of Henry III, and largely responsible for the victory of his forces at Evesham (1265). The tomb is decorated with Limoges enamel, in splendid preservation. It is odd to see in the floor a slab commemorating a modern—Edward Bulwer, first Baron Lytton—but did he not write *The Last of the Barons?* Perhaps the most interesting monument is to Lady Elizabeth Russell. She points at a skull, and it used to be said that the protruding finger was an indication that she died of a poisoned finger, the result of a prick whilst sewing on Sunday. Addison's Sir Roger de Coverley heard this from a guide. Dickens was probably thinking of it when he made Little Nell show such a figure in Mrs. Jarley's Waxworks.

Next is the Chapel of St. Nicholas, with a number of imposing tombs including those of Sir George and Lady Villiers, parents of the famous Duke of Buckingham, who was Charles I's favourite and was murdered at Portsmouth in 1628. We now reach Henry VII's Chapel. Immediately to the right is a narrow doorway leading to the south aisle. Here the principal tomb is that of Mary Queen of Scots. She was first buried at Peterborough Cathedral but brought to Westminster by her son James I, that she might have "like honour" and a "like monument" to the queen who beheaded her. Upon the north wall is a bronze medallion of Sir Thomas Lovell who built the old gateway of Lincoln's

Inn which still stands. Upon the altar steps small stones record the names of those in the vault beneath—Charles II (d. 1685), Mary II (d. 1694), William III (d. 1702), Queen Anne (d. 1714) and her husband Prince George of Denmark (d. 1708). To the left of the altar pavement is a monument to General Monk (d. 1670), so largely instrumental in the restoration of the Stuart dynasty.

We now enter Henry VII's Chapel. A short study of its rich ornamentation and beautiful tracery will justify its being characterized as "The Wonder of the World." It was originally intended by Henry VII to be the shrine of Henry VI, for whose canonization he applied to the Pope. The terms were too hard for the parsimonious king, and so Henry VI's bones were left at Windsor and it was made the place of Henry VII's sepulture. It was not until 1519—ten years after his death—that it was completed. In the fine bronze gates at the entrance, as also round his tomb, will be seen the various badges and devices of the king. The tomb, of black marble, was the work of Torrigiano and English assistants. It is strange that Henry VIII was not buried here instead of at Windsor. In the same vault lies James I (d. 1625). Close by is the vault of Edward VI and George II, the last king buried in the abbey. In the East Chapel is a stone slab recording the burial there of Cromwell and other regicides. Their bodies were exhumed at the Restoration. In one of the side chapels is the Coronation Chair, used for Mary II in 1689, and close by is an oak pulpit said to have been used by Cranmer when preaching before Edward VI. A little farther along is a slab in the floor with the name of Elizabeth Claypole. This was the favourite daughter of Oliver Cromwell, whose death—a few weeks before his own —greatly affected him. Her body was undisturbed. In the North-east Chapel is buried the wife of James I, Anne of Denmark, and in the North Chapel is the large tomb of the first Duke of Buckingham, murdered in 1628. The banners over the stalls are those of the Knights of the Bath who were installed in 1913, the first formal installation since 1812. To right and left, on entering the chapel, are the stalls and banners of the Sovereign and of the Great Master of the Order. The coats of arms are fixed between the seats of the upper tier of stalls; the misericords or hinged seats of the lower tier merit examination.   In the north aisle is the monument to Queen Elizabeth.   The sculptor, while the queen lived, would hardly have dared to carve so unlovely a face as that of the imperial votaress.   Her sister Mary is in the same vault, and a Latin inscription at the west end may be translated: "Tenants alike of throne and grave, we sisters, Elizabeth and Mary, lie sleeping here in hope of the resurrection."   Exhibited upon the tomb is the famous ring presented by Queen Elizabeth to Essex and which, it is said through the malice of the Countess of Nottingham, failed to reach the queen in time to save the earl's life.   In the east wall is a small urn containing the bones supposed to be those of Edward V and Richard of York, who were murdered in the Tower.   They were placed here in 1674 by Charles II.   Close by, Princess Sophia (who died at three days in 1606) and Princess Mary (d. 1601 at two years) are commemorated; one by a cradle, the other reclining on her elbow on a small altar-tomb.   This is often called "The Innocents' Corner."   In this chapel is the grave of Addison, next to the monument to his patron Lord Halifax. He was buried—in 1719—by torchlight.

We now descend the steps of the chapel and mount a wooden stair leading to the Chapel of Edward the Confessor. At its entrance is the mutilated wooden effigy of Henry V. The effigy formerly covered with plates of silver, had also a silver head.   Sir Roger de Coverley attributed its disappearance to "some Whig," and added, "You ought to lock up your kings better."   His helmet, shield, and saddle hang on a beam in accordance with the king's wishes.   A modern altar, with an ancient slab, covers the remains of Henry's queen, Catherine of Valois (d. 1437).   She was originally buried in the Lady Chapel but disinterred on its demolition. The coffin was placed next to her husband's tomb and for more than two hundred and seventy years she remained exposed to the vulgar gaze.   This is how it came about that Samuel Pepys in 1669 "had the upper part of her body in my hands, and I did kiss her mouth, reflecting upon it that I did kiss a queen."   The tomb of Edward the Confessor is of Purbeck marble, and was formerly decorated with gold and glass mosaic, of which the chief remnant is on the twisted pillar at the north-west corner.   The mosaic pavement dates from 1268. The recesses are said to have been for pilgrims to pray in. The body of Edward was seen and robbed of its gold cross and chain by one of the choirmen at the coronation of James II.

Opposite the altar, against the fifteenth-century screen, is the Coronation Chair with the State Sword and Shield of Edward III beside it. This chair was made for Edward I, and every sovereign since, excepting Edward V—king only in name—has been crowned upon it. It has only once left the abbey—when Cromwell caused it to be removed to Westminster Hall for his installation as Lord Protector. Robert Bruce appealed to Edward II for the restoration of the famous Stone of Scone, upon which Scottish kings were crowned and which is beneath the seat, but in vain. A recent agitation in Parliament with the same object was similarly unsuccessful. A number of other royal tombs are near Edward the Confessor's. Edward III and his queen, Philippa, lie side by side; also Richard II and his queen, Anne of Bohemia. After his death in Pontefract Castle in 1390, Richard was first buried at King's Langley (Herts), and brought to the abbey many years later by Henry V. In the eighteenth century some of these royal tombs were shockingly neglected, and in 1766 a Westminster schoolboy removed Richard's jaw-bone. It was returned to the custody of the abbey in 1906 and replaced inside the tomb. Other tombs are of Henry III, Edward I, and Queen Eleanor (d. 1290), who is commemorated by three crosses, still remaining, at Northampton, Geddington, and Waltham.

Opposite the tomb of Eleanor is the Chapel of St. Paul; next—to the right—the Chapel of John the Baptist. Neither calls for special mention. Immediately to the right of the latter is the Chantry Chapel of John Islip, Abbot of Westminster, 1500–32. The only remains of his tomb are a slab forming a table under the window on the north side. On the frieze and elsewhere is his rebus—an eye on a slip of a tree. In the upper chapel are the wax effigies. In earlier times it was customary to carry in the funeral procession of a king or queen an effigy clad in the royal apparel. They were either made of wood or modelled in wax. The first on record is that of Henry III. Those now shown are Charles II; the Duchess of Buckinghamshire with

her little boy; the Duke of Buckinghamshire, her last
surviving son; Frances, Duchess of Richmond (in coronation dress) with her parrot; Queen Anne; William Pitt,
Earl of Chatham; William III and Mary II; Queen Elizabeth;
and Lord Nelson. The Duchess of Richmond sat for the
figure of Britannia on the coins. Nelson with the exception
of the coat, is arrayed in clothes that actually belonged to
him. It must not be assumed that the later figures were
to be seen in funeral processions, for showing them were the
perquisites of members of the choir and they came to be
manufactured for profit.

Turning now to the right we reach the Chapels of St. John,
St. Michael, and St. Andrew. Here is the gruesome monument
to Lady Elizabeth Nightingale, "more theatrical than
sepulchral," wrote Horace Walpole. It is said that a robber
who broke into the abbey one night was so terrified by
Death's figure in the moonlight that he dropped his tools
and fled in dismay from the building. Leaving the chapels
by the north ambulatory gate and passing straight across
the transept we enter the west aisle of the north transept.
At the end is a fine stained-glass window to the memory of
John Bunyan, representing scenes from *Pilgrim's Progress*.
It was unveiled by Dr. Clifford in 1912. We return and
turn to the right into the north choir aisle. Here are
memorials of musicians and scientists, amongst the former,
Dr. Burney (d. 1814) the father of the author of *Evelina*;
amongst the latter, Sir Isaac Newton, Alfred Russel Wallace,
and Darwin (buried close to his monument).

We walk down the nave past the choir screen. The outer
screen was put up in 1831, but the inner stonework is thirteenth
century. In the centre is the grave of David Livingstone.
A pulpit of early Jacobean carving stands against a pillar.
Farther west a stone marks the place where, in an upright
position, Ben Jonson was buried. At the far end, next
to the huge East India Company's monument to Major-
General Lawrence, is Campbell-Bannerman, wearing a
delightful smile. On the west wall is Joseph Chamberlain,
looking the reverse. Close by is a black marble altar-tomb
(erected by Parliament in 1909) to the memory of his
political chief, the Marquis of Salisbury. On one side are
bronze statuettes of his great Elizabethan ancestors, Lord

and Lady Burleigh, with their son, the first Earl of Salisbury, and his wife Elizabeth.   The earl holds a model of Hatfield House.   Over the great west floor is the monument of Pitt, and in the enclosure on the left, sometimes called "Little Poets' Corner," are busts of Wordsworth, Keble, F. D. Maurice, Dr. Arnold of Rugby, Matthew Arnold, Charles Kingsley, and Henry Fawcett, the blind Postmaster-General.   In the middle of the nave is the grave of "An Unknown Warrior" —buried on 11 November, 1920, in the presence of the King and the Royal Family.   The coffin was covered with earth brought especially from France, and the Union Jack was used at Vimy Ridge, Hill 60, and on the Somme.   There are a few interesting monuments in the South Choir Aisle. On the right is Major Andre's (see page 204) and opposite is Canon Barnett's, first warden of Toynbee Hall.   Next to this is Thomas Thynne's.   He was murdered in the Hay-market in 1682, and the crime is realistically represented in bas-relief.   The assassins were in the pay of Count Königs-marck, the Count hoping by his death to obtain the hand of his bride, the heiress of the Percy family.   On the right-hand side are monuments to Isaac Watts and the Wesleys, whilst opposite is a fine shelf tomb with an alabaster figure to the memory of Thomas Owen, an Elizabethan judge (d. 1598), and Flaxman's bust of Paoli.   The Corsican general, who was buried in the island, was Boswell's hero before Johnson.   On the other side again is the much-criticized monument to Sir Cloudesley Shovel, who was drowned off the Scilly Isles in 1707.   He appears as a beau in a long periwig, reposing upon velvet cushions under a canopy of state.   Horace Walpole declared that the mere sight of it made "men of taste dread such honours."   He supposed the sculptor was Bird.   He might have been more shocked had he known it was Grinling Gibbons.   We now go through the door that leads to the cloisters and turn right along the North Walk.   On a tablet, in the second section of the arcading, is a tablet to William Laurence, who died at the age of twenty-seven in 1621.   He was private secretary to one of the prebendaries, and the epitaph says:

> Short Hand he wrote: His Flowre in prime did fade,
> And hasty death Short Hand of him hath made.

A little farther on, also on the wall, is a tablet to the memory of Ephraim Chambers, author of the first English encyclopædia. In the Latin epitaph he describes himself as "familiar to many, himself known to few: one who walked betwixt light and shade, neither erudite nor ignorant, who passed his life in devotion to letters." Turning into the West Walk, a little way past the centre, on the floor is a slab to the memory of John Broughton who died in 1789. He was a prize-fighter, but, in deference to the protest of the Dean and Chapter, he is described as "Yeoman of the Guard." It is said that the space beneath his name was intended to be filled with his greater claim to fame. We turn now into the South Walk and notice on our right the Gothic doorway, dating from Edward III's time, which once led into the Abbey's refectory. Near this are four niches, formerly used as towel aumbries. A little farther on, in the floor, is a slab to the memory of some nephews and nieces of John Wesley. Their father was at the time an undermaster at Westminster School. It is pleasing to notice next an unusually large inscription to an abbey plumber, and at the end of this walk is the large blue gravestone called "Long Meg," marking the supposed resting-place of twenty-six monks who died of the Black Death in 1348–9. The stone received the name of Long Meg as being, according to another old tradition, the grave of the famous giantess "Long Meg of Westminster," who lived in Henry VIII's reign. Opposite this, and cut on the bench, are the names of the abbots from the time of the Norman Conquest until 1222, who were, with one exception, buried here. The names were recut in 1752, but the dates are incorrect and the names not rightly placed. There are three stone effigies. One of Gislebert Crispinus (1114) is in a good state of preservation; the others are badly disfigured. Turning left, just past the Chapter-house, is the flat gravestone of Tom Brown (d. 1704), a wit and a scholar who is known to-day as the author of the epigram about Dr. Fell. A little farther on in the walk is the inscription which is the most appealing of all in the abbey: "Jane Lister, dear child. Died Oct. 7, 1688." The father of Jane, a Dr. Lister who was physician to Queen Anne, evidently thought that brevity was the soul of grief, for when he buried his wife in the old parish church of Clapham he inscribed a stone (which still remains) "Dear Wife." Almost below it is a slab in memory of Mrs. Aphra Behn, the only woman dramatist and novelist interred at Westminster. Neither her character nor her work merited this distinction. These cloisters are mainly fourteenth-century work.

We now return to the Chapter-house, entering through a thirteenth-century archway which has lost much of its original beauty. The stone statues of the Virgin and Child over the arch have crumbled away, and part only of the two angels, which used to be on either side of the entrance, is left. On the left as we enter is a Roman sarcophagus, with a cross on the lid, found in 1869 on the north side of the abbey, with an inscription to the effect that it was made by the sons of Valerius Amandinus in memory of their father. On the right are memorial tablets to James Russell Lowell and Walter Hines Page. The Chapter-house was built between 1250 and 1253. It is fifty-eight feet in diameter —one of the largest in England. In 1540, on the dissolution of the monastery, the Chapter-house passed under the jurisdiction of the Crown, and it is still Crown property. From the reign of Edward I until 1547 when they commenced to use St. Stephen's Chapel of the Palace of Westminster, the House of Commons met here. It was completely restored by Sir Gilbert Scott in 1865, its beauty having been largely impaired by its use for about three centuries as a Record Office. It then had wooden galleries and a wooden floor. Happily the latter protected the beautiful tiled pavement laid down in 1250. Its colours are still remarkably brilliant, and on some tiles—on the right of the central pillar—there are depicted Edward the Confessor giving his ring to a beggar (i.e. to the disguised St. John the Evangelist); a king on a throne (Henry III), playing with his hound; a queen (his wife, Eleanor of Provence) with a hawk on her hand; an abbot with hand upraised in blessing. Few traces remain of the mural paintings. Those on the west wall, where a few remain, were of scenes from the Apocalypse which were executed by the order of John of Northampton, who was a monk here from 1372 to 1404.

South of the Chapter-house, we come to the Chapel of the Pyx. We enter through a Norman arch, enclosing a

heavy oak doorway with six locks. This vaulted chamber,
also under the jurisdiction of the Crown, was built between
1040 and 1100. The altar—the only stone one left *in situ*
at Westminster—with a thirteenth-century piscina on the
column near by, shows that it must have been used as a
chapel at some time before the fourteenth century when it
was the monastic treasury. We know of its use then from
a famous crime. Whilst Edward I was on his Scottish wars,
money hoarded up for supplies and jewels were stolen from
this little chapel. The abbot and forty-eight monks were
taken to the Tower and tried. The abbot and the rest of
the fraternity were released, but the charge was brought
home to the sub-prior and the sacrist. The sequel is truly
melodramatic. Inside and outside of the door by which
the passage is entered were found under the iron cramps
fragments of what was declared to be the skin of a human
being. Presumably this was to terrorize any other weak
clerics with the horrors of wrath in this world as well as
that to come. In this chamber was afterwards kept the
"pyx," or box, containing the standard pieces of gold and
silver, and here once a year took place the trial of the pyx—
the testing of the current gold and silver coinage which now
takes place in the Mint. The circular indentation in the
altar is probably the place where the metal was poured.

Leaving the chapel and continuing to the left we enter
the dark cloister, from which a doorway leads to the Norman
undercroft of the dormitory, now the abbey museum. Here,
in glass cases, are some more effigies of royal personages;
the most ragged of the "ragged regiment." Figures of
Edward III and his Queen Philippa, Henry VII and Elizabeth of York, are there. An attenuated lady is known as
Catherine of Valois, and two headless effigies, one with
doublet and hose, the other practically unclothed, are called
James I and Prince Henry. The rails in the centre formerly
enclosed the tomb of Mary Queen of Scots. Other interesting
relics are remains of the old Norman sacrarium and a model
of the abbey made for Sir Christopher Wren when he
proposed to erect a central tower. It was evidently to
resemble that of Salisbury Cathedral.

We may now turn to the left, on leaving the undercroft,
and again to the left down another cloister to the Little

Cloister. Here is cloistered peace indeed, and although it is mostly modern, the visitor would fain linger. We may now return to the abbey by way of the Great Cloister, once noisier than now. In the eighteenth century the Westminster schoolboys used to play football on the grass.

St. Margaret's Church is well worth a visit. An old tradition ascribes its foundation to Edward the Confessor, and there was certainly a church here early in the twelfth century. Before the Reformation various restorations took place and in 1548 Protector Somerset, planning to build his Strand palace, decided to obtain material by pulling down St. Margaret's. The parishioners, however, immediately appeared in its defence, armed with bows and arrows, and so frightened his workmen "that they ran away in great amazement, and never could be brought again upon that imployment." They were not so successful in preventing a sale of brass during the Commonwealth. In 1742, the chancel floor was levelled and later in the same century all "exterior projections, buttresses, finials, niches, crocketed tabernacles and pinnacles" were swept away and "a plain, neat exterior of smooth Portland stone" substituted, while the old pointed roof was sawn up and transformed into the present one. In 1876 and subsequent years, more desirable improvements were made, such as the removal of the triple galleries and the renewal of the tracery of the side windows. In 1905, as the west wall was unsafe, a restoration was necessary, and this had the effect of lengthening the chancel by six feet and providing a new porch at the east end.

.St. Margaret's has been the official church of the House of Commons since 1614, and in 1642 the anti-Royalist section of the House, together with representatives of the Scottish Covenanters and the Assembly of Divines, pledged themselves to uphold the Solemn League and Covenant, and swore with raised hands to extirpate "Popery, prelacy, superstition, schism, and profaneness," after which a Mr. White "prayed near upon an hour." Members of Parliament have the status of resident parishioners and the consequent right to have their names placed on the electoral roll and to sit on the parochial council.

The East window is the most historical of London windows. It was made in Flanders about 1500 as a gift from Ferdinand

F

and Isabella of Spain to Henry VII on the occasion of the
betrothal of their daughter Catherine to his eldest son
Arthur, and was designed for Henry VII's Chapel.   Shortly
after his marriage Arthur died, and by the time the window
reached England Henry was also dead.   Henry VIII, having
married Catherine, naturally had no use for a window which
portrayed her with Arthur, and he sent it to the Abbey
Church of Waltham.   There it remained until the dissolution when it was moved to the private chapel of New Hall
in Essex, which eventually came into possession of General
Monk.   He buried it during the Civil War to preserve it
from Puritan iconoclasm, and, being replaced in the chapel,
it remained there until about 1735.   In 1758, it was the
property of Mr. Conyers of Copt Hall (Essex), who had
purchased it, and he then sold it to the churchwardens of
St. Margaret's for four hundred and twenty pounds.   The
window was again buried for safety during the Great War.
The central scene is the Crucifixion.   Three angels are shown
holding chalices to receive the blood, and on one side the
soul of the penitent thief—in the guise of a new born babe
—is being transported to Paradise, on the other a devil is
carrying off the soul of the impenitent thief to Hades.
On the left of the window, above the kneeling figure of
Prince Arthur, stands St. George, and in the corresponding
position on the other side is St. Catherine, who bears in
her hand the sword with which she was beheaded by the
Emperor Maximilian after the miraculous destruction of the
wheel on which he had intended she should die.   The
wheel—her emblem—is seen beneath her feet beside the
head of the emperor.   In one of the small top lights is
the Tudor Rose.

The coloured centre piece of the triptych over the altar
was carved in 1753 and is a copy in lime wood of Titian's
famous picture, "The Supper at Emmaus."   On the south
wall of the chancel is a memorial brass to Sir Walter Raleigh,
who was executed in Old Palace Yard in 1618 and interred
in this church.   On the south of the east door is a tablet
to the memory of Caxton, who was buried in the churchyard,
and over the east door is a window placed there in 1882 by
London printers.   On either side of Caxton are the Venerable
Bede and Erasmus, while below is Tennyson's quatrain. East

of the vestry door is a slab. This is all that remains of the tomb of Dame Mary Billing, the fifteenth-century bene-factress of St. Margaret's. It was reduced to its present nakedness during the restoration of 1742. Directly above this tomb is the monument to Thomas Seymour (grandson of the Protector Somerset) and his wife. The window above the vestry door was presented by an American lady in memory of Arabella Stuart who, for marrying without the king's permission, was imprisoned in the Tower of London, where she died in 1615. Her offence was due to the fact that she was a possible claimant to the throne. To the west of the vestry door is a brass memorial to one Cole. It has possibly the longest elegaic verse in London. In line with the chancel steps is an alabaster tomb of Lady Dudley, sister of Lord Howard of Effingham who commanded the English fleet against the Spanish Armada. She died in 1600. In the south-west corner is the font, designed in 1641, and above it is a window dedicated to Lord Frederick Cavendish who was murdered in Phœnix Park, Dublin, in 1882. The inscription on the bronze tablet below was written by Mr. Gladstone. Over the raised pew to the south of the west door is one of the oldest monuments: that to Blanche Parry who "died a maide in the eighte two years of her age the twelfe of Februarye 1589." She was an influential courtier of Queen Elizabeth's. Her heart is deposited at Bacton in Herefordshire, where there is another monument. The Raleigh window dates from 1882 and cost six hundred pounds—collected in America. The window contains full-length figures of Queen Elizabeth, Prince Henry, Edmund Spenser, Sir Walter Raleigh and his half-brother Sir Humphrey Gilbert, while various incidents in Raleigh's life are depicted. Below are some lines of Lowell's, American Minister in London when the window was pres-ented. The next window is in memory of Milton. He lived in Petty France, Westminster, from 1651–60. In 1657, his second wife and her child were laid to rest here. The window depicts scenes from *Paradise Lost*, and Milton as a boy at school, on a visit to Galileo, and dictating *Paradise Lost* to his daughters. Appended are some lines of Whittier's. To the north of the west door is a monument to Lady Dorothy Stafford. The long inscription tells us that she died at seventy-eight in 1604 and "served Q. Elizabeth 40 yeares, lying in her bedchamber, esteemed of her, loved of all." A little farther along is the Susanna Gray Memorial. A curious inscription headed "Halleluiah" recalls the death in 1654 of Susanna Gray near ten years. This is a fitting pendant to Susannah Barfoot's (see page 57). To the right of the north door is part of an old doorway which originally led to the Tower, and belongs to the early years of the sixteenth century. Below the window to W. H. Smith, once leader of the House of Commons, is a tablet to Wenceslaus Hollar, the famous engraver who died in this parish in 1677. Hollar executed many invaluable engravings of London. Near the east end is a window dedicated to Admiral Blake. He was originally buried in the Abbey, but his body, with those of Cromwell and others, was disinterred at the Restoration and thrown into a trench in St. Margaret's Churchyard. The lower light represents the scene at Malaga where Blake is said to have addressed a priestly envoy in the following words: "I would have the whole world know that none but an Englishman shall chastise an Englishman." Below are lines by Lewis Morris.

The western porch of the church was erected in 1891, by public subscription, from the design of J. L. Pearson, R.A., then architect to the abbey. The graveyard is now paved over. Nobody now, with the noise of buses and taxis dinning companionship in the ear, would like the youthful Cowper, then a Westminster schoolboy, want to whistle to keep his courage up in walking across it! Cowper then found a gravedigger at work by lantern light who threw up a skull which struck him on the leg. This gave an alarm to his conscience; and, says Southey, "he reckoned the incident as amongst the best religious impressions which he received at Westminster."

A short walk, or a penny bus ticket, will take us down Victoria Street, opposite the west door of the abbey, to Ashley Place which leads to Westminster Cathedral. The site—that of the old Tothill Fields Prison—was purchased by Cardinal Manning in 1883, and it was erected between 1895 and 1903. The architect, John F. Bentley, died before its completion, and the first public service held in the cathedral was the requiem of its founder, Cardinal Vaughan.

The type of architecture adopted was the Early Christian Byzantine, this being justified as more economic than Gothic.

The central doorway, only opened on special occasions, has sculptured medallions containing demi-figures of twelve Archbishops of Canterbury. The most familiar to the non-Catholic visitor are the first, St. Augustine (597), associated with the conversion of the English, the third St. Mellitus (619), associated with the erection of the first St. Paul's Cathedral, and the tenth St. Thomas à Becket (1162), whose magnitude in the eyes of medieval Londoners is illustrated elsewhere in this book. The usual entrance is in Ambrosden Avenue, and on either side are medallions—on the left St. Augustine of Hippo (430), and St. Gregory (604), and on the right St. Francis of Sales (1622), and St. Alphonsus Liguori (1787).

Immediately within the porch, on the left, is the lift by which the campanile may be ascended. It is two hundred and seventy-three feet in height, and above it rises a metal cross, eleven feet high, alleged to contain a relic of the true Cross. On entering the cathedral itself, one has mixed feelings. The eye passes from some rich tint, such as that of the Norwegian granite columns at the west end of the nave, intended to be symbolic in their colour of the blood of Christ, to the barest of bricks, twelve and a half million of which are said to have been used in constructing the building. These bricks are, however, purposely left rough to afford a satisfactory surface for the adherence of the marble and mosaic which it is hoped will some day cover them. The extreme length of the cathedral is three hundred and sixty feet. The eight monoliths of dark-green marble which support the galleries were hewn from a quarry from which, in A.D. 563, Justinian drew the marbles for the great basilica of Saint Sophia in Constantinople. On these pillars are the fourteen Stations of the Cross.

Turning sharply to the left, past the statue of St. Peter holding the keys, a copy of the famous one in Rome—we come to the first of the side chapels—the Holy Souls. The next chapel is dedicated to St. George and English Martyrs, including the St. Alban commemorated in our cathedral, who was beheaded by the Romans in A.D. 286. On the

walls are inscribed the names of soldiers and sailors who
fell in the war for whom Chantry masses have been founded
in this chapel. Next is the Chapel of St. Joseph, with a
fine marble altar bordered with mother of pearl. The
statue of St. Anthony of Padua on the right of the aisle
is a reminder of the story that once when he was studying
the Gospels the Child Jesus appeared to bless and encourage
his efforts. On the left wall is a mosaic of St. Joan of Arc,
given by the women of England in the year of her canonization. We now reach the Chapel of St. Thomas of Canterbury (otherwise à Becket); it is also the Vaughan Chantry.
A recumbent effigy of the cardinal faces the altar, but his
body lies at the missionary college which he established at
Mill Hill. The cardinal's red hat hangs over the statue to
remain there, according to Roman custom, until it decays.
Crossing the Blessed Sacrament Chapel, reserved for worship
only, we arrive at the nave and can view the High Altar,
a solid twelve-ton block of Cornish granite. The stone
itself can be seen only on Maundy Thursday, and Good
Friday, when the ceremonial stripping of the altar forms
part of a special service. The altar crucifix stands seven
feet three inches high and is so heavy that it takes five
men to lift it. The Metropolitan Throne of the Archbishop
of Westminster on the left is modelled on the Papal Chair
in the Lateran, and was given to Cardinal Vaughan by the
Catholic Bishops of England. On either side of the sanctuary
are stalls for the cathedral canons and chaplains. They
are of oak inlaid with ivory and contrasting woods. The
foundation stone of the cathedral is at the base of the
pillar on the extreme left of the sanctuary. Walking
southwards, we reach the Lady Chapel. To the right of
the Lady Chapel is a passage leading to the crypt. In
an outer lobby is the portrait of John Francis Bentley, the
architect. Facing the altar in the crypt is a curious chair,
the first Metropolitan Throne of Westminster. An inscription gives its history. In the deep recess opposite lie the
bodies of Cardinal Wiseman (d. 1865) and Cardinal Manning
(d. 1892). The former's tomb was designed by Edward
Pugin and erected on the cardinal's grave in Kensal Green
Cemetery and moved here, when, in 1907, both Wiseman
and Manning were re-interred. The red hats will again

be noticed. Here is an altar of St. Edmund, the last canonized Archbishop of Canterbury. On the walls of the crypt are four relic chambers screened with gilt metal grilles and red hangings. Among the most interesting are said to be the mitre of St. Thomas à Becket; a piece of the hair shirt of Sir Thomas More; and a bone of the Archbishop of Armagh, the last Catholic martyr, who was hanged, drawn and quartered at Tyburn in 1681. Returning to the cathedral, the first chapel, walking westward, is dedicated to St. Paul. Above the altar is a triptych of bronze gilt showing the apostle bearing his sword, the instrument of his martyrdom. This sword appears in the arms of the City of London. Next is the Chapel of St. Andrew and the Saints of Scotland. As he was a fisherman the marble mosaic flooring shows waves and fishes. Then comes the Chapel of St. Patrick and the Irish Saints. It is protected by a white marble balustrade in which are introduced the shamrock of St. Patrick and the oak leaves of St. Bridget—to whom St. Bride's Church, Fleet Street, is dedicated. The last of the chapels is dedicated to St. Gregory and St. Augustine, the latter having been dispatched by the former on a mission to convert England. Above the reredos we see St. Gregory sending St. Augustine and his companions to England, and higher still the reception by Ethelbert of the missionaries. On the north wall are shown St. Edmund, king and martyr, with the arrows of his martyrdom, and the Venerable Bede with book and pen. Two panels are in the arches separating the chapel from the aisle. One shows St. Gregory in the market-place of Rome declaring that the Anglo-Saxon child slaves should not be Angles but Angels. This was erected by the choir school of the cathedral. On the opposite wall is the Judgment of Solomon, appropriately commemorating the donor of the chapel, Henry Hawkins, Lord Brampton.

Turning to the left, on leaving the cathedral, we come again into Victoria Street. Keeping straight on, and turning right when we reach Buckingham Palace Road, we reach the palace. It derives its name from a Duke of Buckingham who erected a mansion here in 1703. It was purchased by George III in 1761. Here all his children, except George IV, were born, and here took place that interview between the king and Dr. Johnson, so vividly recorded by Boswell.

It was remodelled in 1825, and whilst William IV would not live there, Queen Victoria made it her residence, and here Edward VII was born (1841) and died (1910). The front was reconstructed in Portland stone from designs by Sir Aston Webb in 1913. There is a model of the palace before the reconstruction in the basement of the London Museum. It was previously more ornate, having, amongst other decorations, a figure of Britannia on the façade. The king's private apartments are on the north side of the palace, no part of which is shown to the public. The Queen Victoria Memorial in front of it was designed by the late Sir Thomas Brock, R.A. The central figure of the queen (thirteen feet high) is carved from one solid block of marble and has to left and right groups representing Justice and Truth, while facing the palace is a group symbolic of Motherhood. A winged figure of Victory surmounts the whole, and it is poised on a sphere supported by figures of Courage and Constancy. The four bronze groups represent Peace, Progress, Agriculture, and Craftsmanship.

If we leave the palace behind and walk down the Mall a path on the left, across the Green Park, leads to Stafford House, now the home of the London Museum. It was originally built for the Duke of York whose column, pointing to the skies, is the best known to Londoners after Nelson's. He did not live to see the house completed, and the property passed in 1841 to the Duke of Sutherland. It was regarded as the finest private residence in London, and Queen Victoria, on visiting the duchess, remarked on entering the magnificent entrance hall: "I have come from my house to your palace." The late Lord Leverhulme bought the lease of the house in 1913, and gave it to the nation for the London Museum.

The collection, admirably arranged, starts with prehistoric London, in the corridor on the left of the entrance hall. Turning right there, first we will look at the case marked one (though the second in order). Here is evidence of the state of London in the days when its site was covered by dragons of the slime. Boars were to be found in the neighbourhood until the thirteenth century, and as Bishop Creighton once sadly remarked, in a prize-giving speech at Highgate, "My predecessors hunted boars in the Middlesex forest. Now they hunt me—in my own palace." Here are the remains of uglier beasts than boars—the milk tooth of a mammoth found in Pall Mall, the tooth of a rhinoceros found in the Old Bailey, etc. The cases opposite and to the left show specimens of Neolithic implements, and the case with a row of skulls at the top takes us a stage farther —to the Bronze Age. One skull, it will be noticed, has been trepanned. This operation, according to Pepys, was carried out upon Prince Rupert. Edward VII was fond of a story of a civil servant who had a part of his brain scraped away and said it mattered little as he was employed at the War Office! In a case on the other side of the entrance door is a fine bronze shield and relics believed to appertain to pile-dwellings, found at Isleworth. The case next to it brings us to the Iron Age, the era of the Ancient Britons where history as taught in elementary schools usually begins. In the side of the case will be seen the currency bars and coin mentioned in our historical sketch. The corridor leads into the first of two Roman rooms. Just inside the door on the left is a vase with the only inscription found in London referring to the goddess Isis. In the centre of the room are some fine specimens of amphora or wine jars, pointed at the end, to be fixed in the ground. Over the mantelpiece is a collection of domestic implements, and opposite are some fine examples of Samian ware. In this room, over the door, is a relic of Stafford House. It is a medallion of Mazzini recording his vist here. Turning left, we find, just outside the second Roman room, a conjectural picture of Roman London showing the bridge and the Basilica in Leadenhall. The most interesting objects in this room are the burial groups, the memorial stones to Romans who died in London (one with a Greek inscription is at the far end of the room), and the relief representing the Persian god Mithra stabbing the sacred bull. From the bull's mouth springs the life of the earth which is represented by a serpent about to drink the holy blood. Mithraism was at one time a serious rival to Christianity in the Roman Empire, and there were remarkable similarities in the respective rites of the two religions. A case that deserves close examination is in the far right-hand corner. There is a Roman curse and small images of various gods. In a case near the door may be seen not only specimens of styluses but ink-wells. Crossing the first Roman room and a large room used for rest and reading, we arrive at the Anglo-Saxon room.   Here is an interesting specimen of a Celtic bell, and many Viking swords.   The most interesting case is in the corner near the corridor.   It contains the contents of some Saxon graves (see page 17), and through the entrance door, on the right, is one of the skeletons laid out as found.   We now cross the entrance hall where are some interesting relics of Charles I.   Also worth attention are a pair of pictures: "A Bayswater Omnibus" (1895), and "Les Misérables, London Cabs" (1888).   Both bring back memories of a Victorian London that is dead. We turn to the right on going upstairs, and after looking at the cradles in the corridor, enter the medieval room. In a case is a volume dated 1497 printed by Wynkyn de ·Worde.   The page at which it lies open gives the story of London as being founded by Brute and called New Troy. Over the mantel is a cake mould in the form of St. Catherine dating from the fifteenth century and found in the Old Bailey.   In the case in the right-hand corner is a shoe with a long pike (see page 151), whilst there are also spoons and pitchers, and fragments of carving from the ceiling of Crosby Hall (see page 134).   In the corridor are a collection of pilgrims' signs, i.e., souvenirs sold at the various shrines, a visit to which was accounted a great act of piety.   They were worn usually on the hat.   The cul-de-sac room has, on the far wall, two bosses from the old Grey Friars Priory (see page 23), and in the case just inside the door is a good specimen of an aquiminale, the vessel used for washing the fingers at meals before forks were introduced.   Passing across the previous room we reach the Tudor collection. Here are spoons, pots, slashed shoes, apprentices' caps, and an ornamented plate with the inscription: "The rose is red, leaves are green.   God save Elizabeth our Queen."   Near the exit door is a pedlar's pack, similar to the one George Eliot's Bob Jakin used to carry, and a copy of the window in Lambeth Church (see page 190).   In the corridor leading from this room is a death-mask of Cromwell, and the room into which it leads is notable chiefly for Cromwellian relics, including a pocket Bible bearing his signature on a fly-leaf. His watch was stolen from this room about two years ago and has not been recovered.   The next two rooms are eighteenth century and largely devoted to crockery. They lead to the costume galleries, which are of greater interest. The eighteenth-century dinner-party staged in a glass case at the end is particularly attractive. Turning left there, we arrive at a room which contains a collection of clothing worn by various members of the royal family and the coronation robes. We then arrive at the outside corridor and may go to the top floor. If, however, time is very limited it may be better to miss this and go straight to the basement. If we decide to go to the top we turn right, and when we reach there, turn left. The first room is devoted to bridges, and there are models of London Bridge and Tower Bridge. Passing on, we can enter a room brought from an eighteenth-century house at Clapham Common, after which we come to part of a splendid collection of water-colour paintings of old London. These are continued in the next room, and there will be found—to mention a few places referred to elsewhere in this book—pictures of Keats's House at Hampstead (wall on left), two pictures of the George Inn and one of the Cheshire Cheese (far wall), and of the Churches of St. Andrew Undershaft, St. Catherine Cree, St. Helen's, Bishopsgate, St. Bartholomew the Great, and Chelsea Old Church (right-hand wall). We may pass across the next room without stopping and enter a much larger one which contains (near the entrance) the famous dagger which Burke threw upon the floor of the House of Commons, a Woolsack from the old House of Lords, and a case of Gladstone relics. The next room contains more water-colours, including the Tabard, with that sign and the sign of the Talbot hanging below one another. The room following has some old pianos and a model of the Church of St. Martin-in-the-Fields. Returning by way of the previous room we reach a room devoted to theatrical exhibits, including a death-mask of Sir Henry Irving. At the end, turning right, we find the Children's Room. Here are dolls' houses and other toys used by members of the royal family and an extraordinary collection of articles which, in pre-war London, could be bought for a penny, made by Mr. Ernest King and presented to the Museum in 1918. We are now close to the staircase, but before descending we should turn left and look at the only room we have missed, one containing models of the old London gates. On top of the staircase is a well-known picture of the Great Fire.

On reaching the ground floor, we turn right across the entrance hall into the corridor, then turn left and descend to the basement. First we notice a collection of knockers, and opposite, an eighteenth-century shop front brought from Holborn. Then, after a few tradesmen's signs, we come to the post-chaise used by Wellington at Waterloo. Turning left brings us to the models of old London which probably attract more attention than any other exhibits. They are fully described over the cases. If we turn left and then right, on leaving these, we see a double doorway brought from Seething Lane, and an opening nearly opposite takes us to the old Roman boat (see page 17). The adjacent cases show some of the objects found with the boat, and pictures on the wall indicate how it was removed. It was found in 1910, twenty-one feet six inches below high-water mark, and was probably, when complete, sixty feet long. It was dried by glycerine, and this drying process was so effectual that a piece of wood weighing seventeen and half ounces after two months was reduced to five and three-quarter ounces. On the other side of the boat is a canoe cut out from a tree trunk, and close by a stake taken from the Thames at Brentford. There is a similar stake in the Guildhall Museum, and they are supposed to have been derived from a protective palisading erected by the Britons to repel Cæsar's army in 54 B.C. Mr. Gordon Home, however, advances good reasons for believing that the Romans crossed at Chelsea, where coins and weapons were found during the construction of the bridge in 1854–5. A beam from Westminster Hall, showing the work of the beetle, is displayed here and, close by, a model of Buckingham Palace, previously mentioned. On leaving this room we turn left, and in cases in the room at the end of the corridor are models of an omnibus and a coach and a group of vehicles, in one of which is the Princess of Wales, afterwards Queen Alexandra, at Piccadilly. The rest of the room is given up to an old fire-engine and fire appliances. In the next room is a fine model of the Tower of London, and in the one following, a Stuart parlour which would be all the better if heads were supplied for the figures. Here are some rare signs such as a fine specimen of the Half Moon. On the left is a model of what purports to have been Izaak Walton's house in Fleet Street. It was in fact one next door to his. Hogarth's house at Chiswick, of which there is also a model, still stands and is a museum. On the right is a good stone mantelpiece from Chelsea, and a curious fresco of Jonah and the whale from Waltham Abbey. In the division following are some old water pipes and some good specimens of wood-carving. Then follows the museum's "Chamber of Horrors." Here is a cell from Neptune Street Prison, a place from whence prisoners were sometimes taken to the hulks for transportation by subterranean ways without the knowledge of relatives. On the other side is a wall carved with names. One, "Edward Ray 1758," occurs twice. Round the walls of this room is a splendid collection of the broadsides sold in the streets on the morning of executions and giving details of the crime and sometimes verse alleged to have been written by the deceased. The door of the condemned cell at Newgate is also shown, whilst there is an interesting oil-painting showing Fauntleroy being manacled on the morning of his execution. A cheque drawn upon the bank of which he was one of the directors is underneath. This execution—for the crime of forgery—created a great sensation. There is an amusing reference to the event in one of Lamb's letters to Bernard Barton, a bank clerk and a Quaker: "You are as yet upright. But you are a banker, at least the next thing to it. I feel the delicacy of the subject; but cash must pass thro' your hands, sometimes to a great amount. If in an unguarded hour . . . but I will hope better. Consider the scandal it will bring upon those of your persuasion. Thousands would go to see a Quaker hanged, that would be indifferent to the fate of a Presbyterian, or an Anabaptist. Think of the effect it would have on the sale of your poems alone; not to mention higher considerations!" The corridor outside this room leads us to the stairs. Before ascending, however, we may notice the stone tablets brought from some of London's street corners, a balustrade from Dr. Johnson's house in Johnson's Court (see page 164), and—by turning for a minute into the corridor beyond the staircase—an eighteenth-century printing press and some old "bone-shakers."

On leaving the museum, we may turn right and look at the front of St. James's Palace. It was erected in 1535 by Henry VIII. Here Queen Mary died in 1558, and Charles II and James II were born respectively in 1630 and 1633. It ceased to be used by the sovereigns after George III acquired Buckingham Palace in 1761. Returning by the way we came, we reach Victoria Station and take a penny tram or bus to Grosvenor Road. On alighting, we turn left and arrive shortly at the Tate Gallery.

This gallery was the gift of Sir Henry Tate and was built upon the site of Millbank Prison and opened in 1897. It has recently been extended and enriched, and now contains good examples of the best modern artists.

Note especially the following pictures:

Room 1. *Hogarth's* "Marriage à la Mode.' A noble *Wilson* (110); *Gainsborough*; *Morland*; and *Reynolds's* "Robinetta."

Room 2. *William Blake's* dream, prophecy, and fancy.

Room 3. *William Müller* (1463); *David Roberts* (401); *Constable* (327 and 1274); a lovely *Cotman* (3661); *David Cox* and *De Wint*, the pillars of early English water-colour.

Room 4. *The Pre-Raphaelites. Windus* (3597); *Hughes* (2475). *Millais's* early vigour and earnestness. *Holman Hunt*, (who remained loyal to P.R.B.) principles. "Claudius "and "The Triumph of the Innocents" in Room 17. The colour and detail of *J. F. Lewis*; *F. Madox Brown's* rich colour and powerful design.

Room 5. *Rossetti*, that master painter (3053–4), exotic taste and brilliant colour, and the mystic memorial to his wife (1279). *Burne-Jones's* ascetic but workmanlike "King Cophetua."

Room 6. *Turner.* Filled with great canvases. Particularly (483) London from Greenwich, (485, 490, 512, and 528).

Room 7. *Turner.* All dream and vision, showing an unrivalled love and knowledge of nature. See especially the quiet harmony (199).

Room 11. (*The New Extension*). *Daumier* (3244), whose interest is in essentials only. *Daubigny's* "Willows" (2621). The "Impressionists." *Pissarro* (3266); *Sisley*; *Berthe Morisot*, and *C. Monet's* translucent dreams. (Monet carried Impressionism to its logical conclusion). *Manet* the inspired "rebel" (3295). The movement, colour, and life of *Degas*. The realism and gaiety of *Renoir* (3268) and the defiant *Gauguin* (3470) with his sensuous colour.

Room 13. Seurat's broken tones and vividness. *Cézanne*, whose feeling for mass and volume has transformed modern art. *Matisse's* simple line and colour patterns. *Van Gogh's* restless soul and love of sunlight. Note his gorgeous "Sunflowers."

Room 14. Sargent. His powerful brush, vigour, sureness, and brilliant colour. The beautiful early "Carnation Lily." "The Wertheimer Family." "Ellen Terry." The solid landscapes and masterly Venetian studies.

Room out of 14. A typical *Joseph Isräels* (2713). *James Maris's* "Amsterdam," full of local truth, and *William Maris's* veiled visions. A sparkling *Alfred Stevens* (Belgian) (3270).

Room 15. Dicksee's "Harmony." *Albert Moore's* "Blossoms." *G. H. Mason's* "Cast Shoe." *Waterhouse* and *Leighton.*

G. F. Watt's Room. The foundation stone of Watts's philosophy, "Life's Illusions." That symbolic harmony "Hope." The trilogy "Woman." "Love Triumphant," and "The Court of Death."

Opposite is the *Alfred Stevens Room.* Stevens who might have been an English Michelangelo! Here his range and genius can be studied. Especially the models for "Dorchester House."

Room 19. Orchardson's scholarly (1524). *Fred Walker's* rich ochre and gold "Old Gate." *David Murray's* "Summer Haze." *Professor Tonks's* accomplished self-portrait. *Nicholson's* "Miss Jekyll." *Lavery's* sparkling "Dressing Room at Ascot." *W. Russell's* "Mr. Minney," and *R. Brough's* elegant "Fantasia."

Room 20. C. W. Furse. Müller and *Fred Walker's* studies. *Brabazon's* visions and *Charles Holmes*, luminous slag heaps.

Room 21. Rothenstein's masterly (3189). *Whistler's* harmony (1959). *McEvoy* (3170). *Wilson Steer's* "Chepstow," and (4422) all light and air. *Augustus John's* "Madame Suggia." *Sickert* (3182 and 3846). *D. Y. Cameron's* solid (3813). *Nicholson's* beautiful "Bowl" (3178) *W. Russell's* "Amber Beads." *Greaves's* "Hammersmith Bridge," and *F. Yeats's* Irish animation (4076).

Room 22. Stanley Spence's "Resurrection." *Muirhead Bone's* iridescent "Snow."

Room 23. Jaggers's realistic "No Man's Land." *Ethel*

Walker's masterly cartoon and *Arthur Melville's* opulent colour (4043).

Room 24. *Conder.* "Spring," a lovely dream. *Spencer Gore's* subdued (3839). *McEvoy's* vivid (4200) and (4230). *Philip Connard's* "Summer." *Wilson Steer's* vibrating light (2872). *Arnesby Brown's* designed "Line of the Plough." *Orpen's* sparkling "Dame Kendal." *Lavery's* "Pavlova." *Clausen's* "Gleaners," and "Winter Morning." *R. G. Eves's* "Thomas Hardy," and *Charles Sims's* decorative panel (2933).

In Sculpture see *Epstein's* gaunt and powerful "Visitation" (in Centre Hall), "Mrs. Phillips" and the alive "Kramer" in the Sculpture Hall, and *Gilbert's* "Eros." In the small room off the Central Hall the bust "Shaw." *Rickett's* "Orpheus and Eurydice," *Mestrovic's* powerful head, and *Reynolds Stevens's* interesting "Royal Game."

WALK IV: *British Museum—Dickens's House—Johnson's House—Public Record Office Museum—Temple.*

For the British Museum we will take tube to Tottenham Court Road station and turn left on reaching the street. The museum originated in 1753, with the purchase of the library and collection of Sir Hans Sloane and of the manuscripts collected by Sir Robert Cotton, an eminent English antiquary (1571–1631), and Robert Harley, Earl of Oxford, the famous minister of Queen Anne. Busts of the first two are on the main staircase. It was opened, in Montagu House, in 1759, but being speedily augmented, notably by the famous Elgin marbles (1816) and by the magnificent library collected by George III, a new building was erected between 1823 and 1847. The great Reading-room was built in 1857, and here may be seen daily a motley throng of students, some evidently prosperous, others Grub Street writers in spirit if not in fact, such as George Gissing described in his novel. A copy of every book published has to be sent to the museum, and there are nearly four million volumes covering some sixty miles of shelving. The number increases at the rate of fifty thousand per annum. A reader's ticket is necessary for admission, and special short-term tickets are issued if it can be justified, upon application to the Director. Those who wish to see the

Reading-room may do so in charge of an attendant. A new wing was added to the museum in 1884 and the King Edward VII Galleries were added in 1914.

It is impossible, in a guide of this size, to give much assistance to a visitor who has a "world of wonder and delight" to explore here. He will be guided by the subjects that most appeal to him. He cannot do better than attach himself to one of the two parties that, twice a day, are officially conducted. If, however, he finds it most convenient to go at some other time, he will find some assistance in the threepenny guide which draws attention to the most important items in each collection. There is one collection that has perhaps a particularly human interest upon which some comment may be made, particularly as the official guides do not include it in their itinerary, i.e. the MSS. This collection is reached by taking the right-hand door from the entrance hall. In Case I is a letter of Henry V, reporting upon the prisoners taken at Agincourt and mentioning the Duke of Orleans who was imprisoned in the Tower (see page 45); a slip of vellum with one of the few signatures of the young and uncrowned King Edward V; a letter from Anne Boleyn to Wolsey; a letter from Sir Thomas More to Henry VIII from "Chelchith" (Chelsea); a page from Edward VI's diary (one of the earliest known), and a letter from Lady Jane Grey. The last is revealing. It shows that that lady was not quite the innocent tool of others as we are sometimes led to believe, as she wrote of "the fayned and untrewe clayme of the Lady Mary bastard daughter to our great Uncle Henry the 8. The first year of our reign." In Case II there is a letter from the lady thus stigmatized, signed "Mary the Queene"; a letter in the beautiful Italian hand of Elizabeth to the sister thus designated, discountenancing rumours of her disloyalty; and a most interesting document—a rough plan prepared by Lord Burleigh of the hall of Fotheringay Castle as it was to be arranged for the trial of Mary Queen of Scots. Below is a report to Burleigh of the execution, mentioning the pathetic conduct of the little lap-dog, an incident of which Froude made such dramatic use. In the same case is a report of the Spanish Armada from the English commander, Lord Howard of Effingham. In Case III is a letter of Cromwell's

G

to the Speaker of the House of Commons, reporting the Battle of Naseby. In Case IV are letters of Edmund Burke and George Washington — the latter's most legible. In Case VII are letters of Fielding, Johnson, Boswell, and Richardson, the latter's dated 1754, from Salisbury Court. In Case IX is a small book inscribed by the Duke of Somerset on the night before his execution, and a manual of prayer believed to have been used by Lady Jane Grey on the scaffold. In Case X is *The Booke of Sir Thomas More*, a play written by Anthony Munday in 1593 or 1594, and with amendments in another hand, considered by some authorities to be Shakespeare's. Here is also the original draft of Ben Jonson's *Masque of Queenes*; a page of Raleigh's journal of his last voyage; Milton's Family Bible and Commonplace Book; a page of one of Swift's letters to Stella; some of Pope's MS. of his translation of the Iliad and Odyssey, mostly upon scraps of letters sent to him; the MS. of Defoe's *Complete English Gentleman*; the draft of Johnson's *Irene* (see page 90); one of Chatterton's *Rowley Poems*; a fair copy in Gray's handwriting of the famous *Elegy*; a copy in Cowper's handwriting of *John Gilpin*; a page of Gibbon's *Autobiography*, in which is the well-known passage about the idea of writing the decline and fall of Rome coming to him while he "sat musing amidst the ruins of the Capitol, while the barefooted friars were singing vespers in the Temple of Jupiter." Here are also Matthew Arnold's fine sonnet to Shakespeare; a letter in Thackeray's neat handwriting; a letter of Lamb's and one of Carlyle's unusually well written—he was a young man then—and letters of Dickens and Browning of unusual interest. Dickens's is to George Eliot on the publication of *Scenes from Clerical Life*, and he says that although he addresses the letter thus ("George Eliot Esq.") he suspects feminine authorship. Yet Mrs. Carlyle had guessed the relative of a curate with a large family! Browning (1868) defends himself against the charge of wilful obscurity, and adds: "I never pretended to offer such literature as should be a substitute for a cigar or a game of dominoes to an idle man." In Case E are some interesting old English books: the Anglo-Saxon *Chronicle*; *Pearl*, a fourteenth-century elegy for a dead child; *Ancren Riwle* (rules for anchoresses), thirteenth century; also the

York and Coventry Mystery Plays. In the room which leads to this most fascinating collection of MSS. are some old Bibles in Tyndale's and Miles Coverdale's translations, and a First Folio Shakespeare.

On leaving the museum we turn left, walk on until we reach Southampton Row. Then we turn right until we reach Theobald's Road. Then we turn left and a few minutes' walk along Theobald's Road brings us to John Street. Doughty Street is a continuation of this thoroughfare. The Dickens House (No. 48) was opened in 1925. Dickens lived here from March 1837 until the end of 1839, and during that period wrote Parts XIV to XX of *Pickwick Papers, Oliver Twist, Nicholas Nickleby,* and the opening chapters of *Barnaby Rudge.* It was here that his second and third children were born—Mamie in March 1838 and Kate in October 1839. The latter died in 1929. Here also died his sister-in-law Mary Hogarth (see page 203).

The following are the most interesting exhibits. Front room (the dining-room of Dickens's day): Letter from Dickens to his sister Fanny—showing the strenuous life he lived. Playbill of performance at Tavistock House Theatre in 1857 by the Dickens Dramatic Company. Painting of Dickens as "Sir Charles Coldstream" in a play entitled *Used Up.* A lock of Dickens's hair. A clock formerly the property of Moses Pickwick (see page 163), and portraits of Sir Henry Fielding Dickens (the only surviving child), Mrs. Perugini, Alfred Tennyson Dickens (died at New York in 1912), and Miss Georgina Hogarth, the sister-in-law who became Dickens's housekeeper after the separation from his wife.

In the back room is an original ticket admitting to Watts's Charity, Rochester, made famous by Dickens's *Seven Poor Travellers.* In the basement is the "Dingey Dell Kitchen" with its pewter ware, gun and night-shade, warming pans and clock. The first-floor back was Dickens's study. Over the mantelpiece is a portrait of Dickens at the time he lived there. On the left is a collection of Dickens's letters presented by Sir Charles C. Wakefield, Bt., C.B.E. (now Lord Wakefield of Hythe). Below is a writing table used by Dickens.

From this room we enter the library, Dickens's drawing-

room. Here is the famous reading desk which Dickens
valued so much that it accompanied him to America on his
last tour. There is also a copy of *A Christmas Carol*,
autographed by John Dickens, a first edition of *The Haunted
Man*, a note written by Dickens when a boy at school (it
will be found in Forster's *Life*), and a long letter written by
Dickens to Macready in 1868. The second-floor back room
contains a series of thirty-one proof illustrations, after
George Cruikshank, for *Sketches by Boz* and the little attic
window from the house in Bayham Street, Camden Town,
occupied by Dickens as a boy of eleven in 1823. The most
interesting exhibits in the top front room are two balusters
from the White Hart Inn (see page 181), and the desk at
which Dickens sat as a youth in Messrs. Ellis & Blackmore's
office, Gray's Inn (see page 177). At No. 14 Doughty Street
is a tablet commemorating the residence there—from
1803–6—of Sidney Smith, the witty cleric who became a
canon of St. Paul's. He was a friend of Dickens, who gave
his name to his fifth son.

On leaving Doughty Street, we return to Theobald's Road
and turn left; at Holborn Hall we turn right and go down
Gray's Inn Road. On arriving at Holborn we cross the
road and turn left and walk down Fetter Lane until we
reach West Harding Street, which leads to Gough Square.

At No. 17 Gough Square Dr. Johnson lived from 1748 to
1758. Here he wrote *The Vanity of Human Wishes*, and
from this massive front door he emerged arrayed in "scarlet
waistcoat, rich gold lace and gold-laced hat," to see the
first performance of *Irene*. It was not a success, and Sir
Leslie Stephen said it was "only read by men in whom an
abnormal sense of duty has been developed." A visitor to
the house once delightedly informed the custodian that she
was going to see *Irene*. What she thought was a revival of
Johnson's dead tragedy was a popular musical comedy! Here
he wrote the *Rambler*. It was published twice a week at
the price of twopence, and consisted of a single essay. It
was brought to an end after two years upon the death of
his wife in 1752. It was here the famous *Dictionary* was
completed, and probably here also that *Rasselas* was written.
At a later date the house was occupied by Hugh Kelly, an
actor and playwright to whom there are several references

in Boswell's *Life*. Carlyle visited it upon writing his essay on Boswell's *Life*. "It is a stout old-fashioned, oak balus-traded house," he wrote, and he was told by the landlord: "'This bedroom was the Doctor's study, that was the garden' (a plot of delved ground somewhat larger than a bed quilt)—now covered by the caretaker's house—'where he walked for exercise: these three garret bedrooms' (where his three copyists sat and wrote) 'were the places he kept his pupils in. I let it all in lodgings, to respectable gentlemen by the quarter, or the month, it's all one to me.' To me also whispered the Ghost of Samuel, as we went pensively our way." In W. Hale White's (Mark Rutherford) *Selections from the "Rambler"* are pictures of the exterior and interior of the house in the nineteenth century. Late in that century it was in the occupation of Messrs. Waller & Baines, printers, and when the owner, Lord Calthorpe, died in 1910, there was some danger of its disappearance. Mr. Cecil Harmsworth, with a laudable public spirit, purchased the house and had it fitted up as a Johnson Museum. There is none of John-son's furniture here, for there is little in existence, but the fittings have all been carefully chosen to harmonize with the period.

All the exhibits are labelled and there is no need to mention more than a few. In the room on the right is a copy of the first edition of the *Dictionary*. The large cupboard in the corner was probably a powder closet. This was a necessity to prevent furniture and carpets getting sprinkled when wigs were worn. On the stairs is a picture of St. Clement Danes' Church in Johnson's time. It is interesting to compare this with the present church. The only notable differences are the posts, such as Johnson loved to touch, instead of railings, and the portico on the south side which was removed in the middle of last century. On the first floor (room on the right), is a curious painting representing what is described as Cripplegate Church. It is certainly not St. Giles's. John Wesley is in the pulpit and Johnson in a back pew. It is probably imaginary as had Dr. Johnson ever been in Wesley's audience it would have been recorded in the latter's voluminous *Journal*. On the floor above, behind the door of the left-hand room, is Dante Gabriel Rossetti's picture of Dr. Johnson's intercourse with the Methodists at the Mitre (see page 164). A strange subject for the Pre-Raphaelite painter! In the opposite room is an interesting portrait showing a dinner party at Sir Joshua Reynolds's house—in Leicester Fields as the Square was then called. Sir Joshua is distinguished by the ear-trumpet. Here, as in the Chesterfield picture below, is a black servant. In an article in the *Independent Review* in 1905 it was estimated that there were eighty thousand black slaves in London in 1760. On the landing is a brick brought home from the wall of China by Lord Northcliffe, a member of the Johnson Club. The appropriate passage from Boswell is quoted above. The top room is the *Dictionary* garret. This Johnson had fitted up as a counting-house. On the desk were placed huge volumes containing the words to be included, with liberal space left between for the definitions and quotations. Of six amanuenses, five were Scotch, and he paid them twenty-three shillings a week. When we remember Bob Cratchit's fifteen shillings a week, about seventy years after, we shall be impressed by the generosity of old Samuel. When we note their nationality, we shall realize that his bite at the Scotch was not equal to his bark. It was to this garret Dr. Burney, Fanny's father, was invited after dining with Johnson. He found there five or six Greek folios, a writing desk, and a chair and a half. Johnson gave his guest the entire chair, balancing himself on one with only three legs and one arm. In this garret, on 11 December, 1929, a dinner was held on the occasion of Mr. Cecil Harmsworth's handing over the house to a National Trust. Amongst the speakers were Augustine Birrell, Lord Charnwood and the Lord Chief Justice. Their names will be found in the Visitors' Book, in the ground-floor room. Visitors who have time to spare should tempt the custodians into conversation. They will find them far from being the "unidea'd" ladies whom Dr. Johnson aspersed. They are as full of Johnsoniana as was James Boswell.

Bream's Buildings, Fetter Lane, will take us to Chancery Lane, and turning left there, we reach the Public Record Office.

Its museum occupies the site of the Chapel of the House of Converts. The latter was founded by Henry III in 1232 for the reception of Jews who had embraced Christianity, and the chapel was begun in the following year. After the expulsion of the Jews from England by Edward I, the office of Keeper of this house became a sinecure, and it was usually given to the Clerk of Chancery whose duty it was to keep the rolls and other records. In 1377, Edward III definitely assigned the House of the Converts to the Keeper of the Rolls of Chancery and his successors, and it remained in their possession until 1837 when it was surrendered to the Crown.

In the meanwhile the fabric of the chapel (a place of worship for masters, clerks, and registrars of the Court of Chancery) underwent many changes. The medieval chancel was destroyed in the seventeenth century, possibly by the Great Fire, some windows were blocked up and others denuded of their tracery. Galleries and presses were from time to time put up for the accommodation of the records, the seats for the congregation being made in the form of lockers. Soon after the completion of the first block of the adjacent Public Record Office in 1856 most of the documents stored in the Rolls Chapel were transferred there. The interior of the chapel was then entirely remodelled, and all that now remains of the old chapel in the museum is the glass in the two most westerly windows, excepting only the first panel in the west window, which is modern, the bell in the vestibule, and three monuments on the north wall. The first of the latter, of alabaster and marble, is in memory of Richard Alington of Lincoln's Inn who died in 1561. His wife, who is also shown and who died in 1603, was sister of a Master of the Rolls. The second monument is of Lord Bruce of Kinloss, Master of the Rolls (d. 1611). It is mainly of alabaster, which in places shows traces of the original painting and gilding. Below are four detached figures kneeling on cushions. The smaller of those on the left is that of Christian, daughter of the deceased, so called because born on Christmas Day, 1595. She was married in the Rolls Chapel in 1608, being then "a pretty red-headed wench" of less than thirteen. The other female figure is presumably that of Lady Bruce, who survived her husband and married again. The figure of a young man in armour is that of Sir Edward Bruce, K.B., who succeeded his father in the title and was killed two years later in a duel. The small male figure is that of the third Lord Bruce of Kinloss, afterwards Earl of Elgin. The third monument is the most beautiful. It is that of Dr. John Yong, Master of the Rolls and Dean of York, who died in 1516. The whole recess and the moulding round it were formerly coloured. It is the work of Pietro Torrigiano who designed Henry VII's tomb in his chapel at Westminster Abbey. At the back of the sarcophagus were found mutilated carvings of plumed angels and Tudor roses exactly corresponding with some at Westminster. These having been removed are now exhibited close to the monument. A replica or model of the head of Christ is in the Wallace Collection and a replica of the head of Dr. Yong is in the National Portrait Gallery.

With regard to the exhibits, they are all labelled, and only those of special interest need be mentioned. There is first, of course, part of the Domesday Book, in a case in the centre. In Case G are the signed Depositions of Shakespeare in the case of Bellot v. Mountjoy (see page 36). Case H (98) shows a tally stick (see page 100). Case I (103–4) shows Nelson's signature before and after the loss of his right arm. Case C (43) is an Abbreviation of Domesday Book with some interesting pictures on the fly-leaves representing scenes in the life of Edward the Confessor. One shows the king giving a ring to St. John—also shown on one of the tiles in the Chapter-house of Westminster Abbey. On the pedestal are a number of interesting letters including: (28) A letter from Catherine of Aragon to Wolsey. (29) A letter from Anne Boleyn to Stephen Gardiner, afterwards Bishop of Winchester, and as such associated with the Marian persecutions. It was written at Greenwich Palace. (30) Letter from—Wolsey "poor, hevy, wrechyd prest"—to Henry VIII, daily crying "for grace, mercy, remissyon and pardon." (32) Memoranda by Sir Thomas More. (38) One of the few documents signed by Lady Jane Grey as queen. (43) Letter from John Knox to Sir William Cecil. (44) Letter to the same from Mary Queen of Scots. (45) Letter from Sir Philip Sidney. (50) Letter from the Earl of Essex to Elizabeth: "Hast paper, to thatt happy presence whence only unhappy I am banished. Kiss that fayre correcting hand which layes new plasters to my lighter hurtes, butt to my greatest woond applyeth nothing. Say thou cummest

from shaming, languishing, despayring S.X." (59) Letter
from Ben Jonson. (60) The famous warning letter sent to
Lord Monteagle through which the Gunpowder Plot was
discovered. (61–3) Declarations of Guy Fawkes. (64) Letter
from Sir Walter Raleigh. (77) Petition of John Milton.
(87) Memorial of Sir Christopher Wren. (97) Letter from
Samuel Pepys. (100) Letter from Daniel Defoe.

We may leave the Record Office by the Fetter Lane
gateway, and, turning left under the entrance archway, we
see on our right an arch of the old Rolls Chapel built into a
wall. Fetter Lane has some interesting history. In Nevill's
Court (No. 34) is a house which survived the Fire. In one
like this, which has disappeared since the war, Keir Hardie
lived for many years. In Bream's Buildings, on the left,
is the graveyard of St. Dunstan's-in-the-West. There is a
gravestone, visible to the passer-by, which reads:

Here sleeps our babes in silence heavens thaire rest
For God takes soonest those he loveth best.

Samewell Marshall, the 2nd sonne of Edwd. Marshall
and of Anne his wife dyed May 27 1631 aged two years
Anne Marshall their first daur. dyed 21 of June 1635
aged 1 yr. 9 moneths Nicholas Marshall thr. 3rd sonne
dyed Decr. 5th aged 5 yrs. 6 mos.

Little thought the bereaved parents who erected that stone
(where, one wonders, do they lie?) that three hundred years
after these ravages of death amongst their flock their grief
would still be patent to the inhabitants of the old city where
now few young children live and fewer die. Modern cemeteries
can never lend themselves to the distinction a City churchyard can sometimes give! The Moravian Chapel, on the
right of Fetter Lane, dates back to about 1740. Those
interested in John Wesley will recall how strongly he was
influenced by this small sect.

Walking down Fetter Lane to Fleet Street we turn left
and enter the Temple from Fleet Street through Wren's
classical gateway built in 1684. We pass under the Agnus
Dei—the lamb and flag—the crest of the Honourable Society
of the Middle Temple. A little way down the lane is Middle
Temple Hall, built in 1572. The exterior was dressed with
stone in 1757 and the entrance tower rebuilt in 1832. The

interior displays a double hammer-beam roof and pendants. The walls are wainscoted and adorned with the arms of the Treasurers and Readers. The slab of the serving table below the dais was made from the timbers of Drake's ship the *Golden Hind*. Above the high table is a series of portraits: Elizabeth, Charles I (a replica of Van Dyck's picture at Windsor), Charles II, James II, William III, Queen Anne, and the first two Georges. From the diary of a law student, Manningham, discovered in the British Museum, we know that *Twelfth Night* was performed here in 1602. When the floor was repaired in the eighteenth century the discovery beneath the boards of one hundred small dice was an indication of the fact that the Hall was much used for recreation.

We will now step across to the fountain, charmingly introduced by Dickens into *Martin Chuzzlewit*:

"A pleasant place indeed," said little Ruth, "so shady." They came to a stop . . . the day was exquisite; it was quite natural they should glance down Garden Court, because Garden Court ends in the garden and the garden ends in the river, and that glimpse is very bright and fresh and shining on a summer's day.

Having taken a glance from here at the Middle Temple Library, which stands to the south-west of the fountain— it was erected in 1861—we again pass the Hall and turn left to reach Brick Court. On the second floor of No. 2 is a medallion of Goldsmith. Here he bought chambers with the proceeds of *The Good-natured Man*. Here he entertained his friends, sometimes with games of blind-man's buff, and it is said that Blackstone, the compiler of the great *Commentaries on the Laws of England*, who had chambers beneath, had sometimes to complain of the noise. Upon one occasion Sir Joshua Reynolds found Goldsmith kicking about a masquerade dress. He wanted, he said, to obtain the value in exercise he had not obtained in dress! Here he died in 1774 and "The staircase of Brick Court," wrote Forster, "is said to have been filled with mourners, the reverse of domestic; women without a home, without domesticity of any kind, with no friend but him they had come to weep for; outcasts, to whom he had never forgotten to be kind and charitable." Thackeray occupied these chambers from 1853-9. The sundial we see on the right-hand wall as we face Goldsmith's chambers, bears the motto: "Time and tide tarry for no man." It replaces an older one which perished in the fire at the beginning of the eighteenth century. This one bore the motto: "Begone about your business," said to have been addressed by a treasurer, irritated by the interruption, when the dial maker's boy called for an appropriate inscription. We cross the lane to the north of Brick Court and enter Hare Court. Charles Lamb had chambers in Inner Temple Lane overlooking this court, and thus he described it in a letter in 1809 to his friend Manning: "Our place of final destination— I don't mean the grave, but No. 4 Inner Temple Lane— looks out upon a gloomy churchyard-like court, called Hare Court, with three trees and a pump in it. Do you know it? I was born near it, and used to drink at that pump when I was a Rechabite of six years old." This court brings us to the Temple Church, on the north side of which is a coffin-shaped tomb bearing the words: "Here lies Oliver Goldsmith." It is a mere guess. He was buried in the graveyard of the church but nobody knows the spot. The stone was placed here in 1860. The gravestones near by do not cover any bodies as they were brought from the floor of the church in 1842 when encaustic tiles were substituted.

The Temple Round dates from 1185 and is a model of the original church of the "Brethren of the Militia of Christ and of the Temple" to use the original name for the body of men who bound themselves together to succour the Christian pilgrims to the Holy Land. On the floor are the famous effigies, not of Knights Templars, but of Associates of the Temple who, unwilling to take the vows, yet desired to participate in the spiritual advantages without entirely abandoning the pleasures of the world. These are the figures which to Beaumanoir, the Grand Master of the Templars in *Ivanhoe*, were the only objects in England to be looked upon with pleasure. They are not to be identified with any certainty and it must not be supposed that they are necessarily buried where the effigies lie. The following are some brief notes about them:

Northern group :

(1) Left. (With cylindrical helmet) Geoffrey de Mandeville, Earl of Essex. Constable of the Tower 1144. Mortally wounded at the siege of Burwell Castle (Cambs.).

(2) Right. Effigy in low relief. Believed to be the oldest in the church but not identified.

(3) Left. Purbeck marble. Feet on grotesque heads, perhaps Saracens. Not identified.

(4) Purbeck marble. A fine monument in chain mail. Mouth covered by helmet. Not identified.

Southern group :

(1) Left. Probably William Mareschel, Earl of Pembroke, guardian of Henry III, 1129. The glove on right hand has fingers, as no other in the collection, and the surcoat is fastened at the breast with a circular brooch of the "pin-ring" pattern.

(2) Right. Reigate Stone. Much restored. Probably William Mareschel, the younger, second Earl of Pembroke, 1231.

(3) Left. Also Reigate Stone. Probably Gilbert Mareschel, killed in a tournament at Ware in 1281.

(4) Unidentified.

The figure alone on the south side is probably Robert de Ros, one of the signatories of Magna Charta of Henry III, who died in 1227.

Although No. 4 (south) is labelled a Crusader solely on the ground of the crossed legs, it is not now considered by antiquaries that the deceased had participated in a Crusade. It was probably nothing more than an idea of making the sign of the cross in death.

The choir or eastern extension of the church dates from 1240 and is a fine example of early Gothic. At the south-west corner is a bust of Richard Hooker (1554?–1600), Master of the Temple and author of the *Laws of Ecclesiastical Polity*. He is likely to be known best to the present generation as a subject for that delightful biographer Izaak Walton, who pathetically describes how the learned man was compelled, at the command of a masterly wife, to break off his studies and rock the cradle. Close by is a tablet to John Selden (1584–1654), the great English lawyer and author of a volume of *Table Talk* still read. There is an aumbry at the eastern end of the north wall, and on the opposite wall another by the side of a double piscina. In a recess slightly to the west of it (it is approached by some dark steps from the level of the raised stalls) is a fine effigy of a bishop, in full episcopal vestments. It is believed to be Sylvester de Everdon, Bishop of Carlisle (1247–1255) and sometime Chancellor of England, who was killed by a fall from his horse and buried in the Temple Church in 1255. In the triforium is a tablet to Oliver Goldsmith, erected by the Benchers in 1837, and on the left of the stairs leading to it is the penitential cell, four feet six inches long and two feet six inches wide, so constructed as to render it impossible for a grown man to lie down. "In this miserable cell," wrote Addison, "were confined the refractory and disobedient brethren of the Temple, and those who were enjoined severe penance with solitary confinement. Its dark secrets have long since been buried in the tomb, but one sad tale of misery and horror connected with it has been brought to light." Addison was referring to the fact, elicited by the examination of the witnesses at the Churches of St. Martin-le-Grand and St. Botolph, when the Templars were on trial in 1311, that one was imprisoned here for disobedience to the Master and here died from the severity of his confinement. His body was carried at early dawn from this solitary cell to the old churchyard between the church and the Hall and there buried.

On leaving the church we will go to the south side. From here we can see the house of the Master of the Temple, the preacher being still so called in deference to the Temple's history. It dates from the end of the seventeenth century. In this court is Lamb Building, with the Lamb and Banner, the badge of the Middle Temple, so prominently displayed on its porch. Famous lawyers have lodged here, but it is better known as the residence of Thomas Day, author of *Sandford and Merton,* and as the Lamb Court in which Pendennis and Warrington occupied a set of attics over the chambers of "old Grump of the Norfolk circuit."

We now retrace our steps to the cloisters and to the Hall of the Inner Temple, whose badge is Pegasus, a horse with wings. It is said the wings once were two men, it being a sign of the original poverty of the Templars, for two men to have only one mount. This hall dates only from 1870. Its panelling is covered with coats of arms, and at the east end is Sir James Thornhill's painting of "Pegasus Springing from Mount Helicon," executed in 1709. Beneath are portraits of William III and Mary, George II and Queen Caroline, by Kneller. The Inner Temple Library, with a collection of forty thousand law books, in addition to volumes on the fine arts, architecture, and county topography, adjoins on the eastern side. At the end of the buildings we turn south into King's Bench Walk. On the right is Crown Office Row, and at No. 2, as is indicated by a tablet, Charles Lamb was born in 1775. We may fitly leave the Temple with memories of Lamb who lived here until he was eighteen. The garden gate opposite Crown Office Row, with the date 1730 and the winged horse, will, however, remind us that in the fitness of things he would better have had the place of his "kindly engendure" in the Middle Temple which has a lamb as part of its badge.

WALK V : *Houses of Parliament—United Service Museum—Whitehall—Trafalgar Square—National Gallery—National Portrait Gallery—St. Etheldreda's Chapel—St. Bartholomew the Great's Church—Smithfield—St. Sepulchre's Church—Saracen's Head—Old Bailey.*

The official title for the buildings generally known as the Houses of Parliament is the Palace of Westminster. The first palace was built by Edward the Confessor at about the time he erected the abbey. It was walled, but not moated, and within its area of about twelve and a half acres so many as twenty thousand people—craftsmen, artificers, cooks, courtiers—are said to have been housed in the fourteenth century. The building was much damaged by fire in 1512, and Henry VIII, having acquired Whitehall from Wolsey and built St. James's Palace, no longer required it. In 1547 Edward VI granted its Chapel of St. Stephen to the House of Commons, and there they sat until a fire in 1834 destroyed it and the rest of the palace save Westminster Hall, the Crypt Chapel and the cloisters. The last two are not generally shown to the public, but can be seen through the friendly offices of a member of Parliament. The fire was caused through over-loading a fireplace with the tally-sticks once used, for some inexplicable reason, for exchequer accounts. In Dickens's only political speech—delivered at Drury Lane Theatre in 1855—he waxed very satirical at this holocaust caused by red tape.

A Select Committee of the House of Commons accepted

the design of Mr. (afterwards Sir) Charles Barry, who adopted the Gothic style of the Tudor period. The foundation stone was laid in 1840, the House of Lords first occupied their chamber in 1847, and the whole building was completed in 1852. The stone used was magnesian limestone from Yorkshire and has proved too little immune to the corroding influence of weather and noxious acids, with the result that many tons of stone have had to be picked off the building for safety's sake and large expenditure incurred in repairs. There are over three hundred independent statues on the main façade of the building. They represent the sovereigns of England and the saints and patron saints from pre-Norman times to Queen Victoria. The chronological sequence starts from the north front—between the Clock Tower and river. In the sunk garden on the western side is Hamo Thornycroft's statue of Cromwell. The Liberal Party wanted to vote five hundred pounds for the purpose in 1895, but chiefly through Irish opposition, had to withdraw the motion. When, however, three years later, Lord Rosebery offered a present of one, the House felt it could not look a gift horse in the mouth and the statue was erected. The Clock Tower is about three hundred and twenty feet high to the top of the finial. A clock stood near here in olden days with a great bell known as "Westminster Tom." This bell was given by William III to the Dean of St. Paul's, and recast to make the present great bell of the cathedral. The dials of the clock are twenty-three feet in diameter, the figures are two feet long, and the minute spaces one foot square; the minute hands are fourteen feet long, made of copper, and weigh about two hundredweight; the hour hands are nine feet long and weigh much heavier; the pendulum is thirteen feet long, beating two seconds. The first blow on the bell—"Big Ben"—which weighs thirteen and half tons indicates the hour. It was so called after Sir Benjamin Hall, First Commissioner of Works when the clock, made by Messrs. Dent, was fixed in 1858. The clock is wound by an electric motor, and lit at night by electricity. It is necessary to climb three hundred and seventy-four steps to reach it. A light is kept burning in the Clock Tower while the House is sitting, and George Jacob Holyoake, a stalwart radical and freethinker, claimed the merit of this idea. Adjoining the first floor of the Tower is the room in which refractory members of Parliament are confined. The last prisoner there was Charles Bradlaugh in 1880. The detention ends with the session, if not sooner terminated by the House.

The public entrance is through a door to the east of the Victoria Tower—in Old Palace Yard. At the top of the staircase which confronts us is the Norman Porch, so called because it was proposed to place upon the pedestals the statues of Norman kings. The next apartment is the King's Robing Room. Here His Majesty dons his robes of state before going to the House of Lords for the opening of Parliament. An oak dado runs round the room with eighteen panels of deep carving portraying stories from the Arthurian legend. Above the dado are five frescoes with similar subjects. The fireplace is made of different marbles, of natural colour, from the British Isles, with a metal statuette on either side of St. George fighting the Dragon, and St. George with the Dragon dead at his feet. The Chair of State is surmounted by a canopy of oak, carved with the Rose of England, the Thistle of Scotland, the Shamrock of Ireland, and Queen Victoria's monogram. Behind the chair is a beautiful piece of embroidery, which was executed by the South Kensington School of Art Needlework in 1856. We now pass into the Royal Gallery, traversed by the king in opening Parliament. The two huge paintings were the work of Dickens's friend Maclise. "Wellington and Blücher" was finished in 1863, "Nelson" in 1865, both having taken seven years. Copley's picture is erroneously called "The Death of Chatham," as his death did not follow the seizure in the House of Lords until a few weeks had elapsed. Beside the doorways and the bay window are gilded stone statues of King Alfred and William I, Richard I, and Edward III, Henry V, Queen Elizabeth, William III, and Queen Anne. In the window immediately above the "Wellington and Blücher" picture and a little to the right of the figures is a hole in the glass made by a piece of German shrapnel during the war. Below a beautiful window in the recess is a volume containing a record of members of the House of Lords and their sons who were killed in the Great War. A fresh page is turned over every day. Among recent

events here were the trial of Earl Russell by his peers in
1901 and an address from both Houses of Parliament to the
king on 19 November, 1918, in celebration of the Armistice.

The next room—the Princes' Chamber—is an ante-room
to the House of Lords. Its principal feature is a massive
statue group of Queen Victoria. There are a number of
bas-reliefs commemorating historic events of the Tudor
period, commencing (over the fireplace) with the visit of
Charles V to Henry VIII in 1522. There is also a series of
Tudor portraits commencing (on the right of the Queen
Victoria statue) with Henry VII and his queen, Elizabeth
of York. These were executed by the students of the Royal
School of Art, South Kensington, and cost seventy pounds
per picture.

We now reach the House of Lords, the most impressive
and ornate apartment in the whole palace. The Throne is
beneath an ornamental canopy divided into three compartments, the centre one projecting over the two chairs of
state, behind which is some exquisite carving of the *passant*
lions of England, the Royal Arms, the emblems of the
Garter, the motto *Dieu et mon droit*, the crests of England,
Scotland, Ireland, and Wales. On the right of the Throne
is the chair occupied by the Prince of Wales at the opening
of Parliament. Privy councillors and the eldest sons of
peers may stand on the steps during debates. In the
centre below the Throne is the Woolsack, the seat of the
Lord Chancellor as Speaker of the House. It was a woolsack
in the reign of Edward III—as an indication of England's
staple industry. It is now stuffed with hair! The cross-
benches are occupied by princes of the blood and peers of
independent view. The seat occupied by the bishops is
distinguished by having arms at either end and in resembling
a pew. The galleries are available for peeresses, ambassadors, and other distinguished persons; there is the Strangers
Gallery at the northern end, and a Press Gallery over the
doorway. At the far end of the House—it has the appearance of a dock—is the Bar at which the Commons attend
to hear the Speech from the Throne and the Royal Assent
to bills. The frescoes over the Throne represent: (1) Edward III conferring the Order of the Garter on the Black
Prince; (2) Baptism of St. Ethelbert; (3) Prince Henry

H

acknowledging the authority of Judge Gascoigne. Those behind the Strangers' Gallery are: (1) The Spirit of Justice; (2) The Spirit of Religion; (3) The Spirit of Chivalry. The first and third were the work of Maclise. The House of Lords Lobby is remarkable for the fine stone carving and the doors of oak, mounted with brass. The Peers' Corridor, at which we next arrive, has eight paintings of events during the Stuart period. The Peers' Robing Room which follows is sometimes called the "Moses Room," from the large fresco of Moses bringing the tables of the law from Sinai. We now turn right, into the East Corridor, where are six frescoes depicting episodes of the Tudor period. The one of Latimer preaching before Edward VI certainly shows a more highly decorated pulpit at St. Paul's Cross than we have record of. The Lower Waiting Hall is next, and here is a statue of John Bright, and Bernini's bust of Cromwell. The medallion on the bust bears a representation of the old House of Commons. Cromwell's wart is clearly shown, and the pedestal reveals what is less known, the arms he assumed when he became Lord Protector.

We now turn left, through a long corridor lined with books, and turning left again, walk through a portrait gallery. This takes us to the House of Commons. The Government side of the House is to the right of the Speaker's Chair, and the Opposition to the left. The seating accommodation is for three hundred and sixty-eight members below and for eighty-two in the galleries. At the Table of the House three clerks sit, and there the Speaker and his chaplain stand during prayers. At the lower end of the table are the rests for the mace when the House sits as such; when it is in committee it is placed upon rests below the table. On either side is a large brass-bound box, the one on the right of the chair marks the seat of the Prime Minister, and the one on the left the seat of the Leader of the Opposition. The dents made to enforce their oratory may be seen. Along the floor of the House a strip of carpet runs with a red-edged border, beyond which no member may stand whilst speaking. This is a relic of the times when members carried swords and marks the distance at which two swords might meet. When crossing the Speaker's line of vision members always bow. Some say this is due to the fact that where the Speaker's Chair now is was the altar in the old Chapel of St. Stephen. Others go farther back and attribute the origin to the days when the Commons met in the Chapter-house of Westminster and bowed to a picture of the Virgin which hung against the central pillar. On leaving the chamber we notice the boxes occupied by the door-keepers of the House to prevent unauthorized persons passing the portals. The Crown has no right of access to the Commons and so the practice is, when a message is sent from the Crown to summon the Commons to the House of Lords, for the door to be shut in the face of its messenger, the Gentleman Usher of the Black Rod. He has then to knock three times at the door and the marks of this importunate servant of the peers may be seen on the door. The Members' Lobby contains statues of Sir William Harcourt and Joseph Chamberlain. We go through another corridor with eight frescoes of historic incidents of the Stuart period, and then, turning right, enter St. Stephen's Hall. This stands upon the site of St. Stephen's Chapel, founded by King Stephen about 1141, partially destroyed by fire in 1298, rebuilt by Edward III in the Gothic style and completed in 1364. There are here a number of statues of doughty debaters of old, and opposite Selden's monument is a brass stud in the floor indicating the position of the Speaker's Chair in the old Chapel, whilst between the statues of Pitt and Chatham is a tablet showing where the lobby of that House commenced, and by the same token, where Spencer Perceval was murdered (see page 173). On either side of the doorways are statues of early kings and queens of England; those at the eastern doorway (in the central hall) are Richard I, his consort, Berengaria, and John, Queen Matilda, Henry II, and Queen Eleanor; those at the western doorway are William I, Queen Maud, William II, Henry I, his consort, Queen Matilda, and Stephen. At the east and west ends are two large mosaic panels relating to the history of the chapel. The one at the east depicts St. Stephen holding a stone, in allusion to his martyrdom, with King Stephen, in mail, on his right, and Edward the Confessor, the founder of the old palace, kneeling on his left. These were unveiled in 1925. The mosaic at the west end portrays Edward III handing the design of his chapel to his master mason, Thomas of Canterbury, with representatives of medieval craftsmen standing beside him. It was unveiled in 1926. More recent still are the mural panels illustrative of English history, commencing at the north-west corner with Alfred the Great and ending at the south-west corner with the Union of the Scotch and English Parliaments. They were unveiled by Mr. Baldwin, then Prime Minister, in 1927.

We now reach Westminster Hall. It was erected by William Rufus between the years 1097–9, and it was first divided by a double line of columns, for the Normans could not otherwise roof so wide a space. The hall was remodelled and heightened by Richard II, who rebuilt the north end, removed the columns and erected the oak roof, Chaucer being clerk of the works. The hammer-beam roof is a marvellous example of Gothic open timber work. The ends of the beams are decorated with winged angels holding shields, on which may be seen the badge of Richard II—a chained hart—and the curved beams are richly moulded. The roof was again repaired in 1819, forty loads of well-seasoned oak from old ships, broken at Portsmouth, being utilized. Owing to the ravages of the death-watch beetles (specimens of their work are shown in a glass case) extensive repairs had again to be carried out between 1914 and 1923. This is one of the largest halls in Europe unsupported by pillars.

A number of historical events have taken place here. In 1305 the trial of William Wallace; in 1399 the deposition of Richard II (see Shakespeare's play, Act IV, Scene i); in 1522 the trial of the Earl of Buckingham (see *Henry VIII*, Act II, Scene i); in 1535 the trial of Sir Thomas More; in 1606 the trial of Guy Fawkes; in 1641 the trial of the Earl of Strafford; in 1649 the trial of Charles I; in 1687 the trial of the Seven Bishops; in 1746 the trials of the Scotch lords after the Young Pretender's rising; and from 1788–95 the trial of Warren Hastings. Some of these events are commemorated by brass tablets on the floor. The hall was also used for great state ceremonies and coronation feasts from Stephen to George IV. At the coronation of the latter, the King's Champion—for the last time—rode into the hall with his challenge to any one who disputed the king's right to succeed (see Sir Walter Scott's *Redgauntlet*). Here Mr.

Gladstone's body lay in state, and also Edward VII's, from 17 May to 19 May, 1910. It is estimated that in that period five hundred thousand people passed through the hall. Here also the victims of the airship R 101 laid in state in 1930. Along the south wall of the hall, on either side of the grand stairway, are three statues: those on the east side stood over the Court of King's Bench (at Westminster Hall were the Courts of Justice until 1882 when they were transferred to the Strand); the statues are said to be William Rufus, Henry I, Stephen, Henry II, Richard I, and John. The three statues in the recesses above the small door in the east wall are of thirteenth-century date. They are believed to have come from the north façade of the hall.

On leaving the Houses of Parliament, we walk down Parliament Street. It was driven through the heart of the Privy Garden of the old Whitehall Palace about 1732. There was a narrower thoroughfare along part of the course followed by Parliament Street, called King Street, and here in 1599 died Edmund Spenser "for lack of bread," according to Ben Jonson. When excavations were made for the erection of the Cenotaph there were found remains of a kitchen with a grate, probably belonging to former Government buildings on the site.

On the second floor level of the Red Lion public-house, at the corner of Derby Street, is a medallion of Dickens. This refers to an incident of his boyhood—used in *David Copperfield*. He entered the predecessor of this modern public-house and asked for a glass of the best ale in the house to celebrate his birthday or some other festive occasion. He got a kiss as well—from the landlady! Downing Street takes its name from Sir George Downing, Secretary to the Treasury in the reign of Charles II. The Prime Minister's residence was conferred by George II on Robert Walpole, regarded as the first Prime Minister though not known as such.

At Whitehall was a Tudor palace which was once the residence of Wolsey as Archbishop of York, but after his fall it fell into the hands of Henry VIII. It was known as York Place, and is so referred to in *Henry VIII*:

> You must no more call it York Place—that is past:
> For since the Cardinal fell that title 's lost;
> 'Tis now the King's and call'd Whitehall.

The palace, in which Henry VIII died in 1547, grew dilapidated towards the end of the century, and James I engaged Inigo Jones, as Surveyor-General, to rebuild it. From the plans — still preserved in Worcester College, Oxford — it appears that it would have covered an area of eleven hundred and fifty-two feet by eight hundred and seventy-four feet. The Banqueting Hall was completed by 1622, but owing to lack of funds the rebuilding was not further proceeded with. It was in Whitehall Palace that Cromwell died, and it was here that Charles II and James II kept court. A fire in 1698 almost destroyed all the remaining Tudor buildings, and in 1724 the Banqueting Hall became a Chapel Royal. There the Maundy money used to be distributed until it was dismantled in 1890. In 1895 the United Service Museum was housed in the building.

There is a tablet under the central window stating that on a platform erected in front of it Charles I was executed. Lord Beaconsfield was once asked by a supporter to give a word of advice to his son. "Never ask," said he, "who wrote the *Letters of Junius* or on which side of Whitehall Charles I was beheaded. For if you do, you will be considered a bore, and that is something too dreadful for you, at your tender age, to understand." Much ink has certainly been spilled on the second of these questions. Canon Sheppard, however, who wrote an admirable book upon Whitehall, was satisfied that the blow which Carlyle considered so fatal to flunkeyism was struck near where the tablet says, and that the king passed on to the scaffold by way of an aperture in the north wall, which led to an annexe of the Banqueting Hall, shown in old prints, from which the scaffold was reached.

To visitors of pacific minds the museum is not of great interest, and it is perhaps not without reason that it endeavours to tempt people within by displaying such a tempting object as one of the anchors of the Spanish Armada at its door. A little room immediately opposite the entrance has some relics of savage warfare, including an Ashantee drum decorated with human bones. On top of the staircase is a tablet relating to Charles I's last walk through the Banqueting Hall. Close by is a bust of James I which represents that king as far more imposing than he ever was.

This is a fitting prelude to the approach to the ceiling. One cannot help wishing that such fine art as Rubens here displayed had had a more inspiring subject than the apotheosis of James I. Of the three central compartments, that at the east end represents the British Solomon on his throne, pointing to Prince Charles who is being perfected by Wisdom; the middle compartment shows him "trampling on the globe, and flying on the wings of Justice (an eagle) to heaven"; in the third he is "embracing Minerva and routing Rebellion and Envy." Rubens was paid thirty thousand pounds for the painting. The ceiling has been several times repaired, and in 1907 it was taken down and carefully ironed at the Science and Art Department at South Kensington.

Generally speaking the relics here are restricted to the pomp and circumstance of war, but there is an item that even a pacifist can greet with a cheer. In the left-hand case, just inside the door, is a letter from the Bishop of Rochester in 1798 declining an invitation to bless the colours of the Westminster Volunteer Cavalry. "A ceremony," he wrote, "of very indefinite and doubtful interpretation, and if it be understood to confer anything of sanctity on the colours, slightly superstitious. Those of the Romans indeed, before the conversion of the Empire, were dedicated to their idols, and in the Church of Rome there may have been consecrations of military weapons and of standards by the authority of the Pope upon particular occasions. But I doubt whether anything of the kind was ever heard of among Christians of any denomination before the time of the Crusades." In the case close to the second window on the left are a number of relics of Nelson, including a watch worn during the Battle of Trafalgar, the saw, a crude, fearful looking weapon, wherewith Dr. Auchmuty amputated his arm in 1797, and a specimen of the spirit in which his body was embalmed on the way to England. Readers of Hardy will remember that *The Dynasts* mentions a rumour that the sailors had felt they needed the spirit more and had absorbed some of it! Under the third window are relics of the Spanish Armada, together with one of Queen Elizabeth's petticoats, and under the fourth are objects connected with the mutiny of the *Bounty* (see page 196). Those who were boys in the Victorian era probably became acquainted with that thrilling story in the pages of Ballantyne's fascinating tale, *The Lonely Island*. The case in the next window recalls "The Loss of the Royal George," the theme of Cowper's poem. On the other side of the hall, in the fourth case from the far end, are relics of Wellington and Sir John Moore. A little nearer the entrance is a collection of Civil War relics, including bullets from the field of Naseby, and a scented pastille found in Charles I's pocket after execution. In the last window but one on this side are the Napoleon relics, and in the next will be seen, on the left, a picture of the Banqueting Hall when it was fitted up as a chapel and one of Whitehall showing the Holbein Gate. A contemporary drawing of the execution of Charles I is close by. This shows a platform extending from the fourth to the seventh window from the north side. This need not be taken seriously: it will be noticed that the artist shows a row of eight windows when there are only seven. There are large models of the Battle of Waterloo and the Battle of Trafalgar. There is a similar one of the Spanish Armada in the basement, where are also models of battles from Barnet (1471) to the Great War.

On leaving the museum, we turn right and go down Horseguards Avenue into Whitehall Gardens, behind the Banqueting House. Pembroke House (No. 7) was built soon after the Whitehall fire of 1698 for the Earls of Pembroke, great lovers of art. Unfortunately the original façade with its link extinguishers has been covered up by the modern entrance made for the purposes of the Government departments that occupied it during the War. At No. 2 Disraeli lived for a time after his wife's death, and at No. 4 Sir Robert Peel lived from 1824–46. When Peel had it built, it had, as one of his biographers wrote: "the advantages of almost rural retirement and tranquillity with a fine view over the Thames," and a son of Sir Robert recalled how preparations had been made to remove the family and valuables by boat in view of a threatened attack by rioters. This was of course before the Embankment made the river more distant. The fear was occasioned by the fact that here anti-Reform Bill meetings were held. Peel's popularity returned with the repeal of the Corn Laws, and upon that occasion "they let him pass unaccompanied in silence, took off their hats and opening their ranks to let him pass, accompanied him in silence to the door of his house." Peel was thrown from a horse in Hyde Park, and on being brought home in a carriage, revived at sight of his beloved residence. He collapsed, however, and died after three days' agony. The tablet was placed upon the house by the L.C.C. in 1904. Mr. H. G. Wells once lived in Whitehall Gardens, and now Mr. Bernard Shaw is resident there. If we return to Horseguards Avenue and proceed towards the river we see on the right a gateway leading to a few steps. Ascending the steps we see, in the south-west corner of this enclosure, a piece of the brickwork of the old Whitehall Palace. It probably dates from the fifteenth century.

Returning to Whitehall, we turn right. The Charles I statue, at the junction of Trafalgar Square with Parliament Street, is the best known in London. It was erected in 1635 and was sold, when Cromwell was in power, to a brazier named Rivett, who was ordered to destroy it. He only buried the statue, though it is said he sold knives and forks alleged to have handles made from its brass. Between 1675 and 1677 it was re-erected. The pedestal has been ascribed to Wren and Grinling Gibbons, but appears to have been entirely the work of Joshua Marshall, architect and master mason to the Crown. During the recent war it was sandbagged up at a cost of four hundred pounds. At one time it was decorated with oak boughs on 29 May, Charles II's birthday. Now annually, on 30th January, the anniversary of his execution, a service is held in memory of Charles I by the Royal Martyr's Church Union and other societies, when wreaths are placed round the statue.

Trafalgar Square was laid out between 1829 and 1840 and happily swallowed up a congeries of somewhat sordid alleys. William IV is said to have been responsible for the idea. The statue of Nelson was not completed until about 1852 and the delay in erection was the subject of much irritation. The lions—designed by Sir Edwin Landseer—did not appear until 1867. The column is one hundred and ninety-three feet high, and the figure of Nelson measures seventeen feet. The damage to the plinth on the west side was caused through some colonial soldiers making a bonfire of a watchman's box, tar, and oil soon after the Armistice. On the north side of the square is the standard of measurement, placed there in 1876. The statues do not call for much attention. The best are those of George IV, north-east corner, and Gordon in the centre. The former was the work of Chantrey, and was intended to adorn the Marble Arch. It is unusual in that the horse is entirely at rest, and that the king is riding bare-backed without saddle or stirrups. Chantrey was to receive nine thousand pounds for his work, but only a third had been paid at his death. His executors extracted the rest from the Commissioners of Woods and Forests. Sir Walter Besant, referring to its proximity to the Nelson column, remarked: "This is the first instance of a testimonial representing a sovereign playing second-fiddle to a subject." Gordon has his famous "whangee" cane under his left arm and in his right hand holds a Bible. On the east and west sides are figures in relief of Charity and Justice, Faith and Fortitude, and round the top of the pedestal a list of his engagements from the Crimea through China to Khartoum.

The National Gallery, which was erected in 1838, really commenced in 1824 with the purchase by the Government for the sum of fifty-seven thousand pounds of thirty-eight pictures. The building, erected upon a very limited site, is a curious one from an external view and was once described as possessing a "cupola without size, a portico without height, pepper-boxes without pepper, and the finest site in Europe without anything to show upon it." The gallery is rich in great masterpieces. All the most notable artists are represented. The following are a few of the many great pictures well worth seeing. Bracketed numbers are catalogue numbers.

Room 1. *Leonardo's* forerunner *Piero Della Francesca.* (665 and 908). Purity, simplicity and unity of tone are his great qualities. *Uccello (Paolo)* (583) Pattern, design and foreshortening; note the glazed silver foils! *Masaccio* (3046), a student of nature who loves mass and movement. He earned Leonardo's praise. *Pollaiuolo (A.)* (292). A realist with wonderful anatomy, he pictures the body in action. A composition of marvellous unity. *Perugino (P.),* decorative and simple with great depth and clearness.

Room 2. Fra Angelico's gracious "Annunciation" (1406).
Gozzoli (B.) (591), medieval but gay. The pageantry and
splendour of Florence.

Room 3. Duccio. (1137). Master of the Sienese School,
gives us genuine human feeling with tenderness and
mystery.

Room 4. Orcagna's magnificent altar-piece (569), *Giotto's*
successor, he has deep religious intensity.

Room 5. Leonardo's adorable "Virgin of the Rocks."
Leonardo, scientist, searcher, and here the creator of eternal
beauty.

Room 6. The Bellinis. Gentile (1440) the best portraitist
of his time. *Giovanni:* (189), and (736) with its red twilight
and deep sympathy between man and nature. *Antonello
da Messina:* (1166) is an amazing achievement where space,
tragedy, and tenderness meet. *Giorgione:* (269) a beautiful
and perfect knight. *Basaiti:* (281) the combined brilliance
and softness of Venetian colour.

Room 7. The pomp of Venice in her pride! *Titian's*
opulence and splendour (34 and 35) and the wonderful
heads in the "Cornaro." *Veronese:* (294). Venice in
spacious light and shade. *Tintoretto:* (1313) Master of the
problems of light, shade, and space. *Lotto (L.)* (1105).
Wonderful draughtsman and thinker, follower of Savon-
arola; and the quiet *Moroni* (697).

The New Mond Room has two happy *Botticellis.*
Raphael's decorative grace (3943). Medieval *Pintoricchio*
(911) boneless but charming.

Rooms 9, 10 and 12 are Dutch.

Room 9. Mieris (W.): (841) matchless detail. *Huysman:*
(796) wonderful flowers. *Metsu:* (2591) freedom of touch,
power, and colour. *Ruisdael:* (980) sombre and melancholy.
A. Van der Neer: (2524) poet painter of the twilight.

Room 10. Paul Potter (849). *Jan Steen* (2560). *Wm.
Van de Velde* (871), the greatest Dutch sea painter: and a
copy of Rembrandt's "Night Watch."

Room 12. Vermeer's modelling and power (1383) and
(2548). *Rembrandt,* profound thinker and craftsman, gives
us in (3214) his absorption in the wonder of light; in
(1675) and (775) his tenderness and understanding of old
age; in (45) his wonder, mystery, and light amid the gloom.
Hobbema, (the Dutch Constable) at his best (830) and (832).
Helst (1937). Note the wonderful hands! *Hals's* marvellous
dexterity (2528) and (2529). *De Hooch* (835) and *Cuyp's*

masterpiece (1286). Rembrandt apart, all is Holland and the love of common and intimate things.

Room 14 is Rubens. Late in the sixteenth century the full-blooded Flemish life flows again after two centuries of subjection. Rubens is the ripe fruit of this new vigour. He lived like a king, speaking seven languages and painting three thousand canvases! His aim is nature in action. His tireless brush overflows all, but never lacks order within the flowing line. He gave to Flemish art a soul and a spirit. (What it might have been but for Rubens is seen in (3215) *Jordaens.* All appetite and flesh.) Study especially 38, 187, 194, and 66.

Room 15. Early Flemish. With *Jan van Eyck* (186) we go back two hundred years! Note its realism, light, colour, and space; its simplicity and peace. *Roger Van der Weyden* (654) and his pupil *Memling* (686) and (747). *Memling* paints the soul and combines subtle colour harmonies. *David* (1045) heads and copes. (1432) the wonderful child. *Patinir* (1082 and 1084) earliest among landscape painters. *Bouts* (D.) (664) human feeling and veiled landscape. Rich colour and well-painted detail are the Flemish keynotes.

Rooms 17 and 18 are Spanish. Silence and space in *Velasquez.* Lover of air and light. A mirror covering with his own distinction the King, the child, and the buffoon; searcher and student always, and at last the supreme master. In (745) note the stillness and austerity, the curl of superiority, the regal pride! Here it is, fixed for ever, steeped in a thin veil of air and light. A perfect example of Velasquez's last manner. *El Greco:* (3476) Dramatic earnestness and convulsive ecstasy. The Inquisition in paint, his colour reflects the barren Toledan landscape. *Zurbaran's* greyness of the monastic spirit in the kneeling Franciscan (230) pouring out his soul. Hard and powerful, rigid and severe. *Murillo* (176) provides the contrast. Sweet and pretty, sentiment and a too obvious symbolism. In *Goya* (1473) we leap a hundred years. Gone is the Inquisition, the dream of Empire is dead. Scepticism reigns and Goya is its spirit.

Room 19 is notable for *Holbein's* workmanlike "Ambassadors" with the elongated skull, and that still picture of maidenhood "Christina of Denmark" (2475).

Room 20 is French. Poussin, who followed the grand style and *Claude.* In the adjoining vestibule Claude and Turner rival each other.

Room 21 *Modern French*. *Manet* the stern realist (3294). *Fantin Latour's* exquisite flowers. *Corot's* morning magic (2625). *Chardin's* homely realism, and the decorative motifs of *Chavannes*.

Rooms 22, 24, and 25 are British.

Room 22. *Constable* (2651) in that bright moment after storm. "The Hay Wain" (1207) with its rolling clouds, and the little gem "A House at Hampstead" (2625). *Cotman's* "Wherries," (1111). Cpulent *Rossetti* (3055). *Watts's* "Love and Death." *Madox · Brown, Millais, Alfred Stevens's* "Mrs. Collmann." and *Whistler's* exquisite "Symphony in White."

Room 24. The quiet glory of "Old Crome." The tonal harmony of (2645) and the space and air of (689). The barber's boy, *Turner*, in all his moods, "Beautiful England" (497), "Frost" (192), "Storm" (472), "Ships" (481), "Golden Legend" (508), and that vision of driving rain shot with sunlight (530) in the next room. *Blake* (1164), mystic and dreamer combine in this slow procession.

Room 25 *Wilson* (2646) and (1290), air and light. *Gainsborough's* typical landscape (80) and "Mrs. Siddons" (683). The accomplished *Reynolds*, cool and elegant in (1259), follower of the Venetians in (78A). *Hogarth* (1162), London's pride. A lovely *Romney* (1667). *Morland* (1030), and "London Bridge in 1745" (313) to connect us with these times.

Room 26. *Raphael* and *Michelangelo* face each other. Compare the serenity and decorative colour of *Raphael* with the vigour and power of *Michelangelo*, whose unfinished fresco is so arresting.

Room 27. *Caravaggio* (172). Bold emphasis on light and shadow. He paves the way for Rembrandt.

Room 29. *Botticelli*: (1033) is just Beauty! (1034) is a happy picture of his last period, tender and mystical. *Lippi* (*Fra F.*) (666) and (667), the first to consider ordinary people. He depicts the Florentine middle class. *Cosimo* (895), first to consider space and distance.

Room 31. *The Duveen Addition*. *Mantegna* (*A.*) (1417). Form, severe draughtsmanship and compact design are his qualities. (274) is a beautiful subdued colour harmony. *Carlo Crivelli's* "Annunciation" (739) rich in accessories.

The National Portrait Gallery is next door—to the left. The Nurse Cavell statue we see to our right as we enter the gallery has an admirable figure but an appalling background. The woman with the child represents Humanity protecting small states.   At the back of the block is an angry British lion in relief.   The words "Patriotism is not enough" were added by the Labour Government in 1924, four years after the statue was unveiled by Queen Alexandra.   The church with cathedral-like proportions is St. Martin's-in-the-Fields. It was erected in 1722 and George I made a contribution towards it, partly because it was then the parish church of Buckingham Palace.   The royal arms over the portico indicate this phase of its history.   Now St. James's is a parish in itself.   In the old church were baptized Francis Bacon and Charles II; Nell Gwynne was buried here, also · Jack Sheppard at a time when the victims of the hangman were buried by their friends, a privilege allowed in that crueler age but denied now.   The church has a crypt which is open all night as a shelter for the homeless, and since the war, thanks largely to its former popular vicar, the Rev. H. R. L. Sheppard, and the broadcast services, is perhaps as well known as any London church.

The National Portrait Gallery was opened in 1896, at a cost of ninety-six thousand pounds, eighty thousand pounds of which was the gift of Mr. W. H. Alexander.   Most people to whom the gallery is new, and many to whom it is old, enjoy an hour studying the art of the portrait painter from medieval anonymities to Sargent.   The historical portraits are on the top floor, and it is best to commence there. Actually the earliest is the electrotype cast of the effigy of Robert, Duke of Normandy, at the head of the main staircase, the original of which, carved in bog-oak and probably of the period of Henry II, is in Gloucester Cathedral. All of these casts are worth examination; that of Lady Margaret is one of the most beautiful.   It is by Torrigiano. There is also on the right of the staircase a cast of the death-mask of Dr. John Yong.   There are three portraits of Richard II.   One is by an unknown artist (565), then the electrotype from his effigy at Westminster (330), and lastly, the copy by J. Randall of the original painting in Westminster Abbey (1676).   The portrait of Richard III (148) does not confirm the Crookback of Shakespeare and legend, but who has drawn a monarch faithfully?   They do not ask — like Cromwell — for the warts!   Mr. John Steegmann, official lecturer at the gallery, gives the palm to the portrait of Henry VII (416), the work of some Flemish artist. The whole character of the king, he says, is well brought out—"crafty, unscrupulous, so excessively business-like." Henry VIII is represented by a fine copy of the portrait by Holbein, now at Althorpe. The original is on a small panel, and shows the king placed against the familiar background, while this copy is painted on copper on a dark ground, "otherwise," says Mr. Steegmann, "there is no difference in kind and only a little in degree." We have here also a fine portrait of Lord William Russell (see page 176), whilst side by side are Samuel Pepys and John Bunyan, perhaps the strongest antithesis to be found in the gallery. Bunyan's portrait, by Sadler, confirms the literary portrait of George Cokayne, a contemporary Nonconformist minister: "tall of stature, strong-boned, though not corpulent, somewhat of a ruddy face, with sparkling eyes, wearing his hair on his upper lip, after the old British fashion; his hair reddish, his nose well set, but not declining or bending, and his mouth moderately large; his forehead something high, and his habit always plain and modest." The portrait was painted in 1684 when Bunyan was fifty-six. Pepys's portrait was painted in 1666, and there are numerous references to its progress in the *Diary*. Pepys is represented in a gown, "which I hired to be drawn in; a morning gowne," and holding in his hand a piece of music, with the words "Beauty Retire." Readers of the *Diary* will know that this was of his own composition and a source of great pride to the composer. Pepys was "mightily pleased" with the picture, and it was made at some cost of money, time, and comfort. "I do almost break my nek looking over my shoulder to make the posture for him to work by," he wrote in the *Diary*. Close to Pepys is Faithorne's engraving of John Milton. This is the one that one of his daughters recognized in 1725, fifty years after Milton's death, as such a faithful one. "O Lord! that is the picture of my father. Just so my father wore his hair." The portrait of Shakespeare is that known as the Chandos, it having been in the possession of the dukes of that name for more than a century. It cannot be traced back to Shakespeare's time, but it was in existence soon after his death. It was probably painted, in the opinion of Sir Sidney Lee, from fanciful descriptions of him. The face with its beard and adornment of rings has an Italian look. Another portrait of interest is that of Dr. Donne (see page 31), and also Casaubon (see page 61). Those who have seen the tomb of Sir Julius Cæsar in St. Helen's, Bishopsgate (see page 144), will be interested to see his likeness. The eighteenth-century portraits on this floor demand attention. There are two of Reynolds's portraits of Johnson (1597) and (1445). With regard to the latter, Mr. Steegmann justly says: "The absence of the wig enables one to see the fine head, and where other portraits of Johnson give one an impression of physical strength as of an ox, this shows physical weakness and intellectual strength." Here are portraits of three well-known eighteenth-century architects, Sir John Soane, who designed the Bank of England, and left the museum in Lincoln's Inn Fields to the nation; James Gibbs, who designed St. Martin's-in-the-Fields; and William Chambers, who was responsible for Somerset House. There is one specimen of the work of Joseph Nollekens, the famous eighteenth-century sculptor—a bust of Rev. Laurence Sterne. This was one of Nollekens's first successes, and he was painted leaning upon Sterne's head.

The floor below attracts most attention, the portraits including those of many people well within living memory. On the right-hand wall of the first room is a painting of Keats in a room at Hampstead, which those who visit the museum there will see. Here is also William Hazlitt's fine portrait of Lamb as a young man, and Phillips's portrait of William Blake—represented as if wrapped in some mystical vision. The portrait of George Eliot (1849) is more attractive than usual. More interesting still, are pictures of the Brontë sisters and one of Emily alone, both painted by the "ne'er-do-well" brother Patrick Branwell. This is probably the "rough common-looking oil painting" which Mrs. Gaskell says, in chapter xxvii of her famous biography, Charlotte Brontë showed her.

From here we take a bus to Ludgate Circus and walk through St. Bride Street; on reaching Holborn we cross the road, leaving the polite statue of the Prince Consort on the left, find Ely Place, through the pathway to the left.

St. Etheldreda's Chapel is all that remains of the palace of the Bishop of Ely, erected here about 1290. In this palace John of Gaunt died in 1381, as described by Shake-speare in *Richard II*, after making (in the play) the familiar speech about England. It is again referred to in *Richard III*:

Gloster.	When I was last in Holborn, I saw good strawberries in your garden there: I do beseech you send for some of them.
Ely.	Marry, and will, my lord, with all my heart.

(Act III, Scene iv.)

This incident is also in Sir Thomas More's *Life of Richard III*. In the cloisters of the palace Henry VIII first met Cranmer. In 1576 Sir Christopher Hatton, a favourite of Queen Eliza-beth, forced Bishop Cox to lease him portions of his property, and in the garden and orchard built himself a mansion. In 1619, Gondomar, the Spanish Ambassador, lodged here. It continued to be the London residence of the bishops until 1772, when they found quarters in Dover Street, Piccadilly. It was then disposed of to the Crown, and some of the houses here now date from about that period when it was laid out for residential purposes. At one time Ely Place enjoyed some peculiar privileges, such as exemption from rating. Even now it levies its own rates, and looks to a beadle to enforce law and order. This beadle closes the gate from Hatton Garden at 11 p.m., and patrols Ely Place calling out the hour and the weather like the old watch. City con-stables never come down Ely Place unless summoned, and even then make any necessary arrest outside its area.

The chapel has a west window to the memory of Catholic martyrs, including Thomas à Becket, John Houghton, the last Prior of Charterhouse, and Sir Thomas More. There is no London window so large as this, and in size it compares with those of York Minster. There is a beautiful screen, the work of J. F. Bentley, the architect of Westminster Cathedral. In the vestibule is a holy-water stoup, found during excavations hereabouts, which some authorities date back to Roman times, some even earlier. There is reason to believe there was a British church on this site. St. Ethel-dreda's is unique in one respect. It is the only building now used for Catholic worship which was so used before the Reformation. The royal arms (now in the vestibule) were in the chapel at the time it was again acquired by the Catholics—from the Welsh Episcopalians—in 1874. It was

I

re-opened by Cardinal Manning in 1879. Evelyn, as recorded
in his *Diary*, came here in 1693 for the marriage of his
daughter. There is a crypt, the walls of which are seven
feet thick.

After leaving the chapel, we may turn down Mitre Court,
leading off Ely Place on the right. Here is a modern public-
house with the old sign of the Mitre and the date 1546.
No doubt this and the sign hanging over the pavement
have a much longer history than the present building, even
if they do not go back to Tudor times. Inside the tavern
is a cherry-tree, alleged to date from the reign of Elizabeth.

From Holborn we turn left, and on reaching Giltspur
Street turn off. This turning takes us to Smithfield, on the
far side of which is the Church of St. Bartholomew the
Great. It was founded by Rahere, one of the courtiers of
Henry I. He made a pilgrimage to Rome in about the
year 1120 and fell ill of malaria. In his distress he vowed
that if he recovered he would, as a thank-offering, establish
a hospital for the poor. His prayer was granted, and during
his convalescence St. Bartholomew came to him and indicated that he should found the church (the hospital apparently
was not mentioned) at Smithfield, a desolate place in which
the one dry spot was utilized for executions. Rahere commenced to build a church and priory—of which he became
the first prior—in 1123, and of the church, by the time of
his death in 1144, the choir, the apse, and the eastern part
of the clerestory, of which the present is a modern repro-
duction, had been completed. In 1930, nightly for some
weeks, a most impressive pageant play was performed, with
torches lighting up the dark recesses of the church, setting
out the history of Rahere, in aid of the hospital he founded.

The priory was one for Canons Regular of St. Augustine,
and Rahere's successor as prior erected transepts and the
easternmost bays of the nave. It was probably completed
during the next half-century in the Early English style. On
the dissolution of the priory, the nave was at once pulled
down, and the choir reserved for the use of the parish. The
church subsequently grew into such a state through exploit-
ation and neglect that in 1791 the Lady Chapel was filled
up with modern tenements, the north transept more or less
destroyed, the south transept was without a roof and used

as a burial ground, the eastern side of the cloister, all that remained, was used as a stable, the site of the north cloister was occupied by a blacksmith's forge, a public-house, and private offices, the south and west being covered with store-rooms and coach-houses. And still there is more to follow. A chapel, dating from Edward III's time, was used as a store-room for hops, and at one time in the eighteenth century there was a fringe factory in the Lady Chapel and a Nonconformist school in the triforium. It has taken over a hundred years and much money to reclaim the church property. Six thousand five hundred pounds were paid to the owner of the fringe factory and two thousand pounds to the blacksmith. Only two years ago was the last of the cloisters bought back by the church.

No other City church has the atmosphere of St. Bartholomew's. It takes us back by a glance to the days when even churches were made by the Normans of a strength massive as castles. It recalls Milton's famous lines about the "studious cloister's pale," and "high embowed roof":

> With antique pillars massy proof,
> And storied windows, richly dight,
> Casting a dim religious light.

Strangely enough there is not a scrap of stained glass in the church, but the dimness is almost too manifest—it is so difficult to read the inscriptions on the monuments.

We notice in the choir, not only the perfect horseshoe pattern of the Norman arches, but the characteristic billet moulding, continuing without a break from pier to pier. The clerestory is a reconstruction by Sir Aston Webb, in 1885. On the left of the choir is the tomb of the founder. He is attired in the black habit of the Augustinian Canons, the hands are joined in prayer and the head rests upon a tasselled cushion. At the feet an angel with flowing black hair, and crowned, is represented rising from clouds, holding towards the recumbent figure a shield on which the priory arms are embossed and illuminated. On each side of the effigy a kneeling monk of the same order is reading from a book, opened at Isaiah li, 3. The passage is obviously chosen as a reference to the state of Smithfield when Rahere founded his church: "For the Lord shall comfort Zion. He will comfort all her waste places; and he will make her wildernesses like Eden, and her deserts like the garden of the Lord; joy and gladness shall be found therein, thanksgiving, and the voice of melody." The figure may date from the twelfth century, but the canopy and panelling were added in the fifteenth century. The arms on the tomb—from left to right—are those of the City of London, St. Bartholomew's Priory, and Sir Stephen Slaney, Lord Mayor in 1595.

From here we get a good view of the oriel window, designed for Prior Bolton about 1530. His rebus—a bolt in a tun—is prominently displayed. From here we may, if we climb to the triforium, obtain an excellent view of the altar and the founder's tomb, and it was probably for this reason that the window was made. We may now pass round to the rear of the apse, carefully restored by Sir Aston Webb, to view the Lady Chapel which is a restoration of one built in 1410. It was recovered from the fringe manufacturer in 1885, and owing to its condition then, much of the work is new. The sanctuary is paved with Roman tesseræ and coloured marbles, in agreement with the pavement beneath the high altar, but of a less elaborate pattern.

The ambulatory, with its low vaulting, leads one to muse upon the procession of the canons, and to think of a great passage in Ruskin: "The greatest glory of a building is in its age, and in that deep sense of voicefulness, of stern watching, of mysterious sympathy, nay, even of approval or condemnation, which we feel in walls that have long been washed by the passing waves of humanity." If we turn to the south ambulatory, on leaving the Lady Chapel we come to Prior Bolton's doorway—with the rebus in the spandrel. West of this is the fine marble altar-tomb of Sir Walter Mildmay who founded Emmanuel College, Cambridge, in 1585, and was one of the commissioners at the trial of Mary Queen of Scots in 1586. A short distance from this is the tomb of Captain John Miller, who traded in the east and died in 1660. A quaint epitaph commences:

Many a storm and tempest past
Here he hath quiet anchor cast
Desirous hither to resort
Because this parish was the port
Whence his wide soul set forth and where
His father's bones intrusted are.

The pulpit was erected under the will of Mrs. Charlotte Hart, a pew-opener, who surprised her friends by leaving nearly three thousand pounds, including six hundred pounds to the restoration fund. On the wall above is the monument of Sir Robert Chamberlayne, representing Sir Robert kneeling in prayer within a circular pavilion, the curtains of which are held up by an angel on either side. The crest of the deceased is on the pediment. He died in 1615, at the age of thirty-five, between Tripoli and Cyprus, and the epitaph tells us that the monument was erected by a friend and concludes, "Heaven covers him who has no sepulchre," from which we may assume that particulars of his interment were unknown. Opposite is the monument to the memory of Percival Smalpace and Agnes, his wife. The Latin inscription informs the reader that their deaths occurred respectively on 2 February, 1568, and 3 September, 1588, and that Michael and Thomas erected the memorial jointly to the best of parents. Underneath are nude figures of the departed lying upon a couch in their last sleep. The lines give the moral:

> Behold yourselves by us;
> Such once were we as you:
> And you in time shall be
> Even dust as we are now.

Charles Lamb once wrote of this kind of epitaph: "Every dead man must take upon himself to be lecturing me with his odious truism that 'Such as he now is I must shortly be.' Not so shortly, friend, perhaps as thou imaginest. In the meantime I am alive. I move about. I am worth twenty of thee. Know thy betters." One more epitaph may be noticed. It is in the north ambulatory, on the west side of a window recess. It commemorates John and Margaret Whiting who died respectively in 1681 and 1680. The epitaph reads:

> She first deceased, He for a little tryd
> To live without her, lik'd it not and died.

The tomb to Edward Cooke, philosopher and doctor, in another part of the church, made of "weeping marble" (it exudes moisture in wet weather), has an inscription which commences:

> Unsluice, ye briny floods. What! can ye keep
> Your eyes from tears, and see the marbles weep?

but it is far less touching than this small monument.

The font—in the south transept—dates from the early fifteenth century. William Hogarth was baptized here in 1697, his father being a corrector of the press in the neighbourhood, and two of his sisters in 1699 and 1707.

The cloisters are worth a visit. The doorway leading to them is Norman, but the doors probably fifteenth century. The cloisters were originally Norman, but rebuilt in the fifteenth century and the restoration, on recovery from the stables, has left little old work in the vaulting. The arms on the bosses are the royal arms, the arms of the diocese, the priory, the rector at the time of restoration (Sir Borrodaile Savory), and the City of London.

As we leave the church we notice the one bay of the nave still remaining with a cluster of early English columns. The porch through which we emerge is worthy of attention. It was built in 1893. In the niche above the apex of the arch, and on a bracket displaying the priory arms, upheld by two angels, stands a figure of Rahere with his left hand raised in benediction and in his right a model of the church. The design of the edifice is taken from one of the ancient seals and shows the central tower. Rahere's features are copied from the effigy on the tomb. Along the path will be seen some fragments of the bases of the early English columns of the nave. On a flat gravestone in the churchyard an interesting ceremony takes place every Good Friday morning. Twenty-one sixpences are laid thereon to be picked up by twenty-one widows of the parish. The practice goes back to the eighteenth century, and the tomb is believed to be that of the founder of this modest feast. It can be called such as now, in addition to extra sixpences, a hot-cross bun is also given!

The tower dates only from 1628, but the gateway probably from the first half of the thirteenth century. It is believed by some to mark the site of the original west front. Only in 1916, when a few tiles were removed by an air-raid, were the original Tudor timbers revealed. These belonged to a half-timbered house erected in 1595 above the gateway. The figure of St. Bartholomew was inserted by Sir Aston Webb in memory of his son, Lieut. Philip E. Webb.

On leaving the church and crossing the road we see, on our left, a tablet to the memory of the Protestant martyrs who perished in Smithfield in the reign of Queen Mary. They numbered forty-three in all, seven suffering in one day—27 June, 1558. The last martyr in England perished here in 1611. He was Bartholomew Legate, what we should call to-day a Modernist. In 1849, when excavations were being made for a new sewer, three feet below ground, there were found unhewn stones, blackened as if by fire, covered with ashes and human bones charred and partially consumed. At the same time were found some strong oak posts, also charred, and a staple and ring. There seems little doubt that these were relics of those dark days. The Church of the English Martyrs, referred to in the inscription, is in St. John Street, Clerkenwell. Its façade includes panels representing martyrdoms and projecting buttresses with statues of martyrs thereon.

Walking straight on we reach the entrance to St. Bartholomew's Hospital. It was founded by Rahere at the time of the priory, but the buildings are modern. The gateway dates from 1702, when the statue of Henry VIII was erected in honour of the fact that after depriving the citizens of the hospital, at the time of the dissolution of the priory, he returned it to them. The hospital is a parish in itself, and inside the gateway is the small octagonal church of St. Bartholomew the Less. It was practically rebuilt in 1823, but there has probably been a church upon the site for as long as St. Bartholomew the Great has existed. In the old church in 1573, Inigo Jones, the famous architect, was baptized.

Crossing the road, on the right, we reach Cock Lane. Every reader of Boswell's *Johnson* knows that this was the scene, in 1762, of the most famous ghost story of the eighteenth century; one that attracted men like Walpole, Goldsmith, and Dr. Johnson. "Scratching" Fanny's father stood in the pillory at the end of the Lane, as a small part of the penalty inflicted, but sympathetic neighbours refrained

from using missiles and in fact got up a subscription for
his benefit! There are one or two old houses left, but it
is impossible to say whether one of them was the alleged
ghost's haunts. The gilded and naked boy will be noticed.
He was erected, formerly outside the Fortunes of War
tavern, to mark one of the places where the Great Fire
ceased. This was called Pie Corner, and the fact that the
Fire commenced at Pudding Lane gave occasion to some
Puritan preachers to attribute it to the judgment of God
upon the gluttony of London's citizens. There is little
doubt, however, that this name was derived from the court
of *pied poudré*, or the dusty-footed. This was a court of
summary jurisdiction held in connection with fairs, and a
few years ago *Headway*, the organ of the League of Nations
Union, suggested that such a court would be useful for
settling disputes upon small matters in which continental
travellers became involved. St. Bartholomew's Fair was
instituted in Henry I's reign, whilst Rahere was still alive.
For several weeks it was the scene of all kinds of revels and
marketing. It gives its name to one of Ben Jonson's plays,
and Pepys in 1668, at this fair, met an extraordinary per-
forming horse, "the mare that tells money, and many other
things to admiration; and among others, come to me when
she was bid to go to him of the company that most loved
a pretty wench in a corner. And this did cost me 2d to the
horse which I had flung him before, and did give me
occasion to kiss a mighty *belle fille*." The fair was not
closed until 1855, and in 1923 there was a revival in aid of
St. Bartholomew's Hospital.

Passing Cock Lane, we arrive at St. Sepulchre's Church.
The old Watch House is of interest. To these watch houses
nocturnal offenders were conveyed until early morning.
There is a sundial on the south wall of the church. The
church was rebuilt in the fifteenth century, but there have
been many alterations since, and only the lower part of the
tower and the south porch remain intact of the original
building. The pinnacles of the tower were rebuilt in 1875.
James Howell aptly wrote: "Unreasonable people are as
hard to reconcile as the vanes of St. Sepulchre's tower which
never looked all four upon one point of the heaven." The
proximity of this church to the Old Bailey connects it

closely with crime. Here, in the days of Tyburn, the criminal was presented with a nosegay, and its most interesting relic is a bell which, under the will of one Robert Dowe, who died in 1605, was to be rung outside the condemned cell on the night preceding an execution and before an exhortation to repentance was given. The fund is now vested in the Ecclesiastical Commissioners. In Newgate Street, a little to the east of the Old Bailey, is a tablet upon the site of Newgate. The turning on the west side of the church is Snow Hill. On the wall of the police station, on the right, is a tablet relating to the Saracen's Head. A little farther on, on the premises of Messrs. Ormiston & Glass, is a bust of Dickens and two terra-cotta panels depicting the departure of Nicholas Nickleby from the Saracen's Head for Dotheboys Hall, and Nicholas flogging Squeers. It will be noticed that the inscription "Saracen's Head Hotel" has been partly scored through. The hotel closed in 1909, when Messrs. Ormiston & Glass acquired the premises, and, very laudably, decided to commemorate the Dickens association. This hotel, however, was the successor of the one where Squeers collected his pupils. This was on the site of the police station, as Dickens indicated by saying that "when you walk up the yard you will see the tower of St. Sepulchre's Church darting abruptly up into the sky." This inn was demolished when Holborn Viaduct was constructed in 1868.

In the Old Bailey is the Central Criminal Court; it rose upon the site of Newgate gaol which was demolished in 1902. There had been a prison here since the days of King John. It was destroyed in the Fire and it was about to be rebuilt when the Gordon rioters burned it down in 1780, and compelled a new structure. Among its famous prisoners have been William Penn, Lord William Russell, Anne Askew, Daniel Defoe, Jack Sheppard, Jonathan Wild, Lord George Gordon, and Lodowick Muggleton.

WALK VI: *St. James's Park—Hyde Park—Kensington Gardens—Kensington Palace—Albert Memorial—Chapel of the Ascension—South Kensington Museums—Chelsea.*

It is possible to enjoy a three-mile country walk in London. Start from Charing Cross and enter St. James's Park by way of the Admiralty Arch. St. James's Park derives its name from a leper hospital dedicated to that saint, which stood near St. James's Palace and was suppressed by Henry VIII in 1532. The year previous, Henry had acquired from the Abbot of Westminster about one hundred acres of land, part of which was enclosed with a wall and made into St. James's Park. It was not opened to the public until the reign of Charles II, and then it appears to have been limited to the aristocracy whose mansions bordered upon it. The general right of entry was won gradually, and partly by the difficulty of devising any satisfactory scheme of exclusion.

The tall column on the steps we see on our right in passing down the Mall is in memory of the Duke of York, a son of George III, who was Commander-in-Chief of the British Army from 1798–1827. He was the good old Duke of York associated with the feat of marching his men uphill and marching them down again. He was enormously in debt when he died, and consequently no statue has been more the butt of criticism. One critic asked whether the spike that protrudes from the top of the head was for the purpose of spiking his bills, whilst another suggested that he was placed sky-high in order to be out of the reach of his creditors. The column was said to be erected by the voluntary contribution of the army. In fact a day's pay was stopped of every one of its members from drummer-boy to general. On reaching the end of the Mall, we turn to our right into Green Park. It was once a part of St. James's Park, and only took a separate name when the Mall was made. We keep in a line with Piccadilly, on the right, and emerge at the open space where stands the Duke of Wellington's statue and the noble and realistic war memorial to the Royal Artillery. We cross the road, and after passing between the Achilles statue, to the memory of the Duke of Wellington, and the statue of Byron, turn left and cross Hyde Park in a diagonal direction to a charming spot called the "Dell." Then, bearing to the left, we pass the eastern end of the Serpentine, and continue alongside it and enter Kensington Gardens. Here, on our left, is Sir George Frampton's Peter Pan statue, by the votes of the readers of *John o' London's Weekly* ten years ago, the finest in

London. A little way farther on we reach the fountains with the statue of Jenner. Near here, close to the Hanover Gate, is the Dogs' Cemetery. To this spot, until the ground was filled up, Londoners used to bring their canine pets for interment, and there are a number of memorial stones. The cemetery is not easily visible and is not regularly open. The park-keepers will, however, admit anybody who requests it.

If we turn our backs to the statue of Jenner and take a path that leads off from the fountains, almost at a right angle, we shall pass, on our left, a granite obelisk in memory of Speke, the African explorer, and arrive at the Round Pond of Kensington Gardens. Beyond it is the palace. This is on the site of Nottingham House, where the Earls of Nottingham resided. William III purchased it, with a view to taking up residence at Kensington. The gravel pits there were considered healthy, and the air of Kensington beneficial for his asthma. The house was rebuilt by Wren as Kensington Palace, and is an inferior specimen of his domestic architecture in comparison with Hampton Court. The palace was not finished when Mary, William III's queen, died within its walls (1694), and here he also died in 1702. Queen Anne died at Kensington (1714), as also George II (1760). George III then bought Buckingham Palace, and it ceased to be a residence for monarchs. Queen Victoria was born in the palace and was living there when she succeeded to the throne. Her nursery is amongst the rooms shown to the public, as also her bedroom at the time of accession. The room in which she was born is, however, not open. By reason of Queen Victoria's close association with the palace there is outside a statue of her as a young woman. The state apartments are well worth a visit. There are some fine ceilings and mantelpieces, a curious clock of "The Temple of the Four Great Monarchies—Assyria, Persia, Greece, and Rome"—a dial-hand erected by William III to show the direction of the wind, a doll's house of Queen Victoria's and the Indian clubs she used. There is also an interesting series of paintings, including portraits by Kneller and views of old London. To follow the details of the various rooms the visitor should purchase the book by Mr. Ernest Law. It is a good shillingsworth.

On leaving the palace we notice the beautiful sunk garden and the orangery, erected by Queen Anne in 1705, now a pavilion for visitors to Kensington Gardens. If we now cross to the other side of the Round Pond, leave the palace directly behind us and bear to the right, we reach the Albert Memorial. This was erected in memory of the Prince Consort by means of a vote of the House of Commons of the sum of fifty thousand pounds. The architect was Sir Gilbert Scott. A detailed description will be found in the handbook sold for a shilling. The four lower groups of sculpture represent Europe (bull), Asia (elephant), Africa (camel), and America (bison). There are one hundred and sixty-nine portrait figures on the podium. A few, as being associated with London's history, may be singled out for mention. North front: Sir Charles Barry, architect of the Houses of Parliament; Sir William Chambers, architect of Somerset House; Sir Christopher Wren; Inigo Jones; Palladio (see page 24). West front: Torrigiano; (see page 63). Caius Gabriel Cibber (see page 51); Grinling Gibbons. Opposite is the Albert Hall, the largest in London, with a seating capacity for eight thousand.

If we turn again into the Park and bear right we come to the Serpentine Bridge. If we bear again to the right on crossing we reach the Birds' Sanctuary and Epstein's grotesque sculpture of Rima, in memory of W. H. Hudson. Some wearied pilgrims who have found it with difficulty have hardly thought it worth the pains. If we leave this on our left and keep alongside the motor road, we shall reach the Bayswater Road. On turning right we shall see on our left, after a few minutes' walk, the Chapel of the Ascension. This quiet haven of rest was the result of an inspiration of a benevolent woman, Mrs. Russell Gurney, wife of the then Recorder of the City of London.

Having decided upon the disused mortuary chapel of the old burial ground attached to St. George's, Hanover Square, she sent an architect, Mr. H. P. Horne, to Italy to obtain suggestions for her proposed building, and with him went Mr. Frederic Shields, a Pre-Raphaelite friend of Dante G. Rossetti. By 1894, the building of the chapel was practically completed. For twenty years Mr. Shields was occupied in painting his Biblical subjects on canvas, chiefly at his studio at Merton Park, which still exists. These were then fixed to the walls of the chapel, the paintings in the ante-chapel being frescoes. The work was finished in September, 1910, and in the following February Mr. Shields died. Thus the purpose of Mrs. Russell Gurney was accomplished, which was to provide a place of rest, prayer, and meditation, wherein body, mind, and spirit, oppressed with the hurrying roar of London life, might find repose.

Around the large graveyard at the rear is a passage between walls, formerly patrolled by police to prevent body-snatching. Herein are buried the Rev. Laurence Sterne, M.A, author of *A Sentimental Journey* and *Tristram Shandy*; and Anne Radcliffe (1823) the author of those sensational novels which Jane Austen satirized in *Northanger Abbey*. Continuing along Bayswater Road we come to a continuation of it known as Hyde Park Place. No. 6 is Tyburn Convent, and here ends the procession referred to in our calendar. Next door, at No. 5, Dickens lived for a few months in the spring of 1870; the last he saw, for the purpose of his last readings at St. James's Hall. On the railings of the Park, opposite the west side of Edgware Road, is a tablet referring to the site of Tyburn gallows up to 1783 when executions ceased there.

From Marble Arch we can take an omnibus to Victoria, and from thence travel by tube to South Kensington Station, a very few minutes walk from the Victoria and Albert Museum.

These buildings date from 1860 to 1909. The exhibits are artistic rather than antiquarian, though there is much to appeal to the latter point of view. The new buildings, entered from the Cromwell Road, were designed in the Renaissance style of architecture, with domes and towers. The central lantern has the outline of an imperial crown, and is surmounted by a figure of Fame. The niches between the first-floor windows are occupied by figures of thirty-two famous British painters, craftsmen, sculptors, and architects.

The rooms are all numbered, but it would be a waste of time and energy to attempt to traverse the museum in the numerical order. The visitor cannot do better than obtain the brief guide at threepence. If he is interested in any particular department of art, detailed guides to such collections can also be obtained. Here it is only possible to draw attention to a few items, and priority is given to those with an historical or topographical interest. In this connection the rooms devoted to architecture and sculpture will attract most attention. In Room 48 (west hall) is the front of Sir Paul Pindar's house in Bishopsgate (1600); the façade of Birch's little green shop (see page 139); also that of a house in Enfield in which Keats received part of his education. In Room 56 (left of main entrance) are fine panelled rooms from Great George Street, Westminster (1760), Clifford's Inn (1686), and Hatton Garden (1730); in Room 54 is a panelled room from the Old Palace, Bromley-by-Bow (1606). In the same room—in a case just where it joins Room 55—is a lace cravat, exquisitely carved in wood, by Grinling Gibbons; in Room 53 there is a chair and footstool belonging to Archbishop Juxon, and in the former Charles I is said to have sat during his trial at Westminster Hall. In Room 10 (lower ground floor) are some interesting busts, e.g. Johnson by Nollekens. This was considered by Chantrey the best of his busts, but Johnson did not like the manner in which the head had been loaded with hair. But according to "Rainy-day Smith," who wrote Nollekens's life, the sculptor insisted upon this as making Johnson look more like an ancient poet. The hair, says the same authority, was modelled "from the flowing locks of a sturdy Irish beggar, originally a street pavior, who, after he had sat an hour, refused to take a shilling, stating that he could have made more by begging!" Close by is Roubiliac's bust of Shakespeare. This was executed for Garrick in 1758 and bequeathed to the British Museum. There are also busts of Inigo Jones and Thomas Tyers. The latter was proprietor of Vauxhall Gardens (a street upon the site still bears his name), and author of one of the numerous biographies of Johnson. Other interesting items in this room are a terra-cotta sketch-model for the competition for Lord Mayor Beckford's statue which stands in the Guildhall, fragments of stonework from Temple Church and Westminster Hall, and a carving, in limewood, by Grinling Gibbons of the martyrdom of Stephen. On the main staircase is a bust of Charles I by Le Sueur, who also designed the statue at Charing Cross; one of Charles II by Pelle, and of Henry VII, attributed to the

Italian sculptor Torrigiano, who was responsible for most
of the splendour of his chapel at Westminster Abbey.
Another item of interest to the Londoner is Alfred Stevens's
original plaster model for Wellington's monument in St.
Paul's Cathedral. This is in the central hall. The exhibits
range from the first to the twentieth century in date, and
in size from tiny specimens of ceramics and jewellery to a
colossal figure of the Buddha and casts of Trajan's Column
at Rome. The Forster collection (including many Dickens
busts) is in Room 83. There is an Indian section in Imperial
Institute Road. The other exhibitions in this neighbourhood are the Natural History Museum (Cromwell Road) and
the Science Museum (Exhibition Road), and the Imperial
War Museum in Imperial Institute Road.

On leaving the museums we return to South Kensington and
take a train to Sloane Square Station. We go down Sloane
Street and on reaching Pimlico Road, turn right. We are then
at Chelsea Royal Military Hospital, founded by Charles II in
1682. The graveyard has some interesting graves, notably
that of William Hieseland who, a long inscription intimates,
lived to be one hundred and twelve and married after he had
attained his century, and Dr. Burney, father of the author
of *Evelina*, who was organist at the hospital chapel. The
hospital was designed by Wren, and is in two wings of red
brick. In the centre of one of the quadrangles is a statue of
Charles II in Roman toga by Grinling Gibbons. Accommodation is provided for about five hundred and fifty
inmates in addition to which there is a large number of out-
pensioners. In winter they wear dark-blue coats, in summer
the colour is scarlet. The hall contains a large painting,
showing Charles II with the hospital in the background,
a table upon which the Duke of Wellington's body lay in
state in 1852, some flags and black jacks, etc. The chapel
has a fine altar-piece, and carvings by Grinling Gibbons.
It is the chapel represented in Herkomer's fine picture "The
Last Muster."

Leaving the hospital by the south gate we have access
to Chelsea Embankment. A short walk westward brings
us to the Chelsea Physic Garden, given by Sir Hans Sloane
in 1722 to the Apothecaries' Company as "a physic garden
so that apprentices and others may better distinguish good

and useful plants from those that bear resemblance to them.
and yet are hurtful." Sloane's marble statue, by Rysbrack,
is in the centre of the gardens. It was erected in 1737.
At No. 4 Cheyne Walk lived and died Maclise, the painter,
and here in 1880, after three weeks' residence, George Eliot
died. In the Embankment Gardens is a bust by Ford
Madox Brown of Rossetti, who lived at No. 16 Cheyne Walk
for a short period with Morris and Swinburne. At No. 24
Cheyne Row, a turning leading from Cheyne Walk, lived
Thomas Carlyle from 1834 until his death in 1881, a record
for literary stability in England! This is the most interesting of London's literary shrines, as the house and its
relics are more intimately associated with the writer than is
the case with Johnson's house in Gough Square, or Dickens's
house at Doughty Street. The able and courteous custodian
is a most welcome guide. One relic may particularly
interest some visitors. It is a letter sent by Carlyle to
Mr. W. Hale White (Mark Rutherford) when the latter was
at Cheshunt College. It is in the sound-proof room. In
the course of a long letter to his wife before she had left
Scotland (see Froude's *Early Life of Carlyle*, Vol. I, ch. xviii)
Carlyle gives a detailed description of the house and neighbourhood and mentions "the sturdy old pollarded" (that is,
beheaded) "lime-trees standing there like giants in tawtie
wigs" in front of the house. When Carlyle moved in,
Leigh Hunt was living at No. 4 Great Cheyne Row, which
crosses the top of Cheyne Row, and there is now a tablet
on the house. In the Embankment Gardens at the end of
Cheyne Row is Boehm's fine statue of Carlyle, a replica of
which was, in 1929, given to Ecclefechan, his birthplace,
by his nephew and unveiled by the donor's granddaughter.
Walking westward along the Embankment we reach Chelsea
Old Church, which can vie with some of the City churches
for interest. Various parts of the church are of diverse
dates, fourteenth, fifteenth, sixteenth century. It contains
the tomb Sir Thomas More built for himself, though whether
it contains his body is matter for conjecture; also some
chained books, including a "Vinegar" Bible. Farther on,
near to Beaufort Street, is Crosby Hall. It was first erected
in 1466 in Bishopsgate by Alderman Sir John Crosby (see
page 145), and was occupied by Richard, Duke of Gloucester,

and thus appears in Shakespeare's *Richard III*. It was afterwards occupied by Sir Thomas More. In 1908—it was then used as a restaurant—it was removed and here reconstructed. This beautiful hall with its mullioned windows is now part of an international hall of residence, and a clubhouse for women graduates studying in London under the British Federation of University Women.

At No. 91 lived "Michael Fairless," and here wrote part of *The Roadmender*. A passage in the section entitled "Out of the Shadow" obviously refers to the view from her upper window. At No. 93 Cheyne Walk Mrs. Gaskell was born in 1810. She was only a few months old when she left there on the death of her mother. At No. 96 lived J. M. Whistler, and at No. 118 Turner died. He frequently climbed to the balustraded roof to see the sun rise and set. The tablet on the house was the work of Walter Crane.

WALK VII: *Through the City—Cheapside—Churches of St. Mary le Bow and St. Stephen, Walbrook—Cornhill (St. Peter's and St. Michael's Churches)—Churches of St. Helen, Bishopsgate, St. Andrew Undershaft, St. Catherine Cree, and St. Olave, Hart Street.*

We start from the Cheapside end of Aldersgate Street. On the wall of the Westminster Bank is a tablet commemorating the site of St. Michael-le-Querne Church. The dedication is a reference to the once adjacent corn market. In this church Sir Thomas Browne was baptized in 1605. He once mentioned simpling in Cheapside as a boy! At Wood Street we must make a halt. Here, as a tablet indicates, stood the Eleanor Cross, the only one within the City. It was pulled down by order of the Parliament in 1643. The row of low shops have succeeded a similar row mentioned in a document of 1401. The date 1687 may be seen upon a tablet overlooking the churchyard of St. Peter's, West Chepe, which was not rebuilt after the Fire. A figure of St. Peter bearing a massive key is on the railings. The tree is mentioned in Leigh Hunt's *The Town*, written in 1834–5, and was evidently old then. Clauses in the leases of the shops prevent its destruction. A bird at the corner of Wood Street caused reveries in the mind of Wordsworth's "Poor Susan." It

K

was not, however, in a tree, but in a cage, though the tree may have influenced her feelings. On the fanlight of the premises 128–9 are painted two crossed keys. This was the site of the Cross Keys Tavern, the destination of young Dickens when he first came to London. He wrote afterwards in *The Uncommercial Traveller*: "Through all the years that have since passed, have I ever lost the smell of the damp straw in which I was packed—like game—and forwarded carriage paid to Cross Keys, Wood Street, Cheapside." In *Great Expectations* it was made the bourne of Pip's coach ride from Rochester, and here he waited with manifest impatience for the arrival of Estella. The sign was taken from the arms of the papal see, referred to by Milton in *Lycidas*:

> Two massy keys he bore of metal twain
> (The golden opes, the iron shuts amain).

It was described in 1838 as a house of considerable size, with an arched entrance leading to the coachyard. It was demolished about sixty years ago.

Most of the streets off Cheapside recall the days when it was the great market-place of London: Bread Street, Milk Street, Ironmonger Lane, etc. Wood Street, however, was probably so named after a man who was sheriff in 1491, and a benefactor of St. Peter's Church. It is probable that wood was not purchased but obtained from the forests adjacent to the City walls. Opposite Wood Street is Friday Street. Between it and Bread Street stood the Mermaid Tavern, the praises of which have been sung by Francis Beaumont, Ben Jonson, and John Keats. It is extraordinary that so famous a tavern was never rebuilt after the Fire; it is equally extraordinary that no contemporary drawing is extant.

At the junction of Bread Street with Watling Street is a tablet commemorating the destruction, in 1876, of All Hallows' Church. A medallion of Milton reminds us of his baptism in this church in 1608. He was born in Bread Street, at a house with the sign of the Spread Eagle (the family crest). It was apparently about half-way between the tablet and Cheapside. On reaching Bow Church, a little farther along on the same side, we are again reminded of Milton by an inscription on the west wall. The flattering lines of Dryden's, prefixed to Tonson's edition of *Paradise Lost* (1688), are quoted in full. The tablet was brought from All Hallows' Church. St. Mary-le-Bow Church has a spacious Norman crypt, and probably its name is partly derived from its round-headed arches. The church, rebuilt by Wren, dates from 1680. It is almost square, and, more than any of his churches, suggestive of the Roman basilica. Interlaced "C's" on the pulpit are said to be those of Charles II and his queen. One of the west windows is in memory of Milton. The steeple is two hundred and twenty-one feet high. The bells of Bow Church are famous. In the fifteenth century they rang nightly at nine o'clock for the apprentices to cease work. It is recorded that once the ringer was late and there was inscribed upon the wall of the church the lines:

> Clerke of the Bow bell, with the yellow lockes,
> For thy late ringing thy head shall have knockes.

To which the erring clerk similarly replied:

> Children of Chepe, hold you all still,
> For you shall have Bow bell rung at your will.

It was, of course, the sound of Bow bells, heard at Highgate, which was supposed to have brought Whittington back.

At No. 76 Cheapside, on the second floor over Bird-in-Hand Court, Keats lodged in 1817. Here he wrote the famous sonnets on Chapman's *Homer* and the one commencing "Great spirits now on earth are sojourning." This court leads to Simpson's Restaurant (see page 6). Almost opposite, just past Ironmonger Lane, is Mercers' Hall. This stands upon the site of a house in which Thomas à Becket was born in 1119. As a memorial to him his sister founded here, about 1190, the hospital of St. Thomas of Acon. Its chapel was built upon the site of the house. At the dissolution the hospital was granted to the Mercers' Company, and the chapel reopened for the Mercers' services. Thomas Guy, founder of the famous hospital in Southwark, was bound apprentice to a bookseller in its porch. Hall and chapel were destroyed in the Fire but rebuilt in 1672. Strangely enough the original façade of the hall, designed by Wren, was removed in the middle of the last century and is now part of the Swanage Town Hall.

We now cross the road, walk through Bucklersbury, and turn down by the side of the Mansion House. We then reach the Church of St. Stephen, Walbrook. The River Wall Brook ran a little west of the thoroughfare which now bears its name. The first church here, dated, at latest, from Henry I's reign and it stood upon the other side of the thoroughfare and also on the other side of the stream. A tablet marks its site. In 1439 a church was built on the present site. This disappeared in the Fire. The church we now enter was built between 1672 and 1679. It is generally regarded as Wren's finest City church. Although its dimensions are not large there is a wonderful sense of spaciousness. The substitution of chairs for the old pews (in 1888), whilst much criticized, certainly enhanced this effect. It has a genuine dome, i.e. the inside diameter of it approximates to the outer, which is not the case with St. Paul's. It is generally thought that here Wren was experimenting for the cathedral. Two pictures of the interior of St. Stephen's and the interior of St. Paul's hang together near the vestry door, and enable us to make a comparison. An excellent view of the church can be obtained from the north-west corner. From here all of the Corinthian columns can be seen with ease. Many have been the tributes paid to its excellence. Lord Burlington saw in Italy a church he admired and praised. He had drawings made and was then told it was a copy of St. Stephen's, Walbrook. He could not believe it until, coming late into London, he drove there at once and viewed it by candle light. John Wesley mentions this story in his *Journal*, and adds that the Italian gentleman who thus improved his Lordship's knowledge of London added that they had not so fine a piece of architecture in Rome. Wesley says he did not wonder at the speech. Canova, an Italian sculptor (1757–1822), said he would gladly pay another visit to England to have the pleasure of beholding St. Paul's Cathedral, Somerset House, and St. Stephen's Church.

On the north wall is Benjamin West's painting of the martyrdom of St. Stephen. It was presented by Dr. Wilson, rector in 1779. On a pillar at the south-east is the oldest monument in the church. It is to John Lilbourne, citizen and grocer, who died in 1678. On the north wall is a tablet to Nathaniel Hodges, a physician who wrote a treatise on the Plague and worked indefatigably to arrest it. Some think he was the original of Defoe's Dr. Heath. On a pillar opposite Lilbourne's monument is a memorial to Robert Marriott, a rector. The Latin epitaph states that he was truly a divine man and emigrated to the Celestial Country, 14 May, 1689. St. Stephen's, Walbrook, is strangely destitute of important monuments. Sir John Vanbrugh, dramatist and architect, was buried here in 1726, but has no memorial.

On leaving the church we see on the wall of the Mansion House, near the front, a tablet mentioning the proximity of the site of the Church of St. Mary, Woolchurch Haw, Haw is the old English word for yard, and so we have "bothaw" for boatyard, and "woodhaws" for woodyards in the City. The haw of this St. Mary's Church was the place for keeping the king's beam for weighing the bales of wool, brought up the Wall Brook on barges. The church was not rebuilt after the Fire.

We cross over to the Royal Exchange and walk up Cornhill. On the site of the present Lloyd's Bank was Birch's little green shop. Birch is described in the *Dictionary of National Biography* as a dramatist and pastrycook. He became Lord Mayor in 1814, and his plays were produced at Covent Garden, Drury Lane, and Haymarket. Yet he remains in memory most as a shopkeeper. A replica of the shop front has been erected at Birch's new premises in New Broad Street. The original is in the South Kensington Museum. On this same side of the road, some fifty yards farther on—outside the National Provincial Bank —is a medallion of Thomas Gray. The author of the famous *Elegy* was born in a house on this site in 1716. He nearly died here too, as did eleven of his brothers and sisters, in infancy. His mother saved his life by opening a vein with scissors when he was in a fit. The house was destroyed in the Cornhill fire in 1748. It was rebuilt and bequeathed by Gray to a cousin.

Gray was baptized in the adjacent Church of St. Michael, and there his father was buried. It is a Wren church but much restored. The tower is an imitation of that of Magdalen College, Oxford. The porch was the work of Sir Gilbert Scott, between 1858 and 1860. Freeman's Court, Cornhill, no longer exists. It disappeared in 1848, consequent upon an extension of the Royal Exchange. It was a place where Defoe carried on business as we know from the address given in the proclamation for his arrest (1703) for publishing *The Shortest Way with the Dissenters.* From this court—it stood south of where we stand—was fired a legal shot heard round the world—Messrs. Dodson & Fogg's letter dated 1 August, 1827, to Mr. Samuel Pickwick, intimating their instructions to make him a defendant in a breach of promise action. Newman's Court (No. 73), though consisting of modern offices, seems admirably to give an idea of what Freeman's Court was like, inasmuch as Dickens says of the latter that the clerks caught "as favourable a glimpse of Heaven's light as a man might hope to do were he placed at the bottom of a reasonably deep well." Opposite St. Peter's Church was the office of Smith & Elder. Here, in 1848, came Charlotte and Anne Brontë, from the Chapter Coffee-house (see page 154), to introduce themselves to their publishers. Lucy Snowe in *Villette* greatly enjoys Cornhill.

St. Peter's Church was built by Wren in 1680-1. It has one of the only two rood-screens in City churches. The other is in St. Margaret's, Lothbury, where it was brought from All Hallows', Thames Street, when the latter was demolished. North of the chancel may be seen a monument, much begrimed, to seven children who perished in a fire in 1782—one more fatal than that of 1666. They are represented by a series of cherubs' heads—angels in bliss to the wistful faith of the father and mother. The monument was erected at the expense of a man who was their boon companion on the fateful night when they returned to find their home desolate. In the vestry is a withdrawing communion table used in the aisles after the Reformation, to emphasize variance from Romish practice, a curious old Bible dated 1290, and the keyboard of an organ upon which Mendelssohn played in 1840. More interesting still is a tablet which assigns the origin of a church upon this site to King Lucius (whose history is given in Thackeray's

Roundabout Papers) in A.D. 179. He is also traditionally associated with the early history of Westminster Abbey. It is claimed therefore that it preceded Canterbury as being the metropolitan see, and the late rector declared he was the real "Simon Pure." In this confidence the eighteen hundredth anniversary was celebrated in 1879! If we turn into Gracechurch Street and take the first court on the right we get a view of the churchyard. From here we can see St. Peter's key on the spire and again on the gate. This place has a Dickensian association. In *Our Mutual Friend* Dickens, describing Bradley Headstone's futile courtship of Lizzie Hexam, said: "The schoolmaster . . . emerged upon the Leadenhall region. : . . The court brought them to a churchyard; a paved court, with a raised bank of earth about breast high, in the middle enclosed by iron rails. Here, conveniently and healthfully elevated above the level of the living, were the dead, and the tombstones; some of the latter droopingly inclined from the perpendicular, as if they were ashamed of the lies they told." There is little doubt that this was the court Dickens had in mind. The tombstones are now raised—physically if not morally! We return to Gracechurch Street, turn left, cross the road, and proceed up Bishopsgate Street until we reach St. Helens' Court where is the Church of St. Helen, Bishopsgate. It is one of the oldest and most interesting of the City churches. There is a reference to a church here in 1140, and parts of the present building—the second arch from the east end and the lancet windows—date from the first twenty years of the thirteenth century. The two eastern chapels were built between 1352-4, and the arcade and roofs probably in the latter part of the fifteenth century. The church was one of the few to escape the Fire, and in view of the simple beauty of its Early English architecture and its wealth of monuments—whereby it has been called "The Westminster Abbey of the City"—the deliverance was a mercy.

In the latter years of King John a priory was built on the north side of the church. Of this all that remains is the nuns' church or choir which, soon after the dissolution of the priory in 1538, was thrown into one by the removal of the arcade screen. This explains the peculiar feature of the church in its having two naves.   In the northern wall of the nuns' choir we can still see the arched entrance from the nunnery into the choir; the narrower door opened on to a staircase leading to the prioress's apartment.   There is also a hagioscope or squint, so constructed as to afford a view of the high altar from the outside during the celebrations of the mass for those not able to be present in the choir. There are also, in the same wall, what were first believed to be two aumbries, but upon examination from the outside, proved to be communication grilles between the nuns' church and a sacristy external to it.   On the outside of the north wall is also a piscina belonging to this sacristy.

Commencing a perambulation of the building at the north-west corner, there is the most interesting of the stained-glass windows.   It commemorates the worthies connected with the church—beginning with Sir John Crosby. Proceeding east, the first monument of note is to Alderman John Robinson, Merchant Taylor and Merchant of the Staple of England, who died in 1599.   The inscription states that "the glasse of his life held three score and ten yeares, and then ranne out."   There is also shown on the monument Christian his wife, who "changde her mortall habitation for a heavenly" in 1592.   "They spent together," we read, "36 Yeares in holy Wedlock, and were happy besides other worldly things in nyne sonnes and seaven daughters."   These are shown, properly divided as to sex.   Next to this monument is the tomb of Alderman Hugh Pemberton, Merchant Taylor, who was sheriff in 1490 and died in 1500, and Catherine his wife.   This monument, which has an ornate canopy, was removed from the Church of St. Martin Outwich, when that church—it stood at the south-east corner of Threadneedle Street—was demolished in 1874.   A little farther east is the memorial of Francis Bancroft, an officer of the Lord Mayor's Court, who amassed a considerable fortune and, on his death in 1727, bequeathed over twenty-eight thousand pounds to the Drapers' Company, in trust for the erection and endowment of almshouses for twenty-four poor old men of that company and a school for one hundred boys.   The almshouses, once in the Mile End Road, have been pulled down; the school is at Woodford (Essex).   He caused his tomb to be erected in his lifetime, and settled part of his estate, to quote an inscription he himself drew up, "for the Beautifying and keeping the same in Repair for ever." The tomb was of a square shape, and covered with a lid supplied with hinges so as to admit of its being opened for the purpose of viewing the corpse, which was embalmed in accordance with Bancroft's instructions. A solemn inspection of the body by the officials of the Drapers' Company took place periodically up till quite recent times, but it became so unsavoury a task that it was abandoned. At the last restoration the tomb—an ugly obstruction—was removed, but its position is marked by a brass border indicating that the grave is the property of the company. Here is the memorial window to Shakespeare. It was discovered that a William Shakespeare paid rates in the parish of St. Helen's in 1598. As the name was not uncommon we cannot be certain this was the dramatist. In view, however, of the close proximity of the Shoreditch theatres, it may well have been he. The window was the gift of a Mr. Prentice of U.S.A. Farther east is an elaborate monument of black marble and alabaster to Captain Bond of the City Trained Bands, at Tilbury in 1588, and subsequently M.P. for the City. He is represented seated at a table in his tent, while outside there is an attendant holding his horse, and two sentinels. We are now in the Gresham Chapel where there is a large altar-tomb of Sienna marble with a top slab of black marble, embellished with a variety of mouldings, and bearing the arms of Sir Thomas. The monument was never completed, and the inscription is simply copied from the parish register: "Sir Thomas Gresham, knight, buried December 15th, 1579." Above the tomb hangs Sir Thomas's helmet which is said to have been carried before his corpse at the funeral. The window, which marks the eastern termination of the nuns' choir, was repaired in 1865–8, and filled with stained glass representing St. Helen and the Four Evangelists by the Gresham Committee in honour of Sir Thomas, who was the founder of Gresham College as well as the Royal Exchange. On the corner of the wall, between Gresham's window and the chancel, is a monument to Sir Andrew Judde, represented kneeling in his armour with other figures, both male and female, at a desk. The inscription runs as follows:

To Russia and Muscoua,
  To Spayne, Gynny without fable,
Traveld he by land and sea,
  Both mayre of London and Staple.

The Commonwealth he norished
  So worthelie in all his days
That ech state full well him loved
  To his perpetuall prayes.

Three wives he had: one was Mary,
  Fower suness one mayd had he by her,
Annys had none by him truly,
  By Dame Mary he had one dowghtier.

. Thus in the month of September
  A thowsand, five hundred fiftey
And eight died this worthie stapler
  Worshipynge his posterytye.

Judde was Sheriff in 1544 and Lord Mayor in 1550. He founded a free grammar school at Tonbridge, his native town, and his London property is commemorated by Judd Street, St. Pancras. One other monument in the nuns' choir calls for comment. It is in memory of Sir Julius Cæsar, a son of Queen Mary's Italian physician, who was born in 1557. He devoted himself to the law, his first appointment being Admiralty Judge under Elizabeth. He married three times, and his last wife being a niece of Bacon's, he was present at the Earl of Arundel's house at Highgate when the great philosopher died in 1626. The curious Latin inscription sets out that Cæsar, "Chancellor of the Exchequer and Master of the Rolls," etc., "by this my act and deed confirm with my full consent that, by the Divine aid, I will willingly pay the debt of Nature as soon as it may please God. In witness whereof I have fixed my hand and seal. February 27th, 1634." Here follows the signature "Jul. Cæsar," and below is another clause: "He paid this debt, being at the time of his death of the Privy Council of King Charles, also Master of the Rolls; truly pious, particularly learned, a refuge to the poor, abounding in love, most dear to his country, his children, and his friends," while lower still is written in large letters: "Irrotulatur Caelo" (It is enrolled in Heaven). This is surely the most legal monument in existence, lacking only in completeness the inscribed signature of a witness as to Cæsar's payment of Nature's debt. On the north side of the chancel is the most magnificent monument—Sir William Pickering's. He distinguished himself as soldier and scholar, under Henry VIII, Edward VI, Mary, and Elizabeth, and the memorial is as handsome a one as can be found in a city church. On the south side of the chancel is the tomb of Sir John Crosby and Agnes his wife. He was member of Parliament, Alderman and Sheriff, and Edward IV appointed him Mayor of the Staple of Calais. His mansion in Bishops-gate is now commemorated by Crosby Place—outside the church—and part of it is now in Chelsea (see page 134). He died in 1475. The figures of Sir John and his wife are very skilfully executed. Sir John wears a helmet and plate armour and his alderman's mantle. In his belt is a dagger, on his fingers are rings, and his feet rest upon a lion. Dame Agnes Crosby is in a close-fitting cap, under which her hair is pulled back, a mantle, and a close-bodied gown with tight sleeves. Her head reclines on a cushion, supported by two angels, and at her feet are two little dogs. She was Sir John's first wife and died in 1466. His second wife survived him. In the vicinity, fastened to a pillar, is a piece of carved woodwork, decorated with the arms of the City and of Sir John Lawrence, Lord Mayor, 1664, and culminating in the arms of Charles II. This was originally attached to the pew occupied by the Lord Mayor when he attended service at St. Helen's, for the accommodation of the civic sword and mace. In the Lady Chapel are the recumbent stone effigies of John Oteswich and his wife, dating from the beginning of the fifteenth century. This monument was formerly in the Church of St. Martin Outwich and was mentioned by Stow. Oteswich had much to do with the building of the church, and probably Outwich is simply a corruption of his name which was added to the dedication. On a bracket attached to the wall of this chapel is a small statue of a woman reading a book. It was formerly covered with black paint, and on its removal was found to be composed of alabaster. It is apparently of Italian workmanship, probably of a date anterior to the sixteenth century. It is impossible to say how it came to be placed here. On the floor of this chapel are fine brasses (covered with mats).

The names are unknown of two of these—a male and female figure dating from about 1400, and a lady of Henry VII's time in elaborate robes, probably a member of a religious order. The remaining five are to the memories of John Brieux and Nicholas Wotton, rectors of St. Martin Outwich, who respectively died in 1459 and 1483; Thomas Williams, gentleman, and Margaret his wife, 1495; John Leventhorpe, Keeper of the Chamber to Henry VII, 1510; and Robert Rochester, Sergeant of the Pantry to Henry VIII, 1514. To the west of the south porch is the monument of Sir John Spencer, Sheriff, 1583, Lord Mayor, 1594, commonly called, on account of his immense wealth, "Rich Spencer." He kept his mayoralty at Crosby Place, which he had purchased. At his death in 1609 the whole of his vast fortune devolved on his only daughter Elizabeth and her husband William, second Lord Compton, created in 1618 Earl of Northampton. The table tomb in the centre of the church is to William Kerwin, freemason, who died in 1594. On leaving the church we walk to the south side and see the old porch, repaired, as the inscription on the keystone of the arch intimates, in 1633. Passing round St. Helen's Place we arrive in St. Mary Axe, and turning to the left, find at its junction with Leadenhall Street, the Church of St. Andrew Undershaft. It dates from 1532, but has undergone a considerable amount of restoration since. The tower was rebuilt in 1830: the chancel reconstructed in 1875. The roof is studded with stars, and the spandrels between the arches were embellished with paintings of scriptural subjects in 1726, at the expense of a parishioner. The west window has some old stained glass, formerly in the east window. It represents five full-length portraits of English sovereigns, Edward VI, Elizabeth, James I, Charles I, and William III. The church contains one of the most famous and time-honoured of City tombs—to John Stow. By researches which cost, to use his own words, "many a weary mile's travel, many a hard-earned penny and pound, and many a cold winter night's study," he produced his great *Survey of London*. A tailor by trade Stow had previously, to quote a contemporary, "stitched up for us our English history." This referred to the *Annals of England*, now extant only in old libraries. Stow, like many another man of letters who has laboured to serve public knowledge rather than to gain private pelf, fell upon evil days and received from James I a licence to collect alms. But, as Strype said, "it is to be feared the poor man made but little progress in this collection." At any rate, what little he received he did not want for long, for he died on 5 April, 1605, of "the stone cholick." His fine black marble and alabaster monument was erected by his widow. Annually, on a date near to the anniversary of his death, a commemoration service, attended by the Lord Mayor and Corporation, is held in this church, in the course of which a new quill pen is put into the hand of the effigy. Other monuments of interest in the church are those of Sir Hugh Hammersley (Lord Mayor in 1627)—farther west than Stow's; Sir Christopher Clitherow (a Lord Mayor 1635), and Sir Thomas Offley (north side of the chancel), over which are some quaint moral lines. On the east wall of the north aisle is a brass to Nicholas Levison, mercer and sheriff (d. 1534), and his wife. He was a liberal contributor to the church. All eighteen children (ten boys and eight girls) are clearly shown. On the south wall is a brass tablet in memory of Holbein, whose portrait of Henry VIII is perhaps the best known English portrait. He is said to have resided in the parish.

A little farther along Leadenhall Street is the Church of St. Catherine Cree. It dates from 1631, when it was consecrated by Laud, then Bishop of London. It has been ascribed to Inigo Jones, but with no conclusive evidence. It is certainly, however much a mixture of Classical and Gothic, a most attractive church. The large east window is constructed in the form of St. Catherine's traditional emblem—a wheel (see page 72). We now remember it most on Guy Fawkes's Day! Strype (1720) stated that he had heard that Holbein was buried in this church. It is not rich in historical monuments, but one is of interest. This is to Sir Nicholas Throckmorton, Chief Butler of England and one of the Chamberlains of the Exchequer, from whom Throgmorton Street takes its name. He narrowly escaped death through his close relationship with Lady Jane Grey, but lived to be ambassador for Elizabeth in France and Scotland, and died in 1571 at the age of fifty-seven. Inserted in the floor, in front of the communion table, is a brass plate which marks the burial place of Sir John Gayer. It was placed there in 1888. Sir John was Sheriff in 1635, and Lord Mayor in 1646. He suffered imprisonment by Parliament as a Cavalier. He was engaged in trade with Turkey and the Levant, and once when travelling he encountered a lion which did not molest him. In order to show his thankfulness for this providential escape he bequeathed at his death the sum of two hundred pounds for the parish, partly for the establishment of an annual sermon called the "Lion Sermon," which is still preached. Mr. Allen Walker, happily, but somewhat impiously, says: "There is no doubt at all that the piety of Sir John Gayer saved his life. Sir John was doing the very best thing in dropping upon his knees and remaining motionless, though it is quite possible that he did not know that beasts of prey have been proved to be unaware of the existence of a motionless human being. This is because their sight seems to take cognizance of moving, rather than of stationary creatures, and hunters of great game have told of similar escapes." The font also was the gift of Sir John Gayer.

A little farther along Leadenhall Street we come to Fenchurch Street. We go down this thoroughfare until we reach Mark Lane, on the left-hand side of which is Hart Street with St. Olave's Church. There has been a church here since the beginning of the fourteenth century, but the present building dates from a hundred years later. The carved pulpit was brought here from St. Benet's, Gracechurch Street, and various other carvings from All Hallows', Staining, when those churches were demolished. The oak panelling around the chancel and the communion table came from St. Catherine Coleman Church when it was demolished in 1923. In the parish register is entered the baptism, in 1591, of Robert Devereux, third Earl of Essex, the commander of the Parliamentary forces at Edgehill, 1642. He was the son of Elizabeth's favourite. He was not baptized in the church but—by Lancelot Andrewes, not then a bishop —in his father's mansion in Seething Lane.

The church is now famous largely as the one attended by Samuel Pepys. Here he heard many sermons and slept under some. He had his pew in a small gallery against the south wall, specially reserved for the Navy Office which was in Seething Lane. The gallery has disappeared, and now upon its site is a monument designed by Sir Arthur Blomfield, inscribed:

SAMUEL PEPYS

born Feb. 23 1632

died May 26 1703

On a lower compartment are his family arms. The memorial was unveiled in 1884 by James Russell Lowell, then American Ambassador, in the absence of Lord Northbrook, First Lord of the Admiralty, who had appropriately been asked to honour one of its faithful servants. Pepys' brother Tom was buried here in 1664, "just under my mother's pew." His wife died in 1669, at the age of twenty-nine, and he drew up the long Latin epitaph which remains. Judging from the bust there was no need for Pepys to look abroad for female beauty. Pepys died at Clapham in 1703, in the house of his friend Hewer, and was buried here in the same vault as his wife, at nine o'clock at night. The service was read by Dr. Hickes, the nonjuring divine.

EVENING WALKS

WALK I: *The Precincts of St. Paul's Cathedral*

WE commence outside the entrance to the cathedral. The scene represented on the tympanum of the porch (supported by Wren's favourite Corinthian columns) is the conversion of St. Paul, and Damascus is shown, in low relief, on the left-hand side. The central figure over it is St. Paul with St. Peter and St. James on either side. The former is easily distinguished by the ominous figure of a cock, ruthlessly represented by the sculptor as in attendance on the apostle.

At the foot of the steps is a slab inscribed: "Here Queen Victoria returned thanks to Almighty God for the sixtieth anniversary of her accession, June 22, 1897." The statue close by is, however, one of Queen Anne. It is a replica of one erected during her reign (1712) which was removed in 1885 and re-erected by Mr. Augustus Hare (author of *Walks in London*) in Holmhurst Park near St. Leonards. Although at the time of the erection of the original statue England had been devoid of any French possession for fifty years, one of the figures represents that country, and the Red Indian, with a headgear of feathers, recalls the time when some of the American states were united to England.

There is a low railing spanning the steps of the cathedral. This is about the height of the rails with which Wren would have encircled the whole building. He was, however, overruled, and what Dean Milman (author of a fascinating history of the cathedral) called "a heavy, clumsy, misplaced fence," was erected instead. This remains for the most part, but the portion outside the west front, together with the entrance gate, was removed in 1874 and sold to Mr. J. G. Howard, a Canadian. It was shipped to Canada, but wrecked in the St. Lawrence River. Some part was recovered, and when his wife died, in memory of the fact that he had courted her in St. Paul's Churchyard, he had some of the railings placed round the tomb in which he was afterwards buried. The inscription on the grave is curious rather than elegant:

> St. Paul's Cathedral for 160 years I did enclose;
> Oh stranger, look with reverence.
> Man, man, unstable man
> It was thou who caused the severance.

Turning to the left and crossing the road we see, at the corner of St. Paul's Alley, the Chapter-house. The lower story is now in the occupation of a bank.

These narrow courts remind us that the churchyard was once enclosed by a wall. It was erected by order of Edward I "in consequence of the lurking of thieves and other bad people in the night time within the precincts of the churchyard," and a number of gates and posterns were provided and regularly opened in the morning and closed at night. These alleys represent the position of the posterns.

After passing Canon Alley a pump will be seen in the roadway with an inscription referring to St. Faith's Parish. Its church, until 1256, stood on this side of the cathedral. The cathedral was then extended towards the east, and the church being demolished, the parishioners were allowed to use its crypt for worship. After the Fire the parishes of St. Faith and St. Augustine's, Watling Street, were united and, as the parishioners had no proper burial place of their own, a portion of the crypt was reserved for their use, until 1853, when the vault was closed up.

On entering the churchyard, the most conspicuous object is the fine open-air pulpit, called St. Paul's Cross. It was erected in 1910, under the will of Mr. H. C. Richards, M.P., whose family were long associated with the cathedral, upon the site of the old cross, the foundations of which were discovered six feet below ground by the cathedral surveyor in 1879. Carlyle rightly called it *The Times* newspaper of the Middle Ages, as it was the official pulpit not only of London but of the country. The first recorded discourse was by one Fitzherbert in 1191. Amongst the more interesting events in its history are the following: In 1469 a Bull of Pope Paul II's was read cursing all shoemakers who

L

made peaks to shoes of more than two inches. The Pope
was probably interested in these piked shoes because their
length made it difficult to kneel at prayer, for which reason
in medieval pictures the devil is often so shod. In 1538
a crucifix from Boxley in Kent, which had moved eyes and
lips and seemed to bow and speak, had its secret springs
exposed after a sermon by Ridley, Bishop of Rochester, and
was thrown down amid derision. In 1603, we read, a "Mr.
Hemming of Trinity College, Cambridge, was very severe on
women." We have perhaps some explanation in another
event at the cross in 1617, when Lady Markham stood in a
white sheet and was fined a thousand pounds for marrying
one of her servants, her husband being still alive." From
about 1633 sermons ceased, and in 1643 it was taken down by
order of Parliament. It was never so elegant as the present
memorial, and at the time of destruction was a hexagonal
structure of wood with a lead roof surmounted by a
cross.

At the east end of the cathedral is a monogram WM in
the stone carving. This stands for William and Mary, the
reigning sovereigns in 1697, the date of the official opening
after the fire. On the other side of the road is a tablet on
the site of St. Paul's School, founded by Dean Colet in
1509 for one hundred and fifty-three boys (the number of
the miraculous draught of fishes), and burned in the Great
Fire. It was rebuilt, but removed to Hammersmith in
1884. Amongst its famous scholars were John Milton and
Samuel Pepys.

Proceeding round the churchyard, we arrive a little way
past the south entrance at some fragments of the pre-Fire
cloister and chapter-house. They were found by the cathedral
architect when sinking a pit in 1878, and the pilasters, of
which we see a few remains, were probably designed by
Inigo Jones. A little farther on stood, until the Great
Fire, the little Church of St. Gregory. This constrained
Fuller, the church historian, to say that St. Paul's was
indeed the mother church, as it had one child in its bosom
(St. Faith's), and another in its arms (St. Gregory's).

The south entrance to the cathedral, best seen from the
end of Godliman Street, recalls an interesting story. When
Wren had decided upon the dimensions of the dome, a

common labourer was ordered to bring a flat stone from a rubbish heap as a direction for the masons. The stone, picked up haphazard, was part of a gravestone with nothing remaining but the single word "Resurgam" (I shall rise again). This word, with the phœnix as its emblem, will be seen carved upon the tympanum. A little farther on is Dean's Court. Here is the Deanery of St. Paul's with a fine door-case adorned with carving by Grinling Gibbons. It was built for Dean Sancroft in 1670. We walk down Ludgate Hill, and get a good view of the dome of the cathedral from Creed Lane. The height to the top of the cross is three hundred and sixty-five feet, and the outward and inward diameters of the dome respectively one hundred and forty-five and one hundred and eight feet, the intervening space being occupied by a course of brickwork and a staircase leading to the lantern.

Creed Lane is opposite Ave Maria Lane, which leads to Paternoster Row. On reaching it and turning left, a wooden gateway leads to Amen Court. These names probably indicate the halting places of religious processions in the Middle Ages. Amen Court, with link extinguishers outside its eighteenth-century houses, is a delightful retreat where reside the minor canons of the cathedral. Those witty clerics Rev. R. H. Barham (author of *Ingoldsby Legends*) and Sydney Smith, resided here, the former from 1831 to 1839, and the latter from 1839 until his death in 1845. One of the latter's witticisms relate to the cathedral. Seeing his little girl stroking a tortoise he remarked "My dear, you might as well pat the dome of St. Paul's to please the dean and chapter." Strangely enough, despite his liberal notions, he opposed the proposal in 1842 to open the cathedral without fees for purposes of inspection. He thought it would become a place of assignation for all the worst characters in the metropolis, and would be a Royal Exchange for wickedness as the Royal Exchange is for commerce. Happily these gloomy predictions have not been fulfilled. The wall immediately facing us is problematical. Some think it is part of the City wall, i.e. medieval work on a Roman foundation—as Ludgate crossed Ludgate Hill south of the Church of St. Martin, the back of which can be seen on our left. It is more likely, however, that when pulled down in 1761, some part of the old wall was used for the foundation of the present one on a different site.

We walk through Amen Court, and on emerging, turn right and then left into Paternoster Row. Now famous for books, it was once celebrated for its drapers. Here in 1663, "with Mr. Creed's help," Mr. Pepys bought his wife a petticoat—"a very fine rich one." The Chapter-house Tavern on the right stands upon the site of a coffee-house associated with Goldsmith, Johnson, and Chatterton—"the marvellous boy who perished in his pride." Charlotte Brontë also stayed here when she came to London in 1848 to reveal the identity of "Currer Bell" to her publishers, and when the old building was demolished, a set of the first edition of her works was bound in wood from the beams. Here Trollope's Rev Septimus Harding stayed, when, most audaciously, he dared to beard Mr. Abraham Haphazard, Q.C., in his den, and was followed by Archdeacon Grantley. The bust over No. 13 is of Aldus Manutius, inventor of italic type, who had a printing office in Venice at the end of the fifteenth century. It was erected by Samuel Bagster, head of a famous Bible emporium in Paternoster Row, in 1820. To conclude, we turn down Panyer Alley, the last court out of Paternoster Row on the left, and see, in a glass case, a boy sitting upon a bread basket or panyer. Here in the Middle Ages was London's bread market. The inscription dated 1688:

> When ye have sought the City round
> Yet still this is the highest ground,

is not quite accurate. Cornhill is about a foot higher.

WALK II: *The Precincts of Westminster Abbey*

The fine equestrian statue of Richard I was the work of Baron Marochetti, a Piedmontese who fled to England during the revolution of 1848. The bas-reliefs represent Richard pardoning the archer whose arrow caused his death (he was in fact flayed alive as soon as the breath had left the king's body), and the onslaught of his armies upon the Saracen defenders of Jerusalem.

From this point an instructive view is presented of the

development of the abbey's architecture. The central tower, covering the sanctuary, displays the stately simplicity of the Early English style; then we see the later and more ornate crossing of the nave, terminating in one direction in the octagonal Chapter-house, and in another in the more beautiful Henry VII's Chapel.

On the left of the Chapter-house is the square structure known as the Jewel Tower, which Dean Stanley thought might have been the monastic prison. It was sold to the Crown in Edward III's reign, and for a time, like the Chapter-house, used as a depository for records and Acts of Parliament. The Victoria Tower opposite, the royal entrance to the Houses of Parliament, attains a higher altitude than any London building, save St. Paul's, viz. three hundred and thirty-six feet. The wall is divided into five divisions. The three central niches have statues: Queen Victoria in the centre with her parents, the Duke and Duchess of Kent, on either side. The shorter pedestals bear figures of Justice and Mercy.

In the adjoining gardens, close to the tower, is Rodin's statue of the Burghers of Calais, commemorating the mercy of the consort of Edward III. When Calais surrendered in 1347 he was minded to destroy the populace. On Queen Philippa's intercession, however, he relented on condition that a deputation should come from the town, one member bearing the key and all having halters about their necks. Happily the king did not accept the vicarious sacrifice thus offered, though the town's valuables were confiscated. This is a copy of a statue in Richelieu Square, Calais. The figures are unhappily dwarfed by the large stage. In the centre of the gardens is a statue of Mrs. Pankhurst, who so bravely and devotedly bore the banner of women's freedom in pre-war days. There is no statue in London with a more naturalistic figure than this. It was unveiled by the Right Hon. Stanley Baldwin in 1930.

On crossing the road and turning right we reach Dean Stanley Street. This leads to Smith Square with the Church of St. John, Westminster, in the centre. It was built in 1728, and has a tower at each corner. Dickens, who gave Jenny Wren (*Our Mutual Friend*) a residence here, describes it as "generally resembling some petrified monster, frightful and gigantic on its back with its legs in the air." The church was one of the fifty proposed to be built with the duty on coal under an Act of Queen Anne's. There is a story that this lady, of whom Pope wrote:

> . . . three realms obey
> Dost sometimes counsel take
> —and sometimes tay,

feeling little disposed for the first, kicked over her foot-stool, and said to the architect: "Build me a church like that," the legs representing the towers. This is probably part of London's ever-increasing apocrypha. The land was marshy, and the towers were erected so as equally to dis-tribute the weight of the building. "In Smith Square," wrote Dickens, "there is a deadly kind of repose, more as though it had taken laudanum than fallen into a natural rest." At No. 5 resided, for many years, the eminent journ-alist and spiritualist, W. T. Stead. He left this house in 1912 on his last ill-fated voyage on the *Titanic*.

Church Street leads to Great College Street, a quiet turning which has on one side the wall of the abbey garden, built by Abbot Litlington in 1363, and on the other a row of eighteenth-century houses. In one of these, as a boy, lived Edward Gibbon, the historian, with an aunt who kept a boarding-house for Westminster schoolboys. Here also, in 1820, Keats took lodgings, hoping that distance from Hampstead would take enchantment from Fanny Brawne. Through the narrow archway (to our left on reaching Great College Street) we reach Dean's Yard. Another archway (thirteenth century) on our right, takes us to Westminster School. There was a grammar school as well as the custom-ary choir school at Westminster before the Reformation, and Queen Elizabeth's remodelled Henry VIII's scheme for what was called—after the abbey—St. Peter's College. The premises include Ashburnham House, the back of which (with a gate dated 1883) is on the left as one faces the stone gateway of the school. This house was built for Jack Ashburnham, a trusted friend of Charles I, who was with him during his escape from Hampton Court and the Isle of Wight. It was purchased by the Crown in 1730 to house, *inter alia*, the famous Cottonian library which narrowly escaped destruction when the house was partly burned in

1731. Among the famous scholars of Westminster School
have been John Dryden, William Cowper, Charles Wesley,
and Warren Hastings. The school is famous for the scramble
for the largest piece of pancake—of one thrown over the
beam in the schoolroom upon Shrove Tuesday (the reward
being one guinea)—and for the performance of Latin plays at
Christmas. The gateway bears the arms of Queen Elizabeth,
in honour of her foundation, but was erected in the eighteenth
century. The names inscribed are those of head boys. The
masters' houses are on the right. The one with a double
staircase probably dates from the first half of the eighteenth
century. These staircases were so convenient for sedan
chairs.

If we return to Dean's Yard and turn right we can
emerge, through an archway, opposite the western towers of
the abbey. An inscription reveals the date of erection—
1735. Designed by Wren and completed after his death in
1723 by the Hawksmoor brothers, they certainly improved
the western aspect of the abbey which had previously had
a most stunted appearance. A path across St. Margaret's
Churchyard brings us to the north door of the abbey. The
design of Sir Gilbert Scott and J. L. Pearson, it was inspired
by the Gothic revival of the mid-Victorian era. Its medieval
predecessor was called "Solomon's Porch," and had "statues
of twelve apostles at full length with a vast number of other
saints and martyrs." There was evidently some idea of
reproducing the ancient splendour. Below the twelve
apostles here presented are—on the east—figures representing the Arts, History, and Philosophy, led by the Church,
and—on the right—War, Justice, and Wisdom, headed by the
three royal builders, Edward the Confessor, Henry III, and
Richard II. Above the side door on the east are statues of
four abbots, including Islip, who built a chapel, and the
corbels above these, commencing on the wall facing east,
support statues of twelve abbey celebrities, Matthew of
Westminster, William Caxton, Walsinus, traditionally the
first abbot, Edwin, first abbot of Edward the Confessor's
foundation, Richard II and Anne of Bohemia, Henry V and
Catherine of Valois, Abbots Ware and Litlington, and Deans
Goodman and Williams. On the upper tier are Bede and
Theodore (Latin and Greek learning), St. Alban and St. Aidan

(primitive church), St. Augustine and Paulinus (Roman Christianity), St. Benedict and St. Dunstan (monastic institutions), St. Boniface and St. Edmund (missions and martyrdom), and Roger Bacon and Robert Grosseteste (medieval learning and science). The four highest figures are the Archangels Michael, Gabriel, Raphael, and Uriel. Over the four side doorways are Lawrence (holding the Papal Bull which granted the mitre to the Westminster Abbots), Langham (the only abbot who became a cardinal and Archbishop of Canterbury), Esteney and Islip (both builders in the abbey).

On the left of the path leading from the north door, and opposite the west end of St. Margaret's Church, is a marble slab. For long regarded as an ordinary gravestone, it is now known, from the inscription T II, to have been a Roman boundary mark. This path takes us to Parliament Square and to a collection of uninspiring statues of eminent Victorians. A few remarks about these will suffice. The statue of the Earl of Beaconsfield is decorated every 19 April with primroses on the assumption—it is nothing more—that this was Dizzy's favourite flower. The Earl of Derby's monument is interesting because the plinth gives an admirable representation of the interior of St. Stephen's Chapel of the Palace of Westminster, the meeting-place of the House of Commons prior to 1834. Readers of Thomas Hardy's *Dynasts* will find a description in Act I, Sc. III: "A long chamber with a gallery on each side supported by thin columns having gilt Ionic capitals. Three round-headed windows are at the farther end, above the Speaker's chair, which is backed by a huge pedimented structure . . . surmounted by the lion and the unicorn. The windows are uncurtained. . . . Wax candles wave and gutter in a brass chandelier which hangs from the middle of the ceiling, and in branches projecting from the galleries." Lord Palmerston's statue, Mr. Desmond MacCarthy thought, "ought to be an object of pilgrimage to all tailors in England. The frock-coat fits like a glove, and though the trousers do not break over the instep enough to suit modern taste, the hang of them is magnificent." The beautiful Gothic fountain in the north-west of New Palace Yard was erected in 1865 by Charles Buxton, M.P., in honour of the efforts of his father, Sir Thomas Fowler Buxton, to secure the emancipation of the colonial slaves.

The eight bronze figures represent some historic rulers, including Caractacus (Britons), Constantine (Romans), Cnut (Danes), Alfred (Saxons), William the Conqueror (Normans), and Queen Victoria.

Passing this fountain and walking towards the abbey, we reach the Middlesex Guildhall, a delightful specimen of architecture. The friezes represent—on the left, the signing of Magna Charta at Runnymede; on the right, Lady Jane Grey accepting the crown from the Duke of Northumberland. The keystone of the arch has a representation of the Great Hall of Hampton Court Palace. On the site of the Guildhall was formerly a strong square Norman tower containing two cruciform chapels, and this comprised the abbey sanctuary, now commemorated in the names of two thoroughfares, Broad and Little Sanctuary. Here Edward V was born— his mother was then the guest of the abbot—in 1470. Here also his younger brother the Duke of York took refuge in 1483. Eventually, his mother consented to resign him to the charge of his uncle, Richard, Duke of Gloucester, and, according to Sir Thomas More's *Life of Richard III*, she said: "'Farewell, my own sweet son, God send you good keeping. Let me kiss you once ere you go, for God knoweth when we shall kiss together again.' And therewith she kissed him and blessed him, and turned her back, and went her way, leaving the child weeping as fast." The system of sanctuary—only latterly permissible for debtors—was finally abolished in 1623. Dean Goodman contended for the continuance of the privilege on the ground that it caused the houses within the district to let well!

We now reach Tothill Street, a name derived from toot-hill—one suitable for a stronghold. In Wyclif's Bible, where the authorized version has, in the second book of Samuel: "David took the stronghold of Zion," we read, "David took the totehill of Zion." Tothill Fields have a long history. It was a place for ordeal by battle, of execution, and of burial. In the latter connection there appears in the accounts of the Church of St. John the Evangelist, Westminster, one for "67 loads of soil laid on the graves in Tothill Fields wherein 1200 Scotch prisoners taken at the fight at Worcester were buried."

Across the end of the modern Victoria Street and where

is now the Crimean monument, stood the Gatehouse Prison, built by Edward III. Here Sir Walter Raleigh spent the night before his execution (1618); here—later in the century —Sir Richard Lovelace wrote his famous lines:

> Stone walls do not a prison make,
> Nor iron bars a cage.

A prisoner in the Gatehouse, in 1682 was Sir Jeffery Hudson, the dwarf who was eighteen or twenty inches high when served up in a cold pie to Charles I and Henrietta Maria, who retained him as a page. He was served up in fiction by Sir Walter Scott in *Peveril of the Peak*. In 1690 Samuel Pepys was a prisoner on the charge of divulging to the French secrets about the navy. Its condition subsequently called down the wrath of Dr. Johnson, and it was pulled down in 1776.

At a point between Tothill Street and Victoria Street, about where is now a hall bearing his name, Caxton set up the first English printing-press. It was in one of two chapels dedicated to St. Dunstan and St. Anne, to whom an amusing reference will be found in Addison's *Spectator*. For this reason the business meeting of journeymen printers is still called a chapel. The title pages of Caxton's first books bear the imprint "In the Abbey of Westminster." Dean Stanley relates that in a hole of the triforium of the abbey were found the corpses of a colony of rats. Successive generations had fed upon paper, beginning with medieval copy-books, going on to Caxton's publications, and concluding with the literature of Queen Anne, when apparently the hole was closed up.

WALK III: *Fleet Street and the Strand*

We start from Ludgate Circus. In Bride Lane, first turning on left, is the mouth of a pump, on the site of the old St. Bride's Well. This was exhausted, according to Hone's *Every Day Book* (1831), on the occasion of George IV's coronation, a number of men from a hotel in Bridge Street, Blackfriars, being engaged in filling thousands of bottles with the "sanctified fluid"—presumably for tea.

St. Bride's Church (the dedication is a corruption of an

Irish St. Bridget), was rebuilt by Wren, after the Great Fire, in 1680. It is disfigured by galleries, but its interior is nevertheless singularly light and attractive. The nave is formed by an arcade of double columns, and its roof is arched, the arches being decorated with handsomely wrought bands. In the church (under pews 12 and 13) is the tombstone of Samuel Richardson, author of *Pamela, Clarissa Harlowe,* etc., who died in 1761 at his house at Parson's Green and was buried here beside his first wife. By reason of the proximity to Fleet Street it has become peculiarly associated with the Press and contains memorials to Sir George Newnes (d. 1910), Sir Arthur Pearson (d. 1921), Sir Edward Robbins, manager of the Press Association (d. 1922).

There is mention of a church on the site in 1122, and the pre-Fire structure had the more interesting associations. In the interior may be seen one pre-Fire relic, a font dated 1615, in the south aisle. An exterior one will be found on the right of the path on leaving the church. It is a vault dated 1657, bearing the name of Holden. Of a member of this family Pepys bought a beaver, costing thirty-five shillings, in 1661. The famous diarist was baptized in the church in 1632. The register is still preserved. He came here for the funeral of his brother, when the grave maker had difficulty in finding a grave, but according to the *Diary* (18 March, 1664), "'For 6d.' (as his own words were), 'I will jostle them together but I will make room for him.'" Other literary men associated with St. Bride's Church were Sir J. Denham (a poet praised by Pope and Johnson), who was interred in the church, and Richard Lovelace who, dying in Gunpowder Alley, Shoe Lane, in extreme poverty, was buried here in 1658. Two quotations from his poems are known to all lovers of literature:

> I could not love thee, dear, so much,
> Loved I not honour more.

and the lines quoted on page 160.

On a building opposite Bride Lane is a tablet referring to the hostelry there of the Abbot and Convent of Cirencester. This is referred to in a will of 1420. At the dissolution of the monasteries it passed into the hands of Henry VIII. The popinjay was the abbot's badge. No. 85 Fleet Street, is called "Byron House," and over the entrance is a beautiful medallion inscribed with Shelley's phrase, "A pilgrim of eternity." In the corridor are a number of tablets giving quotations and curious, if somewhat irrelevant, statistics about the poet, e.g. the number of entries concerning him in the British Museum catalogue, and the small number of false rhymes detected in his works. The enthusiast responsible for all this mural panegyric was Sir J. Tollemache Sinclair. The site is not associated with Byron. Murray, his publisher, had premises at No. 32, some yards farther on. The next turning is Salisbury Court, and on the left, over the White Swan Tavern, is a tablet commemorating the birthplace of Samuel Pepys. Crossing Salisbury Square, we see a tablet at the corner of Dorset Street recording the site of a seventeenth-century theatre. It was pulled down by a company of soldiers under Puritan orders in 1649 but rebuilt in 1660. It was one Pepys frequently attended. Sometimes he calls it the Whitefriars, sometimes Salisbury Court. It was burned down by the fire of 1666, and not rebuilt. A new playhouse, called the Dorset Gardens Theatre, was, however, erected on an adjacent site with a frontage to the Thames.

The head of Samuel Richardson forms the keystone of the arch of Warwick House (Dorset Street), on our left. He was a master printer as well as a novelist, and had his works in Salisbury Square for about thirty-five years. It is said he hid half-crowns among the type to encourage punctuality. From Salisbury Square a fine view of the spire of St. Bride's Church can be obtained. Its telescopic design, with a slight variation at each stage, has been much admired. It is Wren's highest church spire, being two hundred and twenty-six feet high. Prior to being struck by lightning in 1764 it was eight feet higher.

Returning to Fleet Street, *en route* we may notice the jolly little head which forms the keystone of the door of the Chapter-house (13 Salisbury Square). We see on the other side of Fleet Street the Cheshire Cheese. At the side of the entrance (in Wine Office Court) is a list of the sovereigns during whose reign the tavern has been open, and the much worn door-step is protected by a grille. It was rebuilt after the Fire, and is the only old Fleet Street tavern that remains.

There is evidence that Dr. Johnson came here, though not in Boswell, and in the corner where he is said to have sat is a copy of Reynolds's famous portrait over a brass plate. Upstairs are exhibited some interesting relics, including a copy of the famous *Dictionary*, and a chair which is said to have been Johnson's. It is admitted that this did not originally belong to the Cheshire Cheese. It has been associated by some with the Mitre and by others with the Essex Head—both Johnsonian taverns, which have disappeared. Now the Johnson Club holds its dinners at the house in Gough Square. Previously they were held here. Photographs of some of these dinners are in Cheshire Court. For particulars of the famous pudding see page 5. Postcards and a book about the tavern can be purchased.

Crossing the road again we reach Whitefriars Street. It takes its name from the Carmelite Monastery founded here in 1241. It covered practically the whole district at this point from Fleet Street to the Thames. It had a large church, and in *Richard III* the Duke of Gloucester orders the body of Henry VI to be taken there. It was destroyed in 1545, and the hall of the priory eventually became the Whitefriars Theatre. This neighbourhood afterwards became the Alsatia, described by Shadwell in his play *The Squire of Alsatia*, by Scott in *The Fortunes of Nigel*, and by Macaulay in the first volume of his *History*. In Britton's Court, off Whitefriars Street, under the premises of Messrs. E. T. Gething & Co., is an undercroft of the old priory, discovered in 1895, prior to which it had been in use as a coal cellar.

Bolt-in-Tun Court (No. 65) looks brand new, but it has hidden history. A tavern of this name was mentioned in 1443 in a grant to the Carmelite Friars. When Dickens was a young man it was a coach office, and Moses Pickwick's coach ran from here to Bath. Sam Weller notices the name on a coach there and is indignant at what seems to him an unwarrantable liberty. Dickens probably first saw the name in Fleet Street. The coach office was pulled down about three years ago.

Opposite is Bolt Court. In a house at the far corner Dr. Johnson died in 1784. It was destroyed by fire in 1819, but the knocker is preserved at Barclay & Perkins's Brewery in Southwark. No. 3 is an old house and it was occupied by a Quaker physician, Dr. Lettsom, who was acquainted with Johnson. His initial was "J" which, in signing prescriptions, he wrote in the old-fashioned form suggesting an "I," which made a waggish rhymer write:

> If any folks applies to I,
>   I blisters, bleeds, and sweats 'em.
> If after that they choose to die,
>   Well, then, I Lettsom.

In Johnson's Court (No. 166), on the other side of Fleet Street, Dr. Johnson lived from 1765 to 1776. It had that name—derived from a member of the Common Council in the early part of the seventeenth century—when he moved there. In a letter he refers to "Johnson of that ilk." Here he published the *Journey to the Western Isles of Scotland*, his edition of Shakespeare, a new edition of the *Dictionary*, and a prologue to Goldsmith's *Good-natured Man*. The house was demolished in 1899, and a tablet now marks the site.

Crossing the road once more, we reach Serjeant's Inn. Most of the houses here were designed by the brothers Adam, the builders of the Adelphi. A number of their houses remain, together with a pump. At No. 16, Delane, editor of *The Times* for thirty-six years, from 1841–1877, lived in "an old house which had a certain quiet dignity of its own from its good-panelled woodwork and well-designed staircases." He, of course, worked at night, and he is said to have seen more sunrises than any other Londoner.

Mitre Court (No. 37) reminds us of the Mitre Tavern, a favourite resort of Dr. Johnson's. It was there he made his most famous joke about the Scotch, and assayed to convert some pretty Methodists by the unapostolic method of dandling them upon his knee (see page 92). This Mitre was in Fleet Street on the site now marked by a tablet. The tavern in Mitre Court took the name on its demolition in 1829. At the top of a house in Mitre Court lived Charles Lamb, from 1800 to 1809. He said it was "pure airy," and recommended flannel to his visitors. He said by perching himself upon his haunches he could just see the "white sails glide by the bottom of King's Bench Walk." This would be more difficult now.

A little farther on, on the other side of Fleet Street, is St. Dunstan's-in-the-West Church. It dates only from 1831, but there was a church here before 1237. Outside the old church was a famous clock attached to which were two figures of giants which struck the hours. There are many literary references to them. Cowper wrote:

> When labour and when dullness, club in hand,
> Like the two figures at St. Dunstan's stand.

Byron wrote in a letter: "I would have raised all Fleet Street and borrowed the giant's staff from St. Dunstan's Church to immolate the betrayer of trust." Scott in *The Fortunes of Nigel* referred to "Adam and Eve plying their ding-dong," but this was an anachronism as they were not erected until 1671, half a century later than the period of which he was writing. Lamb shed tears at their disappearance in 1830, but they reared their heads again—at St. Dunstan's Lodge, the Marquess of Hertford's villa in Regent's Park—where they still stand. Over the entrance to the school, on the east side of the church, is a statue of Queen Elizabeth, which was on the west side of old Ludgate where it was erected in 1580. Evelyn noted in his *Diary* that it was little disfigured by the Great Fire. After the demolition of the gate in 1760 it was presented to the church as recorded on the tablet. Izaak Walton was a church-warden here, as an inscription beside the porch records. The corbel heads are William Tyndale, a translator of the New Testament, who was martyred at Hamburg in 1536, and Dr. Donne, one time its vicar. He is referred to elsewhere in this book. The bust of Lord Northcliffe was unveiled by Lord Riddell in 1930. There is an interesting monument in the church to Hobson Judkin, Esq., described as "the honest lawyer." A pendant to this is the epitaph recorded by Pennant, which was on the grave of a legal gentleman named Strange: "Here lies an honest lawyer—that is strange." Dickens lovers will remember that "The Chimes" are those of St. Dunstan's Church, and that Trotty Veck had his stand here.

Clifford's Inn (No. 190) derives its name from Robert de Clifford, who owned property here in 1310 and let it to law students. It was one of the Inns of Court until the seventeenth century, and Sir Edward Coke and John Selden were members. The hall and all but one house survived the Fire. In the former Sir Matthew Hale presided over a bench of judges which adjudicated upon claims arising out of it (their portraits are in the Guildhall Art Gallery). The hall was rebuilt in 1766, but the stone archway leading to it probably dates from the fourteenth century. Here (at No. 13, from 1792 to 1824, at No. 14 from then until his death in 1841) Lamb's friend, George Dyer, lived. Later in life he became the fourth husband of his laundress, who lived opposite. She seems to have had some of the supermanly cunning of Bernard Shaw's Anne Whitfield. She said, "She couldn't abear to see the pure gentleman so neglected," and a match was arranged. Here he was visited by Scott, Southey, Coleridge, and Lamb. The latter's last letter was to Mrs. Dyer. It was about a book he thought he had left at Clifford's Inn, and concluded, "If it is lost I shall never like tripe again." Samuel Butler occupied upper rooms in No. 15 (dating from 1663), from 1864–1902. His painting-room overlooked Fetter Lane, where he bought his meat, and his sitting-room faced the garden in the courtyard of which is a pump from which he drew his water. Butler died at a nursing home at St. John's Wood. He had once wanted his ashes to be sprinkled in Clifford's Inn, but his friend and clerk, Cathie, persuaded him that this might lead to trouble, so they were laid in an unknown spot at Woking.

No. 17 Fleet Street—on the other side—is known as Prince Henry's room. He was the eldest son of James I, and his death in 1612 was greatly lamented. The building dates from then, but cannot be connected with him and the Prince of Wales feathers with the monogram "P.H." on the original ceiling (carefully repaired at the School of Art at South Kensington), may only refer to the Prince's Arms Tavern, which were on the site at about the date of his death. In 1795 it was occupied by Mrs. Salmon's waxworks. Between 1900 and 1906 it was carefully restored by the London County Council, who acquired the property, and the carved panels on the façade were again revealed after being long hidden.

Outside Attenborough's at the corner of Chancery Lane

(first floor level) is a statuette of Kaled. He was the page who attended Byron's Count Lara on the battlefield and mourned his death. For what reason it was placed there is difficult to say. The lines inscribed are:

> They were not common links that formed the chain
> That bound to Lara, Kaled's heart and brain.

One writer, however, hazarded a guess that the lines were intended as a touching reminder of a natural attachment between Mr. Attenborough and his clients.

The Devil Tavern (there is a plate on No. 2) is mentioned in Boswell's *Johnson*. Here in 1751 the Great Charm of Literature entertained Mrs. Charlotte Lennox at supper to celebrate the publication of her first novel, and we are told by Sir John Hawkins that "at 5 a.m. his face shone with meridian splendour though his drink had been only lemonade."

The "Griffin" (marking the boundary between the City and Westminster) stands upon the site of Wren's Temple Bar, which was removed in 1878 to Theobald's Park, near Cheshunt. It was threatened in 1787, but one vote in the Common Council kept it standing for ninety-one years longer. In 1921 attempts were made to restore it to London and re-erect it on a more convenient site. This, however, was resisted on the ground that Sir Henry Meux, who acquired it, had been put to considerable expense in removal and that it would be a great loss to the neighbourhood. So long as execution by axe was prevalent, Temple Bar was adorned with heads of which sometimes you could get a close view by paying a halfpenny for the hire of a telescope. Readers of Boswell will remember Goldsmith remarking to Johnson upon these heads: "Perhaps, sir, our names may mingle with these," after the latter had said the same thing a little earlier in Poets' Corner in Westminster Abbey. The bas-reliefs on the Griffin represent (on the south) Queen Victoria going to Guildhall on the first Lord Mayor's Day of her reign—9 November, 1837, (on the north) the procession to St. Paul's to return thanks for the recovery of the Prince of Wales from typhoid, in 1872. Child's Bank, which once used Temple Bar as a store-room (Tellson's of *A Tale of Two Cities*), is the oldest private bank in England. Amongst its clients have been Oliver Cromwell, Charles II, Samuel

M

Pepys, William III, John Dryden. The building is a modern one, but the marigolds in the decoration have an historical significance. The goldsmith who came here in 1560, and afterwards added banking to his business, acquired the site of the Marigold Tavern and adopted the same sign.

The Law Courts were erected in 1868 and the architect was George E. Street, who adopted a pleasing Gothic style. The main hall, of magnificent proportions, is worth a visit. Readers of the *Forsyte Saga* will remember that Val remarked: "By Jove, this 'd make four or five jolly good racket courts." Devereux Court, on the other side of the road, includes a building which was once the Grecian Coffee-tavern, the resort of Addison (who mentions it in the *Spectator*), Sir Isaac Newton, Swift, and Goldsmith. High up in the wall is a bust of Robert Devereux, from whom the court takes its name, with the date 1676. He was the Earl of Essex who led the Parliamentary forces at Edgehill. Twining's Tea Shop, which backs upon the court, has been there since 1710. Devereux Court leads into Essex Street. The "Essex Head" dates from 1890, but supplanted an older tavern, where in 1783—a year before his death—Dr. Johnson made his last stand for clubbability. Reynolds called it a low ale-house and the club failed. The stone archway at the bottom of Essex Street is the water gate of Essex House. Here Queen Elizabeth's favourite retreated after his unsuccessful rebellion, and from here he departed for the Tower of London and death. To bring him to submission a piece of artillery was placed upon the roof of St. Clement Danes' Church—the predecessor of the present building, which was erected in 1681 with assistance from Wren. The church is now principally associated with oranges and lemons and Dr. Johnson. With regard to the first it is the "St. Clemens" referred to in the old nursery rhyme, and thanks to the keen and indefatigable rector, annually on the 31st March a children's service is held, followed by a distribution of oranges and lemons by Danish children. The church is always used for Danish celebrations, and the Danebrog—their national flag—hangs in the chancel. With regard to Johnson, he regularly attended service here, sometimes with Boswell, as the latter records in the greatest of English biographies. His pew in the north gallery is marked by a brass plate and behind it is a stained-glass window in which he is depicted in company with Goldsmith, Burke, Garrick, and Mrs. Carter, whose translation of Epictetus is in Everyman's Library. A service is annually held on the anniversary of Johnson's death. The statue of Johnson at the east end of the church was by Percy Fitzgerald, and is a poor piece of work.

Strand Lane (No. 162A) leads to the "Roman" Bath now in the possession of this church. Some doubt has been cast upon the alleged age of this relic, and no literary reference has been found to it before the eighteenth century. Dickens was early interested in it—he probably found it during his employment in the blacking factory at Charing Cross—and David Copperfield used it.

Arundel Street, with Surrey, Howard, and Norfolk Streets, was built in 1678, upon the site of the mansion of the Earls of Arundel. Here, in 1635, died Old Parr of old age. He was alleged to be a hundred and fifty-two, and a post-mortem examination was conducted by Harvey, the discoverer of the circulation of the blood, presumably to discover why he had not died before. He was a Shropshire lad, and the climate of London, whence he was brought to satisfy the curiosity of Charles I, did not suit him.

The next island church is St. Mary-le-Strand. It has little history. Charles Dickens's father was married here in 1809. It is the successor to one pulled down by Lord Protector Somerset in 1549 to use in the construction of Somerset House. Queen Elizabeth lived at Somerset House during the reign of her half-sister, Mary, and in 1634 Charles I assigned it to his queen, Henrietta Maria. Here, Inigo Jones died in 1652, and in 1658 Cromwell lay in state. At the Restoration Henrietta Maria resumed occupation, and some of the tombs of her attendants are in the vaults of the present building. The latter was erected between 1776–86, and used for the Royal Academy Exhibition and for the meetings of the Royal Society until 1856. The doorway to the left, under the vestibule, was the entrance to their apartments. The three keystone marks within the archway represent the Rivers Dee, Tyne, and Severn. The first Government department to occupy Somerset House was the Admiralty, and then Nelson was a frequent visitor. Readers of Trollope will recall (in *The Three Clerks*) Charlie Tudor's labours at the office of Internal Navigation here. George Crabbe wrote some of his best poetry in the quiet of this quadrangle. The departments now occupying it are the Inland Revenue, Probate Registry, and Registrar-General.

The terrace of Somerset House when (before the construction of the embankment) the river lapped its walls was a quiet rendezvous, and Herbert Spencer, in his *Autobiography*, records his intercourse here with George Eliot, coupled in matrimony in the imagination of their friends.

Crossing Wellington Street one reaches Savoy Hill. On the right is the Chapel of the Old Palace. It was built by Simon de Montfort, the best known of the Earls of Leicester in the middle of the thirteenth century. A little later, however, it came into the hands of Henry III, who presented it to his uncle, Peter of Savoy. The latter soon parted with it, but his name survives. A hundred years later, John of Gaunt, "time-honoured Lancaster," was living here in great state, and amongst his guests were Chaucer, Wycliffe, and Froissart. Wat Tyler's rebels attacked the palace, and the costly plate and rich furniture were flung into the Thames. It then lay in ruins until Henry VII founded here a hospital for poor people. It was untouched by Henry VIII, no doubt in deference to his father, but Elizabeth laid hands upon it and gave favourites of the Crown the right of free quarters. Here, in 1662, the conference took place on the Prayer Book. Some of the scandalous marriages referred to elsewhere took place here in the eighteenth century. Many of the old buildings remained up to the beginning of the nineteenth century, but much was then demolished to make way for the approaches to Waterloo Bridge. The chapel, which dates from about 1504, suffered from fire in 1864, but was restored and has an ornate interior. There is a curious old painting near the door which may have been part of a triptych, and a brass dated 1522 to Gavin Douglas, a Scotch poet. It ceased to be a royal chapel in 1925. There is also a stained-glass window to D'Oyly Carte, the manager of the Savoy Threatre at the time when the Gilbert and Sullivan Operas were at the height of their popularity. It was unveiled by Sir Henry Irving in 1902.

West of the northern arm of Wellington Street and on the

site of the Exeter Hall, so well known to Victorians, was once Exeter House, built by the famous Lord Burleigh. A little farther west, on the other side, were Salisbury House, built by his son, and next, Worcester House where Lord Clarendon lived after the Restoration, at the time when his daughter Anne married the Duke of York, afterwards James II. Higher up at the corner of Agar Street are some anatomical statues. They are the work of Epstein, erected about twenty-five years ago, before he had attained his present notoriety, and designed for the British Medical Institution which has now gone elsewhere.

The Golden Cross which was, until recently, on the north side of the Strand was not the building with Dickensian associations. The front of the hotel, from which Mr. Pickwick started his travels and where David Copperfield stayed, was not far from where is now the Nelson column. Dickens mentions that you had a close view of the Charles I statue from its staircase. That hotel was destroyed when the modern Trafalgar Square came into being, about 1840.

Northumberland Avenue, opposite Charing Cross Post Office, marks the site of Northumberland House, the last of the Strand palaces to disappear. The house originally consisted of three sides of a quadrangle, the fourth side being open with gardens stretching to the river. It was destroyed when the site was compulsorily sold in 1874. The lion with the horizontally poised tail (the badge of the Dukes of Northumberland) which was the top stone of the palace is now over Lion House, Isleworth, where the dukes have their residence, and it can be seen from the river.

Walk IV: *Lincoln's Inn and Gray's Inn*

We commence in Chancery Lane with the old gateway, dated 1518. Of the three shields, that on the north bears the arms of Sir Thomas Lovell, a Bencher of the Inn, Speaker of the House of Commons, and Chancellor of the Exchequer. He was buried in Westminster Abbey. On the south are the arms of the Earl of Lincoln, from whom the Inn takes its name; in the centre those of Henry VIII. The oak doors date from 1564. Passing through the arch, on the right, is the chapel. It was designed by Inigo Jones, one of his few attempts at Gothic, and opened in 1623, when a sermon was preached by the celebrated Dr. Donne. According to one report the crush was so great that a few were carried out dead! The crypt, so happily affording shelter in the pre-umbrella era, was a place for appointments, as sometimes now. Pepys walked there "by agreement," and in Butler's *Hudibras*, which he read so eagerly on publication, is the couplet:

> Or wait for customers between
> The pillar rows of Lincoln's Inn.

This resort of the living was also a place for the dead. In the centre will be seen the tombstone of John Thurloe, a secretary of Oliver Cromwell, who died in 1668. Thurloe, "eager and indefatigable," says John Morley, lived in two sets of chambers in the inn. First in 24, Old Buildings, (there is a tablet on the Chancery Lane side), and, after Cromwell's death, at No. 13. In the ceiling of the latter the Thurloe State papers were discovered by a clergyman lodging there in the reign of William III, who handed them over—they were enough for nearly seventy volumes—to Lord Chancellor Somers. William Prynne was also buried here. A fierce assailant of the stage and of Queen Henrietta Maria, he was sentenced to a fine of five thousand pounds, to stand twice in the pillory, to lose both ears, and to suffer imprisonment. He nevertheless survived until 1669. The chapel has a fine series of stained-glass windows, and Archbishop Laud expressed surprise that so much abuse should have been levelled at his windows at Lambeth Palace whilst these passed unnoticed. The west and north-west windows were damaged by a bomb during the war, and some parts have not been refilled with stained glass. There is an inscription on the north-west window, the stained glass in which was executed by the Flemish artists Bernard and Abraham Van Linge in 1623-6, referring to this event. The second window from the west, on the south side, has a representation of the chapel and its environs, also the Thames and what is apparently the Temple. Other windows contain the arms of the treasurers. In the south-east window will be seen the arms of Prynne and Strode (one of the "Five Members") in the east window, the arms of the king, once treasurer, and in the north-east window those of H. H. Asquith and R. B. Haldane. In the vestibule is a tablet in memory of Spencer Perceval, Prime Minister in 1812, and a member of Lincoln's Inn. The bell was brought from Cadiz by the Earl of Essex in 1594. It rings the curfew (fifty strokes) nightly at 9 p.m. At the porch leading to the stairs to the chapel are two small stone heads—on the left the Bishop of Chichester, who had a palace on the site of the inn in the thirteenth century; on the right Queen Victoria, in whose reign (1883) the chapel was extended westwards. On the north side, close to the west end, will be found a tablet recording the air raid referred to.

The old hall opposite the chapel, as is indicated on a tablet under the archway, was built in 1491 and restored in 1928. It is one of the most charming of Tudor halls. All the stones were numbered, as can be seen on a view of the interior, and the old work for the most part replaced. The clock, which has no figures but the arms of the Inn in lieu, is of great age, and the louvre dates from Edward VI's reign. Round the walls are some fine paintings of distinguished members of the Inn, such as Sir John Fortescue, who was knighted by Henry V for prowess in the French wars and was Chief Justice under Henry VI. Hogarth's "celebrated failure," as Leigh Hunt called the painting of "Paul preaching before Felix," was the result of Lord Mansfield's zeal. The painter received two hundred pounds, the amount of a legacy of Lord Wyndham's for the decoration of the hall. Prior to the erection of the Law Courts in the Strand, Chancery trials took place here, and this was the venue of the interminable action of Jarndyce *v.* Jarndyce in *Bleak House*. Leaving the hall and passing, on our left, some handsome wrought-iron gates, we arrive at the new hall. The initials of the architect, Philip Hardwicke, (he also designed Euston Station), are on the diaper work on the south wall, as also the date 1843. Like the old hall, it received embellishment by a prominent artist. G. F. Watts in 1859 completed a fresco which entirely fills the west wall. It is entitled "Justice"; a hemicycle of law-givers. The figures represented range in date from Moses to Edward I. Minos, Justinian, and Ina had as models respectively, Tennyson, Sir William Harcourt, and Holman Hunt. The artist's reward was a silver-gilt cup, valued at one hundred and fifty pounds, and a purse of five hundred pounds. This hall, the largest in the Inns of Court, has some fine carving, busts of Walpole and Pitt, and a number of statues including John Tillotson, preacher in the chapel until he was made Archbishop of Canterbury in 1691, and Lord Mansfield.

Leaving Lincoln's Inn by the new gateway, erected soon after the hall, and walking westwards, we reach the Royal College of Surgeons, which was rebuilt in 1835. The date 1800 on the cornice is that of the incorporation of the company. Prior to 1809 the Surgeons' Hall was in the Old Bailey, and this was particularly convenient inasmuch as by Act of Parliament the bodies of condemned criminals were conveyed there for dissection. Even then there were gruesome sights, and the *Academy* in 1796 mentioned that two criminals were conveyed in a cart, their heads supported by tea chests for the public to see," which they added, "was contrary to all decency and the laws of humanity." The museum of the college is of interest but can only be inspected by introduction of a member. Here one can sup full with horrors. In happy relief, however, to the sad epitome of the ills that flesh is heir to, are such innocuous exhibits as the skeletons of a ten-year-old dwarf, whose height was twenty inches, of Charles Byrne, an Irish giant who died in 1783 at the height of seven feet eight inches, and of Chunee, the elephant exhibited at Exeter Change Menagerie in the Strand which, becoming unmanageable, was killed in 1826 at the cost of a hundred bullets.

The next turning is Portsmouth Street, with its quaint little "Old Curiosity Shop. Immortalized by Charles Dickens." There is nobody, apart from the shopkeeper, who cannot afford scepticism, who regards this as other than a legend. In 1839, when the novel was written, it was a heraldic sign-painter's, and the inscription was not added until 1868. As Dickens was then resident at Gad's Hill Place, Rochester, and died two years later, he may never have known of it. He told a contemporary that the shop he had in mind was in Green Street, Leicester Square, and the penultimate paragraph of the *Old Curiosity Shop* says "the old house had been long ago pulled down."

Still, it is a picturesque little building, and nobody will regret that it has been shored up for the admiration of posterity.

Retracing our steps we reach Sardinia Street where, until 1909, was a Roman Catholic chapel formerly attached to the Sardinian Embassy. An attack was made upon it when James II provoked anti-Catholic feeling and a medal in the British Museum commemorates the event. It was again attacked in the "No Popery" riots, and is mentioned in *Barnaby Rudge*. Here, in 1793, Fanny Burney married General D'Arblay. A new Roman Catholic chapel in Kingsway bears its dedication—SS. Anselm and Cecilia.

Proceeding north we may look at No. 58 Lincoln's Inn Fields. On this site Pepys's cousin, the Earl of Sandwich, had a house, frequently referred to in the famous *Diary*. It was rebuilt in 1730 and divided into two in 1795. In the half numbered 58 lived Dickens's biographer and executor, John Forster, from 1834 to 1856. A drawing of Maclise shows Dickens in 1844 reading the MS. of *The Chimes*, in this house, to a meeting of literati, including Carlyle. He introduced it into *Bleak House* as the home of Tulkinghorn. "It is let off in sets of chambers now," he wrote, "and in those shrunken fragments of its greatness, lawyers lie like maggots in nuts."

Lindsey House—one of Inigo Jones's—was built for the Earl of Lindsey who was killed fighting for Charles I at Edgehill. It was divided in 1752 and subsequently occupied for 17 years by Perceval, already mentioned.

Newcastle House, at the corner, is, alas, being shorn of its former greatness. Its name is derived from the most distinguished of its many occupants (whose arms until recently adorned the façade)—one of George III's Prime Ministers. Of him, Leigh Hunt tells a delightful tale. One of his supporters having secured election by the single vote of a Cornishman, he promised that voter than when the local supervisor of excise died his son-in-law should succeed him. The duke was one night expecting a dispatch announcing the death of the King of Spain, and, tired of waiting, had retired to bed giving injunctions that any messenger who called was to be at once shown up. At this juncture the Cornishman arrived and was at once shown up. "Is he dead?" exclaimed the duke, rubbing his eyes, "Is he dead?" "Yes, my lord, the day before yesterday, and I hope your grace will be as good as your word and let my son-in-law succeed him." "Is the man drunk or mad?" exclaimed his grace, at the idea of a messenger pleading for the throne of Spain for a relative, when, drawing aside his bed-curtains he recognized his Cornish friend, "making low bows, with hat in hand, and hoping my lord would not forget the gracious promise he was so good as to make in favour of his son-in-law at the last election." There followed peals of laughter—one hopes too the appointment of the son-in-law—but Leigh Hunt does not enlighten us on this point.

We may now enter the gardens. A little way along is a memorial seat to Mrs. Ramsay MacDonald. This pleasing design of a young woman tending happy children, recalls the fact that fifteen years of her married life were spent at No. 3 Lincoln's Inn Fields. From this path we can see the Soane Museum, in the house owned from 1812 to 1837 by Sir John Soane, architect of the Bank of England. It contains a varied collection of statuary and paintings collected by him. Included in the latter are Hogarth's series: "The Rake's Progress," and "The Election." A most remarkable exhibit is the sarcophagus of an Egyptian Pharaoh, dated about 1370 B.C. It was discovered in 1817.

In the shelter, in the centre of these gardens, is a tablet commemorating the execution of Lord William Russell in 1683. He was wrongfully accused of complicity in the Rye House Plot, and the unceasing efforts of his wife to secure his reprieve are poignantly related by Leigh Hunt in *The Town*. The body was taken to Lindsey House prior to being conveyed upon a hearse to Southampton House in Holborn. A less reputable man was also executed in Lincoln's Inn Fields—Babington who plotted in favour of Mary Queen of Scots in 1586. It is piquant now to read that when fearing arrest he hid in St. John's Wood! It is frequently said that, whether by accident or design, the square of Lincoln's Inn is of the same dimensions as the Great Pyramid. This, however, is not correct. The former is eight hundred and twenty-one by six hundred and twenty-five feet; the latter seven hundred and sixty-four feet square.

We will leave Lincoln's Inn Fields by way of Great Turnstile—at the north-west. There is The Ship Tavern with a tablet recording the fact that here was a secret meeting-place of Roman Catholics. As Mr. Popham points out, the fact that the inn could be approached from four different directions would be an advantage. Its proximity to the Sardinian Chapel may also have made it convenient. In *Barnaby Rudge* Dickens gives a vivid presentation of Dennis, the hangman, as a participator in the "No Popery" riots. Dennis was one of the very few historical characters Dickens created, and he was in fact accused of burning houses in Little Turnstile. This is evidence of Roman Catholic associations. Whilst we are given to understand that Dickens's Dennis is hanged, the real one was reprieved. He was, however, deprived of his office, and a wag later wrote that:

> He contracts for ropes
> And lives in hopes
> Of being reinstated.

We emerge upon Holborn and turn right and cross the road. Soon we arrive at Gray's Inn Gate. It was erected in 1594, and the misguided Benchers covered the original red bricks with cement in 1867. We go through into South Square, sometimes known as Holborn Court. At No. 1, Charles Dickens was a clerk with Messrs. Ellis & Blackmore, solicitors, in 1827. He came in May 1827 and left in November 1828. Mr. Blackmore said "he was a bright, clever-looking youth, and several instances took place in the office of which he must have been a keen observer, as I recognized some of them in his *Pickwick* and *Nickleby*." His desk is at Dickens House, and it is said that the petty cash book is still in existence. In it were such names as Weller, Bardell, Corney, Rudge, and Newman Knott. Traddles's address was next door—No. 2. In South Square, also, were Mr. Phonky's chambers. The chapel of Gray's Inn is on our right and the hall on the left. There was a chapel here in the early part of the fourteenth century, but it was largely rebuilt in about 1689. In the chapel the Earl of Birkenhead's body lay in state in 1930. Gray's Inn has its curfew. It rings nightly at 9 p.m. forty times. A man once made a bet with another who did not know there was a regulation number of strokes that it would ring forty. Unfortunately the bell-ringer miscounted and rang forty-one. The hall was built between 1556 and 1560. It is an excellent specimen of Tudor architecture, and has a fine screen, and a minstrel's gallery. It had a narrow escape during the German air raids, the robing room adjoining being set on fire. The toast of Queen Elizabeth is still drunk on special occasions. The statue of Bacon, unveiled by Sir Arthur Balfour in 1912, commemorates his close connection with the inn. We pass through a narrow passage on the left of the hall into Gray's Inn Square. Bacon's chambers until his fall were on the site of No. 1 in the square. They were destroyed in a fire in 1684. At No. 5—the office of his solicitors—Shelley wrote to Southey in 1816 forwarding a copy of *Alastor* in remembrance of his visit to the poet at Keswick. We turn left into Field Court and here get a good view of Gray's Inn Gardens. They are said to have been laid out by Bacon whose essay on gardens was doubtless written here. The catalpa tree—so bowed down—at the north end is said to have been planted by him. At any rate, in that belief slips from it have been planted in America. Here Raleigh walked with Bacon before the latter's departure for "El Dorado." The gardens were a rendezvous of the aristocracy, and Pepys came with his wife "to observe fashions of the ladies because of my wife's making some clothes." Sir Roger de Coverley came here, as also Wesley and Zinzendorf for theological discussion. Charles Lamb wrote of them as "the best gardens of any of the Inns of Court, my beloved Temple not forgotten—have the gravest character, their aspect being altogether reverend and law breathing. Bacon has left the impress of his foot upon their gravel walks." There are one or two old cisterns in use as huge flower vases, and the gates bear the initials of William I. Gilbey, Treasurer, the date of erection, 1722.

WALK V: *Southwark*

We start at the east end of Southwark Cathedral and descend the steps and walk alongside the railings. We proceed along Cathedral Street until we reach St. Mary Overies Dock. To the left of this is Winchester Yard,

once the quadrangle of the palace of the Bishops of Winchester. Here lived the great Cardinal Beaufort of *Henry VI*
at a time when it included a great hall, a chapel and an
extensive park. References to "Winchester geese" in
Shakespeare are to the houses of ill fame under the bishop's
jurisdiction. The palace was destroyed by fire in 1814, but
if we go through the narrow court in the far corner of the
square we shall arrive in Clink Street, and in an archway
see a piece of the old brickwork which still remains. We
go through this arch, and turn left. After a short walk
we turn right and reach Bankside. A tea warehouse bears
the legend "Here stood the Globe playhouse." It stands
very high—higher in altitude than in truth. The playhouse was certainly not so close to the river. With a building
constructed of wood and thatch the risk from the river's
overflow would have been too great. The warehouses
Nos. 8–11 occupy the sites of the houses named "The
Oliphant" and "The Crane." These houses were devised
by will in 1503–4 to the Tallow Chandlers Company. In
Twelfth Night Antonio says to Sebastian, "Hold, sir, here's
my purse; in the suburbs, at the 'Elephant,' is best to
lodge." Probably this was a reference to the hostelry so
close to the Globe where the play was acted. At No. 25
is Rose Alley. This was the name of the first Bankside
theatre, erected about 1587. Here probably Shakespeare
first achieved success as an actor, and first produced *The
Merchant of Venice.* After 1603 it was no longer a playhouse,
and by 1638 had disappeared. Proceeding along Bankside,
we go under Southwark Bridge and reach a turning called
the Bear Gardens. We will turn down here and stand upon
the site of the Bear Pit of Shakespeare's day. There is a
White Bear public-house, and a white bear was included in
a list of animals dated 1638. Slender, in *Merry Wives of
Windsor*, refers to one of the bears, Sackerson, and Macbeth
says:

> They have tied me to a stake; I cannot fly,
> But bear-like, I must fight the course.

This reference would be most apt to an audience standing
watching the play a few yards from the Bear Pit. The
quotation, too, reminds us of the fact that the bear was
tied up and baited by dogs. Later the Bear Pit was rebuilt

as the Hope Theatre. Here plays, bear- and bull-baiting, could be witnessed. It was demolished during the Commonwealth.

Turning left, on leaving the Bear Gardens, and walking along Park Street through a railway arch, on the right, we come upon a tablet recording the site of the Globe Theatre. It was erected in 1598 and burned down in 1613 during a performance of *Henry VIII*, when a too realistic cannon was introduced and set fire to the thatch. It was the "Wooden O" referred to in the prologue to *Henry V*. It had over its entrance the "Hercules and his load," referred to by Rosencrantz, and the Latin motto "All the world's a stage" —the first line of Jaques's famous speech. Shakespeare held shares in the theatre which was rebuilt after the fire and survived until 1644—the period of the Puritan regime— when it was destroyed "to make tenements in the room of it." The Shakespeare Reading Society affixed the bronze tablet in 1909. It admirably represents the rural character of the neighbourhood in the time of Shakespeare. In the forefront the Globe appears, and towards the rear the Rose and the Bear Garden. The medallion-bust of Shakespeare is an adaption of the First Folio portrait by Droeshout. There is still within the brewery, on whose wall the tablet has been fixed, a Globe Alley. Here at the tablet, yearly on the Saturday nearest to Shakespeare's birthday (23 April), scenes from one of the plays are performed.

Walking to the end of Park Street and turning right we reach Barclay & Perkins's brewery, the proprietor of which was once Dr. Johnson's friend Thrale. It was here Johnson was found, when after Thrale's death the premises were sold, bustling about with an ink-horn in his buttonhole. Being asked the price of the property he replied: "We are not here to sell a parcel of vats and boilers, but the potentiality of growing rich beyond the dreams of avarice." Shareholders of the company have since had the doctor's wisdom confirmed! In the company's offices are still preserved a knocker from his Bolt Court house, a chair in which he used to sit, and a copy of the well-known painting of Reynolds which is their trade-mark. If we proceed past the brewery and turn left, we come into Stoney Street. A turn right will then take us to Borough High Street. Crossing that thoroughfare, a little to the left, we find St. Thomas's Street. If we go down it we shall see, on the left, the Chapter-house of Southwark Cathedral. Erected in 1703, it was, until 1865, when St. Thomas's Hospital was removed to the Albert Embankment, its chapel. Passing a terrace of eighteenth-century houses on the left, the gates of Guy's Hospital are seen immediately on the right. The grimy statue in the centre of the courtyard is of the founder, Thomas Guy, and was the work of Scheemakers, a Dutch sculptor. Guy was a native of Southwark, a bookseller, and afterwards M.P. for Tamworth; he lived just long enough to see the completion of the hospital in 1724. Keats walked its wards from 1814–16, and in its lecture-room once "there came a sunbeam and with it a whole troop of creatures floating in the ray; and I was off with them to Oberon and fairyland."

Returning from St. Thomas's Street into the High Street and turning left, we find, alongside a stationer's shop, White Hart Yard. The original inn of this name became the headquarters of Jack Cade in his famous rebellion of 1450. "Will you needs be hanged with your pardons about your necks? Hath my sword therefore broken through London gates that you should leave me at the 'White Hart' in Southwark?" says Cade in *Henry VI*. At the "White Hart" Cade executed one of his victims, and here Cade's body was brought to be identified by the hostess, after a wound, inflicted in the course of his flight, had proved fatal. The inn was destroyed in the great Southwark fire of 1676, after which it was rebuilt in the form so admirably described in chapter x of *Pickwick Papers*, as the place of Sam Weller's employment and the rendezvous of the wicked Jingle and his "dearest of angels," Rachael Wardle. In 1889 it was pulled down. A baluster from the "old clumsy balustrade," to which Dickens refers, is in the Dickens Museum at Doughty Street. A few yards farther on is George Yard. Here chapter x of *Pickwick Papers* can be referred to with more advantage than in White Hart Yard. The "George" (it probably lost its sainthood at the Reformation) has little history. In 1554 it was the property of a Mr. Colet, who represented Southwark in Parliament, and in 1598 Stow mentioned it as one of Southwark's "fair inns."

In 1634 the landlord was reported for allowing drinking during divine service, and in 1645 Sir John Mennes, afterwards Admiral and Comptroller of the Navy, and as such a friend of Pepys, wrote some lines "Upon a surfeit caught by drinking bad sack at the George Tavern in Southwark," which commence:

> Oh, would I might turn poet for an hour,
> To satirize with a vindictive power
> Against the drawer.

From the lines which follow it is clear that the wish was not gratified, even for the moderate period suggested! The "George" disappeared in the fire of 1676. It was rebuilt, and much used by coaches and carriers until 1870, when, in the inevitable process of vehicular evolution, it became mainly a railway depot. The Great Northern Railway Company, who purchased the property, left it largely as it was built, until 1889. The demolition in that year spared only the existing wing. Before then the entrance to the yard was behind the white gate on the right, so the coaches, as they came lumbering in, must also have brushed against the galleries of the inn. The coffee-room has old-fashioned pens, and the bedrooms, with four-posters, open direct on to the galleries. Dickens refers to the inn but once—in *Little Dorrit*. "Tip," the heroine's brother, goes there to write begging letters to Clennam. Jeffery Farnol has a lengthy allusion to it in *The Amateur Gentleman*.

If the "George" is delightful, the "Tabard" by Talbot Yard is disappointing. Only the sign, showing the sleeveless coat of the herald, which hangs high over the pavement, and a history on a card in the window, reminds us of the inn which stood upon the site. The "Talbot" was the name given by the eighteenth-century proprietor (evidently with no sense of history), and the yard still retains it.

Layton's Buildings (No. 199) takes us into the precincts of the Marshalsea Prison. Before the recent rebuilding of the woodshed it bore a turret which once held the bell that warned visitors to leave the prison. Clennam, ignoring this, spent a night within. The house on the right with the flagstaff was probably the governor's.

Returning to the High Street, we find, a little farther on,

a narrow archway leading to Angel Place. A few yards south of this entry was the gate of the prison to which Dickens referred when in *Pickwick Papers* ("The Old Man's Tale about a Queer Client") he first mentions the Marshalsea.

On turning to the right and continuing along the pavement, we find on the left, at the bend, the churchyard of St. George the Martyr, Southwark, which we will enter. It was divided from the church by a roadway in 1907. On the back wall is a tablet referring to the prison. Dickens first knew it when his father was a prisoner in the Marshalsea for three months in 1823, and here the latter gave to his son part of Mr. Micawber's famous advice about the effect upon happiness of proper relations between income and expenditure. Dickens described it in *Little Dorrit* (1856) as an oblong pile of barrack buildings, partitioned into squalid houses, standing back to back. The Marshalsea pump, referred to in the novel, is in the Cuming Museum in Walworth Road. The Marshalsea was discontinued as a prison in 1842 and the prisoners transferred to the King's Bench. Except, however, by indicating that he turned to the right on entering the prison yard, Dickens gives no indication where old Dorrit's rooms were situated. Sir Walter Besant's illustration of the exterior of Little Dorrit's garret, and a painting, at the London Museum, of its interior, represent a garret to be seen on the extreme left as the rambler faces the wall in the churchyard bearing the inscription. This is justifiably regarded as the one mentioned by Dickens (in chapter xxiv) as Little Dorrit's bedroom. It corresponds with Phiz's illustration, and still contains an old cupboard and a casement window.

There has been a church here since 1122, perhaps longer. In the old church were buried many victims of the Marshalsea, including Bishop Bonner. Here (in 1652) was married General Monk, afterwards Duke of Albemarle, the restorer of the Stuart dynasty. This, in the view of society, was a misalliance, as the bride was a farrier's daughter. In the churchyard was buried (in 1676) the author of that arithmetic book (so valued by Dr. Johnson that it accompanied him to the Hebrides), commended in the phrase, "according to Cocker." In 1734 the old church, which figured prominently in Hogarth's picture of Southwark Fair, was pulled down.

N

The present church is famous solely for its Dickens associations. Dickens was certainly most ingenious in associating Little Dorrit with all three of its registers. As a child of the Marshalsea her name appeared in the baptismal register; as the bride of Clennam, when the sun poured through the east window, which can still be seen, it was entered in the column devoted to marriages. If she was not to be "killed for the market," as a ruthless critic said of Little Nell, matters could go no further. But an external connection was a good substitute for an internal one. When Little Dorrit is shut out of the prison, after her "party" she finds refuge in the vestry at the south-east end of the church, and sleeps with the burial register for a pillow. "What makes these books interesting," says the verger grimly, "is not who's in 'em, but who isn't—who's coming, you know, and when." This would certainly have been the view of the man who had Pope's lines put on the table tomb at the entrance to the churchyard:

> How lov'd, how valued once, avails thee not,
> To whom related, and by whom forgot;
> A heap of dust alone remains of thee;
> 'Tis all thou art, and all the proud shall be.

Continuing along Borough High Street and crossing the road we reach Lant Street, where Bob Sawyer held his famous party, and where the boy Dickens had a back attic, when his father was a prisoner. Except that it was at the eastern end of the street, the position of the house is unknown. It was probably demolished in 1877 on the erection of the school where now the Dickens Fellowship annually gives a children's party, and the inscription on the door of No. 53 must be disregarded. There is perhaps not now that repose about Lant Street to which Dickens alluded in chapter xxxi of *Pickwick Papers*, but it may still shed a gentle melancholy upon the soul. If a man were tempted to retire from the world he might not choose it as a hermitage, as Dickens suggested, but he would be as immune as ever from temptation to look out of the window.

On leaving Lant Street, we cross the road and turn down Trinity Street. This leads to Trinity Square, where will be found London's oldest outdoor statue. It represents Alfred the Great, and was brought in 1823, when the church was

erected and the square laid out, from the old Palace of Westminster. It probably dates from the time of Richard II.
One of the hands has disappeared; they originally supported
a book and a sword. We should now retrace our steps and
turn to the left down Swan Street, which brings us to Union
Road, formerly Horsemonger Lane, where the recreation
ground and the L.C.C. Weights and Measures Office stand
upon the site of the county gaol of Surrey from 1791–1879.
Leigh Hunt (Dickens's model for Harold Skimpole) was a
prisoner here from 1812 to 1814 for writing of the Prince
Regent in the *Examiner* that "this 'Adonis in loveliness' was
a corpulent man of fifty." He was visited by Byron, Shelley,
Hazlitt, Lamb, and Keats, who wrote a sonnet to celebrate
his release. Over the main entrance—in Horsemonger Lane
—public executions took place. Dickens witnessed here in
1849 the end of Mr. and Mrs. Manning. The lady wore
black satin for this important occasion, and this material
went out of fashion as a result. The same day Dickens
wrote to *The Times* and said: "I do not believe that any
community can prosper where such a scene of horror as was
enacted this morning outside Horsemonger Lane Gaol is
permitted at the very doors of good citizens and is passed
by unknown or forgotten." It is said that prior to the
abolition of public executions in 1868 the inhabitants of the
old houses opposite made more than their annual rentals
by letting windows for these gruesome spectacles. The
gateway and door of the prison were prior to the fire there in
Madame Tussaud's museum, and the bell now does duty at
St. Michael and All Angels' Church, Lant Street. The tombstone of Mr. and Mrs. Manning, found in the Weights and
Measures Office, is now in the Cuming Museum.

We now turn to the right in Union Road. At its junction
with Newington Causeway there was until 1930 a row of
cottages. Here John Chivery, the turnkey, and his son, the
unsuccessful lover of Little Dorrit, resided. It was, says
Dickens, "a rural establishment, one storey high, which
had the benefit of the air from the yards of Horsemonger
Lane Gaol and the advantage of a retired walk under the
wall of that pleasant establishment."

Opposite Union Road is Borough Road, and immediately
to its right stood the King's Bench Prison, where Smollett,

one of Dickens's fathers in literature, and Mr. Micawber, one of his children in fiction, were confined. This "place of incarceration in civil process," as Mr. Micawber called it, was much larger than the Marshalsea, having two hundred and twenty-four rooms, and a spacious courtyard containing a market. The liberties of the King's Bench, in theory, included about a dozen streets round the prison between it and the "Elephant" and the Obelisk. In the liberties resided Madeline Bray, Nicholas Nickleby's bride. According to Lord Ellenborough, in fact, they extended to the East Indies! The King's Bench was latterly a military prison, and was demolished in 1880.

While Dickens's father was in the Marshalsea, a Mr. Dorrett of Rochester was in the King's Bench. John Dickens may have known him at Chatham. As the name "Dorrett" is in the Dickens memorandum book, for long in the possession of the family of Mr. Comyns Carr, K.C., there is no doubt how the name was derived.

EXTRAS

THE following are places of interest for which space cannot be found for extended reference. Unless visitors are making a long stay in London they may not find it possible to make a special pilgrimage to them, but they are recommended to refer to this list on taking their daily walks abroad to see, by reference to the map, whether any of the places are near to the itinerary they propose to follow.

Adelphi. The Greek word for brothers, and recalls the fact that it was built by four brothers, architects from Scotland, one of whom—Robert—was buried in Westminster Abbey. The foundations of the Adelphi were a series of arches on the river bank, and the work was carried out between 1769 and 1771. These arches, approached from Adam Street, were the favourite resort of the youthful Dickens as of David Copperfield. At 5 Adelphi Terrace David Garrick lived, from 1772 to 1779, when he died in the back room of the first floor. His wife continued to reside there until 1822, when she died in the same room. Here Garrick gave the parties Boswell refers to, and here he was visited by Rousseau. Thomas Hardy studied at a first-floor window of No. 8 as an architect in Mr., afterwards Sir, Arthur Blomfield's office from 1863-7, and Bernard Shaw lived at No. 10 for many years.

Austin Friars (Old Broad Street). Site of the House of the Augustinian Friars, founded in 1253. Many of the medieval nobility were buried here, including Edward, eldest son of the Black Prince, in 1375, and barons killed in the Battle of Barnet, 1471. Erasmus lived here in 1513. Church was granted to Dutch refugees in 1550 and still remains a place of worship for that nationality. The choir, steeple, and transept were pulled down in 1600. The building escaped the Great Fire but was damaged by a smaller one in 1862. Only St. Paul's, of City churches, has a larger floor space.

Billingsgate Fish Market (north side of London Bridge). One of the oldest London markets. Opens at 5 a.m. at the ringing of a bell. Officials of the Fishmongers' Company still inspect fish. About two hundred thousand tons pass through the market annually.

Bloomsbury. St. Giles-in-the-Fields Church dates from 1731 and stands upon the site of a much older one. Here was buried George Chapman, the Elizabethan dramatist, whose translation of Homer Keats praised in the famous sonnet, 1634; Lord Herbert of Cherbury, whose autobiography is still read, in 1648; and Richard Penderel (1672), who helped Charles II to escape after the Battle of Worcester (1651), in a large tomb in the churchyard. His praises are lengthily sung. We are told he is entitled to everlasting fame—which he will not get! Over the west door of this church is a "Resurrection" stone. The Day of Judgment is represented with coffins opening and bodies emerging. It was probably erected about 1670. There is a similar stone outside the Church of St. Stephen, Coleman Street, near the Bank, and there is a similar sculpture on the wall of St. Andrew's Church next to the City Temple, Holborn.

Bunhill Fields Burial Ground (City Road). The burial place or Campo Santo of Dissent, as Southey called it, from about 1665 to 1852, during which time, according to the inscription on the right-hand pillar of the entrance gate, more than one hundred and twenty thousand bodies were buried therein. The more important graves are mentioned on page 203. Others of interest are those of the mother of the Wesleys (left of the central path and near the top end); two graves of Cromwell's relatives close by; the grave of Lady Page, who, we are told in blatant lettering, "in 67 months was tapped 66 times and had taken away 240 gallons of water" (this is conspicuous on the far right-hand side of path); and that of Shrubsole, composer of a well-known hymn tune, "Miles Lane." The first bar of this tune is on the grave (it is usually that of the hymn "All Hail the Power of Jesu's Name"). He was at the time he composed it organist of a Nonconformist chapel in Miles Lane, near London Bridge. There is a sixpenny handbook sold, and it is cheap at the price.

Caledonian Market. Held every Friday. Alight from tram or bus at Brecknock Road. Almost anything can be bought here cheaply.

Charlie Brown's (Railway Tavern, West India Dock Road). Charlie Brown—"mine host"—has collected ivories and other valuables from the East so remarkable as in some cases to be sought after by the British Museum. There are two rooms in the tavern containing these treasures which the genial owner will willingly show, asking only a contribution for the hospitals in return.

Charterhouse (Charterhouse Square). Carthusian Priory founded here in 1371. John Houghton, the last prior, was executed in 1535 for denying the supremacy of the Church to Henry VIII, and his limbs were exhibited over the gateway which still exists. After the dissolution it passed into the hands of Sir Edward North, who built a mansion on the site of the little cloisters. Here he entertained Queen Elizabeth. He died here in 1564, and in the following year Thomas Howard, Duke of Norfolk, bought the place and enlarged it. The house was the scene of a conspiracy in favour of Mary Queen of Scots for which the duke was executed in 1572, and his property sequestered. It was afterwards returned to his son who entertained James I here in 1603. In 1611 it was purchased by Thomas Sutton, a London merchant. Here he founded the Charterhouse School and a hospital for poor brethren, and when he died, in 1611, was buried in the chapel. Charterhouse School remained here until 1872 when it was removed to Godalming (Surrey). The premises were sold to the Merchant Taylors' Company. They demolished most of the old school buildings and built new ones for their school which was located there. Amongst the famous scholars of Charterhouse have been Addison, John Wesley, Thomas Day (author of *Sandford and Merton*), George Grote and Bishop Thirlwall, historians of Greece, and Thackeray. The latter has made Charterhouse always a subject of tender thought, for here Colonel Newcome breathed his last. Thackeray boarded in Charterhouse Square in 1824, when he was thirteen. The hospital remains, together with some parts of the old priory, and it can be visited. The curfew tolls each evening—the rings being equal to the number of poor brethren there.

Chong Chu's Restaurant (Limehouse Causeway). For a Chinese meal in the Chinese quarter before or after visiting Charlie Brown's. English visitors are courteously assisted to choose such dishes as are palatable to them and trained in the art of wielding chop-sticks.

Cleopatra's Needle (Victoria Embankment). With which the famous Egyptian queen had no associations. It was originally one of two obelisks erected at Heliopolis and removed to Alexandria in 12 B.C.. The one here was presented to the British nation by Mohammed Ali in 1819, but many years elapsed before it was brought from Alexandria encased in a cylinder. It was abandoned during a storm in the Bay of Biscay and recovered and erected in 1878. The inscription covers three sides of the base, whilst on the fourth is a memorial tablet to six sailors who perished in a bold attempt to succour the crew of the obelisk ship *Cleopatra* during the storm. The companion obelisk was removed to New York in 1879.

Clerkenwell. The name is derived from the well of the parish clerks. The position is marked by a tablet on 16 Farringdon Road. It was revealed during excavations in 1924, and can be seen upon application to the Finsbury Public Library, Skinner Street. At the well miracle plays used to be performed in the Middle Ages, as mentioned by Arnold Bennett in *Riceyman Steps.* St. James's Church, Clerkenwell Green, was built in 1792 and replaces an earlier one in which two sons of Izaak Walton were buried in 1650 and 1651, their father being resident there, and Bishop Burnet (d. 1715), author of the *History of His Own Times* (in Everyman's Library), and Edward Cave (d. 1754), friend of Johnson and editor of the *Gentleman's Magazine.* In the churchyard (on the south side near the wall) is the tombstone of the Steinburg family who were murdered in 1834.

Cogers. A debating society formed in 1755. Now meets at the Cannon Tavern, opposite Cannon Street Station, on Saturdays at 7.30, the only exceptions being Saturdays before Bank Holidays. The subject of discussion is always an event of the week, but religious issues are excluded. John Wilkes and Daniel O'Connell were amongst the distinguished members in the past. Sir J. B. Melville, K.C., late Solicitor-General, is a member. Male visitors are always welcome, but ladies only on special nights.

County Hall, Westminster Bridge. It was erected on Pedlar's Acre (see pp. 80 and 196) between 1913 and 1922 (building having been interrupted by the war from 1916 to 1919) at a cost of over three million pounds. There is still, however, the eastern wing to complete and this is now in course of construction. There is some beautiful marble, work in the Council chamber and corridors. The members' waiting-room (No. 118) has an old fireplace, removed from 59 Lincoln's Inn Fields. It is believed to date from about 1752. The central panel shows a bear attacking beehives. On the left of the entrance to the council chamber, and forty feet below the floor level, was found a Roman boat (see p. 82). The meetings of the London County Council are on Tuesdays, at 2.30. There is a public gallery, and at stated times the building may be inspected.

Greenwich. The hospital for disabled seamen was the scheme of Queen Mary II, and was opened in 1705 in a palace founded by Charles II. Although principally the work of Wren, it was not completed until the reign of George II, of whom a somewhat disfigured statue by Rysbrack stands in the quadrangle. It was again enlarged in the reign of George IV, and now comprises four blocks named after King Charles, King William, Queen Mary, and Queen Anne respectively. The Great Hall is in King William's Building (on the north-west), and by reason of the emblematic paintings which adorn the ceiling is usually known as the Painted Hall. It contains pictures of illustrious admirals and famous sea fights and some interesting relics of Lord Nelson, including the coat and waistcoat he wore at Trafalgar, his pigtail, cut off after death, his purse and his stockings. There is also Kneller's portrait of William III. The chapel (1698) is in Queen Mary's Building. It has, as altar-piece, Benjamin West's painting of "The Shipwreck of St. Paul." In the centre of the nave is an ornamental compass pointing north. This shows that the altar is north-east; this was made to suit the lie of the palace. The beautiful font was carved by a Chatham prisoner in 1883. There is some fine carving round the galleries, and a charming butterfly window, of Wren's design, in the porch. There, on the left as we leave, we must notice the cleverly designed spiral staircase. Its diameter is only thirty inches. South of the hospital, and facing Greenwich Park is the "Queen's House," now occupied by the Royal Hospital School. It was built by Inigo Jones for Anne of Denmark, queen of James I. The school will shortly be removed to Suffolk, when the building will be used as a National Naval and Nautical Museum. At present this is housed in another apartment in the hospital grounds. There are relics of Franklin's Arctic expedition, and a model of the Battle of Trafalgar.

After leaving the hospital, we proceed north to the main road. A few yards to the right is Greenwich Church. It was built in 1718, but restored in 1860. General Wolfe, of Quebec fame, is buried in the vaults; also the original "Polly Peachum" of Gay's *Beggar's Opera*. Wolfe's family lived at Greenwich when he was young, and a statue, unveiled in 1930, now stands in the park. There the visitor to Greenwich may resort for tea. In the park is Greenwich Observatory, founded by Charles II, and, in part, designed by Wren. It is not open to the public. From Greenwich Park we easily reach Blackheath, and in the south-east corner is Morden College, a delightful example of Wren's domestic architecture. It was designed for the maintenance of "poor, aged, and decayed merchants of England whose fortunes had been ruined by the perils of the sea or other unavoidable accidents." It is open to visitors.

Hampstead. The old-world village of Hampstead is five minutes' walk from the tube station. There are red-brick houses dating from the time of the early Georges. At No. 8 Church Row lived Letitia Barbauld (1743–1825). She was one of Lamb's two bald authoresses—the other being Mrs. Inchbald—and is best known to-day by the hymn "Praise to God, immortal praise," and a poem called "Life" (included in the *Oxford Book of English Verse*). In a poem, published in 1811, she originated Macaulay's New Zealander, and to her Scott attributed the development of his poetic gift.

The parish church blatantly proclaims its date, 1745. It has its chancel at the west end, and, north of it, is a bust of Keats presented by American admirers. In the churchyard (take the path by the wall) are some interesting graves: Lucy Aikin (1781–1864). She wrote memoirs of the Courts of Elizabeth, James I, and Charles I. She would not proceed to Charles II. "He is no theme for me," she remarked, "he would make me contemn my species." Macaulay commended these works, but not her *Life of Addison*. To this he gave the mild chastisement meet for a lady. Joanna Baillie (1762–1851) was a great friend of Sir Walter Scott's. He accordingly called her dramatic works immortal, and detected in them something like a renewal of Shakespeare's inspired strain! John Constable (1776–1837), a great English landscape painter. In the new cemetery opposite, close to the railings, are graves of Du Maurier (1834–96), the great *Punch* artist, inscribed with the closing words of *Trilby*; Sir Herbert Beerbohm Tree (1853–1917); Sir John Hare (1844–1921); and Sir James Barrie's adopted son, who was drowned while bathing at Oxford in 1921. About level with this, but two rows to the left, is the grave of Thackeray's daughter, Mrs. Richmond Ritchie, and from the left-hand path, near the top, will be seen the grave of Sir Walter Besant who wrote so voluminously and delightfully about London.

The small gate leads on to a hill, upon which abuts a Roman Catholic chapel and some small houses dated 1816. Mount Vernon, to which this leads, if we take a turn to the left, provides a view of a delightful corner overlooking Holly Bush Hill. Opposite the triangular green was Romney's studio, now marked by a tablet. Opposite, in the large house with the long front garden, lived Joanna Baillie with her sister. The road to the right of this takes us past Fenton House, built by a merchant of that name in 1793. From the bare dial over the door it is sometimes called Clock House. In the Gothic house on the right lived Du Maurier. In the first turning to the left—opposite One-Tree House—we find Admiral's House, with its square chart-conning room and railed look-out on the roof. From 1856–65 it was the residence of Sir Gilbert Scott, the architect of the Gothic revival who designed the adjacent Christ Church, Hampstead. It was painted by Constable as "A House in Hampstead" (see p. 115). In the house on the left, at right angles to it, Mr. John Galsworthy resides, and here the Forsyte family had birth.

By retracing our steps past the Admiral's House and taking the turning immediately in front we get into Christ-church Road. Turning to the right we reach Well Walk. In a house once next to the Wells Hotel, then called "The

Green Man," Keats lodged with his brother Tom until he died of consumption. "Poor Tom" is underlined in the play of *King Lear* in Keats's Shakespeare, preserved at the Keats House. This is reached by turning left, at the end of Well Walk, and proceeding along East Heath Road until Downshire Hill is reached. On the left is Keats Grove, formerly John Street, where Keats lived for the last four years of his life. The visitor to the house cannot do better than place himself in the hands of the able and enthusiastic curator.

Hampton Court. The palace was built by Cardinal Wolsey, and presented to Henry VIII who spent much of his time here. Here Jane Seymour was married, and here she died shortly after the birth of her son—afterwards Edward VI. It was a residence at times of all the sovereigns up to the death of George II. After that it was used to house various lordly and ducal families and, for that reason, it was not surprising that Dr. Johnson vainly applied for quarters here. In 1828, according to entry in Sir Walter Scott's diary, he went there with Samuel Rogers, Tom Moore, and Wordsworth, with his wife and daughter, where they walked up and down and listened to the band. The grounds were not then, however, open to the public. This did not come about until Queen Victoria's accession.

Now the public can walk through the apartments once used by kings and queens, and admire the pictures and the beds. There is also the Great Hall, with a splendid roof, a great louvre, an oak screen and a minstrels' gallery. The chapel was built by Wolsey and transformed by Wren into a Queen Anne edifice. On the ceiling are painted cherubs supporting the royal crown and the initials A.R. In this chapel Henry VIII married Jane Seymour, the day after the execution of Anne Boleyn. It is said he waited in the palace grounds for the gun which was to announce her death in the Tower of London. Edward VI was christened here with gorgeous ceremonial. Cromwell's daughter Mary was married here by an Independent minister after the ceremony had been already performed privately by an Anglican priest, apparently to gratify her father. At the back of the royal pew is what is known as the Haunted Gallery. It is associated with three ghosts. Catherine Howard's was said to be

heard running up and down in memory of her vain attempts
to implore the mercy of the king as he listened to mass.
Jane Seymour is said to haunt the place where death inter-
vened to rob her of her joy at having borne a male heir
to the king. Lastly, Mistress Sibel Penn watched over the
infancy of the motherless Prince Edward and died here of
smallpox in 1562. It has been said that the noise of her
spinning wheel was heard in an empty chamber of the
prince's lodgings and that she had been seen standing at
the door in a long grey robe and hood, with thin hands
outstretched, as if seeking the child of her love and tears.

The famous astronomical clock was placed on the east
side of Wolsey's Tower by Henry VIII. It consists of three
revolving discs with long pointers which tell the hour of
the day, the day of the month, the month of the year, the
phase of the moon, and the time of high water at London
Bridge. Under the clock, which was only replaced on the
tower thirty years ago, are carved Wolsey's cardinal's hat
and arms. Above it is the still more ancient bell which rings
the hours, and which hung in the Chapel of St. John before
Wolsey built his palace. In the Privy Gardens are beautiful
screens by Tijou, much of whose work is in St. Paul's
Cathedral. The sunk garden was due to William III who
was also responsible for a similar one in front of Kensington
Palace. The maze was also laid out by him. Of recent years
the old Tudor kitchen has been thrown open to the public.

Kew. The brick church which stands on Kew Green was
built in 1784. In the churchyard, Gainsborough, the artist,
was buried in 1788. The Royal Botanic Gardens cover
three hundred acres, and except on bank holidays, the visitor
may enjoy almost as much seclusion in traversing its spacious
lawns as in a private park. Every species of tree, shrub, and
flower is labelled, and we have here for flora what the
Zoological Gardens provides for its fauna. There are also
in the Gardens a "Chinese" pagoda one hundred and sixty-
five feet high, designed by William Chambers, architect of
Somerset House, a Japanese gateway—an exact copy of
the great Buddhist temple of Nishi Hongwanji—and a flag-
pole of Douglas fir from Vancouver Island, presented by the
Government of British Columbia. In the northern part of
the gardens, close to the main entrance, is Kew Palace.

This was the favourite residence of George III, and here in 1818 his consort, Queen Charlotte, died.

Lambeth Palace and Church. There has been a London residence for the Archbishops of Canterbury here since about 1197. The gateway was erected by Cardinal Morton in 1490. The Lollards' Tower, to the north, dates from 1434, the library, a long classically designed building visible from the roadway, was erected by Archbishop Juxon (who attended Charles I at his execution) soon after the Restoration. The chapel dates from 1244–70, but has been much restored. The palace as a whole can be visited only on Saturday afternoons by parties, arrangements being previously made, but the library is open on Mondays, Wednesdays, Thursdays, and Fridays, from 10–4 or 4.30 (Tuesdays 10–1), save for about six weeks from the end of August. It has some interesting exhibits, including a first edition of Sir Thomas More's *Utopia*, and a cookery book of the wife of Archbishop Tenison, with a recipe of a cake liked by Queen Anne and an antiquated specimen of a piece of one made from it!

Lambeth Parish Church adjoining dates from the fifteenth century, but has been much rebuilt. It contains the celebrated Pedlar's window, in the south-east corner. A window of this design is mentioned in 1608, but a new one was erected, apparently the one now to be seen, in 1703. One legend is that a pedlar, who possessed a favourite dog, asked for permission to bury it in holy ground here, and in return gave an acre of land to the church. Another version of the story is that a rich pedlar, whom the church had befriended in days of poverty, gave the land in gratitude for past favours. At any rate, the site upon which County Hall was erected was known as Pedlar's Acre, and the London County Council, when purchasing, realized the value of the gift! In the churchyard are buried a number of archbishops: Bancroft (d. 1610); Tenison (d. 1715); Hutton (d. 1758); Secker (d. 1768); Cornwallis (d. 1783); Moore (d. 1805). A little east of the porch is a large tomb to the memory of John Tradescant, a collector and particularly a botanist, and his son and grandson. They had a house in South Lambeth with a remarkable museum, and the name is commemorated in a road there. Close by is the tomb of Captain Bligh of the ship *Bounty* (see page 109).

London Stone (opposite Cannon Street Station). It is first referred to in connection with the first mayor of London, described as FitzEylwin of Londenestane. It is generally believed to have been the stone from which the Romans measured their distances. In *Henry VI* Cade strikes it with his staff on entering London (as also in Holinshed's *Chronicles*), and Sir Laurence Gomme mentioned that in Bovey Tracey it was a practice of the mayors to strike a certain stone upon election. It probably therefore had some ceremonial importance. In Stow's time it was on the south side of Cannon Street. In 1742 it was removed to the north side, and in 1798 placed in its present position in the church wall, the grille being added in 1869.

Madame Tussaud's (Baker Street). As this waxwork exhibition is open until 10 p.m. the visitor will be wise to devote part of an evening to it rather than to spare the precious hours of daylight. For the waxworks one to one and half hours will suffice. There is, however, now added a first-rate cinema. The sixpenny catalogue is descriptive enough, but attention may be drawn to one or two items which are relevant to allusions in this book. In the hand of Cardinal Wolsey will be seen an orange. This refers to the piquant fact, referred to by his gentleman-usher George Cavendish, in one of the earliest English biographies, his *Life of Wolsey*. The cardinal carried about an orange scooped out and filled with a vinegar-soaked sponge to counteract the odour of the populace. In the Chamber of Horrors (Nos. 4 and 5) are figures of Mr. and Mrs. Manning (see page 185) and (No. 59) Lord George Gordon, the leader of the "No Popery" riots of which Dickens wrote in *Barnaby Rudge*.

"Penny Plain and Twopence Coloured." The shop where juvenile theatres are sold, described by Stevenson in the essay so entitled (*Memories and Portraits*) is at 73 Hoxton Street. B. Pollock, the proprietor mentioned by R. L. S., is still there and welcomes visitors.

Pickering Place (3 St. James's Street). Messrs. Berry's wine business here dates from the days of Queen Anne, and there is a painting of the shop in the London Museum. Inside is a collection of leather wine-flasks and ancient bottles and a pair of great beam-scales. Here you can get weighed and have your weight recorded just as the Prince Regent, Charles Lamb, and Lord Nelson did. Pickering Place is approached by a dark oak-lined passage leading to a tiny quaint square surrounded by some fine houses. In the centre is a sundial, bearing the inscription "William Pickering, Fundator, 1710." The medallion is of a person unknown. Some think it represents Lord Palmerston. In old days this was a favourite place for duels, being so secluded from the street.

Riceyinan Steps (Granville Square, King's Cross Road.) Arnold Bennett's description does not quite apply. There is no Nell Gwynn Tavern thereabouts and never has been so far as can be ascertained, but Bagnigge Wells House close by was the summer residence of that lady. Rowton House is there and "a hell of noise and dust and dirt, with the County of London tramcars" (anybody more plebeian than Mr. Bennett would have said "L.C.C.") and the steps answer to the picture, though one looks in vain for a second-hand book shop and "an abandoned and decaying mission hall."

Richmond. A fine view is to be obtained from the famous terrace, a mile's uphill walk from the station. This was highly praised by Scott in *The Heart of Midlothian*. The park covers two thousand three hundred and fifty-eight acres and is nearly eight miles in circumference. It was first enclosed by Charles I. Nowhere so near London can such solitude be obtained, and the deer wander about undisturbed. The White Lodge, near the Roehampton Gate, was used as a hunting box by George II. Viscount Sidmouth lived there from 1801 to 1844, and was visited by Pitt, Sheridan, and Sir Walter Scott, and also by Nelson when on his way to join the *Victory* for the last time. The present Prince of Wales was born here in 1894. The long avenue in front of the lodge is called Queen's Walk, as it was a favourite promenade of Caroline, wife of George II. It figures in *The Heart of Midlothian* as the scene of the interview between Jeanie Deans and that queen.

On Richmond Green, in the west corner, is the ancient gateway of old Richmond Palace, bearing the arms of Henry VII. Cardinal Wolsey once lived there, and after her divorce from Henry VIII it was assigned as a residence for Anne of Cleves. It was there Queen Mary married

Philip of Spain, and it was the place of Elizabeth's death in 1603. This is traditionally said to have occurred in one of the rooms over the gateway, but probably only because this still remains. Queen Caroline lived here for a time, but by the middle of the eighteenth century the palace had become very dilapidated and ceased to be used as a royal residence.

Royal Academy of Arts. Burlington House, Piccadilly. Summer Exhibition from first week in May to the middle of August (9 a.m. to 7 p.m.) Admission 1s. 6d. Catalogue 1s. Winter Exhibitions, January and February, 9 till 5.

St. Giles's, Cripplegate, Church. Largely a sixteenth-century building. Cromwell was married in the church and Milton buried in it (1674). There is a monument to Milton, also to John Foxe, the martyrologist, Speed, the antiquary, and Frobisher, the explorer. The registers are of great interest. The one recording Milton's burial is still preserved. In the graveyard is a bastion of the Roman wall. The church is introduced by Thomas Hardy into *The Hand of Ethelberta.*

Shepherd Market (Mayfair). Approached from White Horse Street, Piccadilly. A quaint group of shops suggesting a small country town rather than London.

Shoreditch. Derives its name from Sir John Soerditch who held the manor in Edward III's time. There was a church before that—a four-gabled building of which there is a print in the vestry. This was pulled down about 1735 and the present church erected by George Dance. The interesting associations are almost entirely with the old building. Here were buried in 1597 James Burbage who built the first theatre, Richard Burbage, his son, in 1619, the first great Shakespearean actor who, we know from an epitaph, shone in the character of Shylock, and a number of other actors. Their names are on a beautiful grey marble tablet on the north wall, erected by the London Shakespeare League in 1913. Gabriel Spencer, mentioned thereon, was killed by Ben Jonson in a duel at "Hogsden," now Hoxton, in 1598. The entry of his burial and that of many others may be seen in the old registers which the courteous clerk, who lives in a house abutting on the churchyard, will willingly produce. There are also the entries of the burial of Will

o

Somers, Henry VIII's jester, a child of Sir Philip Sidney, who died in 1560, and a son of Robert Green, who wrote the pamphlet "A groatsworth of wit bought with a million of repentance," with its allusion to Shakespeare in 1592. There is an entry of the death of one Thomas Cam, who died in 1588, the year of the Spanish Armada. His age in the register appears to be two hundred and seven, from which it would appear he was born in the year of the Wat Tyler rebellion. It is probably a clerical error. On 24 September, 1801, is the entry of the baptism of three brothers of the poet Keats, George (b. 1797) who went to America, Tom (b. 1799) who died of consumption before the poet (see page 194), Edward (b. 1801) who died in infancy. The family was then living in Craven Street, City Road. Bradlaugh was baptized here on 8th December, 1833, though his father, says his daughter Mrs. Bradlaugh Bonner, was "fairly indifferent on religious matters and never went to church." At the entrance to the vestry is a remarkable monument in wood which shows two most vigorous figures of death pulling down the tree of life. The Latin inscriptions record that the deceased, Elizabeth Benson, was the daughter of a most notable philosopher and sprang from the ancestral kings of Pannonia and from Kentish knights, and that "Death with heavy foot stole on her and the threads of her life were not spent to the full but snapped on the 17th December 1710." As the inscription says she was in her ninetieth year, we are not perhaps impressed by the suddenness of the lady's decease, but doubtless she hoped to become a centenarian.

In the graveyard, on the south side, is a memorial seat to Shakespeare, and on the left-hand side of the entrance path—it can be seen from the pavement—is a large tomb bearing the curious inscription "John Gardner's Last and Best Bedroom," 1807. It is said that this was erected during the lifetime of the deceased, a worm doctor, but that, finding his trade decline upon the assumption of his death, he interpolated the word "intended" after his name, and this was removed after his death. Close by are the old parish stocks. After leaving the church the visitor should explore Crooked Billet Yard. It is only about three minutes walk through the railway arch at the commencement of Kingsland Road, then the first turning on the left. Here a few houses have survived from the end of the seventeenth century. Pathetic in age, dirty in aspect.

Soho. It is said to take its name from an old hunting cry when there were nothing but fields here. This is recalled by the Dog and Duck Tavern. The Duke of Monmouth, who had a house in Soho Square, used it as a battle cry at Sedgemoor in 1685. The Church of St. Anne, Dean Street, dates from 1686, but the tower was added in 1802. There is a tablet, most conspicuously placed upon the front of the tower, to Theodore King of Corsica, who died in Soho a few weeks after release from a debtor's prison, in 1756. The inscription, drawn up by Horace Walpole, who befriended him, gives something of his history. On the other side of the tower is a tablet to the memory of William Hazlitt, who was buried here in 1830. The house in Frith Street where he died is marked by a tablet. This street leads into Soho Square where there are many interesting houses. At No. 32 lived Sir Joseph Banks, President of the Royal Society and a great botanist who gave its name to Botany Bay. He was a fellow traveller with Captain Cook. In Carlisle Street, leading off from the left of the square is a fine eighteenth-century mansion, with link extinguishers at the door, called Carlisle House. This is believed to be the one referred to in *A Tale of Two Cities* as the residence of Dr. Manette. The most foreign aspect of Soho is in Compton Street and thereabouts.

Staple Inn. It was so-called as the inn or house of merchants of the wool staple, but from about the time of Henry V it became an Inn of Chancery, and in Queen Elizabeth's time there were one hundred and forty-five students in term and sixty-nine out of term. In the interior, which has a fine hammer-beam roof, a screen and minstrels' gallery, the date 1581 is carved on a corbel over the oriel window. The date of erection was probably not long before then. The inn passed out of the hands of the lawyers in 1884. Part was acquired by the Government for an extension of the Patent Office, and the two quadrangles and the hall became the possession of the Prudential Assurance Company for sixty-eight thousand pounds. The hall is now in the occupation of the Institute of Actuaries. In the second quadrangle from Holborn is the archway with the keystone "P.J.T."

Here were the chambers of Mr. Grewgious in *Edwin Drood*, and that gentleman used to speculate upon their meaning "perhaps John Thomas" or "perhaps Joe Tyler." In fact they were those of Principal John Thomson who was then President of the Inn. Dickens has a delightful description of the quadrangles:

> It is one of those nooks, the turning into which out of the clashing streets, imparts to the relieved pedestrian the sensation of having put cotton in his ears, and velvet soles on his boots. It is one of those nooks where a few smoky sparrows twitter in smoky trees, as though they called to one another, "Let us play at country," and where a few feet of garden-mould and a few yards of gravel enable them to do that refreshing violence to their understandings. Moreover, it is one of those nooks which are legal nooks; and it contains a little Hall, with a lantern in its roof.

Nathaniel Hawthorne also came here and described it with similar pleasure at his discovery. Up to a few years back there was a tree in the centre of the north quadrangle. A lady was one day sitting on the seat which encircled it, and on rising felt her feet sinking into the ground. This lead to excavations and an old well was found upon the spot. A Latin inscription commemorates the discovery.

Wallace Collection (Hertford House, Manchester Square). Collection of pictures, miniatures, ivories, glass and sculptures formed in the main by the fourth Marquess of Hertford (1800–70) when living in Paris. He bequeathed it to Sir Richard Wallace, who brought it to London and in 1897 the rich treasure was given to the nation by Lady Wallace.

Zoological Gardens. These occupy an area of about thirty-four acres in the northern part of Regent's Park. The greater part of a day is necessary to do justice to this remarkable collection. The Mappin Terraces, the Aquarium and the Monkey Hill are particularly attractive. The great events are the feeding of the lions, tigers, etc., and of the sea-lions. The former are usually fed at four o'clock in summer and 3 o'clock in winter, and the latter respectively at 4.30 and 3.30.

SOME INTERESTING LONDON GRAVES

The following are some of the most interesting graves in London not mentioned elsewhere. An indication of whereabouts is given for the benefit of any who may wish to visit them.

Ainsworth (Harrison). Kensal Green. Square 154. Row 1.

Bunyan (John). Bunhill Fields. Left of path, in centre. Tomb has recumbent statue.

Blake (William). Bunhill Fields. Upright stone. Right of path. Far side from City Road.

Blondin. Kensal Green. Square 140. Row 1.

Clifford (Prof. W.K.). Highgate. Clifford was a brilliant scientist and an atheist, and the epitaph was his own composition: "I was not and was conceived. I loved and did a little work. I am not, I grieve not."

Clifford (Dr. John). Kensal Green. Square 13. Row 1.

Coleridge (S. T.). Highgate School Chapel. Top of Highgate Hill.

Collins (Wilkie). Kensal Green. Square 141. Row 1.

Defoe. Bunhill Fields. Tall obelisk. Left of path, about centre.

Dickens (Mr. and Mrs. John). Parents of Charles Dickens. Highgate. Old Portion. Square 30. Inscription reads: "In memory of John Dickens, aged 66 years, whose zealous, useful, cheerful spirit departed on the 31st of March, 1851."

Dickens (Mrs. Charles, and two daughters, Dora Annie, and Mrs. Perugini (see page 89). Highgate. Old portion. Square 19.

Eliot (Geo.). Highgate. New portion. Square 84. Upright stone with inscription: "Of those immortal dead who live again in minds made better by their presence."

Forster (John). Kensal Green. Square 113. Row 1.

Fox (George). Bunhill Fields Friends' Burial Ground, Roscoe Street.

Gordon (Lord George). St. James's Church, Hampstead Road.

Haydon (Benjamin). Old Paddington Churchyard.

Holyoake (George Jacob). Highgate. New portion. Square 84.

Hood (*Thos.*). Kensal Green. Square 74. Row 1. Bust at top. Inscription: "He sang the Song of the shirt."

Hogarth (*Mary Scott*). Dickens's beloved sister-in-law. It bears his inscription: "Young, beautiful and good,. God in His mercy, numbered her with his angels at the early age of seventeen."

Huxley (*T. H.*). Finchley Cemetery. With epitaph by his wife:

"Be not afraid, ye waiting hearts that weep,
For still He giveth His beloved sleep,
And if an endless sleep He wills, so best."

Hunt (*Leigh*). Kensal Green. Square 121. Row 3.

Lamb (*Chas. and Mary*). Edmonton Churchyard.

Lillywhite (*Frederick W.*). Highgate. Old portion. Sculpture shows broken wicket.

Marryat (*Capt.*). Kensal Green.

Marx (*Karl*). Highgate. Square 111.

Maurice (*F. D.*). Highgate. Square 17.

Napoleon III. Kensal Green. Roman Catholic side.

Owen (*Robert*). Kensal Green.

Siddons (*Sarah*). Old Paddington Churchyard.

Sophia (*Princess*), *Sussex* (*Duke of*). Children of George III. Square 114. Row 1.

Spencer (*Herbert*). Highgate (near Geo. Eliot).

Thackeray (*W. M.*). Kensal Green. Square 36. Row 1.

Trollope (*Anthony*). Kensal Green. Square 138. Row 1.

Watts (*Isaac*). Bunhill Fields. Left of path, towards City Road.

Wesley (*Charles*). Marylebone Churchyard.

Wesley (*John*). City Road Chapel.

AMERICA'S LINKS WITH LONDON

John Quincey Adams. Sixth President of the United States, was married to Louisa Johnson, the daughter of the then (1797) American Consul in London, at All Hallows Barking Church.

Major Andre. Adjutant-General of the British Forces in

America, hanged by Washington's orders as a spy in 1780. His monument in Westminster Abbey (south aisle of nave) was erected at the expense of George III. On the bas-relief Andre is represented presenting the petition vainly imploring Washington for a soldier's death and also on the way to execution. The heads of both figures have often been carried off, and Lamb, writing to Southey, said it was "the wanton mischief of some schoolboy, fired perhaps with the raw notions of transatlantic freedom. The mischief was done about the time that you were a scholar there. Do you know anything about the fortunate relic?" This caused an estrangement between Lamb and Southey who was very sensitive about any reference to his early political principles. In 1821, at the Duke of York's request, Andre's remains were brought from America and buried, after a funeral service, near this monument. The chest in which they were brought is in the Crypt Museum of the abbey.

Boston Tea. On the site of 44 Fenchurch Street was the shop in which was purchased a portion of the tea that was sent to Boston in 1774 and was there thrown into the harbour. The firm was founded by Daniel Rawlinson in 1650, and in 1774 it was Messrs. Rawlinson, Davison & Newman. Davison and Newman were both buried in the Church of All Hallows Staining, and on its demolition the tablet to their memory was conveyed to St. Olave's, Hart Street, where it can still be seen.

Emerson. There is a tablet in the south transept of Southwark Cathedral to William Emerson (d. 1575) described simply as "an honest man." This was probably an ancestor of Ralph Waldo Emerson. There is accordingly an Emerson Street leading off Bankside.

Benjamin Franklin. Lived, on arrival in England in 1724, first at Little Britain, in Bartholomew Close in 1725 when employed in a printing office in St. Bartholomew's Church, in Carey Street, Lincoln's Inn in 1725–6, in Duke Street, Lincoln's Inn Fields about the same time. At this time he was working as a journeyman printer in Watts' printing house in Wild Court, Drury Lane. There is a press which he is said to have worked in South Kensington Museum. From 1757 to 1762 and again, on his return from America, from 1764 to 1772 he lived at 36 Craven Street, Strand, and there is a tablet upon this house. The London County Council publish a pamphlet about it, price twopence.

John Harvard. Born in Borough High Street and baptized in St. Saviour's Church, now Southwark Cathedral, where is now a Harvard Chapel (see page 54).

Abraham Lincoln. Statue opposite Westminster Abbey. Replica of one in Lincoln Park, Chicago. A tower of Christ Church, Westminster Bridge Road is called the Lincoln Tower and so inscribed. It was built with the contributions of Americans. Members of the Booth family, one of whom murdered Abraham Lincoln, are buried in the churchyard of St. John's, Clerkenwell.

Henry Wadsworth Longfellow. Bust in Poets' Corner, Westminster Abbey.

James Russell Lowell. Memorial tablet and medallion with stained-glass window in Chapter-house of Westminster Abbey.

General Oglethorpe. Founder of Georgia. Baptized in St. Martin's-in-the-Fields Church.

W. H. Page. American Ambassador, during the war. Memorial tablet in the Chapter-house of Westminster Abbey, near Lowell's.

Thomas Paine. Started the *Rights of Man* at the "Angel," Islington, then an inn, now a teashop, and wrote another part at Harding Street, Fetter Lane. There is a bust of Paine at Conway Hall, Red Lion Square (Ethical Services on Sunday at 11 a.m.), and one given to Thomas Clio Rickman with Paine's handwriting on the back, in the library of the Rationalist Press Association, Johnson's Court, Fleet Street.

George Peabody. A stone in the centre of the nave of Westminster Abbey marks the spot where his remains rested for a few days before his removal to Massachussetts. He was a great philanthropist who was instrumental in erecting a large number of working-class dwellings in London. His statue is behind the Royal Exchange.

William Penn. He was baptized at All Hallows, Barking,

where, on the south wall, is a brass tablet, and a portrait. At the Central Criminal Court, Old Bailey, is a tablet commemorating the fact that there Penn was tried in 1670 for preaching to an unlawful assembly.

Theodore Roosevelt. In the register of St. George's, Hanover Square, is the entry "Theodore Roosevelt, 28, Widower, Ranchman." The bride was Edith Kermit Carow.

Captain John Smith. "Sometime Governor of Virginia and Admiral of New England," as his monument reads, is buried in St. Sepulchre, Holborn Viaduct. It has a long inscription commencing:

> Here lyes one conquered that hath conquered Kings,
> Subdu'd large Territories, and done Things,
> Which to the world impossible would seem,
> But that the Truth is held in more esteem.

It is proposed to celebrate the tercentenary of his death at the church in June 1931.

Lt. Col. Townshend. Who fell at Fort Ticonderoga in 1758. Monument in Westminster Abbey which has figures giving a weird representation of redskins.

George Washington. There are in London two famous letters written by Washington. One is in the British Museum, and the other in the Record Office. In the Guildhall Museum is a letter from the Association of New York to the Lord Mayor of London, explaining the position of the American Colonies, as a result of which the Corporation protested to the king against the War of Independence. There is a statue of Washington outside the National Gallery. This was the gift of the Commonwealth of Virginia. There is a bust in St. Paul's Cathedral (see page 34).

DAYS AND HOURS FOR VISITING PUBLIC BUILDINGS

All these buildings are closed on Christmas Day and Good Friday. Most city churches are closed on Saturday afternoons. Admission is free except where otherwise stated.

Name	Hours	Remarks
British Museum	10–6. In January, February, November, and December after 4 p.m. and in March and October after 5 p.m. some only of the galleries remain open. On Sundays the Museum is opened at 2 p.m. Admission 1s.; Saturdays 6d.	There is a useful 3d. guide, summarizing the collections: other more expensive guides to various collections. Official guides conduct parties at 12 noon and 3 p.m.
Carlyle House	10–sunset.	There is a useful 1s. guide.
Charterhouse	Monday, Wednesday, Friday, 3–5. Admission 1s.	Official guides conduct
Chelsea Church.	10–1, 2–4.	Interesting guide 1s.
County Hall	Saturdays 10.30–12, 1.30–3.30; Easter Monday, Whit Monday, August Bank Holiday, 10.30–12, 1.30–4.30	There is a good 3d. guide.
Dickens House.	11–1, 2–5. Closed on Sundays. Admission 1s.	A useful guide, written by the Hon. Sec. of Dickens Fellowship, is sold for 6d.
Greenwich Hospital.	10–4, 5, and 6, except Fridays; Sundays after 2. Chapel same times, but closing hour on Saturdays always 4 p.m. Admission 6d. (free on Sundays).	
Guildhall.	10–5 March to October. 10–4 November to February.	A useful 1s. guide is sold. The Guildhall itself keeps open later than the Museum. The Council Chamber and Aldermen's Room may be seen on application.

Name	Hours	Remarks
Hampton Court Palace.	10–6 May to September; till 5 in March, April and October; till 4 November, to February.	There is a 1s. guide.
Houses of Parliament.	Saturdays and Easter Monday and Tuesday, and Whit Monday and Tuesday, 10–3.30.	There is an interesting guide for 1s. 6d.
Johnson House.	10–4.30 or 5. Admission 6d.	
Keats's House.	April to October, 10–6; November to March, 10–4.	There is a handbook sold at 1s. 6d.
Kensington Palace.	April to September, 2–6; October to March, 2–5; November to February, 2–4.	Handbook at 1s.
Kew Gardens.	10–dusk or 9 p.m. (summer time). Houses 1 p.m. to 5 p.m. or sunset. Admission free except on Tuesdays and Fridays (students' days.	
London Museum.	April–October, 10–6; November to March, 10–4. Open on Sundays after 2 p.m. Free Mondays, Fridays (when it is closed until 2 p.m.) and Saturdays. Tuesdays 1s.; Wednesdays and Thursdays, 6d.	There is a 3d. guide to the whole collection and more expensive guides to various sections.
Madame Tussaud's.	10–10. Sundays 2–10, Admission 1s. 3d. Chamber of Horrors 6d	There is a 6d. guide to the whole collection.
Monument.	9–4 or 9–6.	
National Gallery.	10 to dusk, except on Thursdays and Fridays, 6d. Opens on Sundays at 2 p.m.	Official lectures at 11 a.m. and 12 noon. There is a catalogue at 1s. 6d.
National Portrait Gallery.	10 to dusk, except on Thursdays and Fridays, 6d. Opens on Sundays at 2 p.m.	Official lectures at 2.30 and 3.30. except Saturdays and Sundays.

Name	Hours	Remarks
Record Office.	2–4 except Saturdays and Sundays.	A most interesting guide is sold at 1s.
Roman Bath, Strand Lane.	10.30–4.30 and 5.30.6d.	
South Kensington Museums:		
Imperial War.	10–6, Sundays 2.30–6.	
Natural History.	10–6, Sundays 2.30–6.	Summary guide 3d. Guides to various departments 4d., 6d., 1s. and 2s. Official guides 12 noon and 3 p.m.
Science.	Monday, Tuesday, Wednesday, Friday, Saturday, 10–6; Thursdays, 10–10; Sunday, 2.30–6.	Official guides, 12 noon and 3 p.m. Saturdays 2.30 and 4.30 p.m.
Victoria and Albert.	Monday, Tuesday, Wednesday, Friday, 10–6; Thursdays and Saturdays 10–10; Sunday 2.30–6.	Official guides 12 noon and 3 p.m. and 7 p.m. on Thursdays and Saturdays. Brief guide to collection 3d. Guides to collections at various prices.
St. Andrew, Undershaft Church.	12–3.	
St. Bartholomew-the-Great Church.	All day. Admission 6d. Open Saturdays.	A well illustrated account of the church is sold for 1s.
St. Clement Danes' Church.	10.30–5.	There is a very interesting guide for 1s.
St. Etheldreda's R. C. Church.	All day (Crypt 3d.).	
St. Giles' Church, Cripplegate.	10–5, Saturdays 10–1.	There is an interesting 6d. handbook.
St. Helen's Church, Bishopsgate.	11.30–4.	A useful guide is sold for 6d.
St. Catherine Cree Church	12–2.	
St. Margaret's, Westminster.	11–4.	An excellent guide is sold for 1s.

Name	Hours	Remarks
St. Mary-le-Bow Church.	10–4. Crypt 3d., Spire 3d.	A useful guide is sold for 1s.
St. Olave's Church, Hart St.	11–4.	A guide is sold for 1s.
St. Paul's Cathedral.	9–6 April to September, 9–5 October to March. Crypt 6d., Whispering Gallery 6d. Golden Gallery, extra 1s., Ball extra 1s.	There is an excellent guide for 1s. There are official guides inside.
St. Peter's Church, Cornhill.	10–4.	
St. Stephen's Church, Walbrook.	12–5.	
Southwark Cathedral.	7.30–6.	An excellent human guide is the verger, Mr. E. Spice. A good literary one is Rev. T. P. Stevens's 1s. book.
Tate Gallery.	April to September, 10–6; February, March, October, November and December, 10 to dusk; January, 10–4. Sundays 2–6. Winter 2 to dusk.	Official guides at 11 a.m. and 12 noon.
Temple Church.	10.30–1, 2–4, except Saturdays.	The Temple is private property and only residents or attendants at Church are admitted on Sundays.
Tower of London.	May–September, 10–6; October to April, 10-5. White Tower 6d. except Saturdays when it is free. Jewel House 6d. Bloody Tower 6d.	Any ticket admits to Beauchamp Tower. St. Peter's Chapel may be inspected on Monday mornings in company with a Beefeater. A useful guide is sold for 2d.
United Service Museum.	10–5. Admission 1s. Saturdays, after noon 6d.	A guide is sold for 1s.

Name	*Hours*	*Remarks*
Wallace Collection.	10–5. Sundays, 2–5. Closed Christmas Eve. Admission: Tuesdays and Fridays, 6d.; other days free.	(See page 202)
Wesley Museum.	10–1 and 2–4 (closed Sundays). Admission 6d.	There is a 1s. handbook.
Westminster Abbey.	9 or 9.30–5 in March and October. Open till 5.30 in April and September, and in May, June, July and August until 6 p.m. In November, December, January and February it is closed after afternoon service. Fee for ambulatory and chapels, except on Mondays when free, 6d. 6d. for wax-works (3d. Mondays) and 3d. for Undercroft Museum.	Except on Mondays official guides conduct parties round royal tombs at intervals of 15 mins. Guides for the whole of the Abbey (wearing armlets) can be obtained. Charges: four persons up to one hour, 6s.; each additional half-hour, 3s.; 5–10 persons, up to one hour, 10s. each additional half-hour, 5s. There is a short guide by the late Canon Westlake for 1s. 6d. A much more comprehensive one giving details of most of the monuments is sold at the same price.
Westminster Cathedral.	All day. Tower, 6d.; Lift, 1s.; Crypt, 6d.	There is a useful 2d. guide.
Zoological Gardens.	9 to sunset. Admission 1s. On Mondays, Bank Holidays, and other advertised days, 6d. Aquarium, 1s. Children half-price to all. Sundays: Open only to members of the Zoological Society and their friends.	There is a 1s. guide.

BIBLIOGRAPHY

OF the making of books about London there is no end, but there may be of the books worth reading. Many published are "lazy" books. I use an adjective favoured by Mr .Pepys regarding sermons. It is as applicable to the written as the spoken word. The books I have in mind repeat hearsay and commonplace; their authors will give the readers any information not much beyond arm's length of their pens, but cannot be bothered to look up anything that demands labour and patience. I am not so pessimistic as to suggest that, in the spate of London books which for long the press has poured upon us, the following alone are worth perusal. I can say, however, that they have given me pleasure and show signs of a willingness for dust and heat on the part of the writers in the pursuit of knowledge. Where price and publisher are not given the book is out of print.

A History of London, by Rev. W. J. Loftie (2 vols.).

London, by P. H. Ditchfield (Historic Towns, S.P.C.K., 4s.).

A Source Book of London History (Bell, 1s. 6d.).

The History of London, by Sir Walter Besant.

London, by Sir Walter Besant (Chatto & Windus, 7s. 6d.).

London and the Kingdom, by Reginald R. Sharpe, D.C.L. (3 vols.) The author was Records Clerk to the Corporation and this most valuable and reliable work was compiled from the Corporation Records.

Liber Albus or White Book of the City of London.

Wanderings in Medieval London, by Pendrill (Allen & Unwin, 10s. 6d.).

London Life in the Fourteenth Century, by Pendrill (Allen & Unwin, 10s. 6d.).

London, by H. B. Wheatley (Medieval Towns Series, Dent, 5s. 6d.).

London, by George H. Cunningham (Dent 10s. 6d.). A wonderfully comprehensive survey.

The Making of London, by Sir Laurence Gomme.

Stow's *Survey of London,* (Everyman's Library, 2s.).

Unknown London } by W. G. Bell (Bodley
More About Unknown London } Head, 6s. 6d. each).

The Great Plague in London, by W. G. Bell (Bodley Head, 25s.).

The Great Fire of London, by W. G. Bell (Bodley Head, 10/6, abridged edition 3s. 6d.).

Queer Things About London } by C. G. Harper (Cecil
More Queer Things About London } Palmer, 7s. 6d. each).

Quaint Survivals of Old London Customs, by H. E. Popham (Cecil Palmer, 6s.).

Walks in London, by Augustus C. Hare, 2 vols. (Allen & Unwin, 10s.).

Memorable London Houses, by Wilmot Harrison.

The Town, by Leigh Hunt (World's Classics, 2s.).

The Archæology of Middlesex and London, by C. E. Vulliamy (Methuen, 10s. 6d.).

The Times' Book on London, 7s. 6d.

Roman London, by Gordon Home (Benn, 15s.).

London and its Government, by Percy A. Harris, M.A., M.P., L.C.C. (Dent, 7s. 6d.).

London at Home, by M. V. Hughes (Dent, 6s.).

Literary Landmarks, by Laurence Hutton.

Famous Houses and Literary Shrines of London, by A. St. John Adcock (Dent, 5s.).

A Booklover's London, by A. St. John Adcock.

The London of Dickens, by Walter Dexter (Cecil Palmer, 3s. 6d.).

Shakespeare's London, by T. F. Ordish.

The City Churches, by A. E. Daniell. The most completely satisfactory book upon the subject.

Homeland Association, Ltd. (Maiden Lane), publish a Lunch Time Ramble series, price 6d. *Bankside,* by Dr. Martin. *With Charles Dickens in the Borough,* by W. Kent. *Chelsea,* by H. M. Buckingham, *Hampstead* and *The Temple,* both by Prescott Row, and *Cheapside,* by W. G. Morris, are particularly relevant to walks in this guide.

They also publish a most attractive book of views called *Dear Old London* (1s.), and a collection of old pictures entitled *The London of Our Grandfathers* at 3s. 6d.

E. J. Burrows & Co., 43 Kingsway, publish some excellent Borough Guides at 1s.

Messrs. A. & C. Black publish a useful collection of maps of old London at 10s.

The L.C.C. publish booklets on *The Roman Boat, The Site of Tyburn, Prince Henry's Room, The Site of the Theatre at Shoreditch*, and twopenny booklets upon all the houses upon which are affixed memorial tablets. A useful and simple book on architecture which has many references to London is Mr. Allen Walker's *Romance of Architecture* (Philip & Son, 2s. 6d.).

Amongst novels about London may be mentioned Harrison Ainsworth's *Tower of London* (sixteenth century), Scott's *Fortunes of Nigel* (early seventeenth century), Harrison Ainsworth's *Old St. Paul's* (Plague and Fire), Besant's *The Chaplain of the Fleet* (Fleet marriages), Dickens's *Barnaby Rudge*, and *A Tale of Two Cities* (late eighteenth century), and most of Dickens's novels for nineteenth century, particularly *Oliver Twist, David Copperfield, Bleak House*, and *Little Dorrit*, and of his essays, *The Uncommercial Traveller*. Besant's *The Bells of Old St. Paul's* is a tale of Bankside.

For a collection of London's anecdotage, *John o' London's Stories About London* (2 vols.) (Newnes, 2s. each).

P

INDEX TO STREETS AND PLACES SHOWN ON THE MAPS OF MODERN LONDON

The maps are divided into squares, each indicated by numerals along the top and bottom margins and by letters down the side borders. The number following each name in the Index is that of the map in the Atlas; the succeeding letter and numeral that of the square on the map in which the name will be found.

The black figures in Index are text references.

LIST OF ABBREVIATIONS

Ave.: Avenue	Gdns.: Gardens	Sq.: Square
Ch.: Church	Pk.: Park	St.: Street
Cres.: Crescent	Pl.: Place	Sta.: Station
Ct.: Court	Rd.: Road	Ter.: Terrace

Anglesea St., 29, G22
Anhalt Rd., 35, N14
Anley Rd., 32, K9
Annandale Rd., 41, N29
Ansdell St., 30, K12
Anselm Rd., 33, N11
Anthony St., 29, J23
Antrim Grove, 21, D14; Rd., 21, D14
Anwell St., 26, F18
Apollo Theatre, 25, J16
Apostolic Ch., 25, G17
Applegarth Rd., 32, L9
Appold St., 28, H21
Apsley House, 24, K15
Aquinas St., 37, K19
Arbour Sq., 29, H24
Arch St., 38, L20
Archbishop's Pk., the, 37, L18
Archel Rd., 33, M10
Archer St., Lambeth, 37, N17; St., Saint Pancras, 23, E16
Architectural Museum, 36, L17
Argyle Pl., 23, G17; Rd., Hammersmith, 32, L8; Rd., Stepney, 29, G24; Sq., 23, F17; St., 23, F17
Argyll Rd., 33, K11; St., 24, H16
Arkwright Rd., 20, C12
Arlington Gdns., 43, L5; Rd., St. Pancras, 22, E15; Rd., Twickenham, 44, R1; St., Finsbury, 26, F19; St., Westminster, 24, J16
Armada St., 40, N26
Arminger Rd., 32, J8
Armitage Rd., 41, M29
Armourers' Hall, 27, H20
Armoury, 45, Q4
Army Clothing Depot, 36, M16
Arne St., 25, H17
Arnold, Matthew, 67, 88
Arnold Circus, 28, G21
Arnott St., 38, L20
Arnside St., 38, N20
Art School, 32, K8
Arthur St., Chelsea, 34, M13; St., City, 27, J20; St., Holborn, 25, H17; St., Saint Pancras, 26, G18; St., Westminster, 31, K14
Artillery Lane, 28, H21; Row, 36, L16; St., Bermondsey, 39, K21; St., Bethnal Green, 28, G22; Memorial, Royal, 31, K15
Artillerymen's Memorial, 25, K17

Arundel St., 25, J18; Ter., 32, M8
Ascension, Chapel of the, 130; Ascension, Chapel of the, 31, J14
Ash St., 38, L20
Ashburn Gdns., 34, L12; Pl., 34, L12
Ashburnham Grove, 40, O27; Rd., Chelsea, 34, N12; Rd., Greenwich, 40, O27
Ashby St., 26, G19
Ashdown St., 21, C15
Ashford St., 27, F21
Ashley Cottage, 33, L10; Pl., 36, L16
Ashmead Rd., 40, P26
Ashmill St., 22, G13
Ashurst St., 35, N13
Aske St., 27, F21
Aspen Pl., 32, M8
Aspenlea Rd., 32, M9
Assam St., 28, H22
Assembly Passage, 29, H24
Astley St., 39, M22
Astrop Ter., 32, K8
Atterbury St., 36, M17
Attneave St., 26, G18
Atwood Ave., 43, O3
Aubrey Rd., 33, J10; Walk, 33, J11
Auckland St., 37, M18
Audley Rd., 44, Q2
Augustine Rd., 32, L9
Augustus Rd., 32, K8; St., 23, F16
Auriol Rd., 32, L10
Austin Friars, 187; Friars, 27, H20; St., 28, G21
Austral St., 37, L19
Australia House, 25, J18
Australian Ave., 27, H20
Avalon Rd., 34, O11
Ave Maria Lane, 27, H19
Avenue, The, Blackheath, 41, P29; Greenwich Pk., 41, O28; Isleworth, 44, Q1; Richmond, 43, O3; St. Pancras, 22, E15; Rd., Brentford, 42, M1; Rd., Hammersmith, 32, K8; Rd., Hampstead, 22, E13
Averill St., 32, M9
Avery Rd., 24, J15
Avondale Sq., 39, M22
Avonmore Rd., 33, L10
Avonmouth St., 38, L20
Aybrook St., 24, H15
Aylesbury Rd., 38, M20; St., 26, G19
Aylesfort St., 36, M16

Ayliffe St., 38, L20
Aynhoe Rd., 32, L9
Azof St., 41, M29

Baches St., 28, G21
Back Hill, 26, G18; Lane, 40, O27; Ch. Lane, 28, H22
Bacon, Sir Francis, 58, 178
Bacon St., 28, G22
Bagley's Lane, 34, O12
Bagshot St., 39, M21
Baildon St., 40, O26
Baker St., Finsbury, 26, G18; St., Saint Marylebone, 24, G14; St., Stepney, 29, H23; St. Sta., 24, G14
Balaclava Rd., 39, M22
Balcombe St., 22, G14
Balderton St., 24, J15
Baldwin St., 27, G20
Baldwin's Gdns., 26, H18
Baltic St., 27, G20; Shipping Exchange, 28, H21
Bancroft Rd., 29, G24
Bangor Rd., 43, M3
Banim St., 32, L8
Bank, The, 27, H20; of England, 43
Bankruptcy Ct., 25, H18
Bankside, 27, J19; 179
Banner St., 27, G20
Bannerman, H. Campbell, 66
Banning St., 41, M28
Banqueting Hall, Whitehall, 25, K17
Banyard Rd., 39, L23
Barbican, 27, H20
Barclay St., 23, F16
Barclay's Brewery, 38, K20
Barham, Rev. R. H., 34, 153
Bark Pl., 30, J12
Barkston Gdns., 33, L11
Barkworth Rd., 39, M23
Barlow St., 38, M21
Barnabas Ch., 33, K10
Barnardo St., 29, J24
Barnby St., 23, F16
Barnes Cemetery, 45, Q3; Ter., 40, M25
Barnet Grove, 28, G22
Barnham St., 39, K21
Barnsley St., 29, G23
Barons Ct. Rd., 33, M10; Stas., 32, M9
Barrett St., 24, H15
Barron's Pl., 37, K19
Barrow Hill Reservoir, 22, E14; Rd., 22, F13

Bartholomew Close, 27, H19; Lane, 27, H20; Rd., 23, D16; Sq., 27, G20; Villas, 23, D16

Barton St., Fulham, 33, M10; St., Westminster, 37, L17

Basil St., 31, K14

Basinghall St., 27, H20

Bassett St., 21, D15

Bateman's Row, 28, G21

Bath House, 24, K16; St., Bethnal Green and Stepney, 29, H23; St., Finsbury, 27, G20; St., Southwark, 38, L19: Ter., 38, L20

Bathurst St., 30, J13

Batoum Gdns., 32, K9

Battersea Bridge, 34, N13; Bridge Rd., 34, N13; Ch., 34, O13; Pk., 35, N14; Pk. Pier, 35, N14; Pk. Rd., 35, O15; Pk. Rd. Sta., 35, N15; Pk. Sta., 35, N15; Sq., 34, O13; Sq. Pier, 34, O13

Battlebridge Lane, 38, K21

Battle Bridge St., 23, F17

Batty St., 28, H22

Bayer St., 27, G20

Bayham Pl., 23, E16; St., 23, E16

Bayley St., 25, H17

Bayonne Rd., 32, M9

Bayswater, 30, J12; Rd., 30, J12

Bazon St., 37, K18

Beaconsfield, Earl of, 108, 110, 158

Beaconsfield Rd., 41, N29

Beadon Rd., 32, L8

Beagle St., 28, H22

Beak St., 24, J16

Bear Gdns., 27, J20; Lane, 38, K19

Beatrice Rd., Bermondsey, 39, M22; Richmond, 44, Q2

Beauchamp Pl., 35, L14

Beauclerc Rd., 32, K8

Beaufort Gdns., Kensington, 35, L14; Gdns., Lewisham, 40, P26; St., 34, M13

Beaumont, Francis, 57, 58

Beaumont Ave., 44, P2; Cres., 33, M10; Rd., Fulham, 33, M10; Sq., 29, H24; St.,

Saint Marylebone, 24, G15: St., Stepney, 29, G24

Becket, Thomas, 19, 56, 76, 137

Beckway St., 38, M21

Beddome St., 38, M20

Bedford Ave., 25, H17; College for Women, 22, G15; Gdns., 33, K11; Pl., 25, H17; Row, 25, H18; Sq., 25, H17; St., Southwark, 38, M20; St., Stepney, 29, H23; St., Westminster, 25, J17; Villa, 22, G14; Walk, 33, K11

Bedfordbury, 25, J17

Beech St., 27, H20

Beechwood Ave., 43, O3

Belgrave Dock, 36, M16; Mansions, 36, L15; Pl., 35, L15; Rd., 36, L15; Sq., 31, K15; St., Saint Pancras, 23, F17; St., Stepney, 29, H24

Belgravia, 31, K14

Bell Lane, 28, H21; St., Greenwich, 40, N27; St., Saint Marylebone, 31, G13; Wharf Stairs, 29, J24; Yard, 25, H18

Bellot St., 41, M29

Belmont St., 22, D15

Belsize Ave., 20, D13; Cres., 20, C13; Grove, 20, D14; Lane, 20, C13; Pk., 20, D13; Pk. Gdns., 20, D13; Pk. Sta., 20, C14; Sq., 20, D13

Belvedere Rd., 37, K18

Benbow Rd., 32, K8; St., 40, N26

Bendall St., 31, G14

Bennet Pk., 41, P29; St., 24, J16; St., Greenwich, 40, O27; St., Southwark, 37, J19

Bennett, Arnold, 190, 198

Bentinck St., 24, H15

Berkeley Sq., 24, J15; St., 24, J16

Berkley Rd., 22, E14; St., 37, L18

Bermondsey, 39, L21; Leather Market, 38, K21; Sq., 39, L21; St., 39, K21; Wall, 39, K22

Bermuda St., 29, H24

Bernard St., 25, G17

Berner St., 28, H22

Berners Mews, 24, H16; St., 24, H16

Berry St., 27, G19

Berthon St., 40, N26

Bertram St., 21, B16

Berwick St., Westminster, 24, H16; St., Westminster, 36, L16

Berwyn Rd., 45, P4

Beryl Rd., 32, M9

Besant, Sir Walter, 27, 34, 112, 193

Bessborough Gdns., 36, M17; Pl., 36, M16; St., 36, M16

Bethnal Green, 29, G23; Junction, 29, G23; Rd., 28, G22

Betterton St., 25, H17

Betts St., 29, J23

Bevenden St., 27, F21

Bevington St., 39, L22

Bevis Marks, 28, H21

Bicester Rd., 45, P4

Bidborough St., 23, G17

Bifron St., 34, N12

Billingsgate, 187; Market, 28, J21; St., 40, N27

Billiter St., 28, J21

Billson St., 40, M27

Bina Gdns., 34, M12

Bingfield St., 23, E17

Birchin Lane, 28, J21

"Bird in Hand," 20, C13

Bird Sanctuary, Hyde Pk., 31, J13; St., 24, H15

Birdcage Walk, 36, K16

Birkbeck St., 29, G23

Biscay Rd., 32, M9

Bisham Gdns., 21, A15

Bishop King's Rd., 33, L10

Bishop's Rd., 30, H12; Rd. Sta., 30, H13

Bishopsgate, 28, H21

Bittern St., 38, K20

Black Eagle Wharf, 39, K22; Lion Yard, 28, H22

Blackfriars, 23; Bridge, 27; Bridge, 26, J19; Rd., 37, K19; Sta., 26, J19

Blackheath, 41, O28; Ave., 41, O28; Hill, 40, O27; Hill Sta., 40, O27; Rise, 40, P27; Rd., 40, O26; Sta., 41, P29; Ter., 41, O29; Vale, 41, P28

Blacks Rd., 32, L8

Blackwall Lane, 41, M29

Blackwood St., 38, M20

Blake, Admiral, 74

Blake, William, 34, 84, 118

Blake Rd., 34, N11

218

Blakesley St., 29, J23
Blandford Sq., 22, G14; St., 24, H15
Blantyre St., 34, N12
Blendon Row, 38, M20
Blenheim Rd., 43, M4; St., 35, M13
Blind, Institute for, 24, G16
Blisset St., 40, O27
Bloemfontein Ave., 32, J8
Blomfield St., City, 28, H21; St., Paddington, 30, H12
Bloomfield Ter., 35, M15
Bloomsbury, 188; County Ct., 24, G15; Sq., 25, H17; St., 25, H17
Blossom St., 28, G21
Blue Anchor Lane, 39, L22
Blythe Rd., 32, L9; St., 29, G23
Boadicea Statue, 25, K17
Boatmen's Institute, 42, N1
Bolan St., 35, O13
Bolingbroke Rd., Battersea, 34, N13; Rd., Hammersmith, 32, K9
Bollinga St., 36, M17
Bolsover St., 24, G16
Bolton Gdns., 34, M12; Rd., 43, N5; St., 24, J15
Boltons, The, 34, M12
Bolwell St., 37, M18
Bombay St., 39, L23
Bonamy St., 39, M22
Bond St., 26, F18; St. Sta., 24, H15
Boniface St., 37, K18
Bonnington Hotel, 25, H17; Sq., 37, N18
Bonny St., 23, E16
Bonwell St., 29, G24
Boot St., 28, G21
Borough High St., 38, K20; Rd., 38, L19; Sta., 38, K20;
Borrett Rd., 38, M19
Boscastle Rd., 21, B15
Boss St., 39, K21
Bostock St., 29, K23
Boston Pk.Rd.,42, M1; Pl., 22, G14; Rd., 42, M1; St., 22, G14
Boswell, James, 88
Botanic Gdns., Chelsea, 35, N14
Botolph Lane, 28, J21
Boulcott St., 29, J24
Boundary Rd., 32, J9; Row, 37, K19; St., 28, G21
Bourdon St., 24, J15

Bourne's Pl., 34, O13
Bouverie St., 26, J19
Bovingdon Rd., 34, O11
Bow Lane, 27, J20; St., 25, J17
Bowden St., 37, M18
Bower Ave., 41, O28; St., 29, J24
Bowfell Rd., 32, N9
Bowling Green Lane, 26, G19; St.,37, N18; Walk, 28, G21
Boyd St., 28, J22
Boyfield St., 38, K19
Boyle St., 24, J16
Brackenbury Rd., 32, K8
Braddyll St., 41, M28
Bradlaugh, Charles, 200
Bradmore Grove, 32, L8; Pk. Rd., 32. L8
Bradwell St., 29, G24
Brady St., 29, G23
Braemar Rd., 42, M2
Braintree St., 29, G23
Bramber Rd., 33, M10
Bramerton St., 34, M13
Bramham Gdns., 33, M11
Bramshill Gdns., 21, B16
Branch Hill, 20, B12
Brand St., 40, O27
Brandon Rd., 23, D17; St., 38, M20
Branstone Rd., 43, O3
Bray Pl., 35, M14
Bread St., 27, J20
Breakspears Rd., 40, P26
Breams Buildings, 26, H18
Brechin Pl., 34, M12
Brendon St., 31, H14
Brent, River, 42, N1
Brentford, 42, M1; Ait, 42, M2; Bridge, 42, N1; Dock, 42, N2; Sta., 42, M1; Sta. (G.W.R.), 42, N1
Brew House Lane, 29, K23
Brewer St., Westminster, 24, J16; St., Westminster, 36, L16; St. North, 26, F19
Brewery Rd., 23, D17
Brick Lane, 28, G22; St., 24, K15
" Bricklayers' Arms," 38, L21
Bridewell Pl., 26, J19
Bridge Ave., 32, M8; Drive, 35, N14; Pl., 36, L16; Rd., 22, D15; Rd. West, 34, O13; St., Greenwich, 40, N27; St., Rich-

mond, 44, Q1; St., Westminster, 37, K17
Bridgewater House, 24, K16; Sq., 27, G20; St., 23, F16
Bridle Lane, 24, J16
Brig St., 40, M27
Brindley St., 30, G11
" Britannia " P.H., 23, E16
Britannia Gdns., 27, F21; Rd., 34, N11; St.,Saint Pancras,26, F18; St., Shoreditch, 27, F20
British St., 40, M26; Medical Association, 23, G17; Museum, 86, 89; Museum, 25, H17; Museum Ave., 25, G17
Britten St., 35, M13
Broad Sanctuary, 36, K17; St., Holborn, 25, H17; St., Lambeth, 37, L18; St., Stepney, 29, J24; St., Westminster, 24, J16; St. Sta., 28, H21; Walk, Hyde Pk., 31, J14; Walk, Regent's Pk., 22, F15; Walk, The, Kensington Gdns., 30, J12
Broadhurst Gdns. 20, D12
Broadley Ter., 22, G14
Broadwall, 37, K19
Broadway, Deptford, 40, O26; Hammersmith, 32, L9; Westminster, 36, K16
Brodie St., 39, M22
Bromehead St., 29, H23
Bromley St., 29, H24
Brompton, Kensington, 34, M12; Westminster, 30, K13; Cemetery, 33. M11; Rd., 35, L13; Sq., 35, L13
Bromwich Ave., 21, B15
Brontës, 118, 140, 154
Brontë Pl., 38, M20
Bronze St., 40, N26
Brook Green, 32, L9; Green Pl., 32, L9; Green Rd., 32, L9; Lane North, 42, M1; Rd. South, 42, M2; St., Lambeth-Southwark, 37, L19; St., Stepney, 29, J24; St., Westminster, 24, J15
Brookfield Pk., 21, B15
Brooklyn Rd., 32, K8
Brookmill Rd., 40, O26
Brooks Lane, 43, M4

219

Brookshot Rd., 42, M1
Broomfield Rd., 43, N3
Brown St., Saint Marylebone, 31, H14; St., Westminster, 24, J15
Browne, Sir Thomas, **16, 135**
Browning, Robert, **88**
Browning St., 38, M20
Brunswick Ct., 39, K21; Gdns., 33, J11; Pl., St. Marylebone, 24, G15; Pl., Shoreditch, 28, G21; Sq., 25, G17
Brushfield St., 28, H21
Bruton Pl., 24, J15; St., 24, J15
Bryanston Pl., 31, H14; Sq., 31, H14; St., 31, H14
Buccleuch House, 44, R2
Buck Hill Walk, Hyde Pk., 30, J13; St., 23, E16
Buckhurst St., 29, G23
Buckingham Gate, 36, K16; Palace, 77; Palace, 36, K15; Palace Gdn., 36, K15; Palace Rd., 36, L15; St., 25, J17
Buckland Cres., 20, D13
Buckle St., 28, H22
Bucklersbury, 27, J20
Bucknall St., 25, H17
Budge Row, 27, J20
Budge's Walk, Kensington Gdns., 30, J12
" Bull," 23, D17
Bulls Gate, Kensington Gdns., 30, J12
Bulst St., 24, H15
Bulwer St., 32, K9
Bunhill Fields, **188**; Fields, 27, G20; Row, 27, G20
Bunyan, John, **54, 66, 117, 203**
Bunyan Statue, 27, G20
Burdett Rd., 45, P3; St., 37, L18
" Burghers of Calais " Memorial, 37, L17
Burges Grove, 40, O26
Burghley Rd., 21, C16
Burke, Edmund, **88, 169**
Burlington Ave., 43, O3; Gdns., 24, J16; House, 24, J16; Rd., 43, M4
Burman St., 38, L19
Burnaby Cres., 43, M4; Gdns., 43, M4; St., 34, N12
Burne St., 31, H13
Burnett St., 37, M18
Burney St., 40, N27

Buross St., 29, J23
Burr St., 28, K22
Burrell St., 38, K19
Burslem St., 29, J23
Burton St., 23, G17
Burton's Ct., 35, M14
Bury St.,City, 28, H21; St., Holborn, 25, H17; St., Westminster, 24, J16
Busby St., 28, G22
Bush House, 25, J18
Bushwood Rd., 43, N3
Butcher Row, 29, J24
Butchers Row, 40, N26
Bute St., 34, L13
Butler St., 29, G24
Buttesland St., 28, F21
Butts, The, 42, N1
Buxton St., 28, G22
Byng Pl., 25, G17
Byron, Lord, **128, 162, 167, 185**
Byron Statue, 24, K15
Bywater St., 35, M14

Cable St., 29, J23
Cadbury Rd., 39, L22
Cadet Pl., 41, M28
Cadiz St., 29, H24
Cadogan Gdns., 35, L14; Pier, 35, N14; Pl., 35, L14; Sq., 35, L14; St., 35, L14; Ter., 35, L14
Cahir St., 40, M26
Caithness Rd., 32, L9
Cale St., 34, M13
Caletock St., 41, M29
Callow St., 34 M12
Calthorpe St., 25, G18
Calvert Ave., 28, G21; Rd., 41, N29
Camberwell Gate, 38, N20
Cambria St., 34, N12
Cambrian Rd., 44, R3
Cambridge Circus, 25, J17; Gate, 22, G15; House, 22, G15; Pk., 44, R1; Pk. Gdns., 44, R1; Pl., 30, H13; Rd., Bethnal Green-Stepney, 29, G23; Rd., Chiswick, 43, M4; Rd., Hammersmith, 32, L8; Rd., Richmond, 43, N3; Rd., Twickenham, 44, R1; Sq., 31, H13; St., Paddington, 31, H14; St., Saint Pancras, 23, F17; St., Westminster, 36, M15; Ter., Paddington, 31, H13; Ter., St. Pancras, 22, G15; Theatre, 28, H22
Camden Cinema, 23, F16; Gdns., 32, K9; Sq., 23, D17; St.,

Bethnal Green, 29, G23; St., Saint Pancras, 23, E16; New Town, 23, D17; Pk. Rd., 23, D17; Town, 23, E16; Town Stas., 23, E16
Camilla Rd., 39, M23
Camlet St., 28, G21
Camomile St., 28, H21
Campden Grove, 33, K11; Hill, 33, K11; Hill Gdns., 33, J11; Hill Rd., 33, K11; Hill Sq., 33, J10; House, 33, K11; St., 33, J11
Cancel St., 38, M20
Cancer Hospital, 34, M13
Canning Pl., 30, K12
Cannon Pl., 20, B13; Row, 25, K17; St., 27, J20; St. Rd., 29, J23; St. Sta., 27, J20
Canterbury Hall, 37, L18; Pl., 37, L18
Cantlowes Rd., 23, D17
Canvey St., 38, K19
Capella Pl., 40, O20
Captain Cook Statue, 25, K17
Caradox St., 41, M28
Carburton St., 24, G16
Cardigan Rd., 44, R2; St., 37, M18
Cardington St., 23, F16
Cardross St., 32, L8
Carey St. Westminster, 25, H18; St., Westminster, 36, L16
Carkers Lane, 21, C16
Carlingford Rd., 20, C13
Carlisle Pl., 36, L16; St., Lambeth, 37, L18; St., Saint Marylebone, 31, G13
Carlos Pl., 24, J15
Carlow St., 23, F16
Carlton Clubs, 36, K16; Gdns., 36, K16; Hotel, 25, J17, House Ter., 36, K16; Rd., Barnes, 45, P4; Rd., St. Pancras, 21, C15; Rd., Stepney, 29, G24; Sq., 29, G24; St.,Saint Pancras, 21, C15; Theatre, 25, J16
Carlyle, Thomas, **88, 91, 134**
Carlyle House, **134, 208**; Pier, 34, N13; Sq., 34, M13; Statue, 35, N13
Carnaby St., 24, J16
Caroline St., Holborn, 25, H17; St., Stepney, 29, J24; St., Westminster, 35, L15

Carriage Rd., The, 31, K14
Carron Wharf, 28, K22
Carter Lane, 27, J19; St., 38, M19
Carthew Rd., 32, L8; Villas, 32, K8
Carting Lane, 25, J18
Cartwright Gdns., 23, G17; St., 28, J22
Carville Hall, 42, M2
Casson St., 28, H22
Castelnau, 32, M8
Castle Lane, 36, L16; Rd., 23, D15; St., City, 27, H20; St., Finsbury, 28, G21; St., Southwark, 38, K20; St., Westminster, 25, J17
Castlegate, 45, P3
Castletown Rd., 33, M10
Catesby St., 38, M20
Cathay St., 39, K23
Cathcart Rd., 34, M12; St., 21, D15
Cathedral St., 38, K20
Catherine Grove, 40, O26; St., Lambeth, 37, M18; St., Shoreditch, 27, G20; St., Westminster, 25, J18; St., Westminster, 36, L16
Cathnor Rd., 32, K8
Catlin St., 39, M22
Cattle Market, 23, D17
Causton St., 36, M17
Cavalry War Memorial, 24, K15
Cavendish Pl., 24; H16; Rd., 43, N5; Sq., 24, H15
Caversham St., 35, M14
Cavour St., 38, M19
Caxton, William, 72, 160
Caxton Hall, 36, L16; Rd., 32, K9; St., 36, L16
Cayton St., 27, G20
Cedar Rd., 34, N11; Ter., 44, P2
Cedars, The, 45, P5; Rd., 43, M5
Cenotaph, 25, K17
Centaur St., 37, L18
Central Criminal Ct., 27, H19; St., 27, F20
Cephas St:, 29, G24
Ceylon Rd., 32, L9
Chadwell St., 26, F19
Chadwick St., 36, L16
Chalcot Cres., 22, E14; Gdns., 21, D14
Chalk Farm Rd., 22, D15; Farm Stas., 22, D15
Challis Rd., 42, M1

Challoner St., 33, M10
Chalton St., 23, F17
Chamber St., 28, J22
Chamberlain, Joseph, 66, 105
Chamberlain St., 22, E14
Chambord St., 28, G22
Chancellor's Rd., 32, M8
Chancery Lane, 26, H18; Lane Sta., 25, H18
Chandler St., 29, K23
ChandosSt.,SaintMarylebone, 24, H15; St., Westminster, 25, J17
Chapel Alley, 42, M2; Pl., 38, K20; St., Chelsea, 34, N12; St., City, 27, H20; St., Hammersmith, 32, L8; St., Holborn, 25, G18; St., Saint Marylebone,31,H13; St.,SaintPancras,23, F17; St., Westminster, 31, K15
Chapelhouse St., 40, M27
Chapter Rd., 38, M19; St., 36, M16
Charing Cross, 25, J17; Pier, 25, J18; Rd., 25, H17; Stas., 25, J17
Charlbert St., 22, F13
Charles Sq., 28, G21; St., Holborn, 26, H19; St., Kensington,32,J9; St., Saint Pancras, 23, F16; St., Southwark, 38, K19; St., Stepney, 29, H24; St., Westminster, 24, J15; St., Westminster, 25, J16
Charleston St., 38, M20
Charlesworth St., 23, D18
Charleville Rd., 33, M10
Charlotte St., Camberwell, 39, M21; St., Saint Pancras, 24, H16; St.,Shoreditch, 28, G21
Charlton Rd., 41, O28; St., 24, G16
Charlwood St., 36, M16
Charrington St., 23, F16
Charterhouse, 189, 208; 27, G19; Sq., 27, H19; St., 26, H19; Chatham Pl., 38, L20; St., 38, L20
Chatterton, Thomas, 88
Chaucer, Geoffrey, 22, 54, 106, 170

Cheapside, v, 135; 27, H20
Chelmsford St., 32, M9
Chelsea, 81, 133–5, 208; 35, M13; and Fulham Sta. (L.M.S.), 34, N12; Barracks, 35, M15; Basin, 34, O12; Bridge, 35, M15; Bridge Rd., 35, M15; Creek, 34, O12; Embankment, 35, N14; Football Ground, 34, N11; Hospital, 35, M14; Infirmary, 34, M13; Old Ch., 34, N13; Pk. Gdns., 34, M13; P.L. Institute, 35, M13; Reach, 35, N14
Cheltenham Ter., 35, M14
Chenies St., 25, H16
Cheniston Gdns., 33, L11
Chepstow Pl., 30, H11
Chequer St., 27, G20
Cherry Gdn. Pier, 39, K23; Gdn. St., 39, K23
Chertsey Rd., 43, M4
Chesham Pl., 35, L15; St., 35, L14
"Cheshire Cheese" Tavern, 5, 162
Cheshire St., 29, G22
Chesson Rd., 33, M10
Chester Gate, 22, G15; Mews, Lambeth, 37, M18; Mews, St. Pancras, 23, F15; Pl., Paddington, 31, H13; Pl., St. Pancras, 22, F15; Rd., St. Marylebone, 22, F15; Rd., St. Pancras, 21, B15; Sq., 35, L15; St., Lambeth, 37, M18; St., Westminster, 36, L15; Ter., St. Pancras, 22, F15; Ter., Westminster, 35, L15
Chesterfield House, 24, J15; Walk, 41, O28
Chesterford Gdns., 20, C12
Chetwynd Rd., 21, B16
Cheval Pl., 35, L13
Chevening Rd., 41, M29
Cheyne Ct., 35, N14; Gdns., 35, N14; Row, 35, N13; Walk, 34, N13
Chichester Rd., 30, H12; St., 36, M16
Chicksand St., 28, H22
Children's Hospital, Great Ormond St., 25, G18
Childs St., 33, L11

Chilton Rd., 45, P3; St., 28, G22
Chilvers St., 41, M29
Chilworth St., 30, H12
China Walk, 37, L18
Chisholm Rd., 44, R2
Chislehurst Rd., 44, Q2
Chiswell St., 27, H20
Chiswick Rd., 43, L5; High Rd., 43, M3; Pk. Cricket Ground, 43, N4
Chitty St., 24, G16
Cholmondeley Walk, 44, Q1
Christ Ch., Barnes, 45, Q4; Hampstead, 20, B13; Lambeth, 37, L18; Paddington, 30, J12; Poplar, 40, M27; Richmond, 44, P2; Rd., Barnes, 45, Q4; Rd., Hampstead, 20, B13; St., 41, M28
Christchurch St., 35, M14
Christian St., 29, J22; Scientist Ch., 33, J11
Christopher St., 28, G21
Church House, 36, L17; Lane, Battersea, 34, O13; Lane, Hammersmith, 32, M8; Lane, Hampstead, 20, C13; Lane, Stepney, 28, H22; Path, 33, N10; Pl., Paddington, 30, H13; Rd., Battersea, 34, O13; Rd., Hammersmith, 32, L8; Rd., Hampstead, 21, C14; Rd., Richmond, 44, Q2; Row, Bethnal Green, 28, G22; Row, Hampstead, 20, C12; St., Bethnal Green-Shoreditch, 28, G21; St., Chelsea, 34, M13; St., Deptford, 40, O26; St., Greenwich, 40, N27; St., Kensington, 33, K11; St., Saint Marylebone, 30, H13; Walk, Hampstead, 20, C13; Way, 23, F17
Churches: All Hallows, Barking, 43; St. Andrew Undershaft, 81, 146, 210; St. Bartholomew - the - Great, 11, 81, 120–5, 210; St. Botolph's, Aldersgate, 35; St. Bride's, 26, 160; St. Clement Dane's, 11, 17, 168, 210; St. Dunstan's - in - the -

East, 11, 26; St. Dunstan's - in - the - West, 165; St. Ethelburga's, 25; St. Etheldreda's, 11, 118, 210; St. Giles', Cripplegate, 25, 199, 210; St. Helen's, 25, 141-6, 211; St. Katherine Cree, 16, 25, 81, 147, 211; St. Margaret's, 71-4, 211; St. Martin's - in - the -Fields, 81; St. Mary, Aldermanbury, 36, 37; St. Mary-le-Bow, 20, 137, 211; St. Olave's, 148, 211; St. Peter's, 140, 141, 211; St. Sepulchre's, 126; St. Stephen's, Walbrook, 138, 211
Churchill Rd., 21, B16
Churchyard Row, 38, L19
Churton St., 36, M16
Circus, The, 40, O27; St., Greenwich, 40, O27; St., Saint Marylebone, 31, H14
Cirencester St., 30, G12
"Ciro's," 25, J17
City Rd., 27, G20; and Guilds Institute, 34, L13; Temple, 26, H19
Claims and Records Office, 43, N4
Clandon St., 40, O26
Clanricarde Gdns., 30, J11
Clare Market, 25, H18
Claremont St., 40, N27
Clarence Gdns., 23, G16; Gate, 22, G14; Gate Gdns., 22, G14; House, 45, P5; Rd., Chiswick, 43, M3; Rd., Richmond, 44, O3; Rd., St. Pancras, 23, D16; St., 44, P2; Ter., 22, G14
Clarendon Pl., 31, J13; Sq., 23, F16; St., Paddington, 30, G11; St., Saint Pancras, 23, F16; St., Westminster, 36, M15
Clareville Grove, 34, L12; St., 34, L12
Clarges St., 24, J15
Clark St., 29, H23
Clavering Ave., 32, M8
Claverton St., 36, M16
Claxton Grove, 32, M9
Clay St., 31, H14
Claybrook Rd., 32, M9
Clayton Cres., 42, L1; St., Lambeth, 37, N18
Cleaver St., 37, M18

Clement's Inn, 25, H18; Lane, 28, J21; Rd., 39, L23
Cleopatra's Needle, 190; 25, J18
Clerkenwell, 23, 190; Close, 26, G19; Green, 26, G19; Rd., 26, G18
Clevedon Rd., 44, R1
Cleveland Gdns., 30, H12; Row, 24, K16; Sq., 30, H12; St., SaintMarylebone, 24, G16; St., Stepney, 29, G23
Clifden Rd., 42, M1
Clifford Ave., 45, P4; St., 24, J16
Clifford's Inn, 132, 166; 26, H18
Clifton St., Hammersmith, 32, J9; St., Shoreditch, 28, H21; Villas, 23, D17
Clink St., 27, J20
Clipstone St., 24, G16
Clitheroe Rd., 42, L1
Cliveden Pl., 35, L14
Cloth Fair, 27, H19; St., 27, H20
Clyde St., Deptford, 40, N25; St., Kensington, 34, N12
Coal Exchange, 28, J21
Cobden Statue, 23, F16
Cobourg Rd., 39, M21
Coburg St., 23, G16
Cock Lane, 125; 26, H19
"Cock" Tavern, 5
Cockspur St., 25, J17
"Cogers," 190
Coin St., 37, J18
Colchester St., 36, M16
Cold Bath Sq., 26, G18; St., 40, O26
Cole St., 38, K20
Coleherne Ct., 34, M12; Rd., 33, M11
Coleman St., City, 27, H20; St., Stepney, 29, K23
Coleraine Rd., 41, N29
Coleridge, S. T., 203
Colet Ct., 32, L9; Gdns., 32, L9
Coliseum, 25, J17
College Cres., 20, D13; Hill, 27, J20; Lane, St. Pancras, 21, C15; Pl., Chelsea, 35, M14; Pl., St. Pancras, 23, E16; Rd., 22, D14; St., 37, K18
Collerston Rd., 41, M29
Collett Rd., 39, L22
Collingham Gdns., 34, L12; Pl., 34, L12; Rd., 34, L12

222

Collingwood St., Bethnal Green, 29, G23; St., Southwark, 37, K19
Collinson St., 38, K20
Colnbrook St., 37, L19
Colomb St., 41, M29
Colonial Office, 25, K17
Columbia Rd., 28, G22
Colville Pl., 25, H16
Colwith Rd., 32, M9
Colwyn St., 37, L18
Combedale Rd., 41, M29
Comeragh Rd., 33, M10
Comet St., 40, O26
Commercial Rd., 37, J18; Rd. East, 29, H23; St., 28, G21; Sale Rooms, 28, J21
Commerell St., 41, M29
Compayne Gdns., 20, D12
Compton Cres., 43, M5; St., Finsbury, 27, G19; St., Saint Pancras, 23, G17
Comus Pl., 38, M21
Conduit St., 24, J16; Wood, 45, R3
Congreve St., 38, M21
Coningham Rd., 32, K8
Conington Rd., 40, P27
Conley St., 41, M29
Connaught Ave., 45, P4; Pl., 31, J14; Sq., 31, H14; St., 31, H14
Constantine Rd., 21, C14
Constitution Hill, 24, K15
Content St., 38, M20
Convent of the Good Shepherd, 32, M8
Coopers Rd., 39, M22; Row, 28, J21
Copley St., 29, H24
Copperas St., 40, N26
Copthall Ave., 27, H20
Coptic St., 25, H17
Coral St., 37, K19
Coram St., 25, G17
Corfield St., 29, G23
Cork St., 24, J16
Corn Exchange, 28, J21
Cornbury St., 38, M21
Cornhill, 139; 27, J20
Cornick St., 39, L23
Cornwall Gdns., 34, L12; House, 37, K18; Rd., Bethnal Green and Stepney, 29, G23; Rd., Lambeth, 37, K18; St., Fulham, 34, N12; St., Stepney, 29, J23; St., Westminster, 36, M16; Ter., 24, G14
Coronet Theatre, 33, J11

Corporation Island, 44, Q1; Row, 26, G19
Cosway St., 31, G14
Cottesmore Gdns., 34, L12
Cottington St., 37, M19
Coulson St., 35, M14
Coulter Rd., 32, L8
County Hall, 190, 208; Ter. St., 38, L20
Court Theatre, 35, L14
Courtenay St., 37, M18
Courtfield Garage, 34, L12; Rd., 34, L12
Courthope Rd., 21, C15
Coval Rd., 45, P4
Covent Gdn. Market, 25, J17; Gdn. Theatre, 25, J17
Coventry St., Bethnal Green, 29, G23; St., Westminster, 25, J16
Coverdale Rd., 32, K8
Coverley Fields, 28, H22
Cowan St., 38, N21
Cowcross St., 26, H19
Cowley St., 29, J23
Cowper, William, 74, 88, 110, 157
Cowper St., 28, G21
Crampton St., 38, M19
Cranbourn St., 25, J17
Cranbrook Rd., Deptford, 40, O26
Crane Ct., 26, H19; St., 41, N28
Cranley Gdns., 34, M12; Pl., 34, L13
Craven Hill, 30, J12; Rd., 30, H13; St., Shoreditch, 27, G20; St., Westminster, 25, J17; Ter., 30, J12
Crawford Pl., 31, H14; St., 31, H14
Credon Rd., 39, M23
Creed Lane, 27, J19; Pl., 41, N28
Creek Bridge, 40, N27; Pl., 32, L8; Rd., 40, N26; St., 40, O26
Crellin St., 29, J23
Cremorne Rd., 34, N12
Crescent, Vine St., 28, J21
Cresford Rd., 34, O11
Cressage Rd., 42, M2
Cresswell Gdns., 34, M12; Pl., 34, M12; Rd., 44, R1
Cressy Pl., 29, H24; Rd., 21, C14
Crimea Monument, 25, J16
Crimscott St., 39, L21
Crinan St., 23, F17
Crisp Rd., 32, M8
Crispin St., 28, H21
Criterion, 25, J16
Croftdown Rd., 21, B15

Crofton Ter., 44, P3
Crogsland Rd., 22, D15
Crome Rd., 41, M29
Cromer St., 26, G17
Cromwell, Oliver, 80
Cromwell Crescent, 33, L11; Grove, 32, K9; Lane, 43, P5; Pl., 34, L13; Rd., 34, L12
Crondall St., 27, F21
Crooked Billet Yard, 27, F21
Croom's Hill, 41, O28
Crosby Hall, 34, N13
Crosby Row, 38, K20
Cross St., Finsbury, 27, H20; St., Holborn, 26, H19
Crossfield Rd., 20, D13; St., 40, N26
Crown Pl., 21, D16; Ter., 45, P3
"Crown and Garter," 41, M28
Crowndale Rd., 23, F16
Crozier St., 37, L18
Crucifix Lane, 39, K21
Crutched Friars, 28, J21
Cubitt St., 26, G18
Cudworth St., 29, G23
Culford Gdns., 35, M14
Culross St., 24, J14
Culworth St., 22, F14
Cumberland Cres., 33, L10; Market, 23, F16; Rd., 43, N3; St., 36, M15; Ter., 22, F15
Curlew St., 39, K22
Cursitor St., 26, H18
Curtain Rd., 28, G21
Curzon St., 24, J15
Custance St., 27, F20
Custom House and Quay, 28, J21
Cuthbert St., 30, H13
Cutler St., 28, H21
Cygnet St., 28, G22
Cyrus St., 27, G19
Czar St., 40, N26

Dacre St., Westminster, 36, L16
Dalby St., 21, D15
Dale Rd., St. Pancras, 21, C15
Daleham Gdns., 20, D13; Mews, 20, D13
Dalling Rd., 32, L8
Daly's Theatre, 25, J17
Dancer Rd., 45, P3
Dane St., 25, H18
Daniel St., 28, G22
Dante St., 38, L19
Danvers St., 34, N13
Darell Rd., 45, P3
Darling Row, 29, H23
Dartmoor St., 33, J11

223

Dartmouth Grove, 40, O27; Hill, 40, O27; Pk., 21, B15; Pk. Ave., 21, B16; Pk. Hill, 21, B16; Pk. Rd., 21, B15; Pl., 40, O27; Row, 40, O27; St., 36, K17
Dartnell Rd., 39, N21
Dartrey Rd., 34, N12
Darwin, Charles, 66
Darwin Rd., 42, L1; St., 38, M20
Date St., 38, M20
Daventry St., 31, G14
Davies St., 24, J15
Deacon St., 38, L20
Deaf & Dumb Asylum, 38, L21
Dean Farrar St., 36, L17
Dean Hill, 45, P4; St., City, 26, H19; St., Stepney, 29, J23; St., Westminster, 25, H16
Deanery St., 24, J15
Dean's Buildings, 38, M20; Lane, 43, M4; Yard, Westminster Abbey, 36, L17
Decima St., 38, L21
Defoe, Daniel, 16, 25, 88, 95, 139, 140, 203
Defoe Ave., 43, N4
Delamere Cres., 30, G12; Ter., 30, G12
Delancey St., 22, E15
De Laune St., 37, M19
Delhi St., 23, E17
Dell, The, Hyde Pk., 31, K14
Dellow St., 29, J23
Deloraine St., 40, O26
Delorme St., 32, N9
Delverton Rd., 38, M19
Dempsey St., 29, H24
Denbigh Gdns., 45, Q3
Denbigh Pl., 36, M16; St., 36, M16
Denham St., 41, M29
Denman St., 38, K20
Denmark St., 25, H17; St., Stepney, 29, J23
Denning Rd., 20, B13
Dennis St., 23, E17
Denny St., 37, M18
Denton Rd., 44, R1
Denyer St., 35, L14
Deptford Bridge, 40, O26; Creek, 40, N26; Ferry St., 40, M26; Green, 40, N26; New Town, 40, P26; Sta., 40, N26; Town Hall, 40, O26
Derby Lodge, 45, P4; Rd., 45, P4; St., Saint Pancras, 26, F17; St., Westminster, 24, K15

Derbyshire St., 28, G22
Derwent St., 41, M28
De Vere Gdns., 30, K12
Deverell St., 38, L20
Devonport Rd., 32, K8; St., Paddington, 30, H13; St., Stepney, 29, J24
Devonshire Gdns., 43, N4; House, 44, R2; Pl., 24, G15; Rd., 40, O27; Sq., 28, H21; St., Holborn, 25, H18; St., Saint Marylebone, 24, G15; St., Stepney, 29, G23; Ter., 30, H12
Dewhurst Rd., 32, K9
Diamond Ter., 40, O27
Diana Pl., 23, G16
Dickens, Charles, v, 3, 6, 19, 21, 28, 42, 43, 52, 62, 88, 89, 90, 96, 100, 107, 127, 131, 136, 140, 155, 156, 165, 167, 169, 173, 177, 181, 182, 183, 185, 186, 187, 197, 201, 202, 203; House, 89, 90, 208
Dickenson St., 21, D15
Dieppe St., 33, M10
Digby St., 29, G24
Diggon St., 29, H24
Dilke St., 35, M14
Dingley Pl., 27, G20; Rd., 27, G20
Dinsdale Rd., 41, N29
Disbrowe Rd., 33, N10
Distillery Lane, 32, M8; Rd., 42, M2
Distin St., 37, M18
Dock Head, 39, K22; St., 28, J22
Doctor St., 38, M20
Doddington Grove, 38, M19
Dodson St., 37, L19
Dogs' Cemetery, Hyde Pk., 30, J13
Dolben St., 38, K19
Dominion Theatre, 25, H17
Domville Grove, 39, M21
Donne, John, 31, 118, 165, 172
Doon St., 37, K18
Doris St., 37, M18
Dorrington St., 26, H18
Dorset Lane, 32, N9; Sq., 22, G14; St., City, 26, J19; St., Saint Marylebone, 31, H14
Dorville Rd., 32, L8
Doughty Mews, 25, G18; St., 25, G18
Douglas House, 44, S1; Pl., 30, H12; St., 36, M16

Douro Pl., 30, K12
Dover House (Scottish office), 25, K17; Rd., 41, O28; St., 24, J16
Doverton St., 29, G23
Dowgate, 27, J20
Down Pl., 32, L8; St., 24, K15; St. Sta., 24, K15
Downe Ter., 44, R2
Downing St., 25, K17
Downshire Cres., 21, C14; Hill, 20, C13
Doynton St., 21, A16
Draper St., 38, L19
Drapper's Rd., 39, L22
Draycott Ave., 35, L14; Pl., 35, L14
Drayton Gdns., 34, M12
Drewton St., 29, J24
Drummond Cres., 23, F17; Rd., 39, L23; St., 23, G16
Drury Lane, 25, H17; Theatre, 25, J18
Dryden, John, v, 137, 157, 168
Drysdale Rd., 40, O27; St., 28, G21
Ducal St., 28, G22
Duchess St., 24, H15
Duckett St., 29, H24
Dudley House, 24, J15; Rd., 43, O3; St., 30, H13
Dufferin St., 27, G20
Duke St., Bermondsey, 38, K20; St., Lambeth, 37, J19; St., Richmond, 44, Q2; St., Saint Marylebone, 24, H15; St., Stepney, 28, H21; St., Westminster, 24, J16
Duke of York's Monument, 36, K16; Theatre, 25, J17
Duke's Lane, 33, K11; Rd., 23, G17
Dunboyne St., 21, C14
Duncan Rd., 44, P2
Duncannon St., 25, J17
Dundee St., 29, K23
Dundonald St., 36, M17
Dunk St., 28, H22
Dunkirk St., 27, J20
Dunlop Pl., 39, L22
Dunsany Rd., 32, L9
Dunstable Rd., 44, Q2
Durham Row, 29, H24; St., 37, M18; Ter., 30, H11; Villas, 33, K11
Durran Lodge, 45, Q4
Durward St., 29, H23
Dutch Ch., 28, H21
Dutton St., 40, O27
Duval St., 28, H21
Dynevor Rd., 44, Q2
Dyott St., 25, H17

"Eagle, The," 27, F20
Eagle St., 25, H18
Ealing Rd., 42, M2; Rd. South, 42, M2
Eamont St., 22, F14
Ear St., 38, L19
Eardley Cres., 33, M11
Earl Rd., 39, M21; St., 28, H21
Earl's Ct., 33, L11; Ct. Exhibition, 33, M10; Ct. Gdns., 33, L11; Ct. Rd., 33, L11; Ct. Sq., 33, M11; Ct. Stas., 33, L11
Earlswood St., 41, M28
East Dock, 29, J23; Drive, 35, N15; Lane, 39, K22; Lane Stairs, 39, K22; Rd., 27, G20; St., Holborn, 25, G18; St., Islington, 23, E17; St., Saint Marylebone, 24, G14; St., Southwark, 38, M20; Arbour St., 29, H24; Ferry Rd., 40, M27; Heath, Hampstead Heath, 20, B13; Heath Rd., 20, B13; London Hospital, 29, J24; Mount St., 29, H23; Sheen Gdns., 45, P5; Silex St., 38, K19; Smithfield, 28, J22
Eastbourne Rd., 42, M1; Ter., 30, H12
Eastcastle St., 24, H16
Eastcheap, 28, J21
Eastney St., 41, N28
Easton St., 26, G18
Eaton Pl., 35, L15; Sq., 35, L15; St., 37, K19; Ter., 35, L15
Ebenezer Row, 37, M19
Ebor St., 28, G21
Ebury Sq., 35, M15; St., 35, L15; Bridge Rd., 35, M15
Eccleston Sq., 36, L15; St., 35, L15
Eden St., 23, G16
Edge St., 33, J11
Edgware Rd., 30, H13; Rd. Sta., 31, H13
Edith Grove, 34, N12; Rd., 32, L9; Row, 34, N12; Villas, 33, M10
Edmund Pl., 27, H20
Edward St., Deptford, 40, N25; St., Saint Pancras, 23, F16; St., Shoreditch, 27, F20; St., Southwark, 38, K19; St., Stepney, 29, G24
Edwardes Sq., 33, L11
Effingham St., 36, M15
Egbert St., 22, E15

Egerton Cres., 35, L13; Gdns., 35. L13; Rd., 40, O26; Ter., 35, L13
Elaine Grove, 21, C15
Elcho St., 35, N13
Eldon Rd., Hampstead, 20, C13; Rd., Kensington, 34, L12; St., 28, H21
Elephant Rd., 38, L19
"Elephant and Castle" 38, L19
Elephant and Castle Sta., 38, L20
Elim St., 38, L21
Eliot, George, 61, 80, 88, 118, 134, 170, 203
Eliot Hill, 40, P27; Pk., 40, P27; Pl., 41, P28; Vale, 41, P28
Elizabeth Cottages, 43, O3; St., Southwark, 38, N20; St., Westminster, 35, L15
Ellen St., 28, J22
Ellerdale Rd., 20, C13
Ellerker Gdns., 44, Q2
Ellerslie Rd., 32, J8
Elliots Row, 38, L19
Ellis St., 35, L14
Elm Gdns., 32, L9; Grove, 32, L9; Pl., 34, M13; Rd., Barnes, 45, P5; Rd., St. Pancras, 23, E17; Row, 20, B13; St., 25, G18; Pk. Gdns., 34, M13; Pk. Rd., 34, M13; Wood Rd., 43, M5
Elmdale St., 32, M9
Elms, The, 20, A13
Elric St., 32, M9
Elsham Rd., 32, K9
Elsted St., 38, M20
Elswick Rd., 40, P26
Elsworthy Rd., 22, E14
Eltham St., 38, M20
Elvaston Pl., 34, L12
Elverson Rd., 40, P26
Ely Pl., Holborn, 26, H19; Pl., Southwark, 37, L19; Ter., 29, G24
Elystan St., 35, L13
Emba St., 39, K22
Emerald St., 25, G18
Emerson, R. W., 205
Emerson St., 27, J20
Emperors Gate, 34, L12
Empire, Deptford, 40, O26; Music Hall, 29, G24; Theatre, 25, J17
Endell St., 25, H17
Endsleigh Gdns., 23, G17; St., 23, G17
Enfield Rd., 42, M1
England's Lane, 21, D14
Enid St., 39, L22

Ennerdale Rd., 43, O3
Ennismore Gdns., 31, K13
Entick St., 29, G23
Erasmus St., 36, M17
Ernest St., Bermondsey, 39, L21; St., Stepney, 29, G24
Eros Statue, 25, J17
Errol St., 27, G20
Erskine Rd., 22, E14
Esher St., Lambeth, 37, M18; St., Westminster, 36, L17
Esmeralda Rd., 39, M22
Essex St., Stepney, 29, G24; St., Strand, 25, J18; Villas, 33, K11
Estelle Rd., 21, C15
Ethelburga St., 35, O13
Ethelden Rd., 32, J8
Ethelm St., 37, K19
Ethelred St., 37, L18
Eton Ave., 22, D13; Pl., 22, D14; Rd., 22, D14; St., Richmond, 44, Q2; St., Saint Pancras, 22, E15; Villas, 22, D14
Euston Hotel, 23, G16; Rd., 23, G16; Sq., 23, G16; Sq. Sta., 23, G16; Sta. (L.M.S.), 23, F16; Sta. (U.R.), 23, G16; St., 23, G16
Evangelist Rd., 21, C16
Evelyn, John, 25, 120
Evelyn Gdns., Kensington, 34, M12; Gdns., Richmond, 44, P2; Rd., 44, P2; St., 40, N25
Everard St., 28, J22
Everington St., 32, M9
Eversfield Rd., 43, O3
Eversholt St., 23, F16
Ewer St., 38, K19
Exeter St., Saint Marylebone, 22, G13; St., Westminster, 25, J17
Exhibition Rd., 34, L13
Exmouth St., Finsbury, 26, G18; St., Saint Pancras, 23, G16; St., Stepney, 29, H24
Exon St., 38, M21
Exton St., 37, K18
Eye Hospital, 37, L19
Eyre St. Hill, 26, G18

Fair St., Bermondsey, 39, K21; St., Stepney, 29, H24
Fairbank St., 27, F20
Fairclough St., 28, J22
Fairholme Rd., 33, M10
Fairless, Michael, 135
Falcon St., 27, H20
Falkirk St., 27, F21

Falmouth Rd., 38, L20
Fane Pl., 33, M10; St., 33, M10
Fann St., 27, G20
Fanny Rd., 32, M8
Fanshaw St., 27, F21
Fanum House, A.A. Headquarters, 25, J17
Faraday St., 38, M21
Farm St., 24, J15
Farmer St., 33, J11
Farncombe St., 39, L22
Faroe Rd., 32, L9
Farringdon Ave., 26, H19; Rd., 26, G18
Farringdon St., 26, H19; and High Holborn Sta., 26, H19
Fashion St., 28, H22
Fauconberg Rd., 43, M5
Faunce St., 37, M19
Fawcett St., 34, M12
Featherstone St., 27, G20
Felix St., 37, K18
Fellbrigg St., 29, G23
Fellows Rd., 22, D14
Fenchurch St., 28, J21; St. Sta., 28, J21
Fendall St., 39, L21
Fenner Rd., 39, L23
Ferdinand Pl., 22, D15; St., 22, D15
Fernshaw Rd., 34, N12
Ferrand St., 38, L21
Ferry Lane, Brentford, 42, N2; Lane, Kew, 43, M3; Rd., 40, M26; St., 40, M27
Fetter Lane, 95; Lane, 26, H19
Ffinch St., 40, N26
Field Rd., Fulham, 32, M9; Rd., Isleworth, 42, N1; St., 26, F18
Fieldgate St., 28, H22
Fielding, Henry, 27
Fife Rd., 45, Q4
Finborough Rd., 33, M11
Finch St., 28, H22
Finchley Rd., 20, C12; Rd. Sta. (Met.), 20, D12; Rd. and Frognal Sta. (L.M.S.), 20, C12
Finck St., 37, K18
Fingal St., 41, M29
Finnis St., 29, G23
Finsbury Circus, 27, H20; Market, 28, G21; Pavement, 27, H20; Sq., 28, G21; St., 27, H20
Fire, Great, 25; Brigade Headquarters, 38, K19
Firs, The, 45, P5
First St., 35, L14

Fish Ponds, 42, L2; St. Hill, 28, J21
Fisher St., 25, H18
Fishmongers' Hall, 27, J20
Fitzalan St., 37, L18
Fitzgeorge Ave., 33, L10
Fitzjames Ave., 33, L10
Fitzjohn's Ave., 20, C13
Fitzroy Pk., 21, A14; Pl., 23, G16; Rd., 22, E15; Sq., 24, G16; St., 24, G16
Fitzstephen, 19
Fitzwilliam Ave., 42, O3
Flask Walk, 20, B13
Flaxman Ter., 23, G17
Fleet St., 18, 160-7; 26, H18
Fleming Rd., 38, N19
Fletcher, John, 57, 58
Flint St., 38, M20
Flinton St., 39, M21
Flockton St., 39, K22
Flood St., 35, M14
Flora Gdns., 32, L8
Floral St., 25, J17
Florence Grove, 40, O26; Rd., 40, O25; St., 40, O25
Florida St., 28, G22
Flower and Dean St., 28, H22
Foley St., 24, H16
Ford Sq., 29, H23
Fordham St., 29, H22
Fore St., 27, H20
Foreign Cattle Market, 40, M26; Office, 25, K17
Forfar Rd., 35, O15
Fort Rd., 39, L21
Fort St., 28, H21
Fortess Rd., 21, C16
Fortune Theatre, 25, J17
Foster Lane, 27, H20
Fouberts Pl., 24, J16
Foulis Ter., 34, M13
Fountain Dock, 39, K22; The, Hyde Pk., 30, J13
Fournier St., 28, H22
Fox, George, 203
Fox Ct., 26, H18
Foyle Rd., 41, N29
Frances St., 34, O13
Francis St., Chelsea, 35, M14; St., Holborn, 25, G16; St., Westminster, 36, L16
Frank St., Lambeth, 37, M18
Frankham St., 40, O26
Franklin, Benjamin, 205
Franklin St., Saint Pancras, 21, C15

Franklin's Row, 35, M14
Frazier St., 37, K18
Frean St., 39, L22
Freda St., 39, L22
Frederick Rd., 38, M19; St., Saint Marylebone, 22, F14; St., Saint Pancras, 26, G18
Free Trade Wharf, 29, J24
Freeman, J. R., 20
Freemantle St., 38, M21
Freemasons' Hall, 25, H18
Friar St., 38, K19
Friars Lane, 44, Q1; Stile Rd., 44, R2
Friday St., 27, J20
Friendly St., 40, O26
"Friends'" House, 23, G17
Frith St., 25, H17
Frithville Gdn., 32, J8
Frobisher St., 41, N28
Froebel Institute, 32, M9
Frognal, Hampstead, 20, C12; Gdns., 20, C12; Lane, 20, C12; Way, 20, C12
Froude, J. A., 87
Fruit Market, 43, M3
Fulbourne St., 29, H23
Fulford St., 39, K23
Fulham Cemetery, 43, O4; Pl., 30, G12; Rd., 34, N12; Palace Rd., 32, M9; Poor Law Institute, 32, M9
Fuller St., 28, G22
Furnival St., 26, H18

Gables, The, 45, Q4
Gaiety Theatre, 25, J18
Gainsborough Gdns., 20, B13; Rd., 43, O3
Gainsford St., 39, K21
Galena Rd., 32, L8
Galley Wall Rd., 39, M23
Galsworthy, John, 5, 168, 193
Galway St., 27, G20
Gambia St., 38, K19
Garden Row, 45, P3; Row, Greenwich, 40, O27; Row, Southwark, 37, L19; St., 29, H24
Gardnor Rd., 20, B13
Garrett St., 27, G20
Garrick, David, 169, 187
Garrick St., 25, J17
Garvan Rd., 32, M9
Garway Rd., 30, H11
Gaskell, Mrs., 118, 135
Gastien Rd., 32, M9
Gate St., 25, H18
226

Gateforth St., 22, G13
Gatliff Rd., 35, M15
Gay, John, 61, 192
Gayton Crescent, 20, B13; Rd., 20, C13
Gaza St., 37, M19
Gedling St., 39, L22
Gee St., Finsbury, 27, G20; St., Saint Pancras, 23, F16
General Post Office, 27, H19
G.P.O. Sta., 27, H19
Generating Sta. and Depot (C.L.R.), 32, J9
Geological Museum, 24, J16
"George Inn," 181
George Rd., 42, M2; Row, 39, K22; Sq., 27, F21; St., Richmond, 44, Q2; St., SaintMarylebone,31, H14; St., Saint Pancras, 23, G16; St., Westminster, 24, J16
"George and Vulture" Tavern, 6
George's Stairs, 28, K22
Georgiana St., 23, E16
Gerald Rd., 35, L15
Gerrard St., 25, J17
Gerridge St., 37, L19
Gertrude St., 34, N12
Gibbon, Edward, 88, 156
Gibraltar Walk, 28, G22
Gibson St., 41, M28
Giffin St., 40, O26
Gilbert Rd., 37, M19; St., 24, J15
Gillies St., 21, C15
Gillingham St., 36, L16
Gilston Rd., 34, M12
Giltspur St., 27, H19
Girdlers' Rd., 32, L9
Gissing, George, 86
Gladstone, W. E., 2, 60, 73, 81
Gladstone Memorial, 25, J18; St., Battersea, 35, O15; St., Southwark, 37, L19
Glamis Rd., 29, J24
Glamorgan St., 36, M16
Glasgow Ter., 36, M16
Glasshouse Fields, 29, J24; St., Lambeth, 37, M17; St., Stepney, 28, J22; St., Westminster, 24, J16
Glazbury Rd., 33, L10
Glebe Pl., 34, M13; Rd., 39, L23
Gledhow Gdns., 34, M12
Gledstanes Rd., 33, M10
Glen St., 23, F16
Glenforth St., 41, M29

Glengall Rd., 39, M22
Glenhurst Ave., 21, C15; Rd., 42, M1
Glenilla Rd., 20, D13
Glenioch Rd., 20, D14
Glenister Rd., 41, M29
Glenmore Rd., 20, D14
Glenthorpe Rd., 32, L8
Glenville Grove, 40, O25
Gliddon Rd., 32, L10
Globe Rd., 29, G24; St., 38, L20
Gloucester Cres., 22, E15; Gdns., 30, H12; Gate, Regent's Pk., 22, F15; House, 24, K15; Pl., Greenwich, 40, N27; Pl., St. Marylebone,24,H14; Rd., Kensington, 34, L12;Rd., Richmond, 43, N3; Rd., St. Pancras, 22, E15; Rd. Sta., 34, L12; Sq., 30, H13; St., Finsbury, 26, G19; St., Westminster, 36, M16; Ter., 30, H12; Walk, 33, K11
Glover's Island, 44, R1
Glynn St., Lambeth, 37, M18
Goda St., 37, M18
Godfrey St., 35, M14
Goding St., 37, M17
Godolphin Rd., 32, K8
Gold St., 29, H24
Golden Lane, 27, G20; Sq., 24, J16
Golders Hill Pk., 20, A12
Goldhawk Rd., 32, K8
Goldington Cres., 23, F16; St., 23, F17
Goldsmith, Oliver, 96, 97, 99, 125, 167, 169
Goldsmiths' Hall, 27, H20
Goode St., 26, G19
Goodge St., 24, H16
Goodmans Fields, 28, H22
Goods Way, 23, F17
Goodson Rd., 33, M10
Gordon Hospital, 36, L16; House Rd., 21, C15; Pl., 33, K11; Rd., Chiswick, 43, M4; Rd., Richmond, 43, O3; Sq., 23, G17; St., 23, G17
Gore St., 34, L12
Gorleston St., 33, L10
Gosfield St., 24, H16
Gospel Oak Grove, 21, C15; Oak Sta., 21, C15
Gossett St., 28, G22
Goswell Rd., 26, F19
Gouch St., 25, G18

Gough Sq., 26, H19
Goulston St., 28, H22
Government India Stores, 37, K18; Offices, 25, K17
Gower, John, 54
Gower Mews, 25, H17; Pl., 25, G16; St., 25, G16
Gowers Walk, 28, H22
Gracechurch St., 28, J21
Grafton Cres., 23, D15; Pl., 23, G17; Rd., St. Pancras, 21, D15; St., Saint Pancras, 24, G16; St., Stepney, 29, G24; St., Westminster, 24, J16; Ter., 21, C15
Graham St., 35, M15
Granby St., Bethnal Green, 28, G22; St., Saint Pancras, 23, F16
Grand Ave., 28, J21; Junction Rd., 30, H13; Junction Water Works, 33, K11; Junction Water Works, Brentford, 42, M2
Granfield St., 34, O13
Grange, The, 39, L21; Rd., Bermondsey, 39, L21; Rd., Chiswick, 43, M4; Rd., St. Pancras, 22, E15; Walk, 39, L21
Granville Pk., 40, P27; Pl., 31, H15; Sq., 26, G18
Gratton Rd., 32, L9
Gravel Lane, 38, K19
Gray, Thomas, 88, 139
Gray St., Lambeth-Southwark, 37, K19; St., Saint Marylebone, 24, H15
Gray's Inn, 25, H18; Inn Rd., 25, G18
Great Alie St., 28, J22; Barlow St., 24, H15; Bland St., 38, L20; Castle St., 24, H16; Central St., 31, G14; Chapel St., Westminster, 36, L16; Chapel St., Westminster, 25, H16; Charlotte St., 37, K19; Chart St., 28, G21; Church Lane, 32, M9; College St., Saint Pancras, 23, E16; College St., Westminster,37,L17; Cross Ave., 41, O28; Cumberland Pl., 31, H14; Dover St., 38, L20; Earl St., 25,

Hardwick St., 26, G19
Hardy, Thomas, 30, 61, 86, 109, 158, 187, 199
Hardy Rd., 41, N29
Hare St., 28, G22
Harewood Ave., 22, G14
Harley St., Battersea, 35, O13; St., Saint Marylebone, 24, G15
Harleyford Rd., 37, M18
Harmood St., 22, D15
Harmsworth St., 37, M19
Harper St., 38, L20
Harpur St., 25, H18
Harrington Gdns., 34, L12; Rd., 34, L13; Sq., 23, F16; St., 23, F16
Harrison St., 26, G17
Harrow Rd., 30, H12; St., 31, G14
Harrowby St., 31, H14
Hart St., Holborn, 25, H17; St., Westminster, 24, J15
Hartington Rd., 43, N4
Hartland Rd., 22, D15
Harton St., 40, O26
Harvard, John, 54, 206
Harvard Hill, 43, M4; Rd., 43, M4
Harwood Rd., 34, N11; Ter., 34, O11
Hasker St., 35, L14
Hastings, Warren, 157
Hastings St., 23, G17
Hastwick St., 27, G20
Hatfield St., Finsbury, 27, G20; St., Southwark, 37, J19
Hatherly Grove, 30, H12; Rd., 43, O3
Hatton Gdn., 26, H19; Wall, 26, G19
Havelock Rd., 32, K9; St., 23, E18
Haverfield Gdns., 43, N3
Havering St., 29, J24
Haverstock Hill, 20, C14; Rd., 21, C15
Hawkins St., 29, H23
Hawley Cres., 23, E16; Rd., 23, D16; St., 22, D15
Hawthorne, Nathaniel, 202
Hay Hill, 24, J16
Haydon Sq., 28, J22; St., 28, J22
Hayles St., 37, L19
Haymarket, 25, J16; Theatre, 25, J17
Hayne St., 27, H19
Hay's Mews, 24, J15
Hayward's Pl., 26, G19
Hazlitt, William, 118, 185, 201

Hazlitt Rd., 32, L10
Healey St., 23, D15
Hearn Rd., 43, M3; St., 28, G21
Heath, The, Hampstead, 20, B13; Brow, 20, B12; Lodge, 20, A12; St., Hampstead, 20, B13; St., Stepney, 29, H24
Heathcote St., 26, G18
Heathfield Gdns., 43, M5
Heathhurst Rd., 20, C13
Hebron Rd., 32, L8
Heckford St., 29, J24
Helmet Row, 27, G20
Hemming St., 29, G23
Heneage St., 28, H22
Henrietta St., Saint Marylebone, 24, H15; St., Westminster, 25, J17
Henry St., Finsbury, 27, G20; St., Holborn, 25, G18; St., Lambeth, 37, M18; St., Saint Marylebone, 22, F13
Henshaw St., 38, L20
Hepham St., 37, K18
Heralds' College, 27, J19
Herbert Cres., 35, L14; St., 21, D15
Herbrand St., 25, G17
Hercules Rd., 37, L18
Hereford Gdns., 24, J14; Rd., 30, H11; Sq., 34, L12; St., Bethnal Green, 28, G22; St., Saint Marylebone, 31, G14
Heriot Pl., 21, C15
Hermitage Basin, 28, K22; Entrance and Wharf, 28, K22; Rd., 44, Q2
Heron Ct., 44, Q1
Herrick St., 36, M17
Hertford St., 24, K15
Hessel St., 29, J23
Heston St., 40, O26
Hetley Rd., 32, K8
Heygate St., 38, M20
Hibernia Wharf, 27, J20
Hickey's Grove, 45, Q3
Hide Pl., 36, M16
High St., Aldgate, 28, H21; St., Borough, 38, K20; St., Brentford, 42, N1; St., Camden Town, 23, E16; St., Chiswick, 43, L4; St., Deptford, 40, N26; St., Hampstead, 20, C13; St., Holborn, 25,

H17; St., Kensington, 30, K12; St., Lambeth, 37, L18; St., Saint Marylebone, 24, G15; St., Shoreditch, 28, G21; St., Stepney, 29, H24; Holborn, 25, H18; Pk. Ave., 43, O3; Pk Rd., 43, O3
Highbridge, 41, M28
Highgate Cemetery, 21, A15; Ponds, 21, A14; Rd., 21, B15; Rd. Sta., 21, C16
Highmore Rd., 41, N29
Hilbeach Gdns., 33, M11
Hill Rise, 44, Q2; St., Finsbury, 28, G21; St., Richmond, 44, Q1; St., Southwark, 38, K19; St., Westminster, 24, J15; St., Westminster, 31, K14
Hillsleigh Rd., 33, J11
Hillway, 21, A15
Hilmer St., 33, M10
Hinchcliffe St., 37, L17
Hippodrome, 25, J17
H.M. Office of Works, 25, K17
Hobart Pl., 36, L15
Hobury St., 34, N12
Hofland Rd., 32, K9
Hogarth, William, 83, 84, 124, 173
Hogarth Rd., 33, L11
Holbein Pl., 35, M14
Holborn, 26, H18; Circus, 26, H19; Empire, 25, H18; Restaurant, 25, H17; Union, 27, F20; Viaduct, 26, H19; Viaduct Sta., 26, H19
Holcombe St., 32, L8
Holford Rd., 20, B13; Sq., 26, F18; St., 29, G24
Holland House, 33, K10; Lane, 33, K11; Pk., 33, K10; Rd., 32, K9; St., Kensington, 33, K11; St., Southwark, 27, J19; Walk, 33, K10; Pk. Ave., 32, K9; Pk. Gdns., 33, K10; Pk. Mews, 33, K10; Pk. Rd., 33, L10; Pk. Sta., 33, J10; Villas Rd., 33, K10
Holles St., 24, H15
Holly Hill, 20, B12; Lodge, 45, R4; Lodge Gdns., 21, A15; Village, 21, B15; Walk, 20, C12

229

Hollywood Rd., 34, M12

Holme, The, 22, G14

Homes Rd., 21, D15

Holmesdale Rd., 43, O3

Holy Trinity Ch., Barnes, 32, M8; Trinity Ch., Kensington, 30, K12; Trinity Ch., Westminster, 36, M17

Holyoake, G. J., 101, 203

Holyoake Rd., 37, L19

Holywell Lane, 28, G21; Row, 28, G21

Home Office, 25, K17

Homeopathic Hospital, 25, G17

Homer St., 31, H14

Hood, Thomas, 204

Hood Ave., 45, Q5

Hooper St., 28, J22

Horace St., 31, H14

Horn Lane, 41, M29

Horney Lane, 39, L21

"Horns, The," 37, M18

Hornton St., 33, K11

"Horse," 23, D17

Horse Ferry, 40, M27; Guards, 25, K17; Guards Ave., 25, K17

Horseferry Rd., Greenwich, 40, N27; Rd., Westminster, 36, L16

Horselydown Lane, 39, K21; New Stairs, 39, K22; Old Stairs, 28, K22

Hortensia Rd., 34, N12

Hosier Lane, 26, H19; St., 40, O26

Hoskins St., 41, M28

Hotspur St., 37, M18

Houblon Rd., 44, Q2

Houghton Pl., 23, F16

Houndsditch, 28, H21

Houses of Parliament, 37, L17

Howard, John, 30

Howell, James, 3, 13

Howick Pl., 36, L16

Howie St., 35, N13

Howitt Rd., 20, D14

Howland St., 24, G16

Howley Pl., Lambeth, 37, K18; Pl., Paddington, 30, G12

Hoxton Ch., 27, F21; House Schools, 27, F21; Market, 28, G21; Sq., 28, G21

Hudson Memorial, 31, J13

Hugh St., 36, M15

Hughes Fields, 40, N26

Humane Society's House, 31, J13

Humber Rd., 41, N29

Hume Rd., 32, J9

Hungerford Bridge, 25, K18; St., 29, J23

Hunt, Leigh, 135, 176, 185, 204

Hunter St., 23, G17

Huntley St., 25, G16

Hunton St., 28, G22

Huntsworth Mews, 22, G14

Hurlbutt Pl., 38, M19

Hurley Rd., 37, M19

Hutton Rd., 37, M18

Huxley, T. H., 204

Huxton St., 27, F21

Hyde Lane, 34, O13; Pk., 128; Pk., 31, J14; Rd., 44, Q2; St., 40, N26; Vale, 40, O27; Pk. Barracks, 31, K14; Pk. Corner, 31, K15; Pk. Gdns., 30, J13; Pk. Gate, 30, K12; Pk. Pl., 31, J14; Pk. Sq., 31, H13; Pk. St., 31, J13; Pk. Ter., 31, J13

Ibsen, Henrik, 18

Idol Lane, 28, J21

Idonia St., 40, N26

Iffley Rd., 32, L8

Ifield Rd., 34, M12

Ilchester Pl., 33, K10

Iliffe St., 38, M19

Imperial College, 30, K12; Cottages, 34, O12; Institute, 34, L13; Institute Rd., 34, L13; Rd., 34, O12; War Museum, 34, L13

India Office, 25, K17; St., 28, J21

Ingersoll Rd., 32, J8

Ingestre Pl., 24, J16; Rd., 21, C16

Ingleside Grove, 41, N29

Inkerman Rd., 21, D16; Ter., 33, L11

Inner Circle, Regent's Pk., 22, F15

Inverness Gdns., 33, K11; Gate, Kensington Gdns., 30, J12; Ter., 30, H12

Inville Rd., 38, M20

Irongate Wharf, 28, K22

Iron Gate Wharf Rd., 30, H13

Ironmonger Lane, 27, H20; Row, 27, G20; St., 27, G20

Ironmongers' Hall, 28, J21

Island Gdns., 40, M27

Islington Infirmary, 21, A16

Italian Hospital, 25, G18

Iverna Ct., 33, K11; Gdns., 33, K11

Ivimey St., 28, G22

Ixworth Pl., 35, M13

Jack Straw's Castle, 20, B12

Jacob St., 39, K22

Jamaica Rd., 39, L22; St., 29, H24

James Pl., 29, J24; St., Bethnal Green, 29, G24; St., Paddington, 30, H12; St., Saint Marylebone, 24, H15; St., Saint Pancras, 22, E15; St., Westminster, 25, J17; James II Statue, 25, K17

Jamieson St., 33, J11

Jane St., 29, J23

Janeway St., 39, L22

Jeffrey Pl., 23, E16

Jeffrey's St., 23, D16

Jenner Statue, 30, J13

Jermyn St., 36, J16

Jersey St., 29, G23

Jervis Rd., 33, N10

Jewin Cres., 27, H20; St., 27, H20

Jewry St., 28, J21

Jews' School, 28, H21; Synagogue, City, 28, H21; Synagogue, St. Marylebone, 31, H14; Synagogue, Paddington, 30, J11

Joan of Arc, 56, 76

Jocelyn Rd., 44, P2

Jockey's Fields, 25, H18

Jodrell Laboratory, 43, N3

John St., City, 28, J21; St., Fulham, 32, M9; St., Greenwich, 40, P26; St., Holborn, 25, G18; St., Westminster, 24, J15; St., Westminster, 25, J17; Carpenter St., 26, J19; Penn St., 40, O27

Johnson, Dr. Samuel, 19, 83, 88, 90–2, 125, 132, 163, 164, 167, 168, 180, 183, 190, 194

Johnson House, 90–92, 209; St., Poplar, 40, M27; St., Saint Pancras, 23, F16; St., Stepney, 29, J24; St., Westminster, 37, L17

Jonathan St., 37, M18

Jonson, Ben, **88, 95, 199**
Jubilee Pl., 35, M14; Hospital, 33, M11; St., 29, H23
Judd St., 23, F17
Juer St., 35, N13
Julia St., 21, C15
Juniper St., 29, J23

Kassala Rd., 35, O14
Kean St., 25, H18
Keats, John, **81, 118, 132, 137, 156, 185, 188, 192, 194, 200**
Keats Grove, 20, C13; Memorial, 20, C14
Kell St., 38, L19
Kelly St., 23, D16
Kelso Pl., 34, L12
Kemble St., 25, H18
Kemplay Rd., 20, C13
Kempsford Gdns., 33, M11; Rd., 37, M19
Kempshed Rd., 39, N21
Kempson Rd., 34, N11
Kemsing Rd., 41, M29
Ken Wood, 20, A14
Kenley Rd., 42, M2
Kennington, 37, N17; Grove, 37, M18; Oval, 37, N18; Pk., 37, N19; Pk. Pl., 37, M19; Pk. Rd., 37, M19; Rd., 37, L18; Sta., 37, M19
Kensington, 30, L12; Cemetery, 43, L3; Ct., 30, K12; Ct. Mansions, 30, K12; Ct. Pl., 30, K12; Cres., 33, L10; Gdns., 30, J12; Gdns. Sq., 30, H12; Gate, 30, K12; Gore, 30, K13; Palace, **129, 209**; Palace, 30, K12; Palace Gdns., 30, K12; Pl., 33, J11; Rd., 30, K12; Sq., 30, K12; (Addison Rd.) Sta., 33, L10; (High St.) Sta., 33, K11; Union Infirmary, 33, L11
Kent Rd., 43, N3; Ter., 22, G14
Kentish Town, 21, C15; Town Rd., 21, D16; Town Sta., 21, C16; Town West Sta., 21, D15
Kenton St., 25, G17
Kenway Rd., 33, L11
Keppel St., 25, H17
Kerbela St., 28, G22
Kew, **195, 209**; 43, N3; Bridge, 43, M3; Bridge Rd., 43, M3;

Bridge Sta., 43, M3; Foot Rd., 44, P2; Gdns. Rd., 43, N3; Gdns. Sta., 43, O3; Green, 43, N3; Observatory, 44, P1; Palace, 42, N2; Rd., 43, N3
Keyworth St., 38, L19
Kidney Wood, 44, R3
Kildare Gdns., 30, H11; Ter., 30, H11
Kilmarsh Rd., 32, L8
King Sq., 27, G20; St., Chelsea, 35, M13; St., City, 26, H19; St., City, 27, H20; St., Hammersmith, 32, L8; St., Kensington, 30, K11; St., Richmond, 44, Q1; St., Saint Marylebone, 31, H14; St., Saint Pancras, 23, E16; St., Stepney, 28, J22; St., Westminster, 24, K16; St., Westminster, 25, J17; and Queen St., 38, M20; Charles St., 25, K17; David Lane, 29, J23; Edward St., City, 27, H19; Edward St., Lambeth, 37, L18; Edward St., Stepney, 28, H22; Edward VII Memorial Pk., 29, J24; George St., 40, O27; Henry's Rd., 22, E14; James St., 38, K19; James's Stairs, 29, K24; John St., 29, H24; William St., City, 27, J20; William St., Greenwich, 40, N27; William St., Westminster, 25, J17
Kinghorn St., 27, H19
Kinglake St., 39, M21
Kingly St., 24, J16
King's Rd., Chelsea, 34, N12; Rd., Richmond, 44, Q2; Rd., St. Pancras, 23, E16; Arms Gate, Kensington Gdns., 30, K12; College, 25, J18; College Rd., 22, D13; Cross, 23, F17; Cross Rd., 26, F18; Cross Sta. (L.N.E. Ry.), 23, F17; Farm Lodge, 45, P3
Kingsford St., 21, C14
Kingsley, Charles, **67**
Kingston House, Gate, Hyde Pk., 30, K13; St., 38, M20
Kingstown St., 22, E15

Kingsway, Barnes, 45, P4; Holborn, 25, H18
Kingswear Rd., 21, B15
Kinnerton St., 31, K14
Kinnoul Rd., 33, M10
Kintore St., 39, L21
Kipling St., 38, K20
Kirby St., Bermondsey, 38, K21; St., Holborn, 26, H19
Knaresborough Pl., 33, L11
Knightrider St., 27, J20
Knightsbridge, 31, K14
Knott St., 40, N26
Knox St., 31, G14
Kossuth St., 41, M28

Lacks Dock, 37, M17
Ladbrooke Rd., 33, J10
Lady Somerset Rd., 21, C16
Lafone St., 39, K22
Lake St., 29, J24
Lamb, Charles, **30, 45, 83, 97, 100, 118, 123, 164, 178, 185, 204, 205**
Lamb Lane, 40, N27; St., 28, H21
Lambert Ave., 45, P4
Lambeth, 37, L18; Bridge, 37, L17; Church and Palace, 80, 196; Lower Marsh, 37, K18; North Sta., 37, L18; Palace, 37, L18; Palace Rd., 37, L18; Poor Law Institute, 37, L19; Reach, 37, M17; Rd., 37, L18; Sq., 37, K18; St., 28, J22; Walk, 37, L18
Lamble St., 21, C15
Lambolle Pl., 20, D14; Rd., 20, D14
Lambs Conduit St., 25, G18; Passage, 27, G20
Lamerton St., 40, N26
Lamington St., 32, L8
Lamont Rd., 34, N12
Lancaster Gate, 30, J12; Gate Sta., 30, J13; Gate Ter., 30, J13; Pk., 44, Q2; Pl., Hampstead, 20, D13; Pl., Westminster, 25, J18; Rd., 20, D13; St., Paddington, 30, J13; St., Southwark, 38, K19; Walk, Kensington Gdns., 30, J12
Lancing St., 23, F17
Lanfranc St., 37, L18
Langbourne Ave., 21, B15

Q   231

Langdale St., 29, J23
Langham Pl., 24, H16; St., 24, H10
Langland Gdns., 20, C12
Langley Lane, 37, N17; Rd., 32, M8
Langsdale Rd., 40, O27
Langton St., Chelsea, 34, N12; St., Finsbury, 27, G20
Lansdowne House, 24, J15; Pl., 38, L20
Lant St., 38, K20
Larcom St., 38, M20
Larkfield Rd., 44, Q2
Larnaca St., 39, L21
Larnach Rd., 32, N9
Lassel St., 41, M28
Lateward Rd., 42, M1
Latimer St., 29, H24
Laud, Archbishop, 44, 56
Laud St., 37, M18
Launceston Pl., 34, L12
Lavington St., 38, K19
Law St., 38, L20
Lawford Rd., Chiswick, 43, N5; Rd., St. Pancras, 23, D16
Lawn Cres., 43, O3; Rd., 21, C14
Lawrence St., 34, N13
Lawson St., 38, L20
Layard Rd., 39, L23
Laystall St., 26, G18
Layton Rd., 42, M1
Lead St., 40, M27
Leadenhall Market, 28, J21; St., 28, J21
Leake St., 37, K18
Leamore St., 32, L8
Leather Lane, 26, H19
Leatherdale St., 29, G24
Leathwell Rd., 40, P27
Leg of Mutton Pond, Hampstead, 20, A12; Richmond, 45, S3
Leicester Sq., 25, J17
Leigh St., 23, G17
Leighton House, 33, L10
Leinster Ave., 45, P4; Gdns., 30, H12; Pl., 30, H12; Sq., 30, H11; St., 30, H12
Leman St., 28, H22; St. Sta., 28, J22
Lena Gdns., 32, K9
Lennox Gdns., 35, L14
Lenthorp Rd., 41, M29
Leonard St., 28, G21
Leopold St., 37, M18
Leroy St., 38, L21
Lethbridge Rd., 40, O27
Lever St., 27, G20
Leverett St., 35, L14
Leverton St., 21, C16

Lewisham High Rd., 40, O25; Hill, 40, P27; Junction, 40, P27; Rd., Lewisham, 40, P27; Rd., St. Pancras, 21, B15; Rd. Sta., 40, P26
Lewiston St., 22, D15
Lexham Gdns., 33, L11
Lexington St., 24, J16
Leybourne Pk., 43, N3; Rd., 22, D15
Leyden St., 28, H21
Lichfield Rd., 43, O3
Lillie Rd., 33, M11
Lillington St., 36, M16
Lime Grove, 32, K8; St., 28, J21
Limerston St., 34, M12
Lincoln, Abraham, 206
Lincoln St., 35, M14
Lincoln's Inn, 62, 171-7; 25, H18
Linden Gdns., 30, J11
Lindfield Gdns., 20, C12
Lindley St., 29, H23
Lindsell St., 40, O27
Linsey St., 39, L22
Lintaine Grove, 33, N10
Linton St., 31, G13
"Lion," 23, D17
Lion Gate, 42, P3; St., 38, L20
Lionel Rd., 43, M3
Lisbon St., 29, H23
Lisburne Rd., 21, C14
Lisle St., 25, J17
Lismore Circus, 21, C15; Rd., 21, C14
Lissenden Gdns., 21, B15
Lisson Grove, 22, G14; St., 31, H14
Lister Institute, 35, M15
Litcham St., 21, D15
Lithos Rd., 20, D12
Little Albany St., 23, G16; Alie St., 28, H22; Britain, 27, H19; Cadogan Pl., 35, L14; Dorrit's Playground, 38, K20; Earl St., 25, H17; Green, 44, Q2; James St., 25, G18; New St., 26, H19; Newport St., 25, J17; Pulteney St., 25, J16; Saffron Hill, 26, G19; Saint Andrew St., 25, H17; Saint James's St., 24, K16; Sutton, 43, M5; Sutton St., 27, G19; Thames St., 40, N27; Theatre, 25, J17; York St., 28, G21

Liverpool St., City, 28, H21; St., Saint Pancras, 26, F17; St., Southwark, 38, M20; St. Stas., 28, H21
Livingstone, David, 66
Lloyd Sq., 26, F18; St., 26, F18
Lloyds Pl., Kensington, 35, L14; Pl., Lewisham, 41, P28; Row, 26, F19
Loampit Hill, 40, P26
Lochaline St., 32, M9
Lock Sq., 38, M20
Lockwood Rd., 39, L23
Lodge Rd., 22, F13
Loftie St., 39, K22
Loftus Rd., 32, J8
Logan Pl., 33, L11
Lollard St., 37, L18
Loman St., 38, K19
Lombard Lane, 26, J19; St., 27, J20
London and Continental Wharf, 28, K22; Bridge, 14, 27; Bridge, 27, J20; Bridge Sta., 38, K21; County Hall, 37, K18; Docks, 29, J23; Hospital, 29, H23; Museum, 78-83, 209; Museum, 24, K16; Rd., Isleworth, 42, N1; Rd., Southwark, 38, L19; Stone, 197; St., Bethnal Green, 29, G23; St., Greenwich, 40, N27; St., Paddington, 30, H13; University, 34, L13; Wall, 27, H20
Long Acre, 25, J17; Lane, Bermondsey, 38, K20; Lane, City, 27, H19; Water, The, 30, J13
Longcroft Rd., 39, N21
Longfellow, H. W., 206
Longford St., 23, G16
Longley St., 39, M22
Longnor Rd., 29, G24
Longridge Rd., 33, L11
Loraine Rd., 43, N4
Lorne Rd., 44, Q2
Lorrimore Sq., 38, N19
Lothbury, 27, H20
Lots Rd., 34, N12
Loughborough St., 37, M18
Louisa St., 29, H24
Love Lane, Lewisham, 41, P28; Lane, Southwark, 27, J19; Lane, Stepney, 29, J24
Lovegrove St., 39, M22
Lover's Walk, 41, N28
Lowell, J. R., 69

Lower Belgrave St., 35, L15; Berkeley St., 24, H15; Chapman St., 29, J23; Charles St., 26, G19; Grosvenor Pl., 36, L15; Kennington Lane, 37, M19; Mall, 32, M8; Mortlake Rd., 44, P2; Richmond Rd., 45, P3; Sloane St., 35, M14; Ter., 20, B12; Thames St., 28, J21; William St., 22, F13

Lowndes Pl., 35, L15; Sq., 31, K14; St., 35, L14

Lucan Pl., 35, L13

Lucas St., Deptford, 40, O26; St., Stepney, 29, J24

Lucey Rd., 39, L22

Ludgate Circus, 26, H19; Hill, 26, H19; Hill Sta., 26, J19

Luke St., 28, G21

Lulot St., 21, A16

Luna St., 34, N13

Lupus St., 36, M16

Lurgan Ave., 32, M9

Lurline Gdns., 35, O15

Luton Pl., 40, O27

Luxembourg Gdns., 32, L9

Lyall St., 35, L15

Lyceum Theatre, 25, J18

Lyme St., 23, E16

Lyndhurst Gdns., 20, C13; Rd., 20, C13

Lynton Rd., 39, M22

Lyric Theatre, Hammersmith, 32, L8; Theatre, Westminster, 25, J16

Lytton, Bulwer, 62

Macaulay, Lord, 163, 192

Macclesfield St., 27, F20

Macduff Rd., 35, O15

Macfarlane Rd., 32, J8

Mackeson Rd., 21, C14

Macklin St., 25, H17

Macks Rd., 39, L22

Maclise Rd., 33, L10

Macquarie Way, 40, M27

Madame Tussaud's, 197, 209

Maddox St., 24, J16

Madron St., 39, M21

Magazine, Hyde Pk., 30, J13

Magdala Rd., 21, A16

Magdalen St., 39, K21

Magnetic Observatory, 41, N28

Magnolia Rd., 43, M4

Maguire St., 39, K22

Maiden Lane, 25, J17

Maidenstone Hill, 40, O27

Maitland Pk. Rd., 21, D15; Pk. Villas, 20, D14

Major Rd., 39, L22

Makepeace Ave., 21, A15

Malden Cres., 23, D15; Rd., 21, C15

Malet St., 25, G17

Mall, Kensington, 33, J11; The, 36, K16; Rd., 32, M8

Mallord St., 34, M13

Mallow St., 27, G20

Malmsey Pl., 37, M18

Malt St., 39, N22

Malta St., 27, G19

Maltby St., 39, L21

Manchester Rd., 40, M27; Sq., 24, H15; St., Saint Marylebone, 24, H15; St., Saint Pancras, 26, F17

Manciple St., 38, L20

Mandeville Pl., 24, H15

Mann St., 38, M20

Manor Grove, 45, P3; Pk., Richmond, 45, P3; Pl., Paddington, 30, H13; Pl., Southwark, 38, M19; Rd., 45, P3; St., 35, M14

Manresa Rd., 34, M13

Mansell St., 28, J22

Mansfield Rd., 21, C15; St., Saint Marylebone, 24, H15; St., Southwark, 38, L19

Mansford St., 29, G23

Mansion House, 42; 27, J20; House Sta., 27, J20

Manson Pl., 34, L13

Mape St., 29, G23

Maple St., 24, G16

Marble Arch, 31, J14; Arch Sta., 31, H14

Marblehill Pk., 24, R1; River Path, 44, S1

Marchmont Rd., 44, Q3; St., 23, G17

Marcia Rd., 39, M21

Marco Rd., 32, L8

Mardale St., 32, K8

Marden Rd., 39, L23

Maresfield Gdns., 20, D13

Margaret St., Finsbury, 26, G18; St., Saint Marylebone, 24, H16

Margaretta Ter., 35, M13

Margravine Gdns., 32, M9; Rd., 32, M9

Maria Ter., 29, H24

Marigold St., 39, K23

Marine St., 39, L22

Marines' Memorial, 25, K17

Mark Lane, 28, J21; Lane Sta., 28, J21; St., 28, G21

Market Lane, 42, N1; Rd., Islington, 23, D17; Rd., Richmond, 45, P3; St., Bermondsey, 38, K21; St., Paddington, 30, H13; St., Westminster, 24, K15; St., Westminster, 25, J16

Markham Sq., 35, M14; St., 35, M14

Marlborough Gate, Hyde Pk., 30, J13; House, 36, K16; Rd., Camberwell, 39, M22; Rd., Chiswick, 43, L4; Rd., Richmond, 44, R2

Marloes Rd., 33, L11

Marlowe, Christopher, 40

Marlton St., 41, M29

Marquis Rd., 23, D17

Marryat St., 32, M8

Marsden St., 21, D15

Marshall St., Southwark, 38, L19; St., Westminster, 24, J16

Marshalsea Rd., 38, K20

Marsham St., 36, L17

Marsland Rd., 38, M19

Martha St., 29, J23

Martin St., 39, L22

Mary Ann Buildings, 40, N26; Ann St., 28, J22

Marylebone Ch., 24, G15; Lane, 24, H15; Poor Law Institute, 31, G14; Rd., 31, H14; Sta., 22, G14; St., 24, H15

Masboro' Rd., 32, L9

Mason St., 38, L21

Massinger, Philip, 57

Matheson Rd., 33, L10

Mauritius Rd., 41, M29

Mawbey Rd., 39, M22

Maxwell Rd., 34, N12

May St., 33, M10

Mayfair, 24, J15

Maze Hill, 41, N28; Hill Sta., 41, N28; Pond, 38, K20; Rd., 43, N3

Mead Row, 37, L18

Meadow Row, 38, L20

Meadowbank, 44, R1

Meadowside, 44, R1

Meat Markets, 27, H19

Meath Gdns., 29, G24

Mecklenburgh Sq., 25, G18

233

Medburn St., 23, F16
Medcroft Gdns., 45, P4
Medical School, 37, L17
Medway St., 36, L17
Meek St., 34, N12
Melbury Rd., 33, K10
Melina Rd., 32, K7
Melior St., 38, K21
Melrose Gdns., 32, K9; Ter., 32, K9
Melton St., 23, G16
Menotti St., 29, G23
Mercer St., 25, J17
Mercers St., 29, J23
Merchant Service and Fishing Fleet War Memorial, 28, J21
Mercury Rd., 42, M1
Meredith St., 26, G19
Mermaid Ct., 38, K20
Merrick Sq., 38, L20
Merrow St., 38, M20
Merthyr Ter., 32, M8
Merton Lane, 21, A15; Rd., Hampstead, 22, D14; Rd., Kensington, 34, L12
Methley St., 37, M18
Metropole Hotel, 25, K17
Metropolitan Tabernacle, 38, L19; Theatre, 30, H13; Water Board Office, 26, G19; Water Board Reservoirs, Deptford, 40, O26
Meymott St., 37, K19
Middlesex, Guildhall, 36, K17; Hospital, 24, H16; St., 28, H21
Midland Rd., 23, F17
Milborne Grove, 34, M12
Milcote St., 38, K19
Mile End Poor Law Institute, 29, G24; End Rd., 29, H23
Miles St., 41, N28
Milford Lane, 25, J18
Military Hospital, 36, L16; Stores, 36, M16
Milk St., 27, H20; Yard, 29, J23
Mill Stairs, 39, K22; St., 39, K22
Millbank, 37, L17
Milledge St., 39, M23
Miller St., 23, E16
Millfield Lane, 21, A14
Millman St., 25, G18
Millwall Pier, 40, M26
Milman, Dean, 31
Milman's St., 34, N13
Milner St., 35, L14
Milson Rd., 32, K9
Milton, John, 61, 73, 88, 95, 117, 121, 136, 137, 199
Milton St., 27, H20
Mina Rd., 39, M21

Mincing Lane, 28, J21
Minford Gdns., 32, K9
Ministry of Labour, 25, K17; of Transport, 25, K17
Miniver St., 38, K19
Minories, 28, J21
Mint, The, 28, J22; St., 38, K20
Minto St., 38, L20
Mitchell St., 27, G20
Mitchel's Row, 44, P2
Mitre Ct., 26, H19; St., 28, J21
Modbury St., 21, D15
Molyneux St., 31, H14
Monck St., 36, L17
Moneyer St., 27, F20
"Monico," 25, J16
Monkton St., 37. L19
Monkwell St., 36; St., 27, H20
Monmouth Rd., 30, H11
Monnow Rd., 39, M22
Montagu House, 31, H14; Pl., 31, H14; Sq., 31, H14; St., Hammersmith, 32, L9; St., Saint Marylebone, 31, H14
Montague House, 25, K17; Pl., 25, H17; Rd., 44, Q2; St., 25, H17
Montford Pl., 37, M18
Montpelier Row, 41, P29; Sq., 31, K14; St., 31, K14; Vale, 41, P29
Monument, The, 51, 210; 28, J21; Sta., 28, J21; St., 28, J21
Monza St., 29, J23
Moody St., 29, G24
Mooltan St., 33, M10
Moor Lane, 27, H20
Moore Pk. Rd., 34, N11; St., 35, L14
Moorfield St., 27, H20
Moorgate, 27, H20; Sta., 27, H20
Morden Grove, 40, P27; Hill, 40, P27; St., 40, O27
More, Sir Thomas, 44, 46, 87, 88, 94, 106, 119, 134, 135, 159
Morecambe St., 38, M20
Moreland St., 27, F19
Moreton Pl., 36, M16; St., 36, M16; Ter., 36, M16
Morgans Lane, 39, K21
Morley Rd., 44, R1
Mornington Ave., 33, L10; Cres., 23, F16; Pl., 23, F16; Rd., Deptford, 40, O25; Rd., St. Pancras, 23, E16; St., 23, F16

Morpeth St., 29, G24; Ter., 36, L16
Morris, William, 60
Morris St., 29, J23
Mortimer Market, 25, G16; St., 24, H16
Mortlake Rd., 43, N3
Morwell St., 25, H17
Moscow Rd., 30, J11
Motcomb St., 35, L14
"Mother Shipton," 21, D15
Motor Coach Sta., 23, G17
Mount Ararat Rd., 44, Q2; Nod Sq., 40, P27; Pleasant, 26, G18; St., Bethnal Green, 28, G22; St., Stepney, 29, H23; St., Westminster, 24, J15; Vernon, 20, B12
Mulberry St., 28, H22; Walk, 34, M13
Mulgrave Rd., Fulham, 33, M10
Mund St., 33, M10
Munden St., 33, L10
Munster Sq., 23, G16
Munton Rd., 38, L20
Murray St., Saint Pancras, 23, D16; St., Shoreditch, 27, F20
Museum St., 25, H17
Mustard Rd., 33, M10
Mycenae Rd., 41, N29
Myddelton Sq., 26, F19; St., 26, G19
Mylne St., 26, F19
Myrdle St., 29, H23
Myrtle St., 27, F21

Napier Rd., 33, L10
Nasmyth St., 32, L8
Nassau St., 24, H16
Nassington Rd., 21, C14
National Gallery, 112–116, 210; Gallery, 25, J17; Insurance Commissioners' Office, 36, L16; Liberal Club, 25, K17; Portrait Gallery, 116–18, 210; Portrait Gallery, 25, J17
Natural History Museum, 34, L13
Neal St., 25, H17
Neckinger, 39, L22; St., 39, L22
Nelson, Lord, 6, 109
Nelson Sq., 38, K19; St., Finsbury, 27, G20; St., Greenwich, 40, N27; St., Saint Pancras, 23, F16; St., Stepney, 29, H23
Nelson's Monument, 25, J17

234

Netherhale Gdns., 20, C13

Netherton Grove, 34, N12

Netherwood Rd., 32, K9

Netley Rd., 42, M2; St., 23, G16

Nevern Pl., 33, L11; Rd., 33, L11; Sq., 33, L11

Neville St., 34, M13

New College, 20, D13; Cut, 37, K19; End, 20, B13; Rd., Brentford, 42, M2; Rd., Stepney, 29, H23; Sq., 25, H18; St., City, 28, H21; St., Finsbury, 27, G20; St., Pimlico, 36, L16; St., Saint Marylebone, 22, F13; St., Saint Marylebone, 22, G14; St., Southwark, 37, M19; St., Westminster, 25, J17; Bedford Palace, 23, E16; Bond St., 24, J15; Bridge St., 26, J19; Burlington St., 24, J16; Cavendish St., 24, H15; Charles St., 27, F19; Ch. St., 39, L22; Compton St., 25, H17; Crane Stairs and Wharf, 29, K23; Cross Rd., 40, O25; Devonshire House, 24, J16; Gravel Lane, 29, J23; Inn Yard, 28, G21; Kent Rd., 38, L20; King St., 40, N26; Kings Rd., 34, O11; North St., 25, H18; Oxford St., 25, H17; Palace Yard, 37, K17; Quebec St., 31, H14; River Head, 26, F19; River Reservoirs, 21, B16; Scotland Yard, 25, K17

Newark St., 29, H23

Newburn St., 37, M18

Newcastle St., 40, M27

Newcombe St., 33, J11

Newcomen St., 38, K20

Newgate, 127; St., 27, H19

Newington Butts, 38, L19; Causeway, 38, L19; Cres., 38, M19

Newling St., 28, G22

Newman St., 24, H16

Newport St., 37, L18

Newton, Sir Isaac, 66,
168

Newton Rd., 30, H11; St., 25, H17

Nicholas Lane, 27, J20; St., 29, G24

Nightingale Lane, Greenwich, 40, O27; Lane, Richmond, 44, R2; Lane, Stepney, 28, J22

Nile St., 27, F20; Ter., 39, M21

Nine Elms Pier, 36, N16

Niton Rd., 45, P3

"Noah's Ark," 40, N26

Noble St., 27, H20

Noel St., 24, H16

Norfolk Cres., 31, H14; Sq., 30, H13; St., Stepney, 29, G24; St., Westminster, 24, J14; St., Westminster, 25, J18

Norland Gdns., 32, J9; Rd., 32, K9; Sq., 33, J10

Normal School, Westminster, 36, L16

Norman Ave., 44, R1; Rd., 40, N27; St., Chelsea, 35, M14; St., Finsbury, 27, G20

Normand Rd., 33, M10

North Ave., 43, O3; Cres., 25, H16; Ride, 31, J13; Rd., Brentford, 42, M2; Rd., Richmond, 43, O3; Row, 24, J14; "Star," 20, D13; St., Lambeth, 37, L18; St., Westminster, 37, L17; Ter., 35, L13; Audley St., 24, J15; End, 20, A12; End Rd., Fulham, 33, L10; Sheen Sta., 45, P3; Tyssen St., 28, G22; Western Hospital (Fever), 20, C14; Wharf Rd., 30, H13

Northam St., 40, P27

Northampton Inst., 26, G19; Pl., 38, M20; Rd., 26, G19; Sq., 27, G19; St., 26, G19

Northumberland Ave., 25, J17; St., 24, G15

Norton Folgate, 28, H21

Norway St., 40, N27; St., 26, H18

Notting Hill, 33, J11; Hill Gate Sta., 33, J11

Nottingham Pl., St. Marylebone, 24, G15; Pl., Stepney, 29, H22

Nutford Pl., 31, H14

Nutley Ter., 20, D13

Nylands Ave., 43, O3

Oak Hill Park, 20, B12; Hill Way, 20, B12; Village, 21, C15

Oakcroft Rd., 40, P27

Oakden St., 37, L18

Oakfield Cres., 21, C15

Oakford Rd., 21, C16

Oaklands Grove, 32, J7

Oakley Cres., 35, M14; Pl., 39, M21; Sq., 23, F16; St., Chelsea, 35, M13; St., Lambeth, 37, K18

Oakwood Ct., 33, K10

Oat Lane, 27, H20

Observatory, The, 45, Q4; Gdns., 33, K11; Rd., 45, P4

Occupation Rd., 43, L3

Ocean St., 29, H24

Odell St., 39, M21

Ogle St., 24, H16

Okeshott Ave., 21, A15

Old Sq., 25, H18; St., 27, G20; Bailey, 27, H19; Barge House Wharf, 37, J19; Bond St., 24, J16; Brentford, 42, N2; Broad St., 28, H21; Brompton, 34, M12; Brompton Rd., 34, M12; Burlington St., 24, J16; Castle St., 28, H22; Cavendish St., 24, H15; Compton St., 25, J17; Deer Pk., 44, P1; Deer Pk. Cottages, 44, P2; Deer Pk. Gdns., 44, P2; Gloucester St., 25, H17; Gravel Lane, 29, J23; Jewry, 27, H20; Kent Rd., 38, L21; Montague St., 28, H22; Nichol St., 28, G21; North St., 25, H18; Palace Lane, 44, Q1; Palace Yard, Richmond, 44, Q1; Palace Yard, Westminster, 37, L17; Paradise St., 37, L18; Pye St., 36, L16; Quebec St., 31, H14; Queen St., 36, K17; St. Pancras Ch., 23, F17; Swan Pier, 27, J20; Vic. Theatre, The, 37, K19; Woolwich Rd., 41, N28

Oldbury Pl., 24, G15

Oldchurch Rd., 29, H24

Oley Pl., 29, H24

Olive Island, 43, M4

Olney St., 38, N20

Olympia, 33, L10; Theatre, 28, G21

Ongar Rd., 33, M11

Onslow Ave., 44, Q2; Cres., 34, L13; Gdns., 34, M13; Rd., 44, Q2; Sq., 34, L13; St., 26, G19;

Ontario St., 38, L19

Opal St., 37, M19

Ophthalmic Hospital, Finsbury, 27, G20; Hospital, St. Pancras, 25, G18

Oppidans Rd., 22, E14

Orange St., Bethnal Green, 28, G22; St., Southwark, 38, K19

Oratory, The, 35, L13

Orb St., 38, M20

Orbel St., 34, O13

Orchard, The, Barnes, 45, Q4; The, Lewisham, 41, P28; Drive, 41, P28; Hill, 40, O27; Rd., Brentford, 42, M1; Rd., Richmond, 45, P3; St., Saint Marylebone, 24, H15; St., Westminster, 36, L17

Orde Hall St., 25, G18

Orford St., 35, L14

Orleans Rd., 44, S1

Orme Sq., 30, J12

Ormiston Rd., Greenwich, 41, N29; Rd., Hammersmith, 32, J8

Ormond Rd., 44, Q2

Ormonde Rd., 45, P4; Ter., 22, E14

Ornan Rd., 20, C13

Orsett St., 37, M18; Ter., 30, H12

Osborn St., 28, H22

Oscar St., 40, O26

Oscombe Rd., 32, K7

Osman Rd., 33, K9

Osnaburgh St., 23, G16

Ossington St., 30, J11

Ossulston St., 23, F17

Oswin St., 38, L19

Outer Circle, Regent's Pk., 22, F14

Outram St., 23, E17

Oval Rd., 22, E15

Overstone Rd., 32, L8

Ovington Sq., 35, L14; St., 35, L14

Owen, Robert, 204

Owen St., 26, F19

Owens Row, 26, F19

Oxford Circus, 24, H16; Circus Sta., 24, H16; Gdns., 43, M4; House, 29, G23; Rd., 43, M4; Sq., 31, H14; St., Stepney, 29, H23; St. West, 24, H15; Ter., 31, H13

Oxley St., 39, K22

Paddington Ch., 30, H13; Green, 30, H13; Praed St. Sta., 30, H13; Sta. (Gt. Western Ry.), 30, H13; St., 24, H15

Page, W. H., 69

Page St., 36, L17

Pages Walk, 39, L21

Pagoda Ave., 44, P3; Lodge, 42, P2

Paine, Thomas, 206

Pakenham St., 26, G18

Palace Ave., 30, K12; Ct., 30, J11; Gdns., Ter., 33, J11; Gate, 30, K12; Green, 30, K12; St., 36, L16; Theatre, 25, J17

Palissy St., 28, G22

Pall Mall, 36, K16; Mall East, 25, J17

Palladium, 24, H16

Palliser Rd., 33, M10

Palmer St., 37, K18

Palmerston St., 35, O15

Palmerstone Rd., 45, P4

Pancras Rd., 23, F17; St., 25, G16

Panton St., 25, J17

Paper St., 27, H20

Paradise Rd., Richmond, 44, Q2; Row, 32, L8; St., Shoreditch, 28, G21; St., Saint Marylebone, 24, H15; Walk, 35, M14

Paragon, 41, P29; Pl., 41, P29; Row, 38, L20

Parcels Post Office, 26, G18; Post Office, Southwark, 38, K19

Pardoner St., 38, L20

Parfett St., 29, H22

Parfrey St., 32, M9

Paris Gdn., 37, K19; St., 37, L18

Parish St., 39, K21

Park, The, Hendon, 20, A12; Ave., Hendon, 20, A12; Cres., 24, G15; Lane, Richmond, 44, Q2; Lane, St. Marylebone, 22, G14; Lane, Westminster, 24, J14; Pl., Greenwich, 41, N28; Pl., Westminster, 24, K16; Rd., Battersea, 35, N13; Rd., Richmond, 44, Q2; Rd., St. Marylebone, 22, G14; Rd., Twickenham, 44, R1; Row, 41, N28; Shot, 44, Q2; Sq., 24, G15; St., Greenwich, 41, N28; St., Saint Pancras, 22, E15; St.,

Southwark, 27, J20; St., Westminster, 24, J15; Ter., 33, L11; Village East, 22, E15; Village West, 22, F15; Walk, 34, M12

Parker St., 25, H17

Parkers Row, 39, K22

Parkham St., 34, O13

Parkhill, 44, R3; Rd., 21, C14

Parliament, Houses of, 100-7, 209; Hill, Hampstead, 21, C14; Hill, St. Pancras, 21, B14; Hill Fields, 21, B15; St., 107; St., 25, K17

Parr, Old, 61, 169

Parsonage St., 40, M27

Parton St., 25, H18

Pasley Rd., 38, M19

Pasteur St., 29, H23

Patent Office, 26, H18

Pater St., 33, L11

Paternoster Row, 154; Row, 27, H19; Sq., 27, H19

Patshill Rd., 23, D16

Paul St., 28, G21

Paulin St., 39, L21

Pauls Alley, 27, H20; Passage, 38, L20

Paultons Sq., 34, M13

Pavilion Rd., 35, L14; Theatre, 29, H22

Payne St., 40, N25

Peabody Ave., 36, M15; Sq., 37, K19

Peacock St., 38, M19

Pear Tree St., 27, G19

Pearman St., 37, L19

Pearson St., 40, N27

Pedley St., 28, G22

Peel St., 33, J11

Peerless St., 27, G20

Peldon Ave., 45, Q3

Pelham Cres., 34, L13; Pl., 34, L13; St., Kensington, 34, L13; St., Stepney, 28, H22

Pelican Stairs, 29, J24

Pell St., 29, J22

Pelton Rd., 41, M28

Pembroke Gdns., 33, L10; Rd., 33, L11; Sq., 33, L11; Villas, 44, Q1

Pender St., 40, N26

Penelon Rd., 33, L11

Penn, William, 206

Pennard Rd., 32, K8

Pennington St., 29, J22

Penrose St., 38, M19

Pensford Ave., 43, O3

Penton Pl., 38, M19

Penywern Rd., 33, M11

Penzance Rd., 33, J10

People's Palace, 29, G24

236

Pepler Rd., 39, N21

Pepper St., 38, K20

Pepys, Samuel, 19, 25, 42, 64, 95, 117, 148, 154, 161, 162, 168

Perceval Ave., 20, C13

Percival Rd., 45, P4; St., 27, G19

Percy Circus, 26, F18; St., 25, H16

Pereira St., 29, G23

Perham Rd., 33, M10

Perrers Rd., 32, L8

Perth St., 29, H24

Pesthouse Common, 45, Q3

Peter Pan Statue, 30, J13

Peterborough Villas, 34, O11

Petersham, 44, S2; Common, 44, R2; Lodge, 44, S1; Meadows, 44, R2; Rd., 44, R2; Ter., 34, L12

Petra House, 45, P4

Petty France, 36, K16

Petworth St., 35, O14

Peveril St., 35, N13

Phelp St., 38, N20

Philharmonic Hall, 24, H16

Philip Lane, 27, H20; St., 28, J22

Phillimore Gdns., 33, K11

Philpot Lane, 28, J21; St., 29, H23

Phipp St., 28, G21

Phoenix Pl., Kensington, 32, J9; Pl., St. Pancras, 25, G18; St., 23, F17

Physical Energy Statue 30, J12

Piccadilly, 24, K15; Circus, 25, J16

Pickering Pl., 197

Pickle Herring St., 39, K21

Pilgrimage St., 38, K20

Pilgrim's Lane, 20, C13

Pimlico, 36, L15; Gdns. 36, M16; Pier, 36, N16; Rd., 35, M15; Walk, 27, F21

Pinchin St., 28, J22

Pindar St., 28, H21

Pine St., 26, G19

Pitfield St., 27, F21

Pitt St., 33, K11

Plague in London, 24

Planet St., 29, J23

Platt St., 23, F17

Playfair St., 32, M9

Playhouse, 25, J17

Plough Ct., 26, H19

Plumber Row, 28, H22

Pocock St., 38, K19

Point Hill, 40, O27

Poland St., 24, H16

Pole St., 29, H24

Pollard Row, 29, G22; St., 29, G23

Polytechnic, Battersea, 35, O15; St. Marylebone,24,H16; Recreation Ground, 43, N5

Pond Pl., 34, M13; Rd., 41, P29; St., 20, C14

Ponsonby Pl., 36, M17

Pont St., 35, L14

Pope, Alexander, 52, 88

Poplar Grove, 32, K9

Porchester Gdns., 30, H12; Pl., 31, H14; Rd., 30, H12; Sq., 30, H12; St., 31, H13; Ter., 30, H12

Port of London Authority Office, 28, J21; of London Wharf, 40, M27

Porten Rd., 32, L9

Porteus Rd., 30, H13

Portland House, 24, H15; Pl., 24, G15; St., Southwark, 38, M20; St., Stepney, 29, H24; Ter., 44, Q1

Portman Pl., 29, G24; Rooms, 31, H14; Sq., 31, H14; St., 31, H14

Portpool Lane, 26, H18

Portsea Pl., 31, H14

Portugal St., 25, H18

Post Office Savings Bank, 32, L9

Postern Row, 28, J21

Pott St., 29, G23

Potters Fields, 39, K21

Pottery Rd., 42, M2

Poultry, 27, J20

Powell St., 27, G19

Praed St., 30, H13

Pratt St., Lambeth, 37, L18; St., Saint Pancras, 23, E16

Prebend St., 23, E16

President St., 27, G19

Price St., 38, K19

Primitive Methodist Headquarters, 26, G18

Primley St., 29, G24

Primrose Hill Rd., 22, D14; Pk. and Hill, 22, E14; St., 28, H21

Prince St., 39, L21; Arthur Rd., 20, C13; Consort Rd., 30, K13; Consort's Statue, 30, K13; Edward Theatre, 25, J17; of Wales Cres., 23, D15; of Wales

Gate, Hyde Pk., 31, K13; of Wales Rd., Battersea, 35, O14; of Wales Rd., St. Pancras, 23, D15; of Wales Theatre, 25, J17

Princelet St., 28, H22

Princes Gdns., 30, K13; Gate, 30, K13; Mansions, 36, L16; Pl., 33, J10; Restaurant, 24, J16; Rd., Lambeth, 37, M18; Rd., Lewisham, 40, P27; Rd., Richmond, 43, N3; Rd., Richmond, 44, Q3; Row, 36, L16; Sq., Lambeth, 37, M19; Sq., Paddington, 30, J11; Sq., Stepney, 29, J23; St., Bethnal Green, 28, G22; St., City, 27, H20; St., Richmond, 44, Q2; St., Saint Marylebone, 24, H16; St., Southwark, 38, N20; St., Westminster, 24, H16; St., Westminster, 36, K17; Ter., 31, K13; Theatre, 25, H17

Princess Rd., 22, E15

Princeton St., 25, H18

Prior St., 40, O27

Priory Grove, 34, M12; Rd., 43, N3

Prospect St., 39, L23

Providence St., 28, J22

Provost Rd., 22, D14; St., 27, F20

Prudential Assurance Co.'s Offices, 26, H18

Prusom St., 29, K23

Pryors, The, 20, B13

Public Trustee Office, 25, H18

Pulford St., 36, M16

Purchase St., 23, F17

Pyrland Rd., 45, Q3

Pyrmont Rd., 43, M3

Quadrant, The, 44, Q2; Grove, 21, C15; Rd., 44, Q2

Quaker St., 28, G22

Queen Sq., 25, G17; St., City, 27, J20; St., Greenwich, 41, N28; St., Hammersmith, 32, M8; St., Saint Pancras, 23, E16; St., Stepney, 28, H22; St., Westminster, 24, J15; St. Pl., 27, J20; Alexandra's Military Hospital, 37, M17; Anne St., 24, H15; Anne's

237

Rockingham St., 38, L20
Roderick Rd., 21, C14
Rodmere St., 41, M29
Rodney Pl., 38, L20; Rd., 38, L20
Roland Gdns., 34, M12
Rolls Rd., 39, M22
Roman Bath, **169, 210**; Catholic College, 32, L9; Wall, **15, 199**
Romford St., 29, H23
Romney Close, 20, A12; Rd., 40, N27
Rona Rd., 21, C15
Ronald St., 29, J24
Rood Lane, 28, J21
Rookley Rd., 32, K9
Ropemaker St., 27, H20
Rosary Gdns., 34, L12
Roscoe St., 27, G20
Rose Cottage, 45, P4
Rosebery St., 39, M23; Ave., 26, G18
Rosedew Rd., 32, M9
Roseford Gdns., 32,K9
Rosemont Rd., Hampstead, 20, D12; Rd., Richmond, 44, R2
Rosenau Cres., 35, O14; Rd., 35, O14
Rosoman St., 26, G19
Rossetti, Dante Gabriel, **91, 134**
Rosslyn Hill, 20, C13; Pk., 20, C13; Rd., 44, R1
Rossmore Rd., 22, G14
Rotherhithe New Rd., 39, M22; St., 39, K23
Rothsay St., 38, L21
Rothwell St., 22, E14
Rotten Row, Battersea Pk., 35, N14; Row, Blackheath, 41, O29; Row, Hampstead Heath, 20, A13; Row, Hyde Pk., 31, K13
Rouel Rd., 39, L22
Round Pond, Kensington Gdns., 30, K12
Roupell St., 37, K19
Rowan Rd., 32, L9
Rowton House, 38, L19
Royal Academy, 24, J16; Ave., 35, M14; Cres., 32, K9; Exchange, 43; Exchange, 28, J21; Hill, 40, O27; Hospital, 44, P2; Institute, 24, J16; Laundry, 44, P2; Mews, 36, L15; Observatory, Greenwich, 41, O28; Parade, 41, P29; St., 37, L18; Academy of Music, 24, G15; Air

Force Memorial, 25, K17; Albert Hall, 30, K13; Army Medical College, 37, M17; R.A.M.C. Barracks, 36, M17; Automobile Club, 36, K16; Botanic Gdns., Regent's Pk., 22, G15; Botanic Gdns., Richmond, 42, O2; College of Music, 30, K13; College of Surgeons, 25, H18; Cts. of Justice, 25, H18; Free Hospital, 26, G18; Geographical Society, 30, K13; Horticultural Hall, 36, L16; Hospital Rd., 35, M14; Hospital School, 41, N28; Institute of Painters, 25, J16; Mint St., 28, J22; Naval Cemetery, 41, N29; Naval College, 41, N28; Oak Sta., 30, H12; Society of Medicine, 24, H15; Soldiers' Daughters' Homes, 20, C13; Veterinary College, 23, E16; Victualling Yard, 40, M25
Royalty Theatre, 25, H16
Roydon St., 35, O15
Royston Rd., 44, Q2
Rudall Cres., 20, C13
Rufford St., 23, E17
Runham Pl., 38, M20
Rupert St., Stepney, 28, J22; St., Westminster, 25, J16
Rushworth St., 38, K19
Ruskin St., 43, N4
Russell Gdns., 33, K10; Hotel, 25, G17; Rd., 33, K10; Sq., 25, G17; Sq. Sta., 25, G17; St., Battersea, 35, O15; St., Stepney, 29, H23; St., Westminster, 25, J17
Russian Chapel, 24, H15
Ruthin Rd., 41, N29
Rutland Gate, 31, K13; Rd., 32, M8; St., Kensington - Westminster, 35, L13; St., Saint Pancras, 23, F16; St., Stepney, 29, H23; St., Westminster, 36, M16
Ryder St., 24, J16
Rydon Cres., 26, F19
Ryecroft St., 34, O11
Ryland Rd., 21, D15

Sackville St., 24, J16
Sadlers Wells Theatre, 26, F19
St. Alban's Ch., Holborn, 26, H18; Rd., Kensington, 30, K12; Rd., St. Pancras, 21, B15
St. Alphage Ch., 40, N27
St. Andrew St., 26, H19
St. Andrew's Ch., St. Marylebone, 24, H16; Hall, 25, H16
St. Ann St., Westminster, 36, L17
St. Ann's Ch., Kew, 43, N3
St. Anne's Ch., 21, B15
St. Augustine Rd., 23, D17
St. Augustine's Ch., Kensington, 34, L13
St. Austell Rd., 40, P27
St. Barnabas St., 35, M15
St. Bartholomew's Hospital, **125**; 27, H19
St. Botolph's Ch., 28, H21
St. Bride St., 26, H19
St. Bride's Ch., 26, H19
St. Chads Pl., 26, F18
St. Clement's Ch., Westminster, 25, J18
St. Cuthbert's Ch., Kensington, 33, L11
St. Davids St., 38, L20
St. Dunstan's, Regent's Pk., 22, F14; in-the-West Ch., Fleet St., 28, J21; Rd., 32, M9; Works, Headquarters, 22, F15
St. Edmund's Ter., 22, E14
St. Ethelburga's Ch., 28, H21
St. Gabriel's Ch., Hammersmith, 32, J9
St. George Sq., 22, E15; St., 29, J22
St. George's Ch., Holborn, 25, H17; Ch., Southwark, 38, K20; Ch., Westminster, 24, J16; Circus, 38, L19; Hall, 24, H16; Hospital, 31, K15; Market, 38, L19; Rd., Hammersmith, 32, K9; Rd., Richmond, 45, P3; Rd., St. Pancras, 22, E15; Rd., Southwark, 37, L19; Rd., Westminster, 36, M15; Sq., 36, M16; Ter., 22, E14; in-the-East Ch.,

239

St. George's—*continued* 29, J23; Roman Catholic Cathedral, 37, L19
St. German's Chapel, 41, O29; Pl., 41, O29
St. Giles' Ch., Bloomsbury, 25, H17; Cripplegate Ch., 27, H20
St. Helen's Pl., 28, H21
St. James's Pk., 127; Pk., 36, K16; Pk. Sta., 36, L16; Pl., 24, K16; Rd., 39, M22; Sq., Kensington, 32, J9; Sq., Westminster, 36, J16; St., 24, J16; Ter., 22, E14; Theatre, 24, K16; Walk, 26, G19; Ch., Chiswick, 43, L4; Palace, 36, K16; Pl., 33, J10
St. John, Ch.' of, 24, H16; St., 26, F19; Baptist Ch., 32, K9
St. John's Burial Ground, Paddington, 31, H14; Burial Ground, St. Marylebone, 22, F13; Ch., Deptford, 40, P26; Ch., Hampstead, 20, C12; Ch., Hammersmith, 32, L8; Gate, Clerkenwell, 26, G19; Grove, 44, P2; Lane, 26, G19; Pk., Greenwich, 41, O29; Rd., Deptford, 40, O26; Rd., Richmond, 44, P2; Sq., 26, G19; Sta., Deptford, 40, P26
St. Jude's Ch., Kensington, 34, L12; Ch., Stepney, 28, H22
St. Katherine Dock Entrance, 28, K22; Dock Warehouses, 28. H21; Docks, 28, J22
St. Katherine's Lodge, 22, F15; School, 22, F15; Way, 28, J22
St. Leonard St., 36, L16
St. Leonard's Rd., Barnes, 45, P4; Sq., 21, D15; Ter., 35, M14
St. Loo Ave., 35, M14
St. Luke's Ch., Chelsea, 35, M13; Ch., Kensington, 34, M12; Ch., Richmond, 43, O3; Hospital, 27, G20
St. Margaret's Ch., Westminster, 37, K17; Rd., 44, R1

St. Mark's Ch., St. Pancras, 22, E15; Ch., Shoreditch, 27, G20; College, 34, N12; Cres., 22, E15; Hospital, 27, F19; Rd., 34, N12; St., 28, J22
St. Martin St., 25, J17
St. Martin's Lane, 25, J17; Le-Grand, 27, H20
St. Mary Abbots Ch., 33, K11; at Hill, 28, J21; Axe, 28, H21; St., 28, H22
St. Mary's Ch., Fulham, 32, L9; Ch., Kensington, 34, M12; Ch., Lambeth, 37, L18; Grove, Chiswick, 43, M4; Grove, Richmond, 45, P3; Hospital, 30, H13; Sq., 37, L19; Sta., 29, H22; Ter., 30, H13
St. Mathias's Ch., 33, M11
St. Michael's Ch., 35, L15
St. Nicholas' Ch., Greenwich, 40, N26
St. Olave's Ch., Stepney, 28, H22; Grammar School, 39, K21; Union, 39, K21; Wharf, 28, K21
St. Oswald's Pl., 37, M18
St. Oswulf St., 36, M17
St. Pancras Alms Houses, 21, C14; Ch., 23, G17; Gdns., 23, E17; Infirmary, 21, A16; Poor Law Institute, 23, E17; Sta. (L.M.S. Ry.), 23, F17
St. Paul's Cathedral, 26, 29–35, 211; Cathedral, 27, H19; Ch., Brentford, 42, M1; Ch., Deptford, 40, N26; Ch., Hammersmith, 32, L8; Ch., Kensington, 33, K11; Ch., Kensington, 34, M13; Ch., Westminster, 31, K15; Churchyard, 150–3; Churchyard, 27, J19; Cres., 23, D17; Pier, 27, J19; Rd., Brentford, 42, M1; Rd., Richmond, 44, P3; Rd., St. Pancras, 23, E16; Rd., Southwark, 38, M19; Schools, 32, L9; Sta., 26, J19

St. Peter's Ch., Richmond, 44, S2; Ch., Southwark, 38, M20; Ch., Westminster, 36, L15; Rd., Isleworth, 44, Q1; Rd., Stepney, 29, G24
St. Petersburg Pl., 30, J11
St. Philip's Ch., 33, L11
St. Saviour's Dock, 39, K22
St. Stephen's Ave., 32, K8; Ch., Kensington, 34, L12; Ch., Paddington, 30, H11; Gdns., 44, R1
St. Swithin's Lane, 27, J20
St. Thomas's Ch., Hammersmith, 32, K8; Gdns., 21, D15; Hospital, 37, K18; St., 38, K20
St. Vedast Ch., 27, H20
Salamanca St., 37, M18
Sale St., Bethnal Green, 28, G22; St., Paddington, 31, H13
Salem Rd., 30, J12
Salisbury Rd., 44, P2; Row, 38, M20; Sq., 26, J19; St., Bermondsey, 39, K23; St., Saint Marylebone, 22, G13
Samaritan Hospital, 31, H14
Sancroft St., 37, M18
Sandall Rd., 23, D16
Sandford Rd., 38, M20
Sandland St., 25, H18
Sandover Rd., 39, M21
Sands End Lane, 34, N12
Sandwich St., 23, G17
Sandy Rd., 20, A12
Sandycombe Rd., Richmond, 43, O3; Rd., Twickenham, 44, R1
Sardinia St., 25, H18
Saul St., 28, G22
Saunders Rd., 32, J9
Savernake Rd., 21, C14
Saville Pl., 37, L18; Row, 24, J16; St., 24, H16
Savoy Hotel, 25, J18; St., 25, J18
Sayer St., 38, L20
Sayes Ct. Recreation Ground, 40, N25
Scala Theatre, 25, H16
Scarsdale Villas, 33, L11
Sceptre St., 29, G24
School House Lane, 29, J24; of Arts and Crafts, 25, H17; of Hygiene, 25, G17

240

Science Museum, 34, L13
Sclater St., 28, G22
Scoresby St., 38, K19
Scotch Ch., 26, G17
Scott, Sir Walter, 106, 160, 163, 165, 192, 194, 198
Scott St., 29, G23
Scotts Rd., 32, K8
Scovell Rd., 38, K19
Scrutton St., 28, G21
Seabright St., 29, G23
Seagrave Rd., 33, M11
Seamen's Hospital, 40, N27
Seamore Pl., 24, K15
Searles Rd., 38, L20
Seaton St., Chelsea, 34, N12; St., Saint Pancras, 23, G16
Sedlescombe Rd., 33, M11
Sekford St., 26, G19
Selby St., 28, G22
Selcroft Rd., 41, M29
Selwood Ter., 34, M13
Selwyn Ave., 44, P2
Semley Pl., 35, L15
Senior St., 30, G12
Senrab St., 29, H24
Serle St., 25, H18
Serpentine, The, 31, K14
Session House, Finsbury, 26, G19
Sessions House, Southwark, 38, L20
Settles St., 29, H22
Seven Dials, 25, H17
Severne St., 28, J22
Seville St., 24, K14
Seward St., 27, G19
Seymour Pl., Kensington, 34, M12; Pl., St. Marylebone, 31, H14; St., Deptford, 40, O26; St., Saint Marylebone, 31, H14; St., Saint Pancras, 23, F16
Shad Thames, 39, K22
Shadwell, 29, J23; Basin, 29, J23; High St., 29, J23; New Entrance, 29, J24; Old Entrance, 29, J24; Stas., 29, J23
Shaftesbury Ave., 25, J17; Rd., Hammersmith, 32, L8; Rd., Kensington, 33, L10; Rd., Richmond, 44, P2; Theatre, 25, J17
Shakespeare, William, v, 24, 36, 41, 44, 48, 57, 94, 96, 106, 107, 117, 119, 135, 143, 163, 179, 180, 194, 197, 199, 200
Shalston Rd., 45, P4

Shand St., 39, K21
Shandy St., 29, H24
Sharples Hall St., 22, E14
Sharsted St., 37, M19
Shaw, George Bernard, 111, 187
Shawfield St., 35, M14
Sheen Common, 45, Q4; Common Drive, 45, Q4; Lane, 45, Q5; Mount, 45, Q4; Pk., 44, Q2; Rd., 44, Q2; Wood, 45, Q4
Sheendale Rd., 44, P3
Sheffield Ter., 33, K11
Shelley, 178, 185
Shepherd St., 28, H22
Shepherdess Walk, 27, F20
Shepherd's Bush, 32, K9; Bush Green, 32, K9; Bush Market, 32, K8; Bush Rd., 32, L9; Bush Sta., 32, K9; Market, 24, J15; Walk, 20, C13
Sheridan St., 29, J23
Ship Inn, 43, O5; Lane, Barnes, 43, P5; Lane, Lambeth, 37, L18; Lane St., 32, M8; St., Deptford, 40, O26; St., Poplar, 40, M27; Tavern, 40, N27
Shirlock Rd., 21, C14
Shoe Lane, 26, H19
Shooters Hill Rd., 41, O29
Shoreditch, 199; Sta. (L.M.S.), 28, G21; Sta. (U.), 28, G22
Shorncliffe Rd., 39, M21
Short St., 37, K19
Shorts Gdns., 25, H17
Shouldham St., 31, H14
Shroton St., 31, G14
Sidmouth St., 26, G18; Wood, 45, S3
Sidney, Sir Philip, 94
Sidney Sq., 29, H23; St., Finsbury, 27, F19; St., Saint Pancras, 23, F16; St., Stepney, 29, H23
Silk Mills Path, 40, P27; St., 27, H20
Silver Cres., 43, L4; St., City, 27, H20; St., Hampstead, 20, B13; St., Holborn, 25, H17; St., Stepney, 29, H24
Simpson's Rest, 6
Sinclair Gdns., 32, K9; Rd., 32, K9
Singer St., 28, G21
Sion College Library, 26, J19

Skelwith Rd., 32, M9
Skidmore St., 29, H24
Skinner St., 26, G19
Skipton St., 38, L19
Slaidburn St., 34, N12
Slippers Pl., 39, L23
Sloane Ave., 35, L14; Ct. East, 35, M14; Ct. West, 35, M14; Gdns., 35, M14; Sq., 35, L14; St., 35, L14; Ter., 35, L14
Smith, Sydney, 153
Smith Sq., 37, L17; St., Chelsea, 35, M14; St., Finsbury, 26, G19; St., Stepney, 29, H24; Ter., 35, M14
Smithfield, 20, 125
Smyrks Rd., 39, M21
Snow Hill, 127; 26, H19
Snowhill Ave., 41, O28
Snow's Fields, 38, K20
Soane Museum, 25, H18
Soho, 201; Sq., 25, H17
Solander St., 29, J23
Somerford St., 29, G23
Somers Pl., 31, H13
Somerset House, 169; 25, J18; Rd., 42, M1; St., 24, H15
Somerton Rd., 45, P4
South Ave., 43, O3; Cres., Greenwich, 40, P26; Cres., Holborn, 25, H17; Drive, 35, O14; End, 20, C14; Grove, 21, A15; Parade, 34, M13; Pl., 27, H20; Row, 41, P29; St., Finsbury, 27, H20; St., Greenwich, 40, O27; St., Hammersmith, 32, L8; St., Kensington, 34, L13; St., Southwark, 38, M20; St., Westminster, 24, J15; Africa House, 25, J17; Audley St., 24, J15; Bolton Gdns., 34, M12; Devon Wharf, 28, K22; Eaton Pl., 35, L15; End Rd., 20, C14; Hill Pk., 21, B14; Hill Pk. Gdns., 21, B14; Kensington Museums, 131–3, 205, 210; Kensington Stas., 34, L13; Kentish Town Sta., 23, D16; Molton St., 24, H15; Vale Rd., 41, P29; Wharf Rd., 30, H13

Southampton Rd., 21; C14; Row, 25, H17; St., . Holborn, 25, H17; St., Westminster, 25, J17

Southbrook St., 32, K8

Southcombe St., 33, L10

Southern Railway Wharf, 36, N17

Southerton Rd., 32, L8

Southey, Robert, 74, 205

Southolm St., 35, O15

Southwark, 178–86; Bridge, 27, J20; Bridge Rd., 38, L19; Cathedral, 52–8, 205, 211; Cathedral, 38, K20; Pk. Rd., 39, L22; Poor Law Institute, 38, M21; St., 38, K19

Southwell Gdns., 34, L12

Southwick Cres., 31, H13; St., 31, H13

Spa Rd., 39, L22

Spafields Chapel, 26, G19; Ch., 26, F18

Spaniards Rd., 20, A13; Tavern, 20, A13

Sparricks Row, 38, K20

Sparta St., 40, O27

Speedwell St., 40, O26

Speke's Monument, 30, J13

Spelman St., 28, H22

Spencer, Herbert, 170

Spencer Rd., Chiswick, 43, N5; Rd., St. Pancras, 21, B16; St., Battersea, 35, N13; St., Finsbury, 26, G19

Spenser, Edmund, 73, 107

Spicer St., 35, O13

Spital Sq., 28, H21; St., 28, G22

Spitalfields Market, 28, H21

Spring Gdns., Stepney, 29, H24; Gdns., Westminster, 25, J17; Grove, Chiswick, 43, M3; Grove, Richmond, 45, Q3; Grove Rd., 45, Q3; Pl., 21, D15; St., Deptford, 40, O25; St., Paddington, 30, H13

Squire's Mount, 20, B13

Squirries St., 28, G22

Stadium St., 34, N12

Stafford Pl., Richmond, 44, R2; Pl., Westminster, 36, L16; Ter., 33, K11

Stamford Rd., 34, N12; St., Fulham, 34, N12; St., Lambeth-Southwark, 37, K18

Standard St., 38, L20

Stanford Rd., 34, L12

Stangate St., 37, K18

Stanhope Gdns., 34, L12; Gate, Hyde Pk., 31, K15; Pl., 31, H14; St., Paddington, 30, J13; St., Saint Pancras, 23, G16

Stanlake Rd., 32, J8

Stanley Gdns., 21, D14; Rd., Barnes, 45, P4; Rd., Fulham, 34, N12

Stanmore Gdns., 45, P3; Rd., 44, P3

Stannary St., 37, M18

Stanton's Wharf, 28, K21

Stanwick Rd., 33, L10

Stanworth St., 39, L21

Staple Inn, 201; Inn, 26, H18; St., 38, L20

Star Rd., 33, M10; St., 31, H13; and Garter Hill, 44, S2; and Garter Home, 44, R2; Music Hall, 39, L22

Station Rd., 43, O3

Stationers' Hall, 27, H19

Stationery Office, 36, K17

Staunton St., 40, N25

Steam Packet Wharf, 27, J20

Stebondale St., 40, M27

Steedman St., 38, M19

Steele's Rd., 22, D14

Steinway Hall, 24, H15

Stepney, 29, H24; Causeway, 29, J24; Ch., 29, H24; Green, 29, H24; Green Sta., 29, G24

Sterndale Rd., 32, L9

Sterne, Rev. Laurence, 118, 131

Sterne St., 32, K9

Steven St., 39, L21

Stevenson, R. L., 197

Stewarts Grove, 34, M13

Stibbington St., 23, F16

Stile Hall Gdns., 43, M3

Stock Exchange, 28, H21

Stockwell St., 40, N27

Stokenchurch St., 34, O11

Stoll Picture Theatre, 25, H18

Stonecutter St., 26, H19

Stonehill Rd., 43, M4

Stoney Lane, Bermondsey, 39, K21; Lane, City, 28, H21; St., 38, K20

Stonor Rd., 33, L10

Store St., 25, H17

Storks Rd., 39, L22

Stow, John, 24, 146

Stowage, 40, N26

Stowe Rd., 32, K8

Straights Mouth, 40, N27

Strand, 168–71; 25, J17; on the Green, 43, M4

Stratford Pl., St. Marylebone, 24, H15; Pl., St. Pancras, 23, D16; Rd., 33, L11

Strathnairn St., 39, M22

Strathray Gdns., 22, D13

Stratton St., 24, J16

Streatley Pl., 20, B13

Strickland St., 40, O26

Strutton Gdn., 36, L16

Studland Rd., 32, L8

Sturge St., 38, K19

Sturgeon Rd., 38, M19

Styman St., 27, G20

Sudbury St., 37, L18

Suffield Rd., 38, M19

Suffolk St., 25, J17

Sulgrave Rd., 32, K9

Sumner Pl., 34, L13; St., 38, K20

Sun Alley, 44, Q2; St., 28, H21

Sunning Hill Rd., 40, P26

Superintendent's Lodge, Hyde Pk., 31, J14

Surrey Cres., 43, M4; Grove, 38, M21; Lane, 34, O13; Row, 38, K19; Sq., 38, M21; St., 25, J18; Theatre, 37, K19

Sussex Gdns., 30, H13; Pl., Paddington, 30, H13; Pl., St. Marylebone, 22, G14; Sq., 30, J13; St., 36, M15

Sutherland Sq., 38, M20; St., Southwark, 38, M20; St., Westminster, 36, M15; Ter., 36, M15

242

Sutton Lane, 43, M4; St., Lambeth, 37, K18; St., Westminster, 25, H17; St. East, 29, J23
Swain's Lane, 21, B15
Swallow St., 24, J16
Swan Mead, 38, L21; St., City-Stepney, 28, J22; St., Southwark, 38, L20; Walk, 35, M14
Swancombe Pl., 32, J9
Swift, Dean, **88, 168**
Swinton St., 26, F18
Sydney Pl., 34, L13; Rd., 44, Q2; St., 34, M13
Symons St., 35, L14
Syon House, 42, O1; Pk., 42, N1

Tabard St., 38, K20
Tabernacle St., 28, G21
Tabor Rd., 32, L8
Tachbrook St., 36, M16
Tadema Rd., 34, N12
Tadmor St., 32, K9
Tailors' Institute, 21, D15
Tait St., 29, J23
Talgarth Rd., 33, M10
Tallis St., 26, J19
Tamworth St., 33, M11
Tangier Rd., 45, P4
Tanner St., 39, K21
Tanners Hill, 40, O26
Tanswell St., 37, K18
Tanza Rd., 21, B14
Tarling St., 29, J23
Tarn St., 38, L20
Tarver St., 38, M19
Tasso Rd., 32, M9
Tate Gallery, **84, 86, 211**; Gallery, 37, M17; St., 37, M18
Tattersalls, 31, K14
Tavistock Pl., 23, G17; Sq., 23, G17; St., 25, J17
Taviton St., 23, G17
Taylor Ave., 43, O4
Tedworth Sq., 35, M14
Telegraph St., 27, H20
Temperance Hospital, 23, F16
Temple, The, 23, **95–100, 211**; The, 26, J18; Avenue, 26, J19; Bar, **167**; Bar Memorial, 25, J18; Pier, 26, J18; Rd., 43, O3; Sheen, 45, P4; Sheen Rd., 45, Q4; Sheen Villas, 45, Q4; Sta., 25, J18; St., 38, L19
Templeton Pl., 33, L11
Templewood Ave., 20, B12; Gdns., 20, B12

Tench St., 29, K23
Tenda Rd., 39, M23
Tenison St., 37, K18
Tennyson, Alfred, **5, 13, 173**
Tent St., 29, G23
Tenter St., 28, H21; St. East, 28, J22; St. North, 28, J22; St. South, 28, J22; St. West, 28, J22
Tenterden St., 24, H15
Terrace Field, 44, R2; Gdns., 44, R2
Territorial Headquarters, Chelsea, 35, M14; Headquarters, Lewisham, 41, P28
Tetcott Rd., 34, N12
Thackeray, W. M., **96, 140, 189, 204**
Thames House, 37, L17; Police Ct., 29, H24; Rd., 43, M4; St., 40, N27
Thanet St., 23, G17
Thavies Inn, 26, H19
Thayer St., 24, H15
Theobald St., 38, L20
Theobalds Rd., 25, H18
Thermopylae Gate, 40, M27
Thirleby Rd., 36, L16
Thirza St., 29, J24
Thistle Grove, 34, M12
Thomas St., 24, J15
Thorburn Sq., 39, M22
Thornfield Rd., 32, K8
Thornham St., 40, N27
Thornville St., 40, O26
Thrawl St., 28, H22
Threadneedle St., 27, J20
Three Colts Lane, 29, G23
Throgmorton, 27, H20; Ave., 28, H21
Thrush St., 38, M19
Thurland Rd., 39, L22
Thurloe Pl., 34, L13; Sq., 34, L13
Thurlow Rd., 20, C13; St., 38, M21
Thurston Rd., 40, P27
Tiber St., 23, E17
Tilton St., 33, N10
Times Office, 27, J19
Tinworth St., 37, M17
Titchborne St., 31, H13
Titchfield Rd., 22, E14
Tite St., 35, M14
Tiverton St., 38, L19
Tivoli Cinema, 25, J17
Tobacco Dock, London Docks, 29, J23
Tokenhouse Yard, 27, H20
Tollet St., 29, G24
Tolmers Sq., 23, G16
Tonbridge St., 23, F17

Tooley St., 38, K21
Topaz St., 37, L18
Tor Gdns., 33, K11
Torbay St., 23, D16
Torquay St., 30, H11
Torrington Pl., 25, G17; Sq., 25, G17
Tothill St., **159**; St., 36, K17
Tottenham Ct. Rd., 24, G16; Ct. Rd. Sta., 25, H16; St., 24, H16
Toulmin St., 38, K20
Tower, The, 28, J21; of London, **43–50, 212**; Bridge, **50**; 28, K21; Bridge Rd., 38, L21; Hill, 28, J21; St., 37, L19
Town Hall, Bermondsey, 39, L22; Hall, Brentford, 42, N1; Hall, Chelsea, 35, M13; Hall, Finsbury, 26, G19; Hall, Hammersmith, 32, L9; Hall, Hampstead, 20, C14; Hall, Holborn, 25, H17; Hall, Kensington, 33, K11; Hall, Paddington, 30, H13; Hall, Richmond, 44, Q1; Hall, St. Marylebone, 31, G14; Hall, St. Pancras, 23, E16; Hall, Shadwell, 29, J23; Hall, Shoreditch, 28, G21; Hall, Walworth - Southwark, 38, M20
Townley St., 38, M20
Townsend St., 38, M21
Townshend Cottages, 22, F13; Rd., Richmond, 44, Q3; Rd., St. Marylebone, 22, E13; Ter., 44, P3
Toynbee Hall, 28, H22
Tracey St., 37, M18
Trafalgar Rd., Camberwell, 39, M22; Rd., Greenwich, 41, N28; Sq., **111**; Sq., Chelsea, 34, M13; Sq., Stepney, 29, H24; Sq., Westminster, 25, J17; St., 38, M20; Tavern, 41, M28
Tranquil Vale, 41, P29
Tranton Rd., 39, L22
Treasury Office, 25, K17
Trebovir Rd., 33, M11
Tregunter Rd., 34, M12
Trenchard St., 41, N28
Trevanion Rd., 33, L10
Trevelyan, G. M., **21**
Trevor Sq., 31, K14
Trig Lane, 27, J20

243

Wapping—*continued*
Entrance, 39, K22; High St., 29, K23; Sta., 29, K23; Wall, 29, K23
War Office, 25, K17
Warbeck Rd., 32, K8
Ward St., 37, M18
Warden Rd., 21, D15
Wardour St., 25, H16
Warley St., 29, G24
Warner St., Holborn, 26, G18; St., Southwark, 38, L20
Warren St., 24, G16; St. Sta., 24, G16
Warriner Gdns., 35, O14
Warwick Cres., 30, G12; Gdns., 33, L10; Lane, 27, H19; Pl., 30, G12; Rd., 33, L10; Sq., 36, M16; St., Deptford, 40, N25; St., Westminster, 24, J16; St., Westminster, 36, M15
Washington, George, 88, 207
Water Lane, City, 26, J19; Lane, Richmond, 44, Q1
Waterford Rd., 34, N11
Watergate St., 40, N26
Waterloo Bridge, 25, J18; Junction, 37, K19; Pier, 25, J18; Pl., Richmond, 43, M3; Pl., Westminster, 25, J16; Rd., 37, K18; Sta. (S.R.), 37, K18; St., 32, M8
Waterlow Pk., 21, A15
Waterside, 44, Q1
Watling St., 14; St., 27, J20
Watney Rd., 45, P4; St., 29, J23
Watson St., 40, O26
Watts, G. F., 32, 35, 85, 173
Watts, Isaac, 67, 204
Watts St., 29, K23
Waverley Rd., 30, G11
Waverton St., 24, J15
Waycombe Cottages, 43, N3
Weaver St., 28, G22
Webb St., 38, L21
Webber Row, 37, K19; St., 37, K19
Webster Rd., 39, L22
Wedderburn Rd., 20, C13
Weedington Rd., 21, D15
Welbeck St., 24, H15
Well Close Sq., 28, J22; Lane, 45, Q4; Rd.,

20, B13; St., City, 27, H20; St., Stepney, 28, J22; Walk, 20, B13
Wellesley Ave., 32, L8; Rd., Chiswick, 43, M3; Rd., St. Pancras, 21, C15; St., 29, H24
Wellington, Duke of, 28, 34, 82, 128
Wellington Barracks, 36, K16; Rd., Battersea, 35, N13; Rd., Richmond, 45, Q3; Row, 28, G22; Sq., 35, M14; Statue, 31, K15; St., Greenwich, 40, N26; St., Saint Pancras, 22, E15; St., Westminster, 25, J18
Wells, H. G., 50, 111
Wells Rd., Hammersmith, 32, K8; Rd., St. Marylebone, 22, E14; St., Saint Marylebone, 24, H16; St., Saint Pancras, 25, G18
Welsford St., 39, M22
Wemyss Rd., 41, P29
Wentworth St., 28, H22
Werrington St., 23, F16
Wesley, John Charles, 67, 157, 178, 189, 204
Wesleyan College, 44, R2; Methodist Hall, 36, K17
West Drive, 35, N14; Heath, Hampstead Heath, 20, A12; Hill, 21, A15; Lane, 39, K23; Lodge, 43, O4; Rd., 45, P5; Smithfield, 27, H19; Sq., 37, L19; St., 25, J17; Arbour St., 29, H24; Brompton Stations, 33, M11; Cromwell Rd., 33, L11; Halkin St., 35, L14; Hall Rd., 43, O4; Kensington Sta., 33, M10; London Hospital, 32, L9; Pk. Rd., 43, O3; Rd. Ave., 43, O4; Sheen Vale, 44, P3
Westbourne Gdns., 30, H11; Gate, Hyde Pk. 30, J13; Grove, 30, H11; Pk. Cres., 30, H12; Pk. Villas, 30, H11; St., Paddington, 30, J13; St., Westminster, 35, L15; Ter., 30, H12;

Ter. North, 30, G12; Ter. Rd., 30, H12
Westbury Rd., 30, H12
Westcombe Pk. Rd., 41, N29
Westcott St., 38, L20
Western District Fever Hospital, 34, N11
Westgate Ter., 34, M12
Westminster, 154–60; Abbey, 59–71, 154, 205, 212; Abbey, 37, K17; Bridge, 27; Bridge Rd., 37, K18; Cathedral, 74–7, 213; Cathedral (Roman Catholic), 36, L16; City Hall, 25, J17; Hall, 37, K17; Playground, 36, L16; Poor Law Institute and Infirmary, 34, M12; Sta., 25, K17
Westmoreland St., Westminster, 36, M15
Westmorland Pl., 27, F20; Rd., 38, N20; St., Saint Marylebone, 24, H15
Weston St., 38, K21
Wests Wharf, 39, K22
Westwick Gdns., 32, K9
Wetherall Gdns., 20, D13
Wetherby Gdns., 34, M12; Rd., 34, M12
Weymouth St., 24, H15
Wharf Rd., 40, M27
Wharton St., 26, G18
Wheeler St., 28, G21
Whidborne St., 23, G17
Whiskin St., 26, G19
Whistler, J. A. M., 135
Whitcher Pl., 23, D16
Whitcomb St., 25, J17
White, W. Hale, 91, 134
White St., 27, H20; Cross Pl., 28, H21; Cross St., 27, G20; Hart St., 37, M19; "Horse," 21, C14; Horse Gate, Hyde Pk., 31, K15; Horse Lane, 29, H24; Lion St., 28, H21
Whitechapel Art Gallery, 28, H22; High St., 28, H22; Rd., 28, H22; Stas., 29, H23
Whitecross St., 38, K20
Whitefield Memorial Ch., 24, H16; St., 24, G16

MADE AT THE TEMPLE PRESS LETCHWORTH IN GREAT BRITAIN

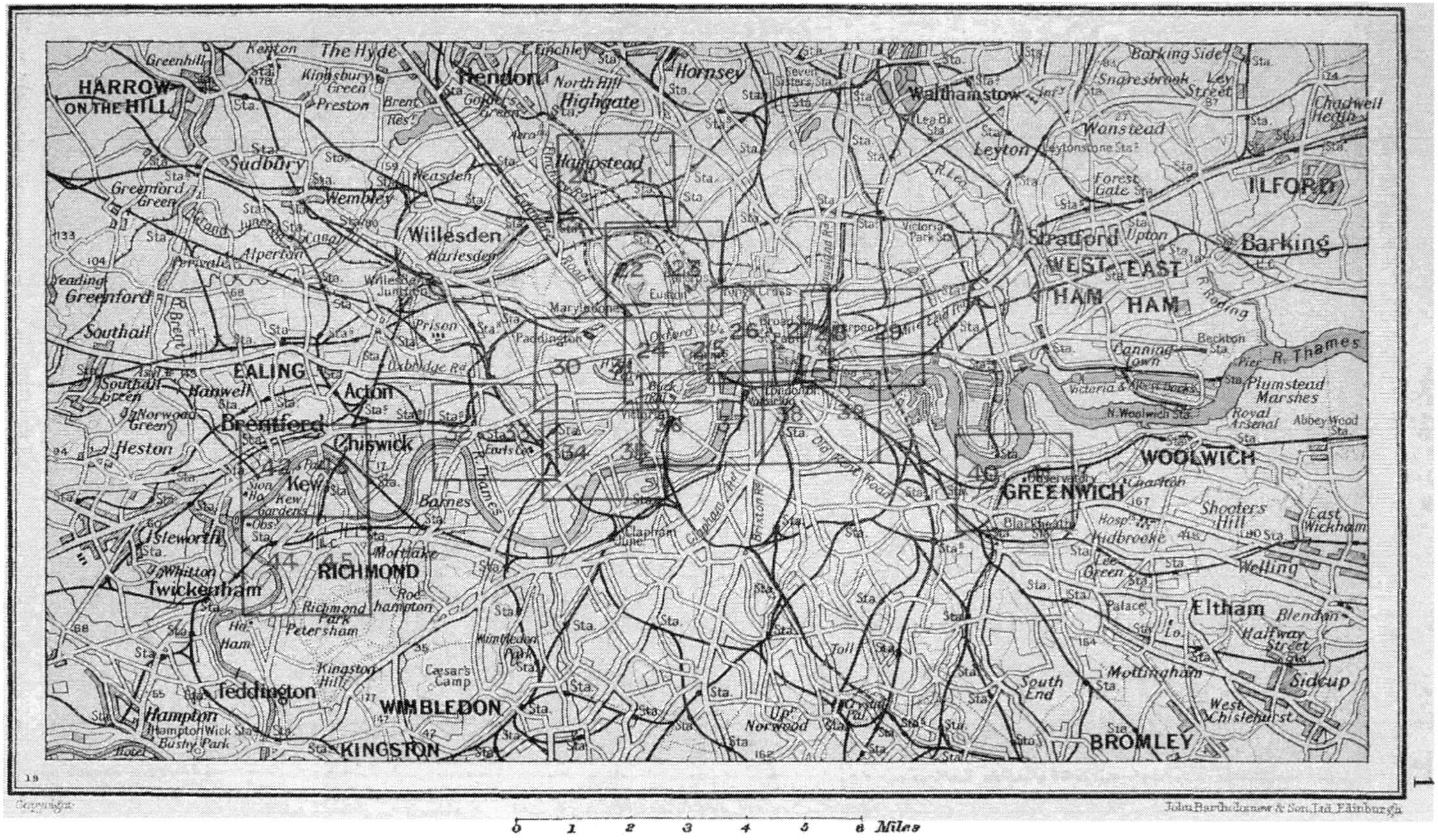
HARROW ON THE HILL
Sudbury
Wembley
Willesden
Harlesden
Hendon
Highgate
Hampstead
Hornsey
Walthamstow
Leyton
Wanstead
ILFORD
Barking
Stratford
WEST HAM
EAST HAM
R. Thames
Plumstead Marshes
Royal Arsenal
WOOLWICH
GREENWICH
Shooters Hill
Eltham
Sidcup
BROMLEY
Greenford
Southall
EALING
Acton
Brentford
Chiswick
Kew
Heston
Isleworth
Twickenham
RICHMOND
Barnes
Petersham
Teddington
Hampton
WIMBLEDON
KINGSTON
Clapham
Norwood
Paddington
Marylebone
Euston
Kings Cross
Victoria
Earls Ct.
20 21 22 23 24 25 26 27 28 29 30 31 32 33 34 35 36 38 39 40 44 45
0 1 2 3 4 5 6 Miles
Copyright
John Bartholomew & Son, Ltd. Edinburgh

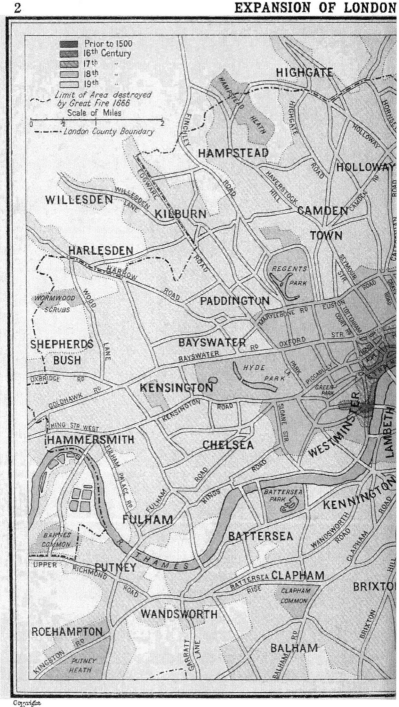

Prior to 1500
16th Century
17th "
18th "
19th "

Limit of Area destroyed
by Great Fire 1666
Scale of Miles
0   ½   1   2
London County Boundary

HIGHGATE

HAMPSTEAD HEATH

HAMPSTEAD

HOLLOWAY

HIGHGATE ROAD

HOLLOWAY RD

HORNSEY

CAXTON RD

WILLESDEN

HAVERSTOCK HILL

CAMDEN
TOWN

KILBURN

WILLESDEN LANE

EDGWARE ROAD

FINCHLEY ROAD

SEYMOUR STR

HARLESDEN

HARROW ROAD

REGENTS PARK

WOOD LANE

WORMWOOD SCRUBS

PADDINGTON

EUSTON RD

COURT RD

TOTTENHAM

SHEPHERDS BUSH

BAYSWATER

BAYSWATER RD

MARYLEBONE RD

OXFORD STR

UXBRIDGE RD

HYDE PARK

PORT

GOLDHAWK RD

KENSINGTON

KENSINGTON ROAD

PARK

PICCADILLY

GREEN PARK

KING STR WEST

SLOANE STR

WESTMINSTER

LAMBETH

HAMMERSMITH

CHELSEA

FULHAM PALACE RD

FULHAM

KINGS ROAD

BATTERSEA PARK

KENNINGTON ROAD

R THAMES

BARNES COMMON

WANDSWORTH ROAD

CLAPHAM RD

BRIXTON

UPPER RICHMOND ROAD

PUTNEY

BATTERSEA

BATTERSEA RISE

CLAPHAM

CLAPHAM COMMON

BRIXTON HILL

ROEHAMPTON

WANDSWORTH

GARRATT LANE

BALHAM RD

BALHAM

KINGSTON RD

PUTNEY HEATH

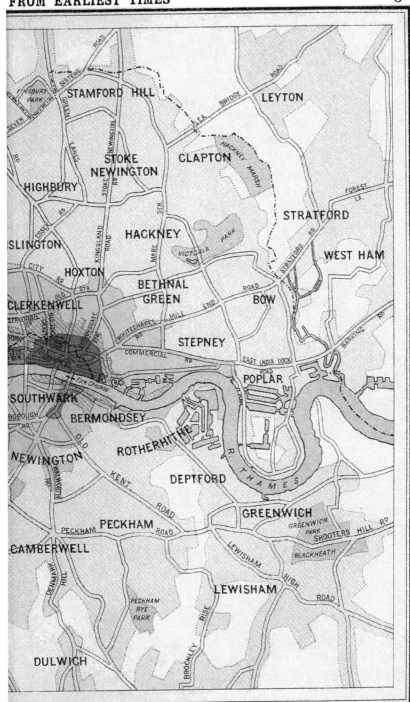

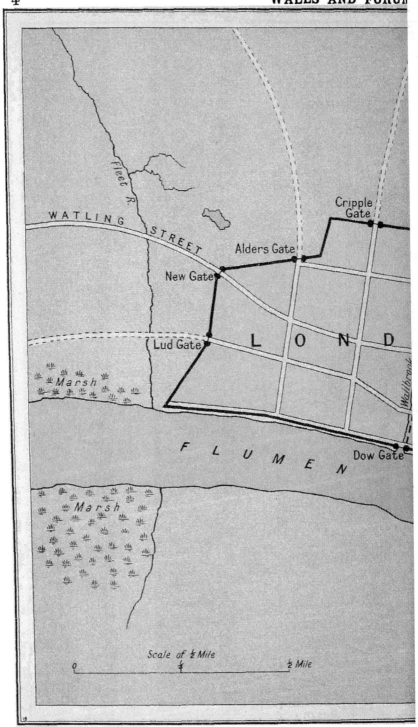

Scale of ½ Mile

0   ¼   ½ Mile

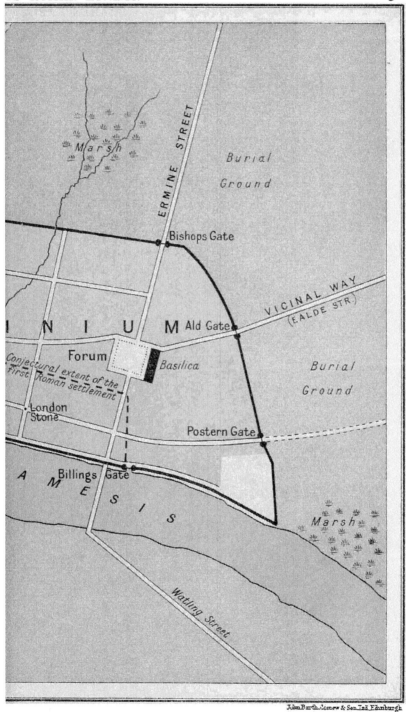

Marsh

ERMINE STREET

Burial Ground

Bishops Gate

VICINAL WAY
(EALDE STR.)

I N I U M Ald Gate

Forum

Conjectural extent of the First Roman settlement

Basilica

Burial Ground

London Stone

Postern Gate

A M E S I S

Billings Gate

Marsh

Watling Street

John Bartholomew & Son Ltd Edinburgh

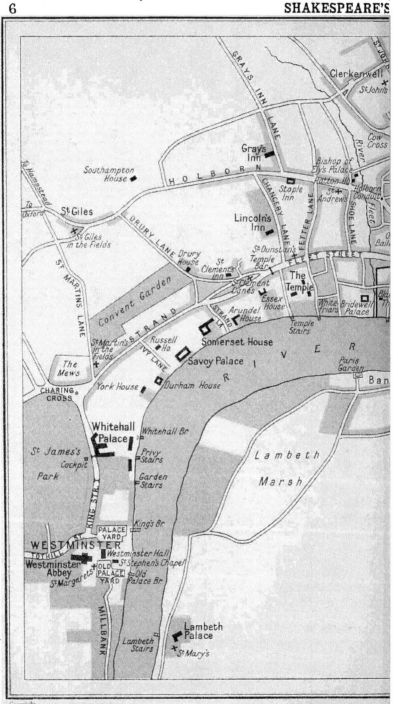

Clerkenwell
St John's
Cow Cross
Grays Inn Lane
Grays Inn
Bishop of Ely's Palace
Patton Ho.
St Andrews
Holborn Conduit
Southampton House
HOLBORN
Staple Inn
Chancery Lane
Fetter Lane
Shoe Lane
Fleet
To Hampstead
To Oxford
St Giles
Drury Lane
Lincoln's Inn
St Dunstan's
Temple Bar
FLEET STREET
Old Bailey
St Giles in the Fields
Drury House
St Clements Inn
The Temple
St Martins Lane
Convent Garden
St Clement Danes
Essex House
White Friars
Bridewell Palace
Black Th.
St Martin's in the Fields
STRAND
STRAND LR
Arundel House
Temple Stairs
The Mews
Russell Ho.
Ivy Lane
Somerset House
R I V E R
Paris Garden
Bank
Charing Cross
York House
Durham House
Savoy Palace
Whitehall Palace
Whitehall Br
Lambeth Marsh
St James's Park
Cockpit
Privy Stairs
Garden Stairs
King St.
King's Br
Palace Yard
Westminster
Tothill
Westminster Hall
St Stephen's Chapel
Westminster Abbey
St Margaret's
Old Palace Yard
Old Palace Br
Millbank
Lambeth Stairs
Lambeth Palace
St Mary's

Copyright

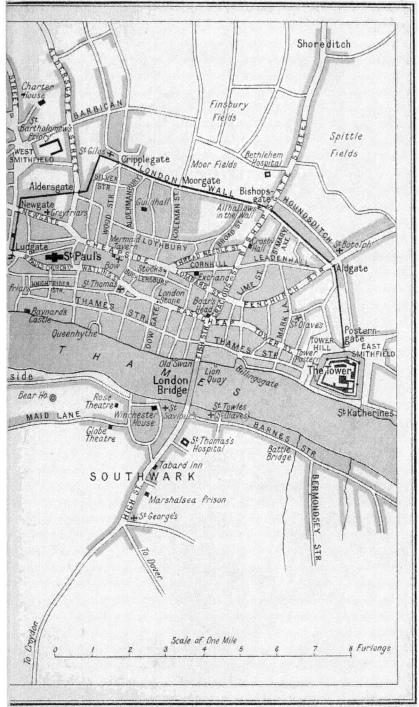

Scale of One Mile

0   1   2   3   4   5   6   7   8 Furlongs

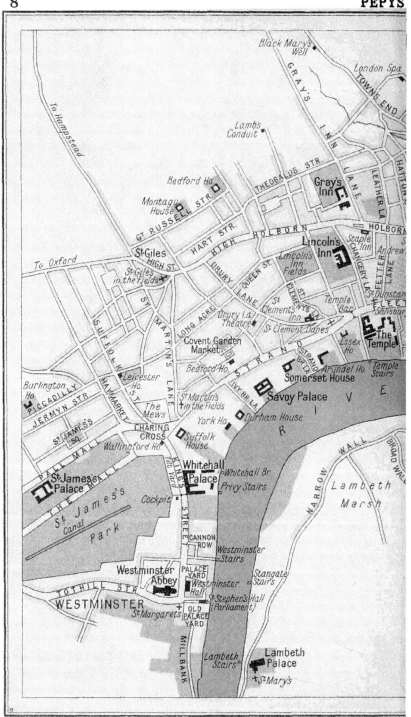

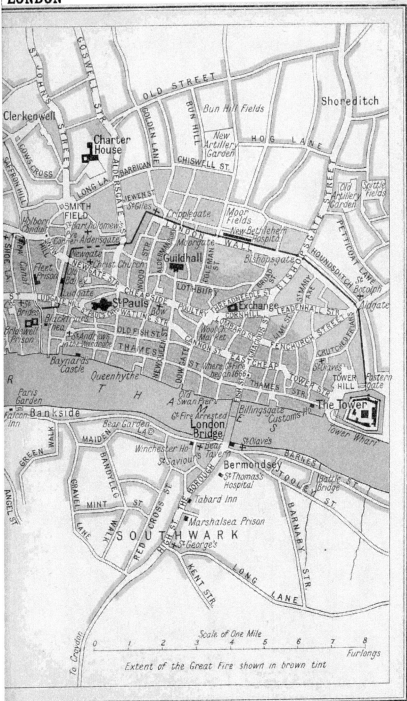

Scale of One Mile

| 0 | 1 | 2 | 3 | 4 | 5 | 6 | 7 | 8 |

Furlongs

Extent of the Great Fire shown in brown tint

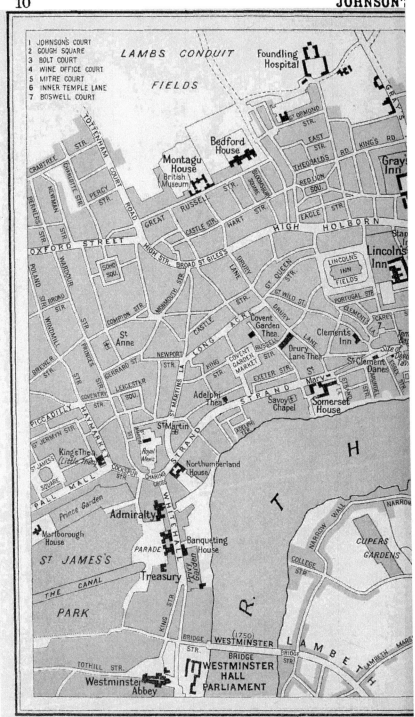

1 JOHNSON'S COURT
2 GOUGH SQUARE
3 BOLT COURT
4 WINE OFFICE COURT
5 MITRE COURT
6 INNER TEMPLE LANE
7 BOSWELL COURT

LAMBS CONDUIT

FIELDS

Foundling Hospital

GRAY'S

GT ORMOND STR.

Bedford House

EAST STR.

THEOBALD'S RD. KING'S RD.

Montagu House

Gray's Inn

Bloomsbury Square

RED LION SOU.

British Museum

RUSSEL STR.

GREAT

TOTTENHAM COURT ROAD

HART STR.

EAGLE STR.

CASTLE STR.

HIGH HOLBORN

CRABTREE

CHARLOTTE STR.

PERCY STR.

NEWMAN

BERNERS STR.

OXFORD STREET

HIGH STR. BROAD ST GILES'S

LINCOLNS INN FIELDS

Lincoln's Inn

SOHO SOU.

POLAND STR.

WARDOUR STR.

BROAD STR.

WINDMILL STR.

COMPTON STR.

MONMOUTH STR.

DRURY LANE

GT QUEEN STR.

GT WILD ST.

PORTUGAL STR.

CLEMENTS

CAREY

St Anne

NEWPORT STR.

CASTLE

LONG ACRE

Covent Garden Thea.

DRURY LANE

Clements Inn

Temple Bar

PRINCES STR.

GERRARD STR.

KING STR.

COVENT GARDEN MARKET

RUSSELL STR.

Drury Lane Thea.

Site of Devil Tav.

BREWER STR.

COVENTRY STR.

LEICESTER SOU.

EXETER STR.

St Clement Danes

ESSEX STR.

PICCADILLY

HAYMARKET

St Martin

Adelphi Thea.

STRAND

St Mary

Savoy Chapel

Somerset House

GT JERMYN STR.

ST JAMES'S

King's Thea. (Little Thea.)

COCKSPUR STR.

CHARING CROSS

ADELPHI TER.

PALL MALL

SQUARE

Royal Mews

Northumberland House

H

NARROW

Prince Garden

WHITEHALL

T

NARROW WALL

CUPERS GARDENS

Marlborough House

Admiralty

Banqueting House

COLLEGE STR.

ST JAMES'S

PARADE

Privy Garden

R.

THE CANAL

Treasury

KING STR.

PARK

BRIDGE STR.

(1750) WESTMINSTER

L A M B E

LAMBETH MARSH

TOTHILL STR.

BRIDGE WESTMINSTER HALL PARLIAMENT

BRIDGE STR.

Westminster Abbey

Copyright

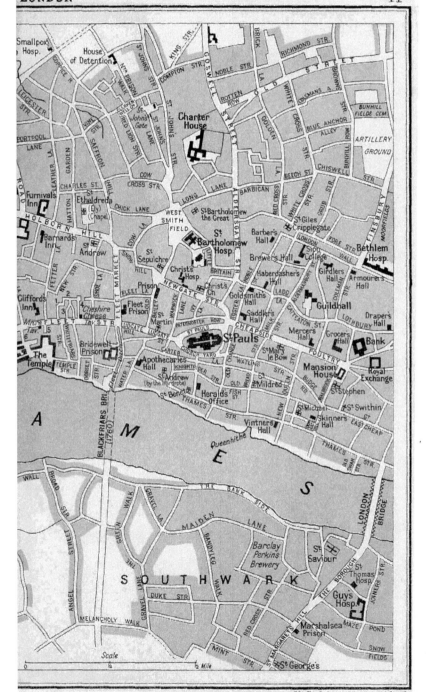

Scale
0   ¼   ½ Mile

John Bartholomew & Son Ltd Edinburgh

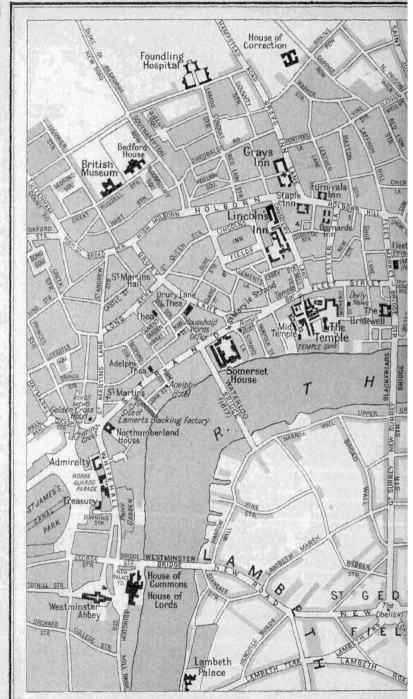

House of
Correction

Foundling
Hospital

BRAINS
ROW

NEW ROAD

DUKE OF BEDFORDS

HAMPSTEAD ROAD

COPPICE
ROW

SAINT

N. PRISON

WALK

WARNER
STR

VINE
STR

SAFFRON

RED LION

SLEEPER
WELL STR

CLERKEN

QUEENS
SQU

SOUTHAMPTON

LAMBS CONDUIT
STR

DOUGHTY
STR

THEOBALDS RD.

GREYS
STR

PORTPOOL
LANE

LEATHER
LANE

HATTON

HILL

CHICK
LA.

British
Museum

Bedford
House

Grays
Inn

Furnivals
Inn

BEDFORD
SQU

BLOOMSBURY
SQU

RUSSELL STR

RED LION
SQU

RED LION

Staple
Inn

GRAYS INN LANE

HOLBORN HILL

SNOW

GT RUSSELL

GREAT

HART STR

HIGH HOLBORN

HOLBORN

Lincolns
Inn

Barnards
Inn

CURSITOR
STR

FETTER

NEW

SHOE

FLEET MARKET

Fleet
Prison

TOTTENHAM COURT RD

OXFORD
STR.

SOHO
SQU

HIGH ST

BROAD

LINCOLNS
INN
FIELDS

CLEMENTS
LA

CAREY
STR

BELL

LANE

STREET

FLEET

LUDGATE
HILL

GREEK
STR

STANDREW

DRURY
LANE

QUEEN STR

DUKE
STR

St Martins
Hall

Drury Lane
Thea.

Temple
Bar

Daily
News

The
Bridewell

BROMLEY

BRIDGE

KING
STR

PRINCES
STR

LEICESTER
SQU

CASTLE ST

LONG
ACRE

BOW
STR

Thea.

COVENT
GARDEN MARKET

St Marylee Strand

Roman
Bath

Mid
Temple

The
Temple

WATER

Household
Words
Office

Adelphi
Thea.

Somerset
House

NORFOLK STR

TEMPLE GDNS

BLACKFRIARS

HAYMARKET

ORANGE
STR

KINGS
MEWS

St Martins

Adelphi
Hotel

WATERLOO
BRIDGE
(1817)

T   H

BRIDGE

PALL
MALL

SPUR
STR

Golden Cross
Hotel

Charing
Cross

Site of
Lamerts Blacking Factory

UPPER

NARROW
WALL

GT SURREY

NEW SURREY

GR

Northumberland
House

R.

BROAD
WALL

Admiralty

WHITEHALL

HORSE
GUARDS
PARADE

VINE
STR

ST JAMES'S
PARK

CANAL

Treasury

DOWNING
STR

PARLIAMENT
STREET

NARROW
WALL

LAMBETH MARSH

WEBBER
STR

ST   GEO

GEORGE
STR

WESTMINSTER
BRIDGE

BRIDGE
STR

NEW
PALACE
YD.

House of
Commons

House of
Lords

NEW ROAD

STANGATE
STR

The
Obelisk

TOTHILL STR.

Westminster
Abbey

ORCHARD
STR.

COLLEGE STR.

ABINGDON

MILL BANK

Lambeth
Palace

HERCULES BUILDS

LAMBETH TERR.

FIEL

LAMBETH

LAMBETH
ROAD

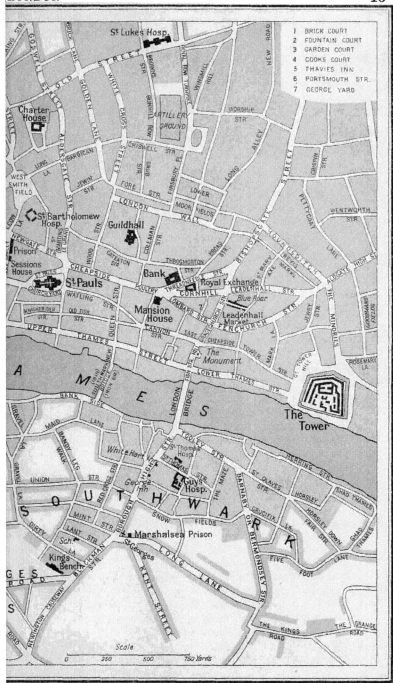

St Lukes Hosp.

1 BRICK COURT
2 FOUNTAIN COURT
3 GARDEN COURT
4 COOKS COURT
5 THAVIES INN
6 PORTSMOUTH STR.
7 GEORGE YARD

GOSWELL STREET
OLD STREET
WHITE CROSS STREET
GOLDEN LANE
BRICK LANE
BROWNS STR.
BUNHILL ROW
WINDMILL HILL
ROYAL ROW TERRACE
NEW ROAD

Charter House

WORSHIP STR.

ARTILLERY GROUND

LONG ALLEY

GRISWELL STR.

WEST SMITH FIELD

CHISWELL STR.
GRUB STR.
FINSBURY STR.
FORE STR.
LOWER
MOOR FIELDS

BARBICAN
JEWIN STR.
WOOD STR.
LONDON WALL
PETTICOAT LANE
WENTWORTH STR.

ALDERSGATE STR.
LONG LA.
St Bartholomew Hosp.
Guildhall
St MARTINS LE GRAND
GATEATON STR.
COLEMAN STR.
THROGMORTON STR.
BROAD STR.
BISHOPSGATE STR.
HIGH STR.

NEWGATE Prison
Sessions House
St PAULS CHURCH YARD
CHEAPSIDE
Bank
Royal Exchange
CORNHILL
LEADENHALL STR.
Blue Boar
ALDGATE
HOUNDSDITCH
BEVIS MARKS
BURY STR.

WATLING STR.
OLD FISH STR.
KNIGHTRIDER STR.
POULTRY
THREADNEEDLE STR.
LOMBARD STR.
Leadenhall Market
FENCHURCH STR.
JEWRY
MINORIES
GOODMANS FIELDS

St Pauls
Mansion House
QUEEN STR.
CANNON STR.
EAST CHEAPSIDE
GRACECHURCH STR.
TOWER STR.
MARK LA.
ROSEMARY LA.

UPPER THAMES STREET
The Monument
LOWER THAMES STR.
GT TOWER HILL

THAMES

BANK SIDE
GRAVEL LA.
MAID LANE
LONDON BRIDGE
The Tower

SOUTHWARK ST

WHITE HART INN
TOOLEY STR.
St Thomas Hosp.
St THOMAS STR.
HERRING STR.
SHAD THAMES

BANDY LEG WALK
UNION STR.
RED CROSS STR.
George Inn
HIGH STR.
St OLAVES STR.
HORSLEY STR.
HORSLEY DOWN
SHAD THAMES

MINT STR.
LANT STR.
Sch.
BOROUGH
Guys Hosp.
SNOW FIELDS
THE MAZE
CRUCIFIX LA.
FAIR STR.
SHAD THAMES

DIRTY LA.
Kings Bench
BLACKMAN STR.
St Georges
Marshalsea Prison
BARNABY OR BERMONDSEY STR.
FIVE FOOT LANE

GES ROAD
NEWINGTON CAUSEWAY
KENT STREET
LONG LANE
THE KINGS ROAD
THE GRANGE ROAD

Scale
0   250   500   750 Yards

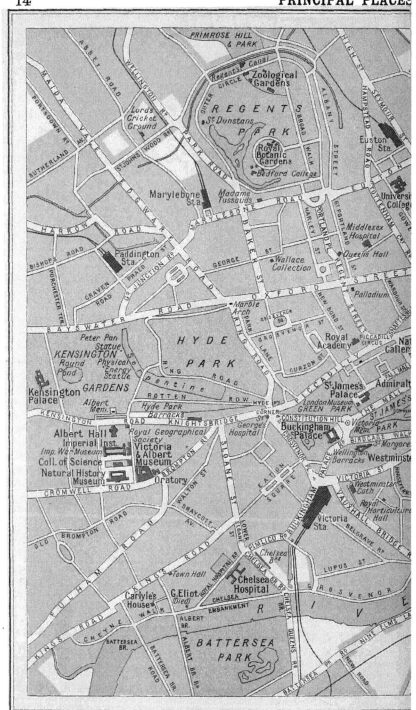

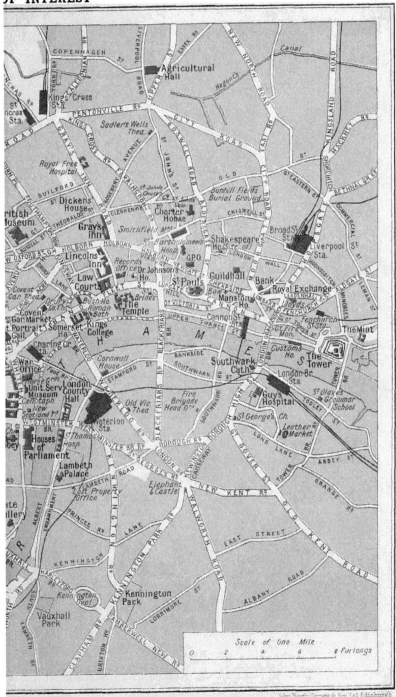

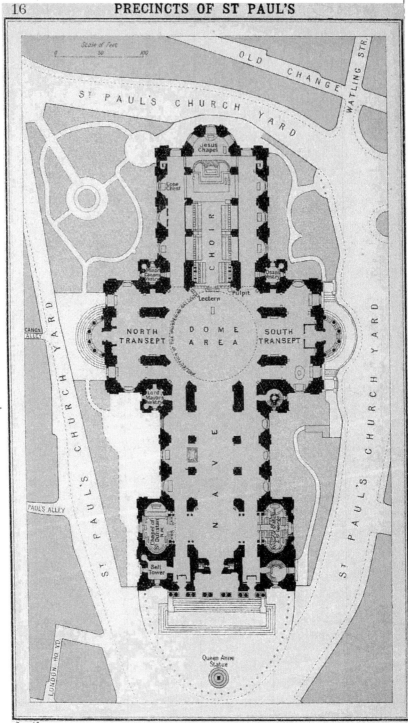

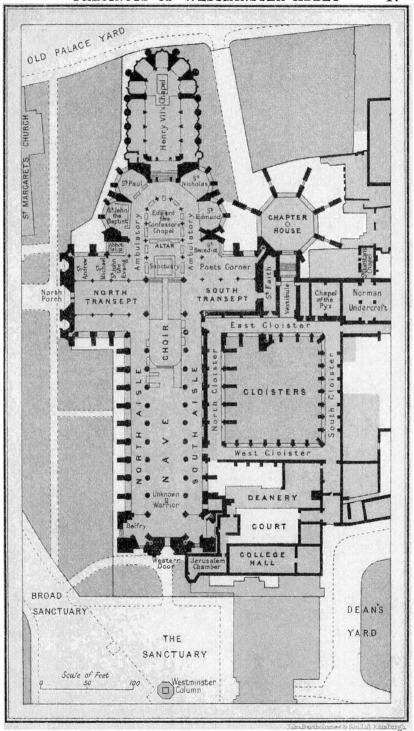

OLD PALACE YARD

ST MARGARET'S CHURCH

Henry VII's Chapel

St Paul
St Nicholas

St John the Baptist
Edward the Confessor's Chapel
St Edmund
CHAPTER HOUSE

Abbot Islip
ALTAR
St Benedict

St Andrew
St Michael
St John the Evang.
Sanctuary
Poets Corner
St Faith
Vestibule
Scholars' Chapel

North Porch
NORTH TRANSEPT
SOUTH TRANSEPT
Chapel of the Pyx
Norman Undercroft

East Cloister

CHOIR

NORTH AISLE
NAVE
SOUTH AISLE
North Cloister
CLOISTERS
South Cloister

West Cloister

Unknown Warrior
DEANERY

Belfry
COURT

Western Door
Jerusalem Chamber
COLLEGE HALL

BROAD SANCTUARY

DEAN'S YARD

THE SANCTUARY

Scale of Feet
0   50   100
Westminster Column

John Bartholomew & Son Ltd Edinburgh

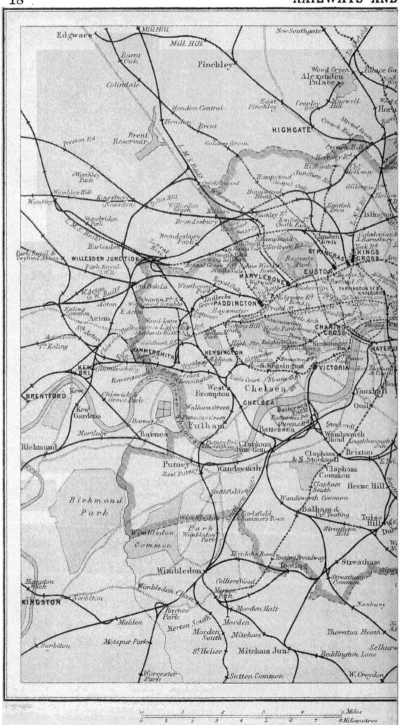

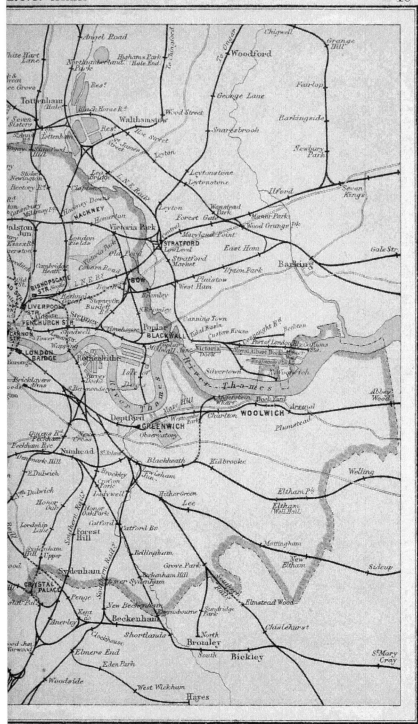

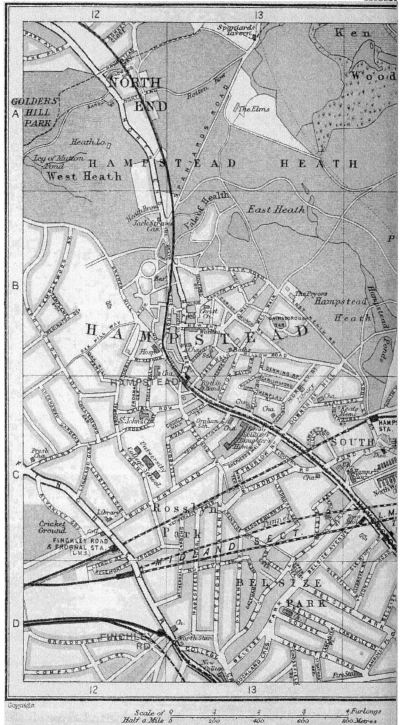

Scale of
Half a Mile

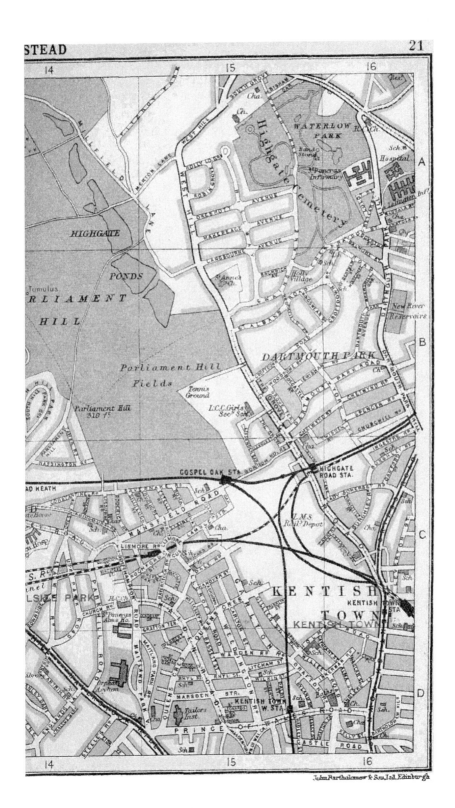

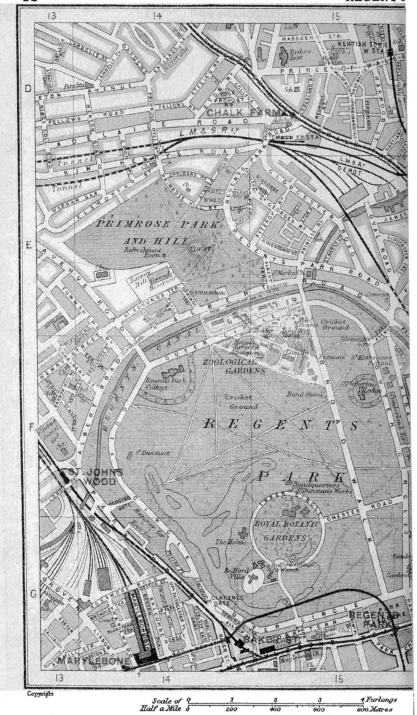

Scale of
Half a Mile

	0	1	2	3	4 Furlongs
	0	200	400	600	800 Metres

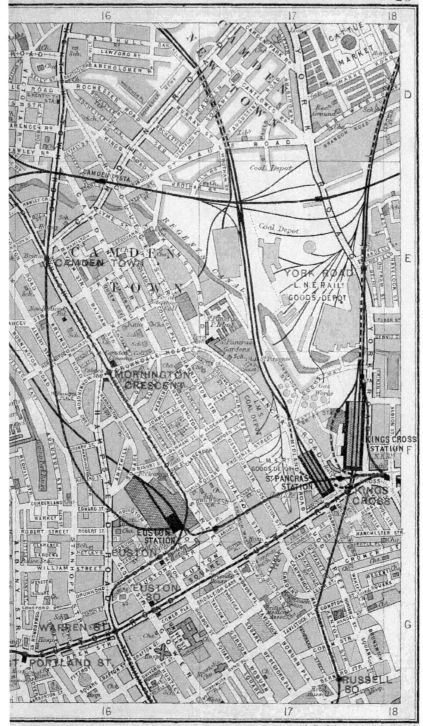

Scale of
Half a Mile

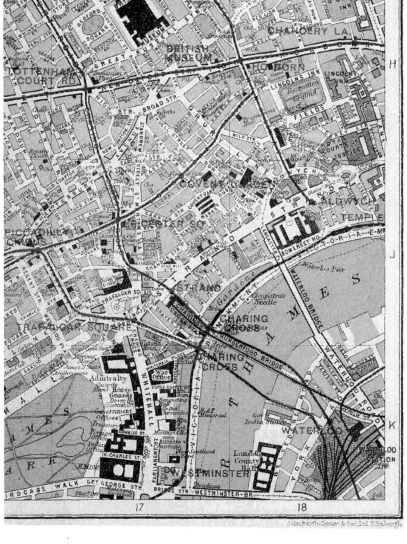

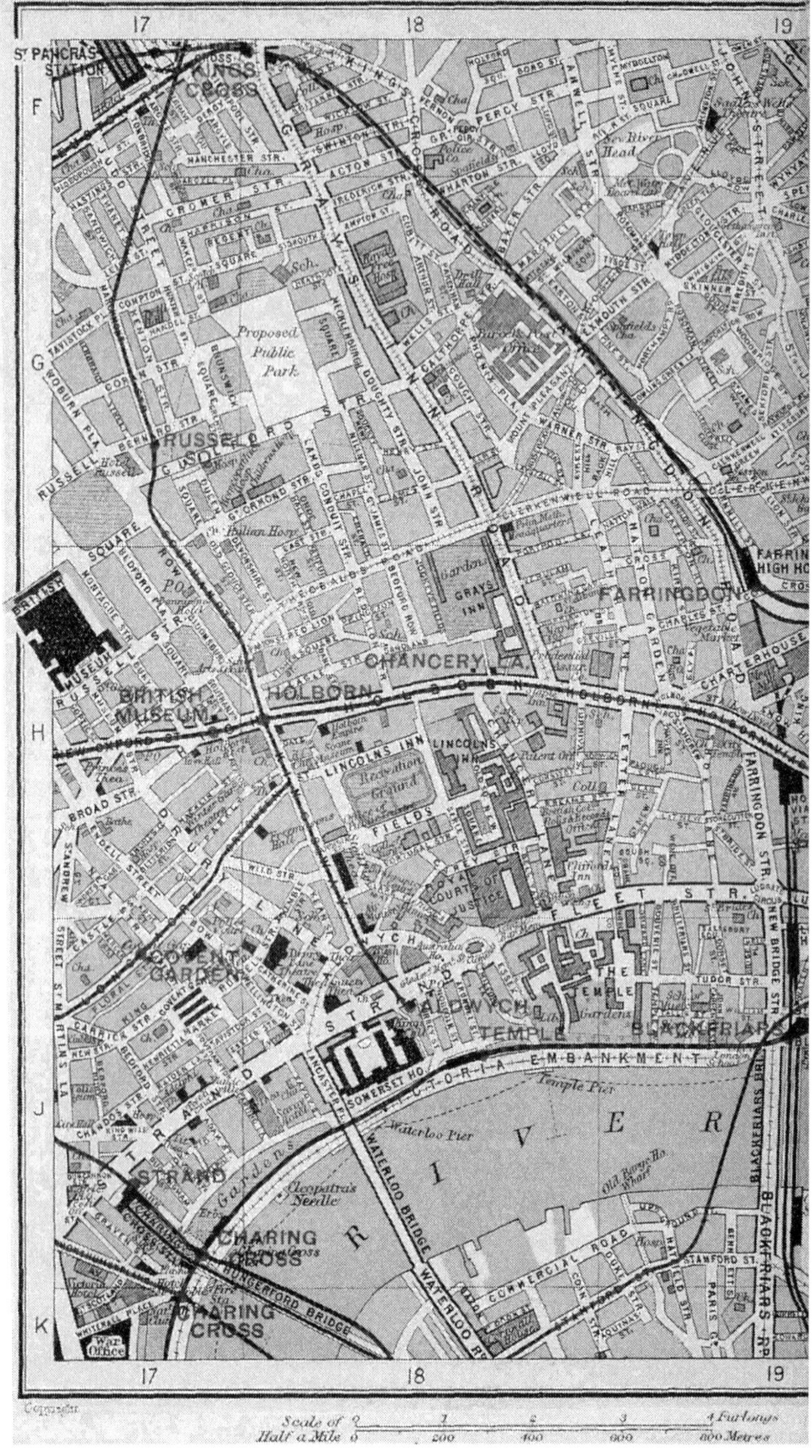

17
18
19
ST PANCRAS STATION
KINGS CROSS
GRAYS INN ROAD
KINGS CROSS ROAD
FARRINGDON ROAD
Proposed Public Park
RUSSELL SQUARE
BRITISH MUSEUM
CHANCERY LA.
HOLBORN
FARRINGDON
GRAYS INN
LINCOLNS INN
LINCOLNS INN FIELDS
ROYAL COURTS OF JUSTICE
FLEET STR.
COVENT GARDEN
ALDWYCH
STRAND
TEMPLE
THE TEMPLE
BLACKFRIARS
VICTORIA EMBANKMENT
SOMERSET HO.
Temple Pier
Waterloo Pier
RIVER
WATERLOO BRIDGE
Cleopatra's Needle
CHARING CROSS
HUNGERFORD BRIDGE
BLACKFRIARS BR.
STAMFORD ST.
COMMERCIAL ROAD
War Office
F
G
H
J
K
Scale of Half a Mile
0 1 2 3 4 Furlongs
0 200 400 600 800 Metres

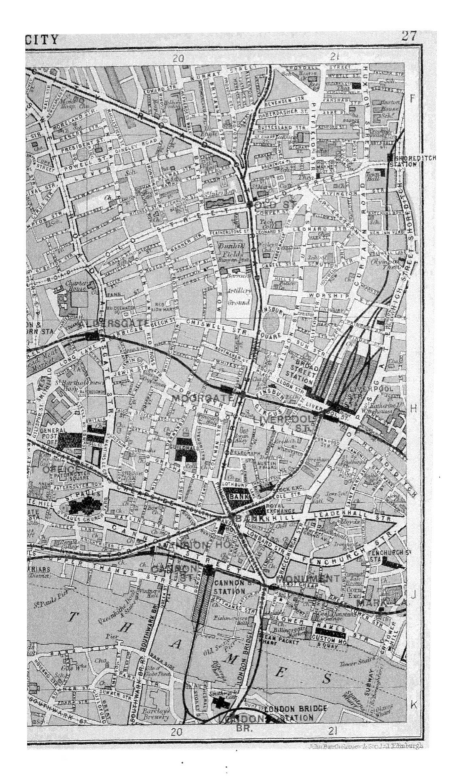

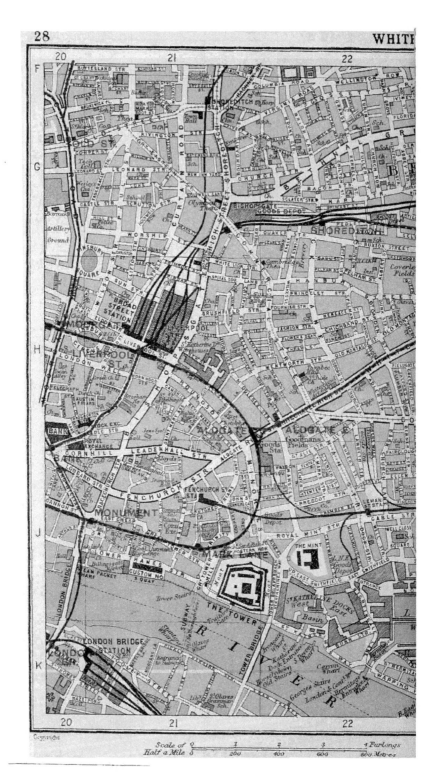

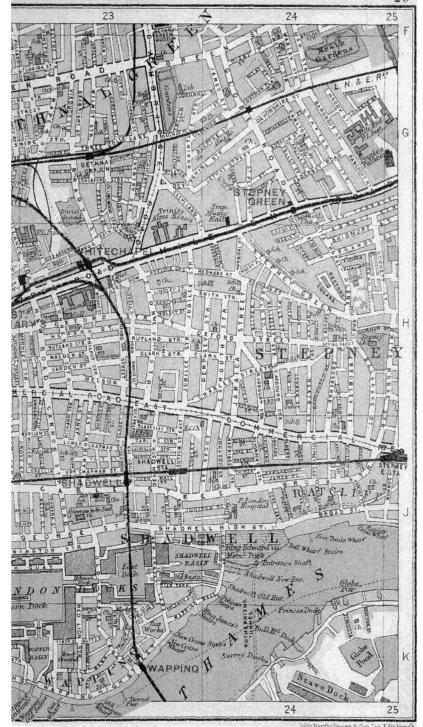

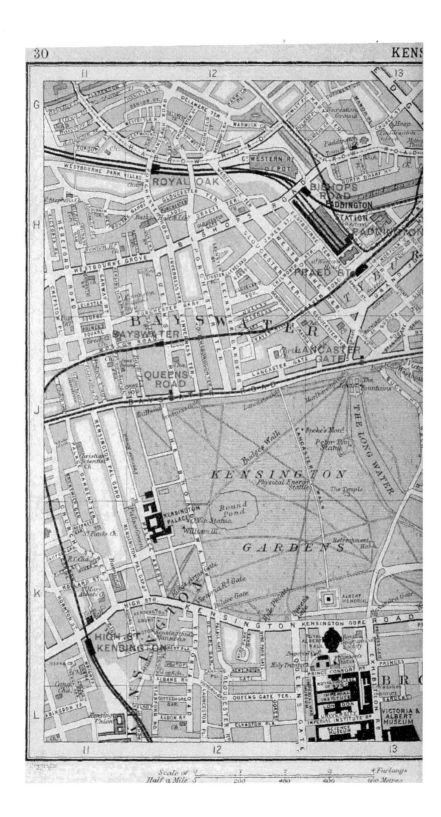

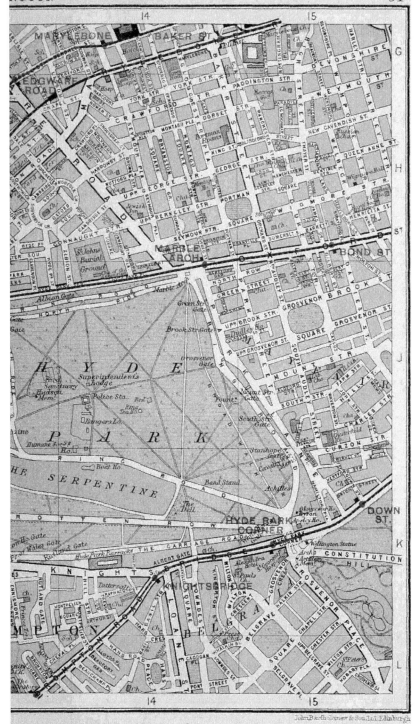

7   8   9

WOOD LANE

J

St Gabriel's
CLIFTON ST.

Generating
Station
& Depot
(C.L.R.)

Cha.

SHEPHERDS BUSH

SHEPHERDS BUSH

UXBRIDGE ROAD

SHEPHERDS BUSH

St Thomas's Cha.

Art Sch.

Baths

Hall

Emp.

K

GOLDHAWK ROAD

Cha.

WESTWICK GAR.

Bap. Cha.

Sch.

Brook Green

Hammersmith Car. Shed

Post Off.
Sch.

P.O. Savings Ban.
R.C. College

St Paul's Sch.
R.C. Cha.
Alms Ho.
Colet Court

L

RAVENSCOURT PARK

N.A. St John's

Lib.

STA. G.W. & M.R.

STA. G.W. & M.R.

Town Hall

W. London
Hosp.

Theatre

Convent

HAMMERSMITH

HAMMERSMITH STREET

St Pauls Sch.

Cha.

Baths

Sch.

St Paul's Ch.

Police Sta.

Convent of the Good Shepherd

Electricity Wks.

BARONS COURT

Hammersmith Cemetery

Cha. Ch.

R. THAMES

M

Filtering Beds

Reservoir

Sch.

Pier

Distillery

Fulham Pl. Inst.

Sch.

Castelnau

Holy Trinity

The Greyhound

Sch.

N

7   8   9

Scale of 0   1   2   3   4 Furlongs
Half a Mile 0   200   400   600   800 Metres

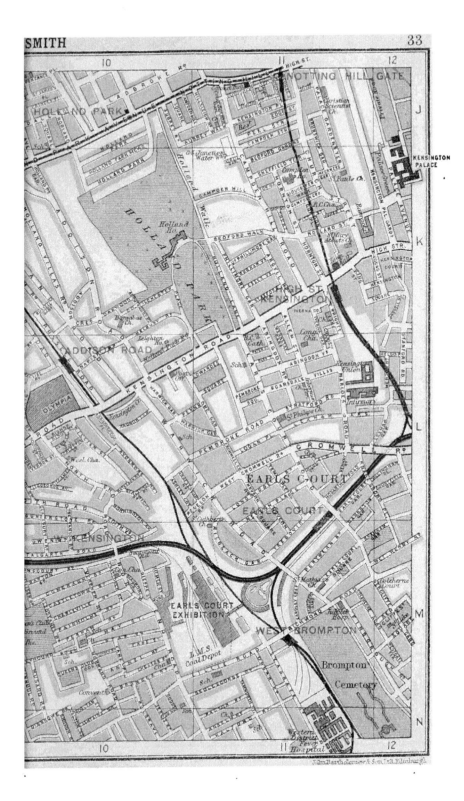

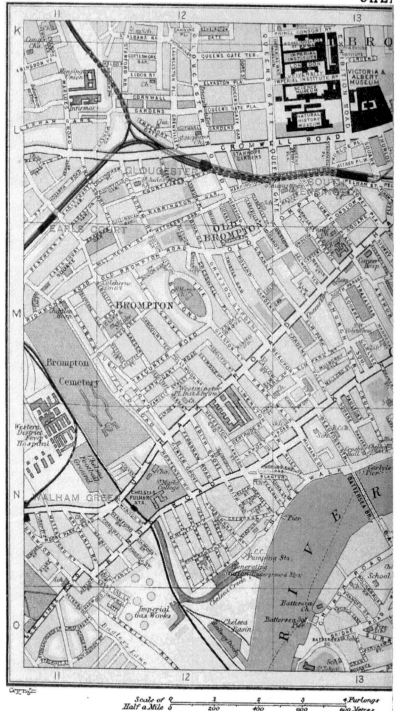

Scale of
Half a Mile

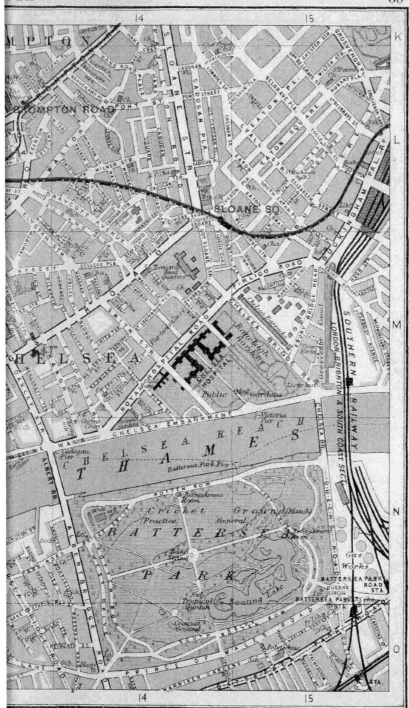

John Bartholomew & Son Ltd Edinburgh.

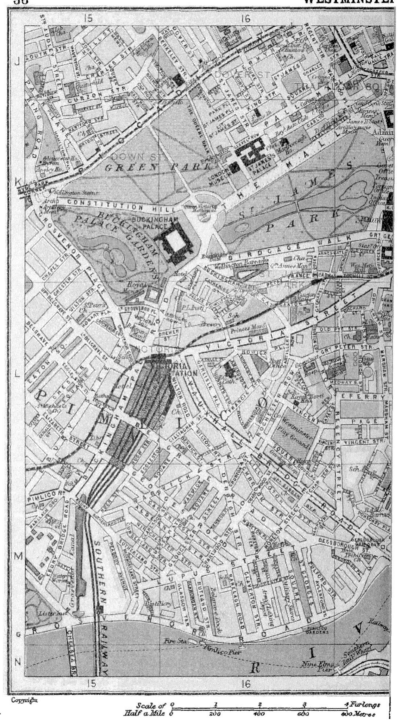

Scale of 0   1   2   3   4 Furlongs
Half a Mile 0   200   400   600   800 Metres

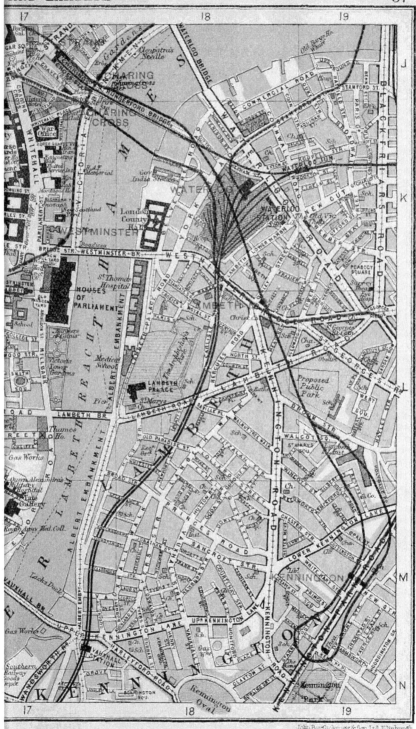

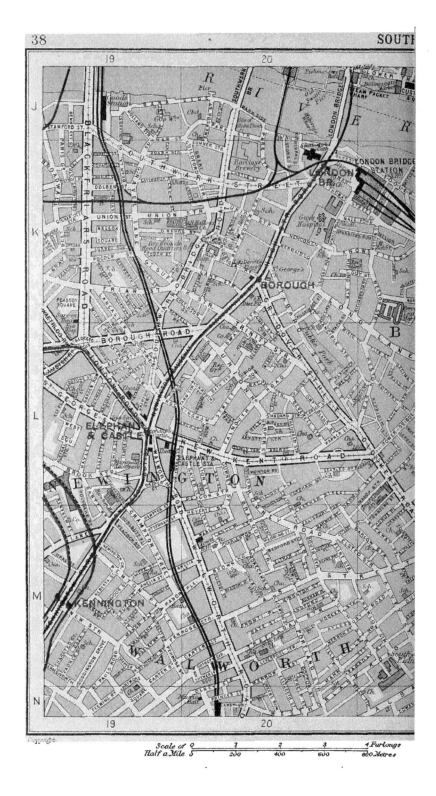

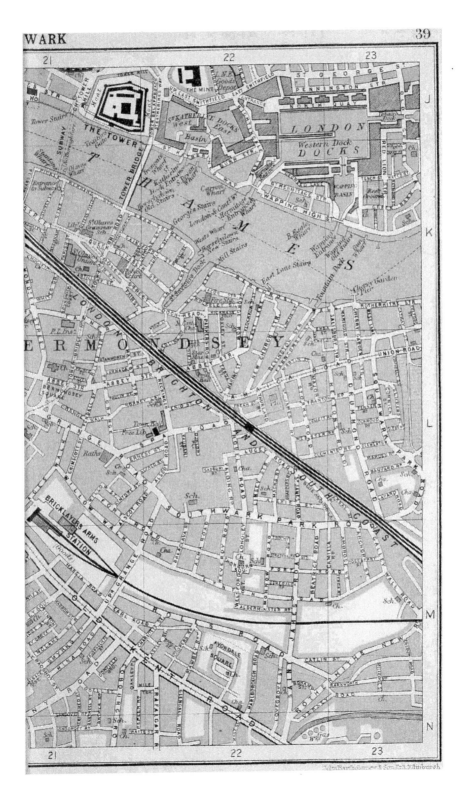

25   26   27

ROYAL VICTUALLING YARD

Millwall Pier

FOREIGN CATTLE MARKET

Dock

R I V E R

GARNET TER.

Saves Court Recreation Ground

PRINCE STR.

EVELYN

STAUNTON ST.

St Nicholas Ch.

DEPTFORD GREEN

G R E E N W I C H   R E A C H

Horse Ferry

Greenwich Pier

Ship Tav.

Gas Wks

THAMES   STREET

BRIDGE   STREET

Ramp Lane

St Alphege Ch.

ROAN STR.

Recreation Ground

Island Gardens

Port of London Wharf

SUBWAY

EAST FERRY ROAD

WHARF

Fire Sta.

EDWARD STR.

WELLINGTON

MARY ANN ST.

HAMILTON

GREEN   ROAD

St Pauls Ch.

MERTON ST.

CHAPMAN ST.

DEPTFORD STA.

Ch.

KIFFIN STR.

TRAFALGAR ST.

WALES ST.

REGINALD

DEPTFORD   CREEK

WOKING STR.

GREENWICH STA.

GREE

Town Hall

Altmn.

ROAD

LONDON STR.

GREENW

NEW CROSS RD. BROADWAY

Empire

DEPTFORD BRIDGE

BLACKHEATH   ROAD

ASHBURNHAM ROAD

Ch.

ASHBURNHAM GRO.

DEVONSHIRE ROAD

GUILDFORD GR.

BRAND ST.

ROYAL

Point Hill

Nightingale

BLACKHEATH HILL

BLACKHEATH HILL STA.

BACK LANE

Hall

Ch.

Mill Water Pond Resr.

RAVENSBOURNE

Sch.

Sch.

DEPTFORD
NEW TOWN

ST JOHNS STA.

St Johns Ch.

LEWISHAM ROAD STA.

Beaufort Gardens

WICKHAM   ROAD

ALBERT RD.

Morden Hill

Hosp.

LEWISHAM JUNC.

ELIOT

25   26   27

Copyright

28 29

Ammunition
Works

MAURITIUS RD

M

Union
Wharf

Trinity Hosp Way

Greenwich
Union Inf.

Royal
Naval
Cemetery

Trinity
Hosp

ROYAL
NAVAL
COLLEGE

TRAFALGAR

MAZE HILL STA.

ROYAL HOSPITAL
SCHOOL

N

HUMBER ROAD

WESTCOMBE PARK RD

VANBRUGH PARK

Ch.

G R E E N W I C H

Magnetic
Observatory

ROYAL
OBSERVATORY

Cha.

ST. JOHN'S PARK

Band
Stand

Nursery

P A R K

Reservoir

BLACKHEATH TER.

O

Golf
Course

Ranger's
House

SHOOTERS HILL ROAD

St Germans
Chapel

Rotten Row

B L A C K H E A T H
Golf Course

Territorial
Head Quarters

ACKHEATH

The
Orchard

Blackheath Vale
Sch.

P

All Saints

Love Lane

Cha.
Avenue

BLACKHEATH
STA.

Cha.

28 29

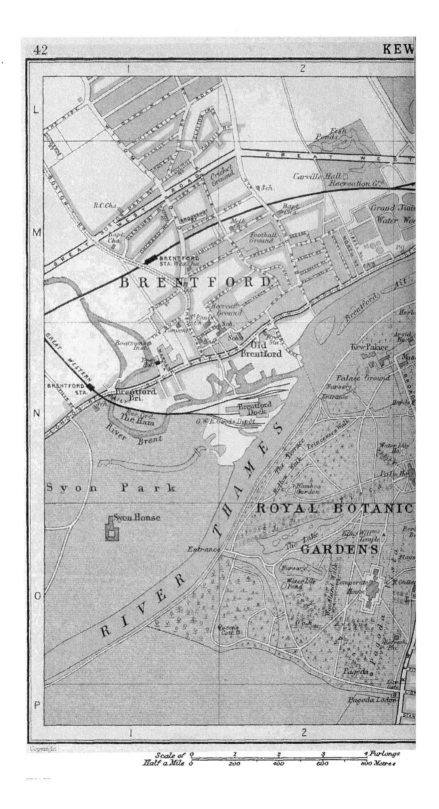

L

M

BRENTFORD

N

O

P

1

2

Fish Ponds

GREAT WEST

Carville Hall
Recreation Gr.

R.C. Cha.

Cricket
Ground

Sch.

Bapt.
Cha.

Grand Tru
Water Wo

Bapt.
Cha.

Meth.

BRENTFORD
STA. West Cha.

Football
Ground

Po

Brentford
Ait

Recreat.
Ground

Herb

St. Paul's
Sch.

Sch.

Sch.

Boatmens
Inst.

Convent
Wha.

Town
Hall

Old
Brentford

Sta.

Kew Palace

Mus

BRENTFORD
STA.

Brentford
Bri.

Palace Ground

Nursery

Arod
Ho.

GREAT

WESTERN

Brent ford

The Ham

Brentford
Dock

Entrance

Hards Ho.

River Brent

G.W.R. Goods Depot.

The Terrace

Water Lily
Ho.

Princesses Walk

Syon Park

RIVER THAMES

The
Hollow Walk

Bamboo
Garden

Path Ho.

Syon House

ROYAL BOTANIC

Entrance

The Lake

King William
Temple

Flags

GARDENS

Nursery

Woodland Walk

Water Lily
Pond

Temperate
House

St. Galle

Queens
Cott. Ho.

Oak

Refresh.
Ho.

Pagoda

Pagoda Lodge

Copyright Art

1

2

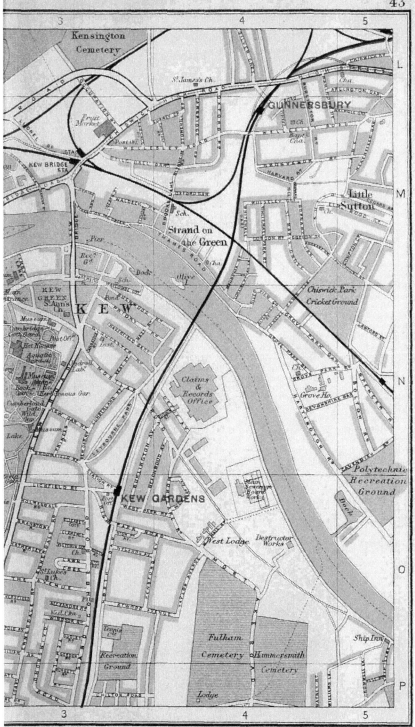

Kensington
Cemetery

KEW BRIDGE STA.

St James's Ch.

GUNNERSBURY

Little Sutton

Strand on the Green

Chiswick Park Cricket Ground

KEW

St Ann's Ch.

Claims & Records Office

Grove Ho.

Polytechnic Recreation Ground

KEW GARDENS

Main Sewage Board Works

West Lodge

Destructor Works

St Luke's Ch.

Ship Inn

Fulham Cemetery

Hammersmith Cemetery

Recreation Ground

Lodge

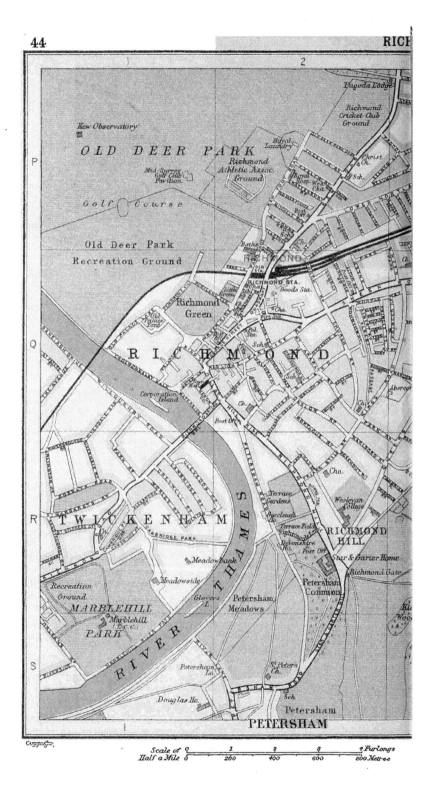

Scale of | 1 | 2 | 3 | 4 Furlongs
Half a Mile 0 | 200 | 400 | 600 | 800 Metres

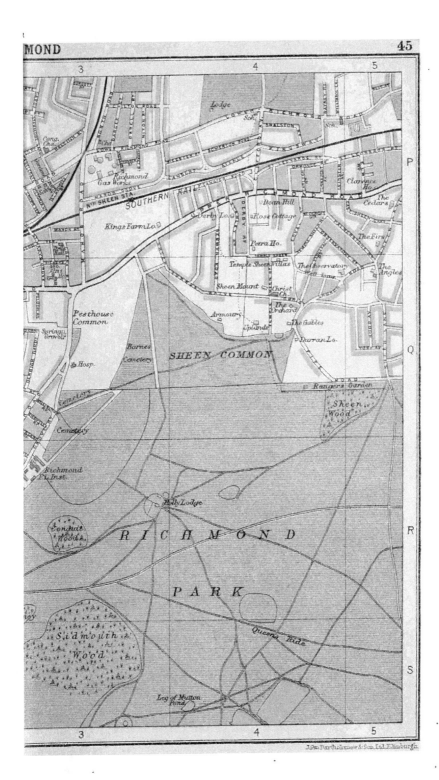

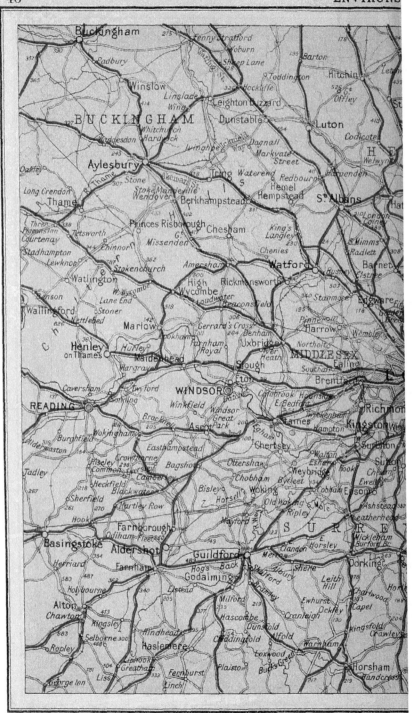

0   5   10   15   20 Miles

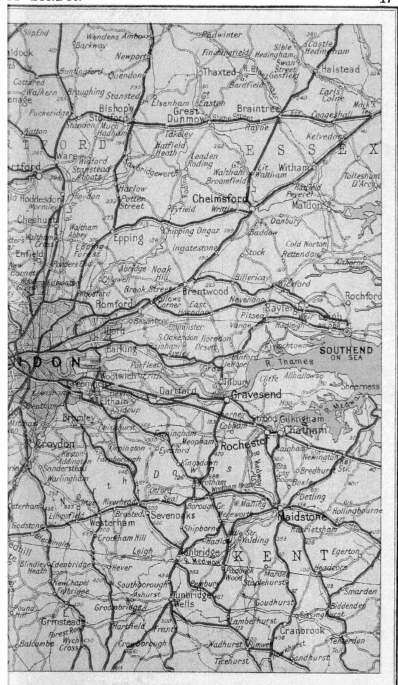

SOUTH EAST OF ENGLAND

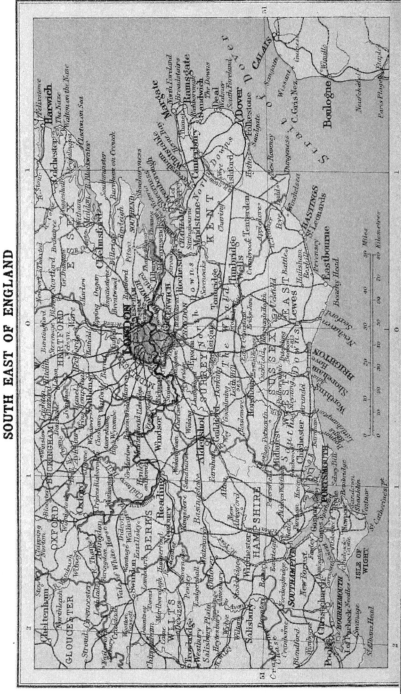

CPSIA information can be obtained
at www.ICGtesting.com
Printed in the USA
BVHW052349080223
658190BV00005B/104